THOMAS JEFFERSON

ALSO BY M. ANDREW HOLOWCHAK

Framing a Legend: Exposing the Distorted History of
Thomas Jefferson and Sally Hemings

THOMAS JEFFERSON

UNCOVERING HIS UNIQUE PHILOSOPHY AND VISION

M. Andrew Holowchak

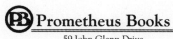

Prometheus Books

59 John Glenn Drive
Amherst, New York 14228

Published 2014 by Prometheus Books

Cover design by Jacqueline Nasso Cooke
Cover image © John Parrot / Media Bakery

Inquiries should be addressed to
Prometheus Books
59 John Glenn Drive
Amherst, New York 14228
VOICE: 716–691–0133
FAX: 716–691–0137
WWW.PROMETHEUSBOOKS.COM

18 17 16 15 14   5 4 3 2 1

Library of Congress Cataloging-in-Publication Data

Holowchak, Mark, 1958-
    Thomas Jefferson : uncovering his unique philosophy and vision / by M. Andrew Holowchak.
        pages cm
    Includes bibliographical references and index.
    ISBN 978-1-61614-952-9 (hardback) — ISBN 978-1-61614-953-6 (ebook)
    1. Jefferson, Thomas, 1743-1826—Philosophy. 2. Jefferson, Thomas, 1743-1826—Political and social views. I. Title.

E332.2.H664 2014
973.4'6092—dc23
[B]

                                                                        2014023879

Printed in the United States of America

This book is dedicated to former president William Jefferson Clinton.

CONTENTS

PART 4. JEFFERSON ON EDUCATION

PREFACE

"I have sworn upon the altar of god, eternal hostility against every form of tyranny over the mind of man."
—TJ to Benjamin Rush, September 23, 1800

efferson has been treated seriously as a biologist, paleontologist, agrarianist, architect, meteorologist, and philologist among other things but seldom as a philosopher.[1] Moreover, except for reading his Declaration of Independence, he is mostly disregarded by philosophers. Such disregard I find strange because his addresses, messages, and letters are suffuse with philosophical content. Nonetheless, Jefferson has been given many philosophical labels. He has been called an Epicurean, a Lockean, a Hobbesian, a Rousseauian, a Stoic, a Christian, a Humean, and even a Machiavellian; a deist and an atheist; a liberal, a communitarian, and a libertarian; a filiopietist and a progressivist; a philanthropist and a wastrel; a rationalist, an empiricist, a skeptic, and a neo-Positivist; a democrat and an aristocrat; a pacifist and a confrontationist; a revolutionist and a conservative; and an expansionist and an agrarianist. Who was the real Jefferson?

Today's revisionist literature, which often suggests he was all things to all persons because the person behind writings is inaccessible through the writings,[2] has served more to confuse than to resolve the issue. Though a complex person and acutely mindful of the needs and sensitivities of his correspondents, he was no chameleon as many revisionists today fashion him to be, and he was anything but unauthentic or disingenuous.

Any attempt to work through the collage of labels and find out who the real Jefferson was will meet with certain ineliminable difficulties—that is, certain discrepancies between Jefferson's actions and words, and to a much lesser extent, other discrepancies between his words in one place and his words in another. This work, however, is not chiefly an attempt to unearth the real Jefferson—the historical Jefferson. It is instead mostly an attempt at disclosure of the dimensions of Jefferson's vision for a new-forming nation—the United States of America—and it is a vision in which the people are to play

9

a substratal role. That vision, I argue, is fundamentally philosophical and has not just parochial but also global implications.

Ever an optimist, Jefferson had one remarkable capability that often goes unrecognized—an uncanny capacity to see things as they could be. That comes out politically, for illustration, in his Sixth Annual Message as president. He says, "Our duty is to act upon things as they are, and to make a reasonable provision for whatever they may be."[3] That also comes out beautifully in Barbara McEwan's description of Jefferson as landscaper. "[Jefferson] had the uncommon facility of being able to visualize in considerable detail the end result he wished. Others saw only bare ground, perhaps with stakes; he saw mature trees and shrubs, walkways, and even garden buildings. For all the disorder he might live in without complaint, he was in truth a very orderly man."[4]

What McEwan says of Jefferson the landscaper is applicable to Jefferson the person. As one of the architects of the American Revolution, he was a creator of much of the social and political disorder in which he would live thereafter. Yet as perhaps the premier architect of the building of the early American nation, he had a lucid, clean, and simple vision of order. Wedded to the notion of placing the concerns of his state and his country before his own, he served as member of the Virginia House of Burgesses, delegate to the Continental Congress, member of the Virginia House of Delegates, governor of Virginia, ambassador to France, secretary of state, vice president, and finally president before he ultimately retired to Virginia in 1809 very nearly at the age of sixty-six to resume, and essay to repair, his much-neglected personal life, riddled with debt. In his mature years, he was guided by an image of an expanding nation, covering the whole North American continent, and that expansive nation was to be a thriving unity—a model of democratic ideals for all nations that showcased full participation of citizens, regard for their rights, opportunities for human flourishing, enticements for scientific advance, and most significantly self-sufficiency—namely, minimal or no involvement in the affairs of other, especially belligerent, nations. That sanguine vision comes out plainly in numerous letters, and for instance in his decision to move forward with the Louisiana Purchase, even though there is no need of the land at the time of its purchase.[5]

In spite of that pristine, orderly vision, Jefferson generally lived amid disorder. Nonetheless, he did so in a very prudential sort of way, because he had an orderly mind, possessed a profound curiosity and fecund imagination, and was an unflappable optimist.

First, Jefferson was perhaps almost pathologically obsessed with order.[6] Writes the great Jefferson scholar Dumas Malone, "One of the most systematic of men, he was in character as a cataloguer."[7] Categorizing flora into trees, plants, fruits, and vegetables, he subdivided each of them into four classes—the medicinal, the esculent, the ornamental, and those useful for fabrication—in an effort to separate the useful from the ornamental and put each, even the ornamental, to fullest use.[8] Symmetry, balance, and order characterized Monticello's gardens.[9] Moreover, he collected books by the thousands all his life and struggled continuously to find the most efficient classificatory scheme for them.[10] Again, he put together a handbook for decorum in matters pertaining to proceedings in the Senate—his *Manual of Parliamentary Practice for the Use of the Senate of the United States*. Jefferson says, "It is much more material that there should be a rule to go by, than what the rule is; that there may be an uniformity of proceeding in business, not subject to the caprice of the Speaker, or captiousness of the members."[11] Very probably doing the lion's share of the work, he helped draft 126 bills to reform the laws of Virginia. Prior to his political career was his legal career. Writes professor of law William G. Merkel of Jefferson's meticulousness in the case *Bolling v. Bolling:* "Jefferson's brief to the court—written without the assistance of a clerk, the aid of online search engines and databases, and access to compiled reports of decisions—surpasses in thoroughness, logic, and depth of understanding any memorandum from a large modern law office that I have seen."[12] As each illustration shows, obsession with order was no rope of sand. It tied neatly into an equally strong obsession for efficiency, exemplified by his distaste for political wrangling, without any intention of compromise.[13]

Second, Jefferson had a child's curiosity and was almost boundlessly imaginative. He collected Native American languages in an effort, among other things, to learn whether they were descendants of Eastern Asians, or the converse; he organized and sanctioned the Lewis and Clark expedition to find and efficient route to the Pacific Ocean and learn as much about the climate, terrain, biota, and peoples on the way; and he even kept a caged grizzly bear on the lawn of the White House;[14] among other things. Moreover, he advised his friend Robert Skipwith on a "gentleman's library"; he invented an improved plow mold board for efficient plowing; and he decimalized the US monetary system. One might say that he was ever in the business of seeing things cloaked in their various potentialities and of trying to actualize, when his talents and resources allowed and when the scenario was optimal, the best

of those potentialities. In that regard, he was no mere visionary but an actu-
alist. Nonetheless, his curiosity and imagination were the bases for lifelong
reproaches, satire, and ridicule.

Last, Jefferson was unbendingly but realistically optimistic, in spite of the
uncertainty of the times in which he lived. Writes historian Alf Mapp: "A tem-
pered optimism was characteristic of Jefferson at every stage of his life except
for the period immediately succeeding his wife's death. Ordinarily he tackled
each problem with hope but without the easy assumption that success could be
won without effort."[15] That optimism expressed itself especially concerning the
fate of his newly forming nation. He firmly believed in participatory republicanism, which involved a belief that each person could manage his own affairs
without governmental intervention. He firmly believed in the continued moral
and intellectual progress of humans over time. He firmly believed, misfortunes notwithstanding, that life on the whole was worth living—even reliving,
should the prospect avail itself. Finally, he firmly believed that the universe
was created and maintained by a benevolent deity.

Jefferson's orderliness, curiosity and imagination, and optimism were in
service of his humanism. He has been called by scholar Karl Lehmann "one
of the greatest humanists of all time" because of his "concrete grasp of human
experience, in the records and works of the ancient world, in its integration in
individual, progressive personalities who are aware of their duties toward the
human society of their time."[16]

Jefferson's talents as visionary were aided by his curiosity as experimen-
talist. He was unsettled in any environment with which he was unfamiliar and
found comfort only when he examined scientifically all its elements and could
coordinate them neatly in his own mind, which was inordinately plastic.

Jefferson's most profound vision concerned his republicanism, which can
be taken as a political alternative to the centralized and big-government federalism of Hamilton and other ultraist Federalists. (Throughout I adopt the convention of capitalizing *Republicanism* and *Federalism*, and their variant forms,
only when referring to the political parties of Jefferson and Hamilton not to
the philosophical visions underlying them.) That view is, in some measure,
beyond contention, yet I hope to show that it is also too narrow. His republicanism, I contend, is a practicable philosophical vision, rich in substance and
broad in application. His republicanism is a schema for any people-based government where happiness and progress are ends and where the means to them
involve liberty, equality, full political participation on behalf of all citizens,

and government by the best—that is, the most virtuous and most talented. His republicanism has naturalistic, political, moral, and educative components.

This book is not a historical work. Following the tack I took in *Dutiful Correspondent: Philosophical Essays on Thomas Jefferson*—a collection of essays on philosophical aspects of Jefferson's writings on issues from philology and liberalism to war and race—I treat Jefferson as a philosopher and aim to show that he is a significant American political and educational philosopher whose contribution to philosophy has largely gone unnoticed because he never concretized his philosophy in published formal treatises. Historian Merrill Peterson writes: "Men called him a philosopher, and demanded of him more thorough and timeless wisdom than he could supply. He never had the occasion, probably never the desire, to work out a systematic statement of his philosophy. So he appeared before posterity with his rich intellectual garments dangling and disarrayed."[17] Though the rich intellectual garments are dangling and disarrayed, perusal of his writings, I hope to show, indicates that Jefferson held largely consistent views on the cosmos, human nature, politics, morality, and education. Thus, *Thomas Jefferson: Uncovering His Unique Philosophy and Vision* is an outgrowth of my work in *Dutiful Correspondent.* Aiming to disclose Jefferson's thoughts on the issues of humans in the cosmos, politics, morality, and education through scrutiny of his writings, this book is an effort—and the first of its kind—to expatiate on and systematize the philosophical content of Jefferson's writings. With expatiation and systematicity as my chief aims, the book is more expository than critical of Jefferson's philosophical thinking. Nonetheless, there is critical engagement at times with Jefferson and significant critical engagement with the works of other scholars, though some of it is relegated to the endnotes.

Qua philosopher, Jefferson was a philosopher of the people. He was their liberator, bulwark, salvager, and benefactor, and all such things not because of a tendency to mingle and curry favor with the people but because of his unaffected, people-friendly policies and words, expressed via his quill. Shunning public attention and direct personal involvement, Jefferson preferred to prompt change indirectly—through bills, proposals, declarations, and, of course, his thousands of letters. His merit and legacy, then, lay in his symbolism—what he represented to the people as a visionary political figure who refused to believe that the answer to the problem of good government is lain in the mawkish, saccharine thoughts of humans' ancestors.

Thomas Jefferson is divided into four parts: Jefferson's naturalism, Jefferson's political thought, Jefferson's moral thought, and Jefferson's educative thought. Part 1, "Jefferson on Nature," examines his physicalism and naturalism in one chapter. Part 2, "Jefferson on Politics," comprises three chapters, which critically look at Jefferson's republicanism, liberalism, and his political progressivism. Part 3, "Jefferson on Morality," comprises three chapters, which analyze his notion of the nature of man, his moral-sense theory, and his view of "natural aristoi." Part 4, "Jefferson on Education," comprises three chapters that critically spell out his thoughts on education.

Overall, I argue that Jefferson's "great experiment"—his vision of a government as responsibly representative of its people and functioning for the sake of them—is interlarded and undergirded by his philosophical thoughts on humans and their place in the natural order of things, which are remarkably consistent over time.[18] Humans, given a general education, are fully capable of managing their own affairs and participating, at least, in local government.[19]

Jefferson's philosophical speculations, however, are not mere metempirical intuitions that function to underpin and drive his empiricism. They are more of the nature of scientific hypotheses—novel, numerous, and fruitful—which either can be discarded, if put to the test and proven false, or can be accepted (at least, provisionally), if put to the test and confirmed. In stating that Jefferson is fundamentally an empiricist, I reject any sort of unmanageable eclecticism that typifies other attempts at grappling with the philosophical content of Jefferson's writings.[20]

Because Jefferson's philosophical speculations are best taken as hypotheses, it is mistaken to see his republicanism as a mere political vision that is founded a priori—that is, founded on unwavering intuitions. It is also mistaken to see his republicanism as Republicanism—namely, a mere political alternative to Federalism. His republicanism is a scientific theory in the literal sense and it is to be confirmed or disconfirmed by the test of time, hence his preference for the term *experiment*.

I have two notes of methodological significance.

First, I have mostly taken the liberty in this work not to add the Latin *sic* to differences of language extant in Jefferson's day or accidental (or even intentional) misspellings: for example, "it's," "compleat," "Kaims" for Kames, "sais," "percieve," "decieve," "knolege," "expence," and "interprizing." I leave it up to readers to recognize conventional differences and misspellings in Jefferson's writings. I also here note that readers should be aware that Jefferson often begins sentences in his letters without capitalizing the first word, except when it is *I*; he also places periods after numerals. Here again I avoid use of *sic*.

Second, there is a methodological concern before closing. There are several major compilations of Jefferson's writings, several of which I list below.

- *The Writings of Thomas Jefferson: Being His Autobiography, Correspondence, Reports, Messages, Addresses, and Other Writings, Official and Private: Published by the Order of the Joint Committee of Congress on the Library, from the Original Manuscripts, Deposited in the Department of State*, 9 vols., ed. Henry Augustine Washington (Washington, DC: Taylor & Maury, 1853–1854);
- *The Works of Thomas Jefferson*, ed. Paul Leicester Ford, 12 vols. (New York: Putnam, 1902);
- *The Writings of Thomas Jefferson, Definitive Edition*, 20 vols., ed. Andrew Adgate Lipscomb and Albert Ellery Bergh (Washington, DC: Thomas Jefferson Memorial Association, 1907); and
- *The Papers of Thomas Jefferson*, 42 vols. (to date), ed. Julian Boyd et al. (Princeton: Princeton University Press, 1950–).

There are also several one-volume compilations of Jefferson's writings—the best of which is Merrill D. Peterson's *Thomas Jefferson: Writings* (New York: Library of America, 1984). Moreover, many of Jefferson's writing are readily available online—for instance, the Hathi Trust Digital Library, the Online Library of Liberty, and Founders Online. Thus, I have adopted the convention here, as in other publications, of labeling Jefferson's epistolary writings by reference only to his correspondent and the date of the letter, thereby giving readers the opportunity to refer to the edition most readily available to them. Nonepistolary writings, in contrast, are fully referenced throughout this book.

INTRODUCTION

*"My theory has always been, that if we are to dream, the flatteries
of hope are as cheap, and pleasanter than the gloom of despair."*
—TJ to François Barbé-Marbois, June 14, 1817

A letter by Jefferson to Dr. Benjamin Rush (January 16, 1811) relates
the story of Jefferson's dinner engagement with Alexander Hamilton
and John Adams. At some point in the conversation, Adams asserts that the
British system of government would be the most perfect system of government, should some of its "defects and abuses" be corrected. Hamilton counters
that it is the most perfect form of government with its vices and would only be
made impracticable by correction of its vices. Jefferson adds:

> The room being hung around with a collection of the portraits of remarkable
> men, among them were those of Bacon, Newton and Locke, Hamilton asked
> me who they were. I told him they were my trinity of the three greatest men the
> world had ever produced, naming them. He paused for some time: "the greatest
> man," said he, "that ever lived, was Julius Caesar." Mr. Adams was honest as
> a politician, as well as a man; Hamilton honest as a man, but, as a politician,
> believing in the necessity of either force or corruption to govern men.[1]

The passage suggests much about Jefferson's political, moral, and even
epistemological ideals. It suggests that his political ideals excluded force
and corruption. It suggests that his moral ideals demanded honesty in both
personal and political affairs, which suggests that his political ideals were
answerable to moral ideals. In addition, it suggests that his epistemological
ideals—given that Bacon, Locke, and Newton were dyed-in-the-wool empiricists—were empiricist.[2]

Jefferson—qua architect, lawyer, farmer, inventor, astronomer, statesman,
classicist, anthropologist, musician, surveyor, philologist, naturalist, economist, and philosopher, among other things—was intimately involved in the
world around him and a consummate empirical investigator of it.[3] Whatever

he did, he did with investment and zest, and would show himself over time to be no dilettante.

One such experiment stood out from all the others and was a lifelong obsession with broad implications—Jefferson's republicanism. In several of his writings, Jefferson, like others of his contemporaries, spoke of the making of the American nation as an "experiment" or the "great experiment." For Jefferson, the experiment was literally an experiment—a hypothesis concerning governance by the people, through reason and regard for truth to be put to the test of experiment.

In a letter to John Tyler (June 28, 1804), Jefferson mentions an "experiment" of representative government in which America is involved.[4]

> No experiment can be more interesting than that we are now trying, and which we trust will end in establishing the fact, that man may be governed by reason and truth. Our first object should therefore be, to leave open to him all the avenues to truth. . . .
>
>   I hold it, therefore, certain, that to open the doors of truth, and to fortify the habit of testing everything by reason, are the most effectual manacles we can rivet on the hands of our successors to prevent their manacling the people with their own consent.

After his ascendency to president, Jefferson writes to Joseph Priestley (March 21, 1801) of a second revolution of the American people. The experiment is now a "great experiment": "We can no longer say there is nothing new under the sun. For this whole chapter in the history of man is new. The great experiment of our Republic is new." Jefferson's "Draft Declaration and Protest of the Commonwealth of Virginia, on the Principles of the Constitution of the United States of America, and on the Violations of Them," written in December 1825, also mentions a "great experiment."

> We owe every other sacrifice to ourselves, to our federal brethren, and to the world at large, to pursue with temper and perseverance the great experiment which shall prove that man is capable of living in society, governing itself by laws self-imposed, and securing to its members the enjoyment of life, liberty, property, and peace; and further to show, that even when the government of its choice shall manifest a tendency to degeneracy, we are not at once to despair but that the will and the watchfulness of its sounder parts will reform its aberrations, recall it to original and legitimate principles, and restrain it within the rightful limits of self-government.[5]

Jefferson's vision for America was more than setting out a new manner of living, driven by revolution, for different sorts of people in a different land. America was Jefferson's vision of a modern Arcadia and the experimental results therein obtained would be generalizable to humans worldwide.[6] "Nor are we acting for ourselves alone, but for the whole human race," he writes to Governor David Hall (July 6, 1802). "The event of our experiment is to shew whether man can be trusted with self-government. The eyes of suffering humanity are fixed on us with anxiety, as their only hope, and on such a theater for such a cause we must suppress all smaller passions and local consider-ations." As John Taylor neatly sums in a letter to Jefferson (December 26, 1804), the president essayed to "subdue tyranny by intellect" and thereby make a display of republicanism "in an experiment, fair, full and final."

Jefferson has planned, scholar Robert Faulkner rightly states, "for a great democratic nation of private individuals who are protected by a government that is their agent. The plan can be not only definite, but also a future-oriented and universal project to improve the world. For its politics and science of basic needs can be expected to attract most people, and it can also reconcile them to superiors who seem but representatives and experts in service to the public or to humanity at large."[7] Jefferson historian Dumas Malone adds that the vision was shared: "Nothing was more characteristic of the Patriots at the birth of the Republic than the conviction that the American people were unique in their character, their opportunity, and their mission, and that their experiment in self-government was destined to set an example for the world. To that faith and vision Jefferson purposed that the country should return."[8]

Jefferson was conducting, simply stated, a parochial experiment with global implications. He saw America as a sort of political proving grounds for his view of the human condition—humans as free, rational, and progressive beings.[9] Given that, he wished to establish a minimal political structure that invited some measure of political participation from all persons and allowed for virtue and talent, not wealth and birth, to govern. America would instan-tiate everything great from England and France—especially their science and technology—while avoiding the pitfalls of the excesses and deficiencies of each. It would be the rebirth of Greco-Roman agrarianism within a liberal, noncoercive, and progressive framework. Jefferson sums in a letter to John Adams (February 28, 1796): "Never was a finer canvas presented to work on than our countrymen. All of them engaged in agriculture or the pursuits of honest industry, independent in their circumstances, enlightened as to their rights, and firm in their habits of order and obedience to the laws. This I hope will be the age of experiments in government, and that their basis will be founded on principles of honesty, not of mere force."

The point is made starkly and poignantly by historian Adrienne Koch: "One is struck by Jefferson's belief that American political procedures represent something novel in the history of civilization. Jefferson appreciated fully 'the American experiment,' crediting it partly to the spontaneous adaptation of immigrants of Scottish and English ancestry to a new soil and fresh problems, but tending to view the 'experiment' with the eyes of a classicist and scholar,"[10] and I add, a normativist.

This book examines Jefferson's great experiment—his participatory republicanism—and its several naturalistic, political, moral, and educative components. Jefferson's great experiment, I maintain, does not involve instantiation of any particular form of government, but instead a basic mostly bottom-up schema that allows for honest, representative government in a liberal, progressive frame. Like the philosophical and scientific contributions of his three fellow empiricists—Bacon, Locke, and Newton—Jefferson's project is amazingly grand in scale, ambitious, and comprehensive. His overall aim is that measure of human happiness to be gained through scientific and moral progress by breaking the mold of bad, centralized, and coercive government. Jefferson's new mold is liberal because it allows significant free space for human individuality while it encourages free choice of political participation. It is also moral in that Jefferson's individuals are essentially communal beings duty-bound to each other by ties of benevolence.

FOUR SUBSTRATAL THESES

Jefferson's republican experiment is a general schema of a thriving political unit, undergirded by a liberal vision of the good life—what I elsewhere call his "liberal eudaemonism."[11] As Jefferson's unique notion of liberalism is the focus of much of chapters 2 through 4, in the remainder of this introduction I cover four complementary substratal theses—empiricism, eudaemonism, meritocracy, and progressivism—which will get fleshed out in the course of exposition.

Empiricism

Jefferson had what we would acknowledge today to be a scientist's, not a rationalist's, curiosity concerning the world around him. Following British and Scottish empiricists of his day—for example, Francis Bacon, John Locke, Lord Kames, David Hume, and Adam Smith—his attitude was unmistakably experimental.[12] His writings—the *Notes on the State of Virginia* especially—show him to be incurably scientific. A hard-shell empiricist in the manner of Bacon, Locke, and Newton—called by historian Gilbert Chinard "the herald of positivism"[13]—he was always formulating hypotheses apropos of all sorts of difficulties,[14] testing them against data, and essaying to subsume them, when confirmed, under more general and well-corroborated hypotheses. In short, ever-curious and empiricist-oriented, Jefferson was always engaged in varied scientific experiments of one sort or another—whether they concerned the viability of the American whaling industry, testing foreign crops in American soils, establishing an isochronic pendulum to be used as a measuring instrument, or assessing the moral and rational faculties of Native Americans and African Americans.[15] "I am myself an empiric in natural philosophy," he writes to George F. Hopkins (September 5, 1822), "suffering my faith to go no further than the facts. I am pleased, however, to see the efforts of hypothetical speculation, because by the collisions of different hypotheses, truth may be elicited and science advances in the end."[16]

Jefferson's *Notes on the State of Virginia* begins, at times with stunning descriptive and aesthetic detail, with an analysis of Virginia's physical characteristics—its geography, rivers, minerals, mountains, fauna, flora, and so on—before it moves to its human elements—constitution, laws, colleges, religions, manners, manufactures, history, and the like. Sprinkled throughout the book is a running commentary by Jefferson on the state of things not only in Virginia but also in other parts of the country. Query VI shows Jefferson's intent in the *Notes on the State of Virginia* is to disprove the celebrated French naturalist Le Comte de Buffon's theory that nature belittles what she produces in America, whether human or animal, in terms of size, overall numbers, and capacity to be domesticated. Jefferson offers in reply General George Washington, Benjamin Franklin, and self-taught astronomer David Rittenhouse as examples of American genius, and the bones of the wooly mammoth as an illustration that animals in North America are every bit as large as those in Europe.[17] In addition, he investigates subjects such as sea shells in the mountains (Query VI), the mammoth (Query VI), medicinal springs (Query VI), American-Indian burial mounds (Query XI), and even the formation of moisture on houses with walls of stone or brick (Query XV).[18]

Eudaemonism

Eudaemonism, drawn from Aristotle's view of eudaimōnia (commonly translated as "happiness"), is the view that the best manner of living is to live well or to flourish. Etymologically, it comes from the Greek word *eu*, meaning "good," and the Greek word daimon, meaning "lesser deity." The sense here literally is that of being favored by a god (i.e., being fortunate); less literally, but more in keeping with Greek use of eudaimōnia by the time of Aristotle (384–322 BCE) is that of happiness in the sense of living well or flourishing. The two most prominent eudaemonist schools of thought in antiquity are that of Aristotle and that of the Stoics, which came into being shortly after Aristotle and was prominent for some five hundred years.

For Aristotle, human flourishing is critically linked with the concept of aretē ("virtue" or, more generally, "excellence"), which has both political and apolitical senses. Human flourishing involves politically—in the sense of the *polis* or Greek city-state—the exercise of excellence of character (ethikē aretē) through generous, courageous, magnanimous, just, and friendly actions, among others. Apolitically, human flourishing involves the exercise of excellence of thought (dianoētikē aretē) through contemplation of unchanging truths.[19] Both sorts of excellence are manifestations of psychical equanimity.

For Aristotle, other factors outside of human control influence human flourishing, for the goods that comprise it, though preeminently psychical, are also external (e.g., wealth and fame) and bodily (e.g., health and beauty). Human flourishing involves some measure of all goods, but a complete stock of psychical goods without bodily and external goods prevents one from being miserable, though one will not be happy, while a complete stock of bodily and external goods without psychical goods leads to misery, as if one were without goods of any sort.[20]

For the Greek and Roman Stoics, in contrast, human flourishing is solely a matter of internal, psychical goods—that is, the expression of internal stability through virtuous activity. External and bodily goods are not goods per se, because, as Seneca says, "[they] can be put to wrong use," and whatever can be put to wrong use is not an unqualified good.[21] Though Aristotle's external and bodily goods are not categorized as "goods" for Stoics, they are deemed "conveniences" (Gr., proēgmena; L., commoda) in that it is better for one to have them, but they nowise influence one's happiness. Thus, psychical goods are sufficient for human happiness.[22]

Jefferson is a eudaemonist of some persuasion—though, as we shall see, for him morally correct action is mostly independent of reason. His addresses and correspondence especially show that he has a very definite notion of the good life, which critically involves virtuous activity through exercise of the moral sense as well as some stock of bodily and external goods. As is the case with Aristotle and the Stoics, human happiness for Jefferson involves no separation of political and private dimensions. Hence, authenticity is essential for happiness.[23]

Democracy/Meritocracy

For Jefferson, good government is moral government through a virtuous citizenry—what I have called elsewhere Jefferson's "Platonic thesis."[24] Four tiers of government—wards, counties, states, and the nation—will be in place so that everyone has some participatory role in governing. The citizens must contribute to their fullest capacity. That entails election of, oversight of, and, if necessary, recall of governing officials, as well as political involvement at local levels of governing—the democratic component of Jefferson's republicanism. Key, however, he writes to John Adams (October 28, 1813), is that the most capable and the morally superior—that is, the natural aristocracy[25] ("natural aristoi")—must be encouraged to govern at the higher levels—the meritocratic component of Jefferson's republicanism. The way to ensure that the naturally best and not the artificially best rule is to leave the election of governors in the hands of the people, suitably educated. Jefferson even claims axiologically that having the best rule—the best genius and most virtuous—is the best test of a good government.

Given that good government requires a virtuous citizenry and virtuous governors, Jefferson's political ideals are inescapably normative. That is not merely to say Jefferson's political views have a normative or moral dimension. I argue that Jefferson's political views are essentially moral views. Jefferson has a definite conception of the human organism and how it functions best. Humans for Jefferson have a well-defined, fixed nature that is capable of improvement and refinement through exposure to the right sorts of experiences. Human improvement and refinement require the right sort of political milieu—one that is participatory, free, and progressive.[26]

Progressivism

As his 1813 letter on the natural aristoi with Adams shows, Jefferson's political experiment is untrivially revolutionary. He is proposing government of the best—the most virtuous and talented—elected by and responsible to the people. Adams, the realist and Federalist, cannot do other than see things as they have been. For Adams, history shows that humans are incapable of escaping their past. Jefferson, the idealist and Republican, sees things as they might and ought to be. For Jefferson, history is morally and intellectually progressive and is a guide to future avenues of possible human exploration. History is on the move, humans are progressing, and Jefferson's republicanism, a meritocratic admixture of aristocratic and equalitarian ideals, is a result of that moral and intellectual advancement.

Jefferson's writings show that he consistently clung to the belief that humans as a whole were progressive beings, though progress was tortuous and sometimes had retrogressive stages. In keeping with the general trend of Enlightenment thinking, Jefferson believed that the human mind and the moral sense, an innate moral capacity, were massively underdeveloped, and thus capable of substantial improvement. Apropos of the human mind, there were Bacon in philosophy; Boyle, Brahe, Galileo, Kepler, Rittenhouse, and Newton in science; and Locke, Sidney, and Tracy in political theory. Apropos of moral theory, there were Kames, Priestley, Sterne, and Hutcheson. Following the lead of such progressors, Jefferson's republican ideals were directed toward maximizing human improvement to promote human flourishing.[27] Progress was not posited metaphysically; it was instead observed over time. Thus, Jefferson's progressivism was a hodgepodge of sorts: Aristotelian teleology tamed by Baconian empiricism.

One of the most important implications of Jefferson's republicanism as it relates to progressivism is this. His republicanism qua political philosophy is decidedly at odds with a politics of coercion or power. In linking liberty to science, Jefferson presciently envisaged at least the possibility of a global community of nations, freely exchanging goods and ideas to promote human flourishing. In that regard, Jefferson, like Kant, was far in advance of others of his day and may be called a philosopher of peace.[28]

In the ensuing chapters, I give what I take to be the first full view of the philosophy undergirding Thomas Jefferson's writings. It is my hope that this book
will give rise to heightened critical discussion of the merits and demerits of
the philosophical content of Jefferson's writings. I hope that my philosophical
findings, if they pass the test of time, will create a sound platform on which
other scholars might build. If they do not pass the test of time, I hope that the
mistakes I have made will lead to judicious and more refined critical assessment of Jefferson qua philosopher.

PART 1

JEFFERSON ON NATURE

CHAPTER 1

"I CANNOT REASON OTHERWISE"

Jefferson's Cosmos

"I like the dreams of the future better than the history of the past."
—TJ to John Adams, August 1, 1816

John Adams, at the end of a letter to Jefferson (September 14, 1813), writes: "Now, my Friend Jefferson, suppose an eternal self-existent being existing from Eternity, possessed of infinite Wisdom, Goodness and Power, in absolute total Solitude, Six thousand Years ago, conceiving the benevolent project of creating a Universe! I have no more to say, at present," he adds, as if to dismiss that notion as bunkum. In the closing paragraph of the letter, Adams adds: "It has been long, very long a settled opinion in my Mind that there is now, never will be, and ever was but one being who can Understand the Universe. And that it is not only vain but wicked for insects to pretend to comprehend it."

Like Adams, Jefferson never professed to have much knowledge on matters of deity and the cosmos. Though there is no evidence that he ever will-fully embraced atheism, he was reviled as an atheist by others—especially by political opponents and no more than during the elections of 1800 and 1804. The reasons were chiefly three: he authored the Virginia Statute for Religious Freedom, deemed heretical; he championed French philosophy and science, deemed atheistic; and he wrote *Notes on the State of Virginia*, deemed het-erodox.[1] Nonetheless, Jefferson seemed consistently to be a believer in some sort of superior power that, at least, created the cosmos and set it to order. "When the atheist descanted on the unceasing motion and circulation of matter through the animal, vegetable and mineral kingdoms, gifted with the power of reproduction," he writes thoughtfully years later to Adams (April 8, 1816), "the theist, pointing 'to the heavens above, and to the earth beneath, and to the waters under the earth,' asked, if these did not proclaim a first cause pos-sessing intelligence and power."

This chapter is an introduction to Jefferson's philosophical thinking by introducing his cosmos. It comprises two sections. The first section concerns his physicalism. I begin with Jefferson's materialism and then go on to depict his idea of deity—a material being that created the cosmos, set its parts in motion, and in some sense superintends it. The second section concerns his naturalism. I show how men in society differ from men in the state of nature. I then explicate Jefferson's notion of natural rights. Finally, I have something to say about how science, for Jefferson, enables humans to penetrate nature's hidden modus agendi.

JEFFERSON'S PHYSICALISM

Jefferson's physical universe is based on an empiricist epistemology, expressed neatly in a reply (August 15, 1820) to a letter of John Adams (May 12, 1820).[2] He begins on assumption of the veridicality of sensory impressions: "A single sense may indeed be sometimes deceived, but rarely: and never all our senses together, with their faculty of reasoning." The implications are that the senses work intimately with reason and that the totality of impressions gives reason information sufficient to guard against being mistaken, though reason is certainly not an infallible guide.

Jefferson then offers Adams a playful, Cartesian sketch of his epistemology.

> "I feel: therefore I exist."[3] I feel bodies which are not myself: there are other existencies then. I call them *matter*. I feel them changing place. This gives me *motion*. Where there is an absence of matter, I call it *void*, or *nothing*, or *immaterial space*. On the basis of sensation, of matter and motion, we may erect the fabric of all the certainties we can have or need. I can conceive *thought* to be an action of a particular organization of matter, formed for that purpose by its creator, as well as that *attraction* is an action of matter, or *magnetism* of loadstone.

The use of "feel" and not "think" is intentional and in keeping with the thinking of philosopher Destutt de Tracy,[4] but the barebones structure is, of course, Newtonian. In *Principia Mathematica*, Isaac Newton begins by defining "mass" and "motion," and the forces of or that act on bodies—the "innate force of matter," "impressed force," and "centripetal force." He then writes of "absolute time," "absolute space," "absolute place," and "absolute motion" without offering definitions because they are "well known to all." Next he offers his celebrated three laws of motion.[5] Newton's aim throughout is not to wax epistemological or metaphysical. Given the axioms, corollaries, and lemmas of his system, the explanatory power of the system speaks for itself. Yet Jefferson, pace Newton, does not essay to give any details of bodily attraction. His aims are more banausic than metaphysical. He wishes to show that the existences in the universe are all material.

The physical universe of Jefferson is similar to that of the third-century BCE Greek philosopher Epicurus, of whom he claimed discipleship in a letter to American ambassador and longtime friend William Short (October 31, 1819). "Everything comprises bodies and void," states Epicurus, "for in every case, sense perception itself testifies that bodies exist, and it is because of sense perception that we must infer through reason what is non-evident." The existence of void-space is clear through reason, for bodies move and they must move in something.[6] Even soul, dispersed evenly throughout the body and responsible chiefly for sensation, comprises tenuous atoms.[7] There is no room for any substance that is immaterial.

Jefferson is likewise an out-and-out physicalist. Perhaps with Epicurus in mind, Jefferson addresses the objection, made famous by Descartes, that thinking is due to some sort of immaterial substance. The mystery of matter, having the mode of action called thinking, is no more mysterious than the sun, having the mode of action called attraction, Jefferson continues in his letter to Adams (August 15, 1820). As attraction is a property of all bodies, so too thinking is a property all types of a certain kind of matter. That might prove puzzling, but it is much less puzzling than explaining how nonmatter can will and put matter in motion. He concludes boldly: "To talk of *immaterial* existences is to talk of *nothings*. To say that the human soul, angels, god, are immaterial, is to say they are *nothings*, or that there is no god, no angels, no soul. I cannot reason otherwise." Matter is endowed by the creator—a thinking material being, since no immaterial being can put matter in motion.

Though he claimed to be a disciple of the Greek philosopher Epicurus,[8] Jefferson's physicalist system is not a commitment to atomism of an Epicurean sort. Epicurus accounted for the range of existences and their diversity by positing invisible "uncuttables" (Gr., atoma)—that is, atoms. Invisible on account of their size, their numbers were infinite, though their kinds were ungraspably large, not infinite, and each moved rectilinearly through void-space on account of its weight. Bodies formed because of collisions between and linkage of atoms, as a result of uncaused swerves—needed posits for the congregation of atoms into visible bodies. Bodies decayed because of the constant bombardment of atoms over time.[9]

Jefferson, in contrast, was not a metaphysical atomist of the Epicurean sort, but a nominalist in the manner of the philosopher John Locke.[10] He expresses his nominalism unequivocally in a letter to New Jersey politician Dr. John Manners (February 22, 1814):

> Nature has, in truth, produced units only through all her works. Classes, orders, genera, species, are not of her works. Her creation is of individuals. No two animals are exactly alike; no two plants, nor even two leaves or blades of grass; no two crystallizations. And if we may venture from what is within the cognizance of such organs as ours, to conclude on that beyond their powers, we must believe that no two particles of matter are of exact resemblance. This infinitude of units or individuals being far beyond the capacity of our memory, we are obliged, in aid of that, to distribute them into masses, throwing into each of these all the individuals which have a certain degree of resemblance; to subdivide these again into smaller groups, according to certain points of dissimilitude observable in them, and so on until we have formed what we call a system of classes, orders, genera and species. In doing this, we fix arbitrarily on such characteristic resemblances and differences as seem to us most prominent and invariable in the several subjects, and most likely to take a strong hold in our memories.

The aim here is biological; the target is the Swedish botanist Carl Linnaeus. Jefferson is responding to Linnaeus's system of biotic classification, which had become the received view in Jefferson's day. He notes that Linnaeus proffers solid practical reasons for the groupings he has made, but there are reasons to be suspicious of the veridicality of the system. Jefferson speaks of "characteristic resemblances and differences as seem to us most prominent and invariable in the several subjects, and most likely to take a strong hold in our memories." That suggests nature's plan is inscrutable to humans, who group together natural objects by convenience, not by their true natural relations. The passage is reminiscent of Aristotle, who contrasts what is better known to humans with what is better known by nature.[11] It also harmonizes with the thinking of Scottish philosopher Lord Kames, who maintains deity has created humans so that their sensory impressions are of utmost use, not necessarily so that such impressions accord neatly with the nature of things.[12] Thus, any attempt at an aboveboard classification is left to fancy, not fact.

In a later letter to Massachusetts politician Edward Everett (February 24, 1823), Jefferson says observed particulars are found to be nothing but concretizations of atoms. He then advises caution. "By analyzing too minutely we often reduce our subject to atoms, of which the mind loses hold."

Is Jefferson here endorsing metaphysical atomism? His phrasing "of which the mind loses hold" suggests that reduction to atoms is due mostly to a certain frustration of mind at the thought of dividing without end, and a human tendency to discontinue the dividing at some point to end the frustration, not any actual state of the cosmos. Here "atoms" are to be taken not in the sense of real irreducible particles, as was the case with Newton, but instead as arbitrary epistemological stopping points. Jefferson seems to be endorsing nothing more than a sort of pragmatic atomist.

Matter and Motion

Though Jefferson's universe is similar to that of Epicurus, his notion of deity is non-Epicurean. Epicurus's cosmos exists independently of deity. For Epicurus, the gods exist—all persons have an innate conception of them[13]—and are blessed and indestructible. Being most blessed and virtuous, they have quasi-human form with quasi blood. Unlike humans, they partake of no labor, no serious occupations, but being freed of all disturbance, they are idle and self-sufficient. They merely "rejoice in their own wisdom and virtue." Being perfect, they nowise involve themselves in the affairs of humans. Thus, supplication is aimless.[14]

Epicurus's deities, comprising atoms like all other existences, are also the accidental products of the collisions of atoms. Due to the unceasing bombardment of atoms on larger bodies, all existences, except the gods, are destructible and ephemeral. Yet each god, indestructible, has a point of its creation, but no point of its dissolution. The coaffection of atoms in divine bodies is, thus, somehow of a permanent sort—impervious to whatever blows they might receive.

For Jefferson, in contrast, the cosmos is no accident. It gives unmistakably evidence of design—cause linked with effect—that is inconsistent with the arbitrary collisions of Epicurean atoms, which form visible bodies.[15] Noting of the surge of liberty across many parts of the globe, he writes in his "Auto-biography": "This is a wonderful instance of great events from small causes. So inscrutable is the arrangements of causes & consequences in this world that a two-penny duty on tea, unjustly imposed in a sequestered part of it, changes the condition of all its inhabitants."[16] One can nearly see the hand of deity at work, either in directly superintending the course of events or through implanting the spirit of liberty so viscerally in humans that the slightest taste of it leads to riotous consequences.[17] Again, he writes in a letter to John Adams (April 11, 1823), "When we take a view of the Universe, in its parts general or particular, it is impossible for the human mind not to be perceive and feel a conviction of design, consummate skill, and indefinite power in every atom of its composition." This argument from design—inclusion of "perceive" and "feel" again is nonaccidental and in keeping Destutt de Tracy's episte-mology[18]—allows the possibility of Jefferson's material deity being subject to the laws governing the cosmos only insofar as it does not close the door on some sort of pantheism.[19] Otherwise the clear articulation of a material creator-deity strongly suggests a being that antedated the cosmos and brought it into being at some point in time.

It is likely that Jefferson, who freely admits to having a fondness of Stoic ethical thinking,[20] had Cicero's *On the Nature of the Gods*—a treatise concerning Stoic cosmology—in mind when writing to Adams.[21] He stated on several occa-sions his love of classical literature,[22] singled out Cicero on several occasions,[23] and listed Cicero among the "most esteemed of the sects of ancient philosophy, or other individuals."[24] Moreover, the Scottish empiricists (e.g., Bolingbroke, Reid, Kames, Stewart, and Smith) who influenced Jefferson considerably drew much inspiration from the Stoics. Even his beloved novelist and sermonizer Laurence Sterne begins volumes 1 and 2 of Jefferson's favorite work of fiction, *Tristram Shandy*, with a quote from the Stoic Epictetus.

In book 2 of *On the Nature of the Gods*, the Stoic apologist Balbus begins with his modus operandi. He aims to show that the gods exist, to explain their nature, to prove that they govern the cosmos, and to demonstrate their concern for humankind.[25]

In his 1823 letter to John Adams, Jefferson is expressly committed to the existence and governance of a deity. Of their nature, he says, little can be known other than their superior intelligence and overall beneficence.[26] That he thinks they concern themselves with human affairs, insofar as they favor humans before other animals, seems unlikely.

Jefferson then offers four arguments in support of the existence of deity. All are inductive. The first two seem analogical but are not to be taken thus. The third is an argument from consensus. The last is an argument from authority. In what follows, I sketch out Jefferson's arguments and compare them to arguments Balbus gives in *On the Nature of the Gods*.

Jefferson's first argument is an argument from design, which essays to depict a cosmos whose parts reveal directly a cause-and-effect pattern that points unmistakably back to an ultimate cause.

> I hold (without appeal to revelation) that when we take a view of the universe; . . . the movements of the heavenly bodies, so exactly held in their courses by the balance of centrifugal and centripetal forces; the structure of our earth itself, with its distribution of lands, waters, and atmosphere; animal and vegetable bodies, each perfectly organized whether as insect, man or mammoth; it is impossible not to believe, that there is in all this, design, cause and effect, up to an ultimate cause, a Fabricator of all things from matter and motion.[27]

Following empirics like Tracy and Kames, Jefferson is not arguing via analogy. Design is directly seen and it speaks directly to the existence of its author.

Balbus argues for the existence of god by virtue of design from II.4 to II.44. He begins at II.4, "When we gaze upward to the sky and contemplate the heavenly bodies, what can be so obvious and so manifest as that there must exist some power possessing transcendent intelligence by whom these things are ruled?" States Balbus:

> When you see a statue or a painting, you recognize the exercise of art; when you observe from a distance the course of a ship, you do not hesitate to assume that its motion is guided by reason and by art; when you look at a sundial or a waterclock, you infer that it tells the time by art and not by chance; how then can it be consistent to suppose that the world, which includes both the works of art in question, the craftsmen who made them, and everything else besides, can be devoid of purpose and of reason?[28]

At II.16, Balbus invokes the authority of the preeminent Stoic philosopher Chrysippus to demonstrate that the design exhibited by the cosmos greatly exceeds the capacities of human intelligence and, thus, bespeaks a deity. The arguments herein contained are numerous and variegated. That the order of the cosmos is causal is a large part of Cicero's explication of Stoic divination in *On Divination* and a point iterated in *On the Nature of the Gods* at II.82 and following.

Next, Jefferson gives an argument from superintendence. Some stars have disappeared; others have come to be. Comets, with their "incalculable courses," deviate from regular orbits and demand "renovation under other laws." Some species of animal have become extinct. "Were there no restoring power, all existences might extinguish successively, one by one, until all should be reduced to a shapeless chaos." Superintendence here need not imply direct intervention on the course of physical events, for to do so would be to invoke supernature—namely, miracles or events not explicable by recourse to existing natural laws. A natural capacity for restoration might be in certain types of matter in the same way that mind is in certain types of matter.[29]

Balbus argues for the governance of the cosmos from II.73 to II.153. He begins by addressing the mistaken notion that deity (Gr., pronoia or "fore-thought") is a sort of fortune-telling fishwife—a deity that sits outside of, observes, and predicts events. The cosmos is governed by the gods in that it and all its parts were "set in order at the beginning" and are "governed for all time by divine providence."[30]

For Stoics, governance is a matter of complete immersion in and fusion with events. "The word 'cosmos' . . . relates to deity himself—the artificer of the cosmos who at times absorbs into himself all of creation and re-cre-ates later" through an infinite series of identically unfolding, recurrent cycles. Thus, the cosmos—interchangeably called Reason, Fate, or Zeus—begins when the fiery deity acts on the passive, precosmic water. Fire, air, water, and earth result and the cosmos comes into being. *Pneuma*—a tenuous, vital, and substratal matter that is pervasive in all cycles—brings order to the basic matters through effecting a certain tension throughout the cosmos. Thus come to be all the existents of the cosmos. At some point, the cosmos matures to such extent that all water is consumed and the cosmos becomes a complete conflagration. Yet in the all-consuming fire, the seeds of the next cosmos are sewn.[31] Cosmic governance, thus, is a matter of self-regulation.

Third, Jefferson gives an argument from consensus. Jefferson writes to Adams (April 11, 1823), "So irresistible are these evidences of an intelligent and powerful Agent that, of the infinite numbers of men who have existed thro' all time, they have believed, in the proportion of a million at least to Unit, in the hypothesis of an eternal pre-existent Universe." Such "unanimous sentiment," he admits, is an argument from likelihood, not a proof, but it makes the existence of deity much more probable, he thinks, than not.

Likewise, Balbus argues on behalf of the Stoics that the firm and permanent fixation of belief in deity in the minds of humans is evidence of existence. "The main issue is agreed among all men of all nations, inasmuch as all have engraved in their minds an innate belief that the gods exist."[32] That belief only gets strengthened over time, while other firmly held beliefs, such as the hippocentaur or the chimaera, are vitiated with time. "For time obliterates the inventions of imagination, while they confirm the judgments of nature"[33]—a most Jefferson-like sentiment.[34]

Finally, Jefferson appeals to an argument from authority as evidence for the existence of deity. At John 2.24 of the Bible, Jesus says that God is spirit (*pneuma*). Jefferson points out correctly that *pneuma*, for the ancients, was deemed a material substance, though a tenuous one. He appeals to Origen, who writes similarly of deity. Book 2 of John speaks plainly the words of Jesus: "In the beginning God existed, and reason [or mind] was with God, and that mind was God. This was in the beginning with God. All things were created by it, and without it was made not one thing which was made."[35] In consequence, appeals to authority show that deity preexisted before the world and that deity, pace the Presbyterians with whom Jefferson perpetually quarreled, is one, not three.[36]

Balbus too employs the argument from authority apropos of deity, by citing arguments from the Stoics Cleanthes, Chrysippus, and Zeno[37] as well as from Plato and Aristotle—all of whom would certainly have been credible authorities to an ancient reader.[38]

Deism or Theism?

By *deism* let us understand the view of the existence of a deity that has created the cosmos, but thereafter sits apart from and is uninvolved with what has been created. By *theism* let us understand the view of the existence of a deity that has created the cosmos and is thereafter in some sense intimately involved with it. Was Jefferson a deist or a theist? The difference can be grasped via analogy of a builder who constructs a house, sells it, and goes off to do something else as contrasted with a builder who constructs a house and thereafter cares for it, because, say, he lives in it.

Letters show that Jefferson's view of deity changed over time. Early on, he believed that the universe was harmoniously and perfectly designed and regulated by a divine artificer and that perceived flaws in the design were attributable to human ignorance, not divine imperfection. Later, upon acceptance of the extinction of species,[39] he adopted a more hands-on view of deity—that is, one that gave the creator a superintending role of some sort in addition to that of creator.

Jefferson was always an open-minded freethinker vis-à-vis the existence and nature of deity and other Gordian issues. He had great tolerance of differences of opinion on such issues. He asked merely that investigators give an honest, evidence-based, and rational effort. He deemed it more ingenuous and exemplary to form the wrong conclusion by following available evidence than to stumble upon the right conclusion by happenstance or sleight of hand. I offer two instances, each related to deity.

First, in Query XVII of his *Notes on the State of Virginia*, published in 1782, Jefferson investigates the issue of religious toleration:

> But our rulers can have authority over such natural rights, only as we have submitted to them. The rights of conscience we never submitted, we could not submit. We are answerable for them to our God. The legitimate powers of government extend to such acts only as are injurious to others. But it does me no injury for my neighbor to say there are twenty gods, or no god. It neither picks my pocket nor breaks my leg. If it be said his testimony in a court of justice cannot be relied on, reject it then, and be the stigma on him. Constraint may make him worse by making him a hypocrite, but it will never make him a truer man. It may fix him obstinately in his errors, but will not cure them. Reason and free inquiry are the only effectual agents against error. Give a loose to them, they will support the true religion by bringing every false one to their tribunal, to the test of their investigation. They are the natural enemies of error, and of error only.

The account was scandalously blunt for the time. Persons are free to believe as they wish, without the intervention of governors, even on issues such as the existence of deity, so long as in holding their religious views they do no injury to others. Many years later, Jefferson laconically defends his bluntness in a letter to lawyer and statesman George Thatcher (January 26, 1824): *deorum injurae, diis curae*.[40]

Second, Jefferson advises his nephew Peter Carr (August 10, 1787) to examine meticulously religious issues. His recipe is to "lay aside all prejudice on both sides, & neither believe nor reject anything because any other persons, or [any] description of persons [that] have rejected or believed it." He says:

> Do not be frightened from this inquiry by any fear of its consequences. If it ends in a belief that there is no god, you will find incitements to virtue in the comfort & pleasantness you feel in its exercise, and the love of others which it will procure you. If you find reason to believe there is a god, a conscious-ness that you are acting under his eye, & that he approves you, will be a vast additional incitement; if that there be a future state, the hope of a happy exis-tence in that increases the appetite to deserve it; if that Jesus was also a god, you will be comforted by a belief of his aid and love.

Jefferson sums, "Your own reason is the only oracle given you by heaven, and you are answerable not for the rightness but uprightness of the decision." What one believes, he seems to be saying, is inconsequential so long as what one believes is the product of guileless, evenhanded rational inquiry. If deity exists and sits in judgment, it will likely judge disuse or deliberate misuse of reason more harshly than drawing a wrong conclusion based on honest effort. He writes to New York veterinarian William Carver (December 4, 1823): "For the use of this reason, however, every one is responsible to the God who has planted it in his breast, as a light for his guidance, and that, by which alone he will be judged. . . . It is better always to set a good example than to follow a bad one." There is more to be said, however. Like Balbus, Jefferson is clear that aboveboard inquiry is, over time, self-corrective. Over time, fictions fade away and the truth is thereby disclosed.[41]

Jefferson's early view of deity suggests a commitment to deism—the belief that deity exists as a material creator of the cosmos, but somehow tran-scends that which was created in the manner of an axe maker who fashions and then sells a handsome double-axe he has made. Deity is an intelligent craftsperson like Plato's *demiourgos* in *Timaeus*—an architect/builder who plans and builds the cosmos and then leaves it to itself.

Overall, Jefferson's early conception of deity is founded on the claim, given observational succor, that the cosmos is orderly, homogenous, self-suf-ficient, and perfect—or nearly so. For instance, he argues via analogy, in a letter to politician and Philadelphian Charles Thomson (September 20, 1787), rocks grow in layers in many directions, following the example of trees. This explanation entices him because it allows for consistency in nature—all things grow and decay—and it is consistent with Stoic vitalism—that there is a "vital, material unity and coherence to the cosmos as there is with all things that are its parts."[42] It also suggests an economic strain in nature: Why multiply causes, if nature can do much with one? Again, when he mentions the mammoth exhumed from American soil in his *Notes on the State Virginia*, he speaks of it as if it still exists somewhere on the continent.[43] He argues that there is thus far neither evidence of nature allowing any one race of animals to have become extinct nor evidence to date of nature forming links that allow for the possibility of being broken.[44] "The annihilation of any species of existence," he says in a letter to Virginian John Stuart (November 10, 1796), "is so unexampled in any parts of the economy of nature which we see, that we have a right to conclude, as to the parts we do not see, that the probabilities against such annihilation are stronger than those for it." So, he at least sees himself to be on grounds as solid as those persons who would argue for its extinction.

The durability of natural things invites Jefferson to speculate on the magnificence of the divine cause of such durability. It also demonstrates Jefferson's early commitment, like other naturalists of his day, to the "great chain of being"—a hierarchy of living things that presupposed that nothing was created in vain, and thus nothing could become extinct without disturbing the fragility of this chain.

Advances in science forced Jefferson to change his mind about deity as well as the chain of being. Perfectionism, early on for Jefferson, entailed that the number of species on the planet was fixed, unalterable, and part of a progressive chain at the moment of creation. In time, the "paleontologists" of Jefferson's day provided sufficient geological evidence—the undeniable existence of numerous fossilized species of biota that no longer exist—to compel Jefferson to relinquish that view. In *Essay on the Theory of the Earth*, for instance, naturalist Georges Cuvier argued that the fossils in the various geological strata were the result of periodic catastrophes—large-scale natural disasters—that devastated the earth and extinguished numerous species of biota. Those remaining species then repopulated the globe. A pupil of Cuvier, Alcide d'Orbigny, posited some twenty-eight global catastrophes, each of which annihilated all living things, and some unknown force to repopulate the globe. Religionists were wont to see the direct hand of deity in such episodes.

Jefferson, if only grudgingly, came to acknowledge the genuineness of biotic extinction. That certainly led him to recognize that nature was less economical than he had formerly envisaged. Yet there is no evidence that it lessened his conviction in the perfection and wisdom of deity or in the fruitfulness of nature. Deity, qua creator of the cosmos, merely took on the added role of cosmic superintendent, and the cosmos, I suspect, merely became more inscrutable. How did acknowledgement of divine superintendence alter his conception of deity and the cosmos?

Jefferson's view of deity's superintendence is expressed succinctly, inchoately, and crudely in his cosmological letter to Adams (April 11, 1823):

> We see, too, evident proofs of the necessity of a superintending power to maintain the Universe in its course and order. Stars, well known, have disappeared, new ones have come into view, comets, in their incalculable courses, may run foul of suns and planets and require renovation under other laws; certain races of animals are become extinct; and, were there no restoring power, all existences might extinguish successively, one by one, until all should be reduced to a shapeless chaos.

There is not only a "superintending power" but also a "restoring power" without which all life, at some point in time, could cease through the gradual extinction of each species over time.

Jefferson never expatiates on deity's restorative capacities. However, there is no reason to believe that divine restoration involves periodic divine intervention in cosmic affairs, consistent with d'Orbigny's catastrophism, in any kind of supernatural manner. Jefferson's insistence that Jesus's true teachings can be extracted from the New Testament simply by eliminating in them what is miraculous or contrary to nature is evidence that he would have found unpalatable an interventionist account of restoration, inconsistent with physical principles of the cosmos.[45] The "restorative" capacities of deity were likely some sort of hitherto-undisclosed and god-imposed laws governing natural bodies. That, of course, does not debar the possibility of pantheism—the equivalence of deity and cosmos.

Overall, though Jefferson agrees with Adams that it is both vain and wicked for "insects to pretend to comprehend [the cosmos]," he does think that the cosmos itself proffers certain clues about the nature of deity. The argument from design shows superhuman intelligence, potency, imagination, and skill. The argument from superintendence shows superhuman innovation or problem solving. Both give evidence of goodness, insofar it is reasonable to assume that a craftsperson, crafting, does not aim to produce something deficient or *déclassé*. What is applicable to a craftsperson is even more applicable of a divine craftsperson.

Jefferson is a staunch naturalist, and his notion of deity, a superhuman material being endowed with mind, reflects that. Like Plato and Aristotle, he needs the concept of deity to make sense of the cosmos, which bespeaks a demiurge.[46] Yet his investigation is not metempirical. He begins with an empirical examination of nature. Seeing it designed, he derives deity from etiological expediency. Like the Stoics, his examination reveals a caring and good deity, both a creator and restorative superintendent.

The notion of superintendence, forced on him through astronomical and biological findings, does not settle the deism/theism debate, depicted at the start of this section. However, two possibilities suggest themselves. First, Jefferson could be committed to the sort of deism in which deity created the cosmos as a self-sufficient entity. Superintendence here denotes the capacity for preestablished cosmic self-regulation comparable to the work of a thermostat in regulating the temperature of a building.[47] Second, Jefferson could be committed to the sort of theism in which (1) deity creates the cosmos and thereafter immerses himself in it, like the dispersion of ink in a cup of water, or (2) deity's creation of the cosmos is an act of self-actualization similar to Stoic pantheism. There is nothing, however, to decide the issue.

The "Ball of Liberty"

Does divine superintendence for Jefferson imply that deity pays especial attention to human affairs?

There are two general views of divine superintendence of human affairs, which can be dubbed interpositionism and noninterpositionism. I begin with the former first.

By *interpositionism*, let us understand the view that deity, at least sometimes and in some slight measure, privileges or intercedes in human affairs for the general good of humans. Here, deity is a sort of guiding figure, a cynosure, which has humans among all things created foremost in mind.[48]

By *noninterpositionism*, let us understand the view that deity, as creator and superintendent of cosmic affairs, neither privileges nor intercedes in human concerns. Deity has created humans in such a way that they can control for themselves at least some measure of their own happiness. Deity's superintendent role amounts merely to regulation of a most general sort—for example, ensuring a sort of cosmic equilibrium, for instance, by keeping through natural mechanisms the number of species and stars constant, or relatively so.[49]

There is much evidence for interpositionism. It is not uncommon for Jefferson to invoke deity in presidential speeches, messages, or addresses—for instance, his First Inaugural Address—for divine guidance in human affairs. Such invocations cannot be taken as bone fide evidence of a belief in divine intervention in human affairs, as they might be instances of ingenuous appeals to popular opinion to allay public apprehension.

The notion of divine superintendence favoring human affairs is also evident in several letters. For instance, in a letter to economist and political economist Tench Coxe (June 1, 1785), Jefferson speaks of the forward motion of the "ball of liberty" as proof of a heavenly god that guides human affairs in a progressive direction.

> I congratulate you on the successes of our two allies. Those of the Hollanders are new and therefore pleasing. It proves that there is a god in heaven, & that he will not slumber without end on the iniquities of tyrants, or their Stadtholder. This ball of liberty, I believe most piously, is now so well in motion that it will roll round the globe. At least the enlightened part of it, for light & liberty go together. It is our glory that we first put it into motion, & our happiness that being foremost we had no bad examples to follow.

Again, to Jean Nicolas Démeunier (ca. June 26, 1786), editor of the *Encyclopedie methodique*, he writes, "When the measure of [slaves'] tears shall be full, when their groans shall have involved heaven itself in darkness, doubtless, a God of justice will awaken to their distress, and by diffusing light and liberality among their oppressors, or, at length, by His exterminating thunder, manifest His attention to the things of this world, and that they are not left to the guidance of a blind fatality." Furthermore, to Benjamin Waring, prominent aristocrat of South Carolina (March 23, 1801), he appeals to deity for guidance in American affairs. Moreover, to David Barrow (May 1, 1815), he says: "We are not in a world ungoverned by the laws and the power of a Superior Agent. Our efforts are in His hand, and directed by it; and He will give them their effect in His own time." The suggestion in each and numerous other passages is that deity not only superintends the cosmos but also is in some sense specifically involved in human affairs. Finally, there are numerous allusions to an afterlife for humans.[50]

Nonetheless, there is also merit to noninterpositionism. Consider, for illustration, this passage from Lord Bolingbroke that Jefferson cites in his *Commonplace Book*: "man is the principal inhabitant of this planet, a being superior to all the rest, but will it follow from hence, that the system, wherein this planet rolls, or even this plane[t] alone, was made for the sake of man? will it follow, that infinite wisdom had no other end in making man, than that of making an happy creature? surely not. the suppositions are arbitrary, and the consequences absurd."[51] Again, consider what Jefferson says to Virginian Miles King (September 26, 1814) apropos of implantation of the moral sense in humans in reply to a lengthy letter from King concerning "vital religion."[52]

> I have trust in him who made us what we are, and know it was not his plan to make us always unerring. He has formed us moral agents. Not that, in the perfection of his state, he can feel pain or pleasure from any thing we may do: he is far above our power: but that we may promote the happiness of those which whom he has placed us in society, by acting honestly towards all, benevolently to those who fall within our way, respecting sacredly their rights bodily and mental, and cherishing especially their freedom conscience, as we value our own.

The sentiments avowed are that deity helps them who help themselves and that each person is empowered to help himself, which cannot occur without helping others.

Finally, there is Jefferson's express aversion to supernatural intervention, when he comments to several correspondents on the ease with which one can separate Jesus's true teachings from the corruptions of later compilers.[53] This aversion to events in the cosmos having anything but a natural explanation strongly suggests that superintendence occurs within the laws of nature—that is, that nature and natural laws superintend or have built-in regulative mechanisms.

How is one to decide between interpositionism and noninterpositionism?

It is best to take a cautious approach to such issues and not to attribute to Jefferson more than can be safely attributed. He believes, as did the Stoics, that the cosmos is "framed on a principle of benevolence" by a perfect demiurge.[54] His cosmos is a good cosmos insofar as a perfect craftsperson is incapable of crafting anything that is not good. Nonetheless, that entails only that the artificer had the best intentions in mind for its overall construction, not that the artificer had in mind the best intentions for any of its parts—for instance, humans. "When great evils happen," he says to Dr. Benjamin Rush (September 23, 1800), "I am in the habit of looking out for what good may arise from them as consolations to us: and Providence has in fact so established the order of things as that most evils are the means of producing some good." Thus, good and bad are meted out to each person and it is up to each person to make the best of circumstances. It is absurd to fret over bad things, he says Stoically to American ambassador William Short (November 28, 1814), that might never happen. Two years later, in a letter to John Adams (August 1, 1816),[55] Jefferson says, "I think, with you, that life is a fair matter of account, and the balance often, nay generally in it's favor. It is not indeed easy, by calculation of intensity and time, to apply a common measure, or to fix the par between pleasure and pain: yet it exists, and is measurable."[56] The reply bespeaks divine benevolence and interest in human concerns.

Overall, there is no reason to see deity's concern with humans for Jefferson to be above and beyond that of any of deity's concern with his other creations. Deity, as a perfect being, created everything out of love and is, thus, deserving of love. Consequently, noninterpositionism seems a more economical attribution than interpositionism.

If noninterpositionism is correct, it follows that one cannot securely ascribe to Jefferson the notion of an afterlife in which good and bad humans are correspondingly rewarded and punished.

JEFFERSON'S NATURALISM

In his famous dialogue between Head and Heart in one of his numerous letters to Maria Cosway (October 12, 1786), a married artist whom he met and with whom he fell in love while in France, Jefferson writes:

> And our own dear Monticello, where has Nature spread so rich a mantle under the eye? mountains, forests, rocks, rivers. With what majesty do we there ride above the storms! How sublime to look down into the workhouse of nature, to see her clouds, hail, snow, rain, thunder, all fabricated at our feet! And the glorious Sun, when rising as if out of a distant water, just gilding the tops of the mountains, and giving life to all nature!—I hope in god no circumstance may ever make either seek an asylum from grief!

The passage is plainly exaggerated—a barefaced attempt to entice his beloved Cosway to consider a visit to Virginia so that the two can see each other once again. Yet it also contains one of thousands of references to "nature" in Jefferson's writings. Here nature is considered from the god's-eye perspective, in which the sublime, which makes men cringe in fear, is tamed by distancing. Monticello sits above: It sits on the Olympus of mountains. Nature herself is "under" one's eye. One sits like an immortal above the mountains, forests, rocks, and rivers, and looks down on the clouds, hail, snow, rain, and even thunder, which are each at one's feet. One rides like an immortal above the storms. Placed so far above nature, there is nothing to fear. It is as if with each step up the mountain to Monticello, the sublime evanesces until it is seen for what it really is: beauty from the perspective of a deity.[57]

Jefferson's views of "nature" have been the subject of extensive study, but there is no received view. I proffer a small sampling from the literature.

Some scholars believe that Jefferson's employ of "nature" and "natural" was political and, presumably, propagandist. One scholar states: "Natural law . . . is the system of governing norms, rules, and duties that bind man—the correlative, in short, of the natural rights which he claims. Natural law in its widest legal sense (what Jefferson . . . referred to as 'the law of nature and nations') included this meaning plus the usages and customs of nations dealing with other nations in the interest of peace and under the controlling ideal of more humane and civilized practice."[58]

A second scholar mentions the effect of climate and habitat on Jefferson's naturalism—especially as it is exhibited in his *Notes on the State of Virginia*—and that makes Jefferson look very much like a Hippocratic. "Jefferson's discussion of climate has two purposes—one critical and another constructive: criticizing the theories advancing the idea of impotence and decay in the New World while, in the process, constructing a scientific vindication of the natural and political constitution of America."[59]

Still another scholar asserts Jefferson's political experiment, essentially Epicurean, involved demystifying nature as well as political propaganda for the sake of a normative vision.

> Jefferson's anthropological thoughts did serve as a proxy for a normative ethics. To promote virtue and to attain success Jefferson needed to represent apparent dangers and real failures, and dangers made visible are the most powerful means to help moral actions. The syllogism is very plain: self-

government is the result of moral rectitude, America needs self-government, hence America desperately needs moral rectitude. To construct America Jefferson needed to persuade Americans that they are mere moral subjects, not supernatural beings, titans, or heavenly spirits to whom an earthly adventure happens. Accordingly, to become a moral subject a human being needs to remember his depravity, the underlying chaos, wilderness, and other enormities.[60]

The most extensive study of Jefferson's use of *nature* is that of American Studies professor Charles Miller in *Jefferson and Nature*. The Enlightenment used *nature* as a means of assaulting tradition. It saw *nature* in the guises of reason and experience. Reason was nature in its orderly, general state; experience was nature in its disorderly, particular state.[61]

In his study of Jefferson's use of *nature* and *natural*, Miller states that the words appear with "great frequency" in his corpus, in "countless contexts," and "with many meanings."[62] So, the project of coming up with any one notion of each term is likely futile. Nonetheless, Jefferson is an outright physicalist. There is no place for "unnatural" or "supernatural," when examining the physical cosmos: "Nature itself consists of matter, and only matter. Nothing else— soul, spirit, or thought—his primary existence or a reality independent of a stuff of nature. . . . Everything has a natural, material explanation. Jefferson is a Lucretian materialist."[63]

As we have seen, the depiction of Jefferson as a Lucretian materialist—Lucretius was a first-century BCE disciple of Epicurus (fl. 290 BCE)—is untenable. Unlike Epicurus's cosmos, Jefferson's cosmos gives evidence of design and superintendence, even if the designer and superintendent is material, as is the case for Jefferson and the Epicureans (for whom the gods are the products of random collisions of atoms). Jefferson's cosmology and naturalism owe at least as much to the Stoics as they do to Epicurus. For Stoics, as we have already seen, nature was a generative force that permeated the cosmos and was a force that regulated both cosmic and human affairs.

Nature versus Society

During Jefferson's time, there were two dominant views of man's relation to nature: those of Thomas Hobbes and of Jean-Jacques Rousseau. Each philosopher recognized a presocial period in which humans existed in the state of nature. The question for each was this: Why is it that individuals in the state of nature, where they were free to do what they wanted to do when they wished to do it, would have left the state of nature for organized civil society with its numerous constraints?

Thomas Hobbes, in *Leviathan*, has readers consider the state of nature—a state without government—as a sort of thought experiment. In nature, due to the natural antagonism between humans, private disputes would abound, and there would be no authority to listen to them and adjudicate between them. Thus, the state of nature would be a state of "war of every man against every man," due to the natural antagonism between humans. It would be a nasty, solitary, brutish, and short life, from which release through accord with his fellow men was needed. The social contract enables humans to escape the continual antagonism in nature. Individuals implicitly contract with a sovereign for security at the expense of freedom. The monarch, once the contract is established, has absolute power. For Hobbes, that such a state of nature did exist (and still exists) is evidenced by the continued conflict of monarch versus monarch, the state of barbarism during times of revolution, and the savagery of Native Americans.[64]

Jean-Jacques Rousseau, in his *Discourse on Inequality*, recognizes two sorts of inequality: natural inequality—differences in age, strength, health, and mind—and political inequality—differences due to convention. Political inequality is unjustified because it does not have the sanction of nature, only the sanction of man. In the state of nature, without the entanglements or entrapments of civilized living, man lives a free and happy life. There is neither virtue nor vice. His goods are nourishment, women, and rest. Social living and the cultivation of reason are responsible for the numerous ills— namely, crimes, wars, murders, miseries, and horrors—from which humans suffer. As a socialized creature, man is "always active and in a sweat, always agitated, and unceasingly tormenting himself in order to seek still more laborious occupations."[65] He takes umbrage in reason, which is a poor substitute for the happiness, tranquility, and freedom he has lost in the state of nature. He becomes unhappy, soft, dependent, and cruel to his fellow humans. Even science is unavailing. The more humans study themselves, the less they know themselves.

Jefferson's view is at odds with Hobbes's, in that Jefferson deems humans, in or outside the state of nature, generally to be good—at least insofar as each congenitally possesses a sensory or quasi-sensory capacity for moral discernment. Moreover, humans for Jefferson are happiest when they are in social settings, but not under the arbitrary rule of a monarchical leader. Yet Jefferson is no Rousseauian, either. It is not social living and the cultivation of reason that leads to human corruption but instead insufficient use of reason and, especially, insufficient cultivation of the moral sense. Humans are happiest in social settings, just because they are social animals. For Jefferson, tiered government, with morally sensitive representatives, and a society that is chiefly agrarian make a political ideal that cultivates progressive living and human happiness.

Jefferson appeals to nature in what one scholar correctly calls a "middle landscape" manner. The happiest state for humans is one that steers clear of what is savage and what is "refined," at least by European standards, and seeks a middle ground. Jefferson's vision of Arcadia in America is a pastoral society that has the freedom of primitivism (because it is neither materialist nor manufacturing), and it has the fortune of land and the trimmings of cultured societies (because it is not primitive and uncultured).[66]

Jefferson's natural-law theory is Stoical, not Hobbesian or Rousseauian. It aims at reconciliation of the state of nature with the state of society. Unlike for Rousseau and Hobbes, for Jefferson, the laws of nature that obtain when man is in the state of nature are the self-same laws that obtain in civil society:

> The moral duties which exist between individual and individual in the state of nature, accompany them into a state of society, and the aggregate of the duties of all the individuals composing the society constitutes the duties of that society towards any other; so that between society and society the same moral duties exist as did between individuals composing them, while in an unassociated state, and their maker not having released them from those duties on their forming themselves into a nation.[67]

The Stoics held that humans were social animals and that the study of nature—both human nature and the nature of the cosmos—indicated through a discovery of its laws the proper course of human action. Appropriate action was always action in accordance with nature; inappropriate action was always action in discordance with nature. The chief difference is that for Stoics right action is driven by reason, while for Jefferson it is determined independently of reason by one's moral-sense faculty—the topic of subsequent chapters.

Nature and Natural Rights

In the Declaration of Independence, a manifesto written as an apologia for the American Revolution, Jefferson lists two self-evident truths: the equality of all men and their god-given endowment of unalienable rights. As human equality is a topic in the next chapter, here I ask these questions: Just what are these unalienable rights and how do they tie into Jefferson's naturalism?

By "unalienable," Jefferson means *inseparable* in that no one can be deprived of such rights and no one can transfer them to another. Moreover, they admit of a more-than-human status, otherwise they would be contingent or conditional truths. They are derived from nature and deity. Derived from nature and deity, only nature or deity can take them away.[68] Being natural, they exist in the state of nature, whether or not humans in that state recognize them. Being natural, they also exist in civic societies even if governments do not allow their expression.

"Rights" are more difficult to grasp, as they are ambiguous and problematic. Writes one scholar, "Rights were understood as *claims* which a person has to be treated in certain ways by others, to be permitted to do certain things without interference, to engage in certain activities and to enter into certain relations with those around him."[69] They are held to obtain, whether or not holders recognize them. Moreover, they are acknowledged to have a moral dimension apart from their obvious legal dimension. There is the moral obligation to obey the law, when its legitimacy is unquestionable. There is also the moral obligation to recognize and uphold the rights of others.

Jefferson, following Locke, mentions three unalienable rights in the Declaration of Independence: life, liberty, and, contrary to Locke, pursuit of happiness.

The right to life constitutes a right to one's own personhood. No one has the right to treat another as mere property—as Aristotle would say (of non-slaves), as a tool, or as Kant would say, as a means and not an end. No one has the right to end arbitrarily or for insufficient reasons the life of another.

The right to liberty entails the right of self-determination through labor, art, and industry. It also entails the right to self-governance. In other words, government must not manage the affairs of its citizens but instead must possess legislative self-restraint. More than that, government has an obligation to promote human flourishing through allowing utmost expression of personal liberty for all citizens.

Finally, the right to happiness cannot be grasped straightforwardly without meaninglessness or absurdity, for no government, especially one whose chief function is as it were to stay out of its citizens' affairs, can secure for its citizenry happiness. Thus it is profitable to make a distinction between "right to happiness" and the "right to pursuit of happiness." I have argued elsewhere that Jefferson is a liberal eudaemonist insofar as he takes happiness (Gr., eudaimōnia, in the Greek sense of human thriving) as the end of all human activity, and (here, going beyond the Greeks[70]) as he deems liberty to be a key component of the good life. In proclaiming a right to the pursuit of happiness, Jefferson merely acknowledges government's obligation to create civic situations both that allow for citizens' autonomy and that maximally encourage political participation to safeguard that autonomy.

Thus, Jefferson's republican schema is an experimental political structure that has happiness as its end. Though good government aims at happiness, it cannot dictate the happiness of all citizens without destroying it—that is, happiness cannot be imposed but must inhale the oxygen of liberty. Happiness is not something one person can give to another or that a government can give to its citizens. Requiring autonomy, happiness is something each person must secure for himself. In that regard, it is like generosity, for involuntary generosity is not generosity. Government, however, can ensure that all persons have a suitable opportunity to secure their own happiness. It can set up a minimal governing structure that allows for political unity, political participation of citizenry, suitable avenues for actualization of human capacities in a progressive (i.e., scientific) frame, and the autonomy of all citizens to entertain and realize their idiosyncratic conceptions of the good life, within the constraints of morally sensitive bounds. In short, government cannot ensure the happiness of its citizens, but it must defend their right to be happy, and it must allow for the pursuit of happiness by creating various salubrious and progressive outlets for human social engagement.

One should, of course, not overlook the right to revolution—perhaps Jefferson's chief reason for writing the Declaration of Independence. That document was a formal declaration of the right of the people, any people, to abolish any tyrannical form of government, given a track record of long abuses. The right to revolution can be seen to follow from the rights to life, liberty, and pursuit of happiness. Tyrannical governments, encroaching on each of those liberties, do not allow for human thriving and progressive living. As such, citizens have a right to revolt, when their substratal rights are breached.

Why was the acknowledgement of individual rights so critical to Jefferson's liberal thinking? One view is that Jefferson was a political atomist. Attribution of unalienable rights to individuals is merely an extension of Newtonian atomism to the moral and political realm. One writer says, "Concern for the value of the individual person as such is not the issue; what is at stake is the validity of conceiving individuality in terms of the model of hard, self-enclosed, impenetrable units which retain identity within themselves and quite independently of the social relations in which they stand."[71] One begins with individuals, gathers them up, and by merely being added together, they make up a social unity.

The problems with political or liberal atomism, covered in greater detail in chapter 3 are numerous. One large difficulty is that no society, which is a mere collection of individuals, can be a functioning unit without some shared goals, values, and duties. That is Plato's point in *The Republic*, and it is a point of which Jefferson is abundantly aware. Without a shared ideology as some level, there is mere anarchy, not unity. Second, liberal atomism implies that government has no significant role beyond that of securing liberties for its citizens. As I demonstrate in chapter 3, Jefferson's notion of "liberty" goes significantly beyond negative liberty—roughly, the right to be left alone to do whatever one wishes to do. Government is not something outside of its citizenry. Government is its citizenry, acting in a morally responsible manner—each person acting with concern for the well-being of every other person. There is a gauzy and loose organicism to Jefferson's political thinking here. His liberalism is in some measure eudaemonist; citizens are social creatures; and citizens' happiness is not to be found outside of progressive, social settings.

Jefferson's gauzy organicism—his commitment to his fellow man and to societal progress—is evidenced by him not admitting a right to one's own ideas. Nature had created men, Jefferson believed, such that each is capable of forming countless ideas. Whoever receives an idea from another receives instruction without diminishing the other's learning. Jefferson writes: "That ideas should freely spread from one to another over the globe for the moral and mutual instruction of man, and improvement of his condition, seems to have been peculiarly designed by nature, when she made [ideas] incapable of confinement or exclusive appropriation. Inventions then cannot, in nature, be a subject of property."[72] In keeping with his thoughts here, Jefferson refused to patent his own invention of a highly innovative, math-designed "mouldboard" for plowing.[73] He claimed that the materials were easily obtained and that he merely followed nature in its design. The benefit he would have derived through a patent, he says, would have been outweighed by the bane that would have been the result of restricted dissemination of the idea.

Nature's Hidden *Modus Agendi*

Upon receipt of the bones of an extinct animal from a cave in Greenbrier County of what is now West Virginia, Jefferson noted the claws were of a great size, and so he decided the animal was a feline carnivore similar to a lion or tiger. He named the animal *Megalonyx* ("Great Claw"). When he later saw a drawing of bones of a Paraguayan animal called *Megatherium*, he immediately noticed the similarity of *Megalonyx* and *Megatherium* and realized that he might not have discovered a new species of animal.[74]

This takes us back to Jefferson's nominalism. "Nature has, in truth, produced units only through all her works," he writes to John Manners (February 22, 1814). "Classes, orders, genera, species, are not of her works. Her creation is of individuals. No two animals are exactly alike; no two plants, nor even two leaves or blades of grass; no two crystallizations." No two particles of matter of any sort are alike, he adds. Jefferson says starkly that no two objects are alike in kind. Even crystallizations escape categorization, as each separate crystallization is sui generis. Thus, the classification of "like" things, based on perceptions of likeness (e.g., *Megalonyx* as similar to or identical with *Megatherium*) is arbitrary—a mere convenience for the sake of ordering our sensations and experiences, which would otherwise go unordered.

It is worth noting that Hobbes too was a nominalist. He writes in *Leviathan*, "Some [names] are common to many things, Man, Horse, Tree; every of which though but one name, is nevertheless the name of divers particular things; in respect of all which together, it is called an *universal*; there being nothing in the world universal but names; for the things named, are everyone of them individual and singular."[75]

Nominalism for Hobbes is apprehensible; nominalism for Jefferson is perplexing. For Hobbes, nature is arbitrary and its arbitrariness is calamitous for man. Thus, it is expedient and beneficial for man to remove himself from the state of nature and form social bonds at whatever the cost—even with an arbitrary sovereign.[76] For Jefferson in *Notes on the State of Virginia*, only nature's first impression is "arbitrary." Nature's first impression is frightening, even overwhelming—evidence of a latent, incomprehensible sublimity. The finishing impression is one of calm and delight—evidence of a simple, comprehensible beauty.[77] Moreover, Jefferson's nominalism vitiates his firm commitments to science and both intellectual and moral progress.

Nominalism makes science, for Jefferson, a mere practical discipline, if not an arbitrary one. A committed nominalist cannot take seriously science as a truth-generating practice. The practice of gathering data, subsuming them under generalizations, and putting the generalizations to the test of further observations to confirm or disconfirm them is a practice that amounts to nothing, he tells Professor Edward Everett (February 24, 1823). Nominalism makes any real categorization of nature impossible, and that leaves no room for a genuine notion of scientific progress.

Yet Jefferson did make purchase of science as a means of categorizing and understanding nature, in spite of an express commitment to nominalism. Here, it seems plausible, he was following Kames, who maintained that deity so shaped human sensory experience to be of utmost use vis-à-vis external objects, not to grasp their essence. In categorizing nature, Jefferson followed Bacon to the letter. His method for categorizing nature was to have detailed, varied, and numerous observations of phenomena. He would then draw generalizations from the data. Finally, consistent with the eliminative part of Baconian inductivism, he would compare his hypotheses to those of others. If any data were straightforwardly inconsistent with a certain hypothesis, he would eliminate that hypothesis. The remaining hypotheses would be evaluated for their fit with the data.

There are many clear illustrations of Jefferson's eliminative inductivism in his *Notes on the State of Virginia*.[78] I give one:

In Query VI, Jefferson takes it upon himself to address the criticisms of Count de Buffon that are directed at the New World. Buffon claims:

1. The animals common to America and Europe are smaller in America.
2. Animals endemic to America are on a smaller scale.
3. Animals, domesticated in America and Europe, have degenerated in America.
4. There are fewer species of animal in America.

The causes of these defects of American animals are the presence of greater water and the lack of heat. The hypothesis under consideration can be framed thus: *In places where water is abundant and heat is scarce, animals will be smaller, degenerate, and fewer.*[79] Buffon's target in part, Jefferson surmises, is the Native Americans. In a country inhospitable to biotic thriving, the Native Americans must be defective, and humans transplanted in America too will degenerate in time.

Jefferson guardedly and soberly begins his refutation of Buffon: "I will not meet this hypothesis on its first doubtful ground, whether the climate of America be comparatively more humid? Because we are not furnished with observations sufficient to decide this question." He then turns to the hypothesis concerning the lack of heat in America. "The truth of this is inscrutable to us by reasonings a priori. Nature has hidden from us her modus agendi. Our only appeal on such questions is to experience; and I think that experience is against the supposition."[80]

What does experience indicate? Jefferson appeals to his experience with husbandry. Husbandry shows, pace Buffon's claim, that vegetables profit from heat and moisture, not heat and aridity. Vegetables, he adds, are the immediate or mediate food of all animals. When there is food in abundance, there are animals in abundance, both in number and in size. There is an abundance of vegetables in America, so there must be an abundance of animals.[81] Reasoning backward, it is sensible to think America is hotter and wetter than Europe— that is, that Buffon's hypothesis concerning heat and aridity being related to biotic thriving is false.

Jefferson then addresses head-on Buffon's claim that America is colder and wetter than Europe. His argument is a form of conditional proof. On supposition that America is both colder and wetter than Europe—coldness and wetness for Buffon being inhospitable for animal growth—American animals, against Buffon, should be as much smaller, less hearty, and less abundant than European animals. Jefferson then appeals simply to observations of American animals to contest Buffon's hypothesis and its implications.

Jefferson refers to three tables: "aboriginals of both" (quadrupeds common to America and Europe); "aboriginals of one only" (animals endemic to each); and "[animals] domesticated in both."[82] The tables, though incomplete, offer weighty evidence against Buffon's assertion of the inferiority of American animals. Jefferson, showing savvy, then appeals to Buffon's assertion, *«J'aime autant une personne qui me relève d'une erreur, qu'une autre qui m'apprend une vérité, parce qu'en effet une erreur corrigée est une vérité»*,[83] and uses it against him.

Nonetheless, Jefferson is not out to one-up Buffon. He merely wishes to show that America can hold its own in any comparison—that its land, climate, and biota are not defective, as Buffon has asserted. His trump card is the fossilized remains of a mammoth, which has bones "as large as those found in the old world."[84] Overall, his observations reveal a country equal to Europe in being hospitable to biotic thriving. "We therefore have reason to believe," he concludes modestly, "[America] can produce her full quota of genius."[85]

PART 2

JEFFERSON ON POLITICS

CHAPTER 2

"PROPHECY IS ONE THING, HISTORY ANOTHER"

Jefferson's Mother Principle

"The abuses of monarchy had so much filled all the space of political contemplation, that we imagined everything republican which was not monarchy. We had not yet penetrated to the mother principle, that 'governments are republican only in proportion as they embody the will of their people, and execute it.'"
—TJ to Samuel Kercheval, June 12, 1816

Jefferson never aimed to place his political thinking into a system.[1] No one of his writings articulates the particulars of a republican system. Although his political thinking was never fully systematized in any single writing, its development, which took an evolutionary form and not a revolutionary form, can be followed in his writings. With Jefferson, "thought long preceded action and determined its direction in advance."[2]

Yet what Jefferson did do was to sketch out, during the course of his life, the general principles that any sort of political system that is equalitarian, democratic, meritocratic, and concerned with individual rights ought to have. That "sketch" reached maturity in his post-presidential years.

In the main, Jefferson's aim was universal, not provincial. As he stated in a letter to Judge John Tyler (June 17, 1812), he regretted having penned his Summary View of the Rights of British America (1774) so narrowly—it was aimed at King George III of England—for in coming from England, "we brought with us the rights of men." Though universal, those principles were not of an a priori nature because they were answerable to experience—that is, proof of their correctness or incorrectness would come in time through the various more-or-less "republicanist" experiments in Europe and the Americas. Writes one scholar of Jefferson's idyllic vision:

Jefferson's vision of republican government was both an extrapolation of conventional Enlightenment ideas about civility and sociability and a projection of his own ever-expanding circle of friends. Political life could be seen as a conversation among friends, recognizing diverse perspectives and interests while seeking a common ground and a common good. Similarly, a harmonious union of free states in America was predicated on the mutual interest and natural sociability of liberty-loving republicans, not on the "energetic" government favored by Federalists—or even on the party organization that Republicans had to develop in order to counter Federalist corruption. In its most extravagant formulation, the fulfillment of Jefferson's project would see the nations of the world substitute peaceful, mutually beneficial exchange for violent conflict.[3]

That vision of "peaceful, mutually beneficial exchange" was grounded chiefly on one political principle. Jefferson had one code of political policy for each citizen, whether acting singly or collectively, and that was to surrender to the will of the majority. "The will of the nation is the only thing essential to be regarded," he tells statesman Gouverneur Morris (December 30, 1792).[4] Yet one must add, as Jefferson does in his First Inaugural Address, "for that will [of the majority] to be rightful [it] must be reasonable."[5] The reasonableness to which he refers here, I show in the remainder of this book, must be presumed to be given an ethical backing.

L'AN 1816

In a letter to Abigail Adams dated January 11, 1817, Jefferson is uncharacteristically chapfallen: "Nothing proves more than this that the being who resides over the world is essentially benevolent, stealing from us, one by one, the faculties of enjoyment, searing our sensibilities, leading us, like the horse in his mill, round and round the same beaten path." With each turn, the senses become satiated and fatigued by "leaden iteration" and the wish to live wanes. With the turn of a new year, Jefferson, it seems, has begun his crepuscular years. He waxes Stoical: "Perhaps however one of the elements of future felicity is to be a constant and unimpassioned view of what is passing here. . . . Mercier has given us a vision of the year 2440,[6] but prophecy is one thing, history another. On the whole however, perhaps it is wise and well to be contented with the good things which the master of the feast places before us, and to be thankful for what we have, rather than thoughtful about what we have not." Resignation seems an irregular, uncustomary sentiment for Jefferson—at least in his letters. Nine months earlier, he had told John Adams a story singularly different and seemingly anti-Stoical. "My temperament is sanguine. I steer my bark with Hope in the head, leaving Fear astern. . . . The perfection of the moral character is, not in a Stoical apathy, so hypocritically vaunted, and so untruly too, because impossible, but in a just equilibrium of all the passions."[7]

Why is there such a quick antipodal shift in perspective? The reason, I suspect—and here I am being slightly tongue-in-cheek—is because of a philosophical hangover of sorts.

Doubtless prompted by global and local events—America survived a Federalist threat of secession in 1814, and the War of 1812 for all intents and purposes ended with a remarkable victory in the Battle of New Orleans in 1815—the year 1816 was an especially philosophical year for Jefferson. His letters reflect a large amount of somber contemplation on contentious issues—foremost among them is the issue of republican government. In no other year does he reflect on the nature of republican government with such optimism and verve in letters. He is essaying to decipher the nature of true republicanism.

On April 24, 1816, he writes to the economist Pierre Samuel Dupont de Nemours that republican government is founded on certain "moral principles"—nine of which are given:

1. Morality, compassion, and generosity are innate elements of all humans.
2. There is a right independent of force.
3. Humans have a right to property.
4. No one has right to obstruct another.
5. Justice is the fundamental law of society.
6. The majority, acting merely by force, has no right to oppress any individual.
7. "Action by the citizens in person, in affairs within their reach and competence, and in all others by representatives, chosen immediately, and removable by themselves, constitutes the essence of a republic."
8. "All governments are more or less republican in proportion as their principle enters more or less into their composition."
9. Republican governments can exist over a greater surface than any other form of government.[8]

Note that Jefferson calls these principles "moral," not political. For Jefferson—and this is a point that I iterate throughout the book and that cannot be reiterated too much—the political is reducible to the moral.

One month later, Jefferson notes the vagueness of "republic" as evidenced by the "self-styled republics" of Holland, Switzerland, Genoa, Venice, and Poland in a letter to statesman John Taylor (May 28, 1816). He offers up a direct-participation definition of *republic* (numbers added):

> Were I to assign to this term a precise and definite idea, I would say, purely and simply, it means a government (1) by its citizens in mass, (2) acting directly and personally, (3) according to rules established by the majority; and that every other government is more or less republican, in proportion as it has in this composition more or less of this ingredient of the direct action of the citizens.

Jefferson's emphasis on majority rule must be qualified by implicit understanding of his sixth principle in his letter to French official and economist P. S. Dupont de Nemours—that the rules established and actions of the majority are to be nonoppressive to any minority, even a minority of one.

What is striking in the direct-participation definition is Jefferson's statement after the semicolon. He emphasizes proportionality and he twice uses "more or less." Those suggest an ideal to be approximated, not something that can be attained. A true republic would have the direct and equal participation of all citizens, but as that is impossible, the best sort of government is one both in which the vast majority of individuals participate (mostly locally) to the best of their capacities and in which elected officials, mindful of the rights and needs of the citizenry, participate in the state and federal governments. Government is comparable to a machine. Useless parts can only hamper its efficiency.

Later in his letter to Taylor, Jefferson offers the qualification to his prior definition that the citizens of a republican government must have control over their agents. He writes: "If, then, the control of the people over the organs of their government be the measure of its republicanism, and I confess I know no other measure, it must be agreed that our governments have much less of republicanism than ought to have been expected; in other words, that the people have less regular control over their agents, than their rights and their interests require."[9] The concessions here are important. Though Jefferson implicitly acknowledges the rights of individuals and the need for them to participate as directly and fully as possible, he also acknowledges, as he does in his letter to Dupont, limits to their capacities and reach. First, though each person is in capacity the moral equal of every other, not all are equals in intelligence. Thus, only the most intelligent are best suited for governance. Second, not everyone has the same political reach. Merchants are bound to their businesses; craftsmen to their crafts; and farmers to their farms.

The final statement in the last sentence of the condition is also highly significant and seems best grasped normatively. It asserts, in effect, that citizens ought to have control over their governors in proportion to their rights and interests. As their rights, which historically have been violated or neglected, are paramount and their interests are varied and many, their control over their governors must be considerable. Elected officials who fail to respect and uphold the rights and interests of citizens must be removed from their offices.

As if to underscore the concessions made in the regular-control amendment, Jefferson ends his letter with a generic, slightly different definition of *republic*—the emphasis here being on control of officials through election (and presumably recall):

> Governments are more or less republican as they have more or less of the element of popular election and control in their composition; and believing, as I do, that the mass of the citizens is the safest depository of their own rights, and especially, that the evils flowing from the duperies of the people, are less injurious than those from the egoism of their agents, I am a friend to that composition of government which has in it the most of this ingredient.

Jefferson, after his definition and mirroring the sentiment in his regular-control amendment, shows that he has little faith in governors to govern effectively—that is, in the interest of the citizenry—if they are not always under the watchful eye of the citizenry, whose moral-sense faculty and intellect, given a modicum of prompting or education, are fully capable of electing, monitoring, and, if needed, recalling officials.

In a letter to Virginia lawyer Samuel Kercheval (July 12, 1816), months later, Jefferson again points to the ambiguity of *republican* and offers another qualification or needed condition for a correct definition, in the form of a "mother principle," which focuses on officials acting pursuant to the will of the people. "In truth, the abuses of monarchy had so much filled all the space of political contemplation, that we imagined everything republican which was not monarchy. We have not yet penetrated to the mother principle, that 'governments are republican only in proportion as they embody the will of their people, and execute it.'" Sentences later, he adds the notion of periodic checks:

> For let it be agreed that a government is republican in proportion as every member composing it has his equal voice in the direction of its concerns (not indeed in person, which would be impracticable beyond the limits of a city, or small township) but by representatives chosen by himself, and responsible to him at short periods, and let us bring to the test of this canon every branch of our constitution.

Further in the letter, Jefferson adds that the function of government is to guarantee citizens' equality through securing their rights. "The true foundation of republican government is the equal right of every citizen, in his person and property, and in their management."

Without question, republicanism is foremost in Jefferson's thinking in 1816. His spirited attempts of defining the term are not quixotic and vain. There are both political and ethical motivations.

Historian Conor Cruise O'Brien writes with petulance of Jefferson's political motivation: "'Republicanism' was just coming into use at this time to refer to the emerging party of Jeffersonian inspiration, opposed to the Federalists under Alexander Hamilton. The choice of the name 'Republican' reflects Jefferson's adroitness as a propagandist. If you were not a republican, then you must be a monarchist."[10] O'Brien's sentiment is misguided. He sees nothing beyond a propagandist, political motivation for Jefferson's musings. *Republicanism* was an emerging party of Jeffersonian inspiration and it was people-friendly and antimonarchical. Nonetheless, attempts at a definition reflect not so much emergence of a political party in opposition to the Federalism, spearheaded by Hamilton many years earlier, but instead a political movement, both democratic and meritocratic in essence, and normative at bottom.[11] For Jefferson, the issue was not political but moral. It was a matter of government embracing fusty obscurantism versus government embracing science-sensitive, people-serving progressivism. That is why Jefferson referred to his election as president in 1801 as a "revolution" in the spirit of the revolution of 1776. That was not an egotistical reaction to being elected president but an assertion that, in electing one with resolute republican principles, "order & good sense" were restored and the will of the people would find expression.[12]

Jefferson, even in the early years of the formation of his views on republicanism, had more in mind than partisan politics. As secretary of state in 1792, he wrestled with a suitable grasp of republican government, and his bouts, driven by sharp disagreements with Hamilton's policies, revealed a philosophical foundation behind the façade of a political agenda. To Gouverneur Morris (November 7), Jefferson says, "[Republicanism] accords with our principles to acknowledge any government to be rightful which is formed by the will of the nation substantially declared." Nearly two months later (December 30), he adds to Morris: "Every [nation] may govern itself under whatever forms it pleases, and change these forms at it's own will, and that it may transact it's business with foreign nations through whatever organ it thinks proper, whether King, convention, assembly, committee, President, or whatever it may chuse. The will of the nation is the only thing essential to be regarded."[13]

The sentiment to Morris smacks of political relativism, but Jefferson was no relativist. Attempts at a definition of *republicanism*[14] instead reflect a philosophical preoccupation with refining his philosophical vision of human flourishing for his youthful nation as well as his Mercier-like vision of a global Arcadia in which public opinion, suitably informed through general education and a free press, is established as the "court of last resort."[15] It is not the attainment of a global Arcadia for which he strives, as his more-or-less formulations years later indicate, but its approximation through convergence toward it that Jefferson is after. Convergence toward an ideal is no fool's paradise. The numerous triumphs of science are proof of that. There does, however, need to be clarification of what it is toward which people, once liberated from the shackles of conservatism, ought to be working. Science offers no help, for, as Jefferson says roundly in his letter to Dupont de Nemours and elsewhere, science is in the service of morality. As he writes in an early letter to nephew Peter Carr (August 19, 1785), "An honest heart being the first blessing, a knowing head is the second." Thus, political reform for Jefferson is for the sake of moral advance.

One thing must be acknowledged. Jefferson was proposing the basic scheme of a morally sensitive government. He insisted that the basic scheme be instantiated according to the will of the majority of its citizens and that constitutions always be representative of that will. The sentiment was expressed neatly and succinctly by James Madison: "The authority of constitutions over governments, and of the sovereignty of the people over constitutions, are truths which are at all times necessary to be kept in mind."[16] As president, Jefferson acted with caution, restraint, with an eye toward compromise, and with the aim of morally correct action. "I see too many proofs of the imperfection of human reason," he writes to Congressman John Randolph (December 1, 1803), "to entertain wonder or intolerance at any difference of opinion on any subject; and acquiesce in that difference as easily as on a difference of feature or form; experience having long taught me the reasonableness of mutual sacrifices of opinion among those who are to act together for any common object, and the expediency of doing what good we can, when we cannot do all we would wish." He was indisposed to impose his vision of a vigorous, flourishing country on an unwilling citizenry because theory, however sound and well intended, always was second fiddle to practicability. "What is practicable must often control what is purely theory and the habits of the governed determine in a great degree what is practicable," he says to the Marquis de Lafayette (January 18, 1802), general during the American Revolution. "The same original principle, modified in practice to the different habits of the different nations, present governments of very different aspects."

LESSONS OF FRANCE AND ENGLAND

Jefferson's republicanism was rooted in certain theoretical convictions on the nature of humans to be tested over time as well as observations on the political struggles and advances of other countries. Jefferson advises John Rutledge Jr. and Thomas Lee Shippen in their travels abroad to make an especial study of each country's laborers—their food, clothing, labor, and liberty—as no country can be well-governed if its laborers are unhappy.[17] With the early American government newly established, Jefferson wished to see instantiated, pace the British monarchical system of government and the French sharp division of classes, a republican government based on liberalism, equalitarianism, thin government,[18] and fullest political participation by all citizens pursuant to the reach and capacities of each. That government was best which governed inconspicuously but honestly. "More blest is that nation," he writes to longtime friend and former French minister Comte Diodati (March 29, 1807), "whose silent course of happiness furnishes nothing for history to say."

Jefferson respected the scientific advances of France and England but found both countries to be morally retrograde, especially on account of the amaranthine fighting between the two nations. He writes to John Adams (January 21,

1812): "As for France and England, with all their pre-eminence in science, the one is a den of robbers, and the other of pirates.[19] And if science produces no better fruits than tyranny, murder, rapine and destitution of national morality, I would rather wish our country to be ignorant, honest and estimable as our neighboring savages are." Each culture too was morally retrograde. French culture was pococurante through excess of leisure. British culture was vulgar through want of leisure. Moreover, Europe was itself wedded to "Old World Imperialism"—that is, "priestly ignorance and military despotism"[20]—and Jefferson realized America would thrive only if it divorced itself from the "never ceasing broils of Europe."[21]

The Hammer or the Anvil

The extent to which Jefferson's republicanism was fashioned by his stay in France as ambassador to that country is still a matter of considerable debate today.

On the one hand, some believe that the foundation for Jefferson's republicanism was set during his time in France. Jefferson's five years in France (1785–1789) were "among the happiest years of Jefferson's life," says one scholar.[22] He involved himself at least as an outsider in French political affairs because he thought the successes of the French Revolution and the American republic were indissolubly linked. So insistent was Jefferson on the success of the revolution in France that he turned a blind eye to the many wicked atrocities committed on its behalf. His attachment to France was mitigated only with the ascendance of Napoleon Bonaparte.

On the other hand, others, including me, maintain that the germ of Jefferson's political thinking was already in place prior to his tenure in France. The philosophical climate of France had little influence on Jefferson, writes another scholar. His character was pragmatic, not speculative. The *philosophes* were "closet philosophers" whose universal speculations were formulated without concern for application. Their fondness of universal truths could have little appeal to the "American empiricist" who lived in the practical, not theoretical, world.[23] Though he was happy to see some of his favorite thoughts embraced by *philosophes*, "it is equally certain that France was to him a living demonstration and a sort of horrible example of all the evils caused by aristocratic, monarchical, and ecclesiastical oppressions."[24]

It is certainly concedable that Jefferson enjoyed his time in France. With the death of his beloved wife (1782), it was a welcome respite—a time for wounds to heal. Again, he was a committed Francophile who believed that the fates of the American and French republics were codependent, until events beginning in the latter part of the eighteenth century[25] proved him wrong. Furthermore, he enjoyed the intellectual stimulation of French society as well as its art and music. Yet he did not enjoy them as one, unfamiliar with the taste of caviar, anticipates with excitement the prospect of experiencing new flavors. In that regard, he was no sensualist. He enjoyed them more in the manner of a scientist who enjoys a new discovery on account of the information it places at his disposal for existing problems. Jefferson might have been an idealist, but he was always axially a practicalist—that is, his ideals were at least in his mind always achievable.

Overall, Jefferson in France was a practical, classical man in an impractical, rococo culture. In art, he preferred architecture, because it was useful art, to paintings and sculpture. In horticulture, he preferred medicinal and esculent plants, because they were useful plants, to ornamental plants. Thus, he wished to learn not for the sake of learning, but for the sake of taking his learning with him back to his fledgling country to improve it.[26] In short, during his stay in Paris, he was always an American in France and never pretended to be otherwise. To James Monroe (June 17, 1785), he writes: "I sincerely wish you may find it convenient to come here [to France]. The pleasure of the trip will be less than you expect but the utility greater. It will make you adore your own country, it's soil, it's climate, it's equality, liberty, laws, people & manners. My God: how little do my country men know what precious blessings they are in possession of, and which no other people on earth enjoy."

What struck him as repugnant was the moral depravity of the culture, due to vast differences between the wellborn and the impoverished prior to their revolution.[27] To James Madison (October 28, 1785), he tells of his chat with a day-laboring woman while both were walking toward a tall mountain. The woman was scarcely getting by financially, and Jefferson assisted her with twenty-four sous—three times her daily wage. Upon leaving the impoverished woman, Jefferson then fell into reflection. He writes, "The property of this country is absolutely concentered in a very few hands, having revenues of from half a million of guineas a year downwards." They employ "the flower of the country as servants" as well as a great number of manufacturers, tradesmen, and husbandmen. Outside of the workers, there are the poor who do not work because there is no work for them. "I asked myself what could be the reason that so many should be permitted to beg who are willing to work, in a country where there is a very considerable proportion of uncultivated lands?" The uncultivated lands, he answers, are kept idle so the rich can hunt. Jefferson concludes, "Whenever there is in any country, uncultivated lands and unemployed poor, it is clear that the laws of property have been so far extended as to violate natural right. The earth is given as a common stock for man to labour and live on."

To fellow Virginian Charles Bellini, Jefferson writes from France (September 30, 1785), "I find the general fate of humanity, here, most deplorable. The truth of Voltaire's observation, offers itself perpetually, that every man here must be either the hammer or the anvil." Even among the wealthy, he notes, happiness, through cultivation of the simplest pleasures, is unknown. Instead, the French cultivate excess.

> Conjugal love having no existence among them, domestic happiness, of which that is the basis, is utterly unknown. In lieu of this, are substituted pursuits which nourish and invigorate all our bad passions, and which offer only moments of ecstasy, amidst days and months of restlessness and torment. Much, very much inferior, this, to the tranquil, permanent felicity with which domestic society in America blesses most of its inhabitants; leaving them to follow steadily those pursuits which health and reason approve, and rendering truly delicious the intervals of those pursuits.

Boredom leads to the continual pursuit of purposeless and unproductive excitements to stave off the ennui of the present. He writes to Philadelphian Anne Willing Bingham (February 7, 1787) of the daily routine *chez madame.* Madame's day begins at 11 a.m.—one can readily imagine Jefferson's revulsion to such complete waste of the morning hours—and only then are the curtains drawn to let in the sun. While propped on pillows, the bulletins of the sick and the billets of the well are read. Madame then writes letters and receives visitors. On days less tumultuous, she might "hobble around" the Palais Royal, but she must hobble quickly, for she will soon meet with her coiffeur and such a meeting often takes her all the way to dinner. After eating, she mingles with acquaintances through the streets for one-half hour and then makes her way to the spectacles for another half hour. After another half hour of visits to friends, it is time for supper, then cards, and then bed. The next day, she begins the routine again. He sums, "Thus the days are consumed, one by one, without an object beyond the present moment; ever flying from the ennui of that, yet carrying it with us; eternally in pursuit of happiness, which keeps eternally before us."

For Americans, in contrast, boredom is not a problem. There is purposive and productive labor to be done each day. Americans cultivate the simple life: husbandry, time with children, and improvement of the house and grounds. "Every exertion is encouraging," Jefferson says, "because to present amusement, it joins the promise of some future good." Moreover time spent with others is not fatuous intercourse or shillyshallying with sycophants, opportunists, and habitués. "The intervals of leisure are filled by the society of real friends, whose affections are not thinned to cob-web, by being spread over a thousand objects."

It comes as no surprise, then, that Jefferson, especially early on, was an ardent supporter of the French Revolution.

Reforming the English Kitchens

In spite of his enumerations of the defects of French culture in numerous letters, Jefferson was avowedly partisan toward French culture: He was a Francophile. He saw in it the promise of greatness and was for the most part an ardent supporter of their revolution. He believed, at least early on, that the fate of France and that of America[28] were in some sense inseparably linked and perhaps even that the fate of the world depended on the successes of the American experiment and French Revolution. He was soured with the French mostly because of the rise and abuses of Napoleon—a man born without a sense of morality.[29] In contrast, Jefferson was never a true Anglophile, as British culture he generally reviled.

Jefferson's writings, especially early on—for instance, Summary View of the Rights of British America (1774) and "The Declaration of the Causes and Necessity for Taking Up Arms" (1775)—betray great hostility toward England. In a letter to lawyer and statesman William Carmichael (December 15, 1787), he says, "I consider the British as our natural enemies, and as the only nation on earth who wished us ill from the bottom of their souls."[30] Jefferson's execration on England is certainly due to the abuses of the mother country, but he was also slighted by King George III, while he and Adams were on a diplomatic mission in England. Though Adams was received cordially by the king, Jefferson was snubbed. Jefferson writes to lifelong friend John Page (May 4, 1786): "That nation hates us, their ministers hate us, and their King more than all other men." Jefferson's "cool" reception, of course, had much to do with his anti-British writings—the vitriolic Summary View especially.

Still, Jefferson always recognized that America would always be inescapably linked to England. To politician William J. Duane (August 12, 1810), he says, "Our laws, language, religion, politics and manners are so deeply laid in English foundations, that we shall never cease to consider their history as a part of ours, and to study ours in that as its origin." He never gave up the hope that someday the colonial settlers would be reunited in a bond of mutual friendship with their mother country. In a letter to John Adams (November 25, 1816), he states, "I should myself feel with great strength the ties which bind us together, our origin, language, laws and manners: and I am persuaded the two people would become in future, as it was with the antient Greeks, among whom it was reproachful for Greek to be found fighting against Greek in a foreign army. The individuals of the nation I have ever honored and esteemed, the basis of their character being essentially worthy."

Abuses of the mother country notwithstanding, there was also a desire for reconciliation that can only be attributed to feelings of loss by separation from the mother country. "I am sincerely one of those [who still wish for reunion with their parent country], and would rather be in dependance on Great Britain, properly limited, than on any nation upon earth, or than on no nation," he writes to John Randolph (August 25, 1775).

Notwithstanding his ambivalence, Jefferson thought Britain was a nation in moral decline. It had become increasingly commercial as a result of parliament's ascendancy after the Revolution of 1688 and the nominal status of the monarchy thereafter. Political scientist Garrett Ward Sheldon neatly sums, "As mercantilist interests grew the former conduct of the old empire diminished: in place of expansion for the honor and virtue of the royal sovereign and his realm, the empire grew for purely commercial purposes; in place of integral dependencies within the royal 'family' of states, the colonies became objects of purely economic concern."[31] Manufacture of goods—that is, economic prosperity for the nation—trumps concern for the British citizenry.

Vice is rampant, Jefferson notes, for both the poor and well-to-do. Involved in drudgery in squalid working conditions many of the hours each day, laborers turn to vice in what little time they have for leisure, if only to drown out the pain of a drudgery-filled existence. Yet cultivation of vice is practiced also by the well-to-do. Jefferson says, "If [a youth] goes to England, he learns drinking, horse racing and boxing. These are the peculiarities of English education."[32] Doubtless in some sense tongue-in-cheek and knowingly taking effect as cause, Jefferson asserts to Abigail Adams (September 25, 1785) that the British love of meat is, at least in part, responsible for their coarseness. "I fancy it must be the quantity of animal food eaten by the English which renders their character insusceptible of civilization. I suspect it is in their kitchens and not their churches that their reformation must be worked."[33]

Jefferson does acknowledge the wondrous gardens and the efficient mechanical arts of the British. "The gardening in that country is the article in which it surpasses all the earth." Nonetheless, it is pleasure gardening, which has for its end ostentation, not use. Moreover, London's mechanical arts, though "carried to a wonderful perfection," are carried to an extreme of extravagance, without which America is better.[34]

Jefferson's coloring of England was influenced by his slanted Whiggish interpretation of their history, reflected by the books in his library, such as Sir Edward Coke's *Institutes of the Laws of England* and philosopher John Locke's *The Second Treatise of Civil Government*. Jefferson was a Saxon sympathizer who saw English history after the Norman conquest as "frequent monarchical encroachments on ancient rights" that led to "Norman treachery and feudalism"—what is often referred to as the "Saxon myth."[35] He saw the emerging American states as Saxon communities of free people. This view is elegantly expressed in A Summary View of the Rights of British America:

> Our ancestors, before their emigration to America, were the free inhabitants of the British dominions in Europe, and possessed a right which nature has given to all men, of departing from the country in which chance, not choice, has placed them, of going in quest of new habitations, and of there establishing new societies, under such laws and regulations as to them shall seem most likely to promote public happiness. That their Saxon ancestors had, under this universal law, in like manner left their native wilds and woods in the north of Europe, had possessed themselves of the island of Britain, then less charged with inhabitants, and had established there that system of laws which has so long been the glory and protection of that country.

These Saxon ancestors, the settlers in the New World, understood only too well their natural right not to bow down to the yoke of Norman sovereignty.[36] Thus, Jefferson wished to instantiate again the germ of the Saxon "system of laws" and their manner of free living.

THE SPIRIT OF THE PEOPLE

France and England, for Jefferson, were examples more of moral than political failures. The lessons of France and Britain showed that countries could be scientifically robust, yet morally retarded. Britain's moral failure is that it placed the economic prosperity of the country ahead of concern of its own people, or at least worked on assumption that the people had to be happy, if the country was prospering economically—a short sight that is applicable equally as well to America today. France's moral failure, especially prior to its revolution, is that it tolerated a sharp division between the wealthy and poor. The wealthy let arable land, which could have been farmed by the poor, go to waste so they could use it for leisure. The real lesson, Jefferson tells us, is that political and economic interests are always answerable to moral interests. That is why he writes to politician Elbridge Gerry (January 29, 1799) of his interest in America's independence from European dissipation: "I am for free commerce with all nations; political connection with none; & little or no diplomatic establishment. And I am not for linking ourselves by new treaties with the quarrels of Europe." Noninvolvement in the affairs of Europe would mean noninvolvement in the continual quarrels of Europe. It would also lead to economic and population growth, self-sufficiency, and political independency. The notion of free commerce with all nations without political involvement was, of course, a pipe dream, and his years as president showed him that.

To serve Jefferson's moral aims, which are progressive, republicanism is not a specific form of government—not a constitution per se—but a schema for governing, whose essence resides in the people. "Where then is our republicanism to be found?" he asks lawyer Samuel Kercheval (July 12, 1816). "Not in our constitution certainly, but merely in the spirit of our people. . . . Owing to this spirit, and to nothing in the form of our constitution, all things have gone well." That is a significant claim, often overpassed by scholars. Constitutions are important for stability, but only in the short term, as they are conservative, while people are morally and intellectually progressive. He adds:

"Laws and institutions must go hand in hand with the progress of the human mind. As that becomes more developed, more enlightened, as new discoveries are made, new truths disclosed, and manners and opinions change with the change of circumstances, institutions must advance also, and keep pace with the times. We might as well require a man to wear still the coat which fitted him when a boy, as civilized society to remain ever under the regimen of their barbarous ancestors." My notion of "schema" is perhaps what Jefferson historian Merrill Peterson had in mind when he said Jeffersonian democracy was more ideals than doctrines. "Democracy was not something Jefferson had dreamed once and for all, and which could be had by the simple expedient of returning to his principles. Nor was it a theory of government or a code of action valid for all time. . . . Jefferson was not about doctrines but ideals. He symbolized the faith that an informed people secure in their inalienable rights are always capable of saving themselves."[37]

Jefferson's republicanism, at least in spirit, constitutes hands-off governing and faith in the people. That libertarianism and that optimism account to a great extent for his great popularity as president. He believes in self-sufficiency—namely, leaving alone the people to do things for themselves.[38] He is a "friend to mankind who would ask no more of his fellows than he had to."[39] That is why he writes to a namesake, Thomas Jefferson Smith (February 21, 1825), late in life, "Never trouble another for what you can do yourself."

It is important to underscore Jefferson's progressivism. Republicanism, for Jefferson, is an ideal to be approximated, not so much a reality to be had. Equal rights are guaranteed all persons by virtue of their equal moral status, not their capacities, which avowedly vary considerably. Yet equal rights allow all persons to actualize fully their capacities if they so choose. Scientific advances offer undeniable proof that people have been using more fully their capacities, and scientific advances and the comforts they bring are proofs that republicanism is a political advance.

Progress in politics as well as in science and morality made Jefferson realize that there could be no one constitution that fit a people for all time. That would be mandating that a man wear the suit that fit him as a boy, which is absurd. Republicanism, thus, was a flexible schema of good governing that mandated merely that governors were elected to serve the interests of the citizens and that people would run their own affairs, without governmental intervention, so long as the *vox populi* was reasonable, and progressive.

One must also recognize that a one-size-fits-all constitution was impractical. Settlers in America from all parts of Europe were not wedded to any one political system. Thus, a union of states was not an imperative; it was an option. Moreover, the individual states in Jefferson's day had an independence they do not have in ours. Each had a unique admixture of ethnicity, each had its own culture, and each had its own laws.[40] To preserve a unity of such independent states required great constitutional pliancy.

Overall, motivation for Jefferson's mother principle lay in the abuses of King George III, the deficiencies of the Virginia Constitution,[41] the notion that Lockean libertarian principles of government have heretofore never been rightly instantiated, and the belief that people were, in the main, sufficiently good, honest, and, given a modicum of education, intelligent enough to determine their own lives.[42]

The keys to the mother principle are the moral equality of all humans and guarantee of their natural rights of life, liberty, and pursuit of happiness.[43] Given those rights, the primary role of government is, paradoxically, inactivity of a sort—acting mostly to secure citizens' rights, which is in large measure nonintervention in citizens' affairs. Justice is, then, mostly a matter of government acting only when citizens' rights are abused.

The mother principle was dependent upon two key political reforms: general education, the topic of the fourth part of this work, and the ward system. He writes to politician and fellow Virginian John Tyler (May 26, 1810), "I have indeed two great measures at heart, without which no republic can maintain itself in strength. 1. That of general education, to enable every man to judge for himself what will secure or endanger his freedom. 2. To divide every county into hundreds, of such size that all children of each will be within reach of a central school in it."

Wards were needed if only because of the size of America. Centralized government was impossible for America because it covered too great an expanse of land. A centralized governing power would, thus, be too remote from much of the country and could only function through the actions of federal agents, empowered by the federal government and spread throughout America. Their diffusion throughout the land, however, would make them insusceptible of answerability. The results would likely be the establishment of numerous local tyrannies, then chaos, and then eventual dissolution of the confederation of states. Wards were seen as the solution to the problem of establishing political unity of a nation and the independency of it citizens. Each ward, as political atoms of the counties within states, would be in some sense politically independent of all others. In that manner, each ward would be self-sufficient and capable of retaining the local interests and customs of its citizens. However, as parts of a county, a state, and the nation, each ward and each citizen would have political ties with all other wards and citizens.[44]

With the foundation of republican government on wards,[45] good government, strictly speaking, was not top-down driven but bottom-up driven. Jefferson says to Virginia politician Joseph C. Cabell (February 2, 1816), "The way to have good and safe government, is not to trust it all to one, but to divide it among the many, distributing to every one exactly the functions he is competent to." The national government ought to be responsible for national defense and foreign and federal relations; state governments, with civil rights, laws, police, and administration of affairs of state; counties, with affairs of county; and wards, with the most provincial affairs. "It is by dividing and subdividing these republics from the great national one down through all its subordinations, until it ends in the administration of every man's farm by himself; by placing under every one what his own eye may superintend, that all will be done for the best."

As a check for corruption at the top, Jefferson envisaged a separation of executive, legislative, and judicial powers—each construed as an equal and independent authority. In a draft of his First Annual Message to Congress, Jefferson writes a memorable passage that was unfortunately excised.

> Our country has thought proper to distribute the powers of its government among three equal and independent authorities, constituting each a check on one or both of the others, in all attempts to impair its Constitution. To make each an effectual check, it must have a right in cases which arise within the line of its proper functions, where, equally with the others, it acts in the last resort and without appeal, to decide on the validity of an act according to its own judgment, and uncontrolled by the opinions of any other department.[46]

Overall, Jefferson's aim was sound government, which entailed morally responsible governors (i.e., officials involving themselves in citizens' affairs only to secure their rights), the fullest participation of citizens in governmental affairs (i.e., local political participation and overseeing elected officials), an educated citizenry for citizens' self-sufficiency, and a mostly bottom-up political schema to allow for self-sufficiency, thin government, and constitutional changes that reflect moral and intellectual advances.

CHAPTER 3

"TURBULENT LIBERTY [OR] QUIET SERVITUDE"

Jefferson on Liberty

"We both consider the people as our children, and love them with parental affection. But you love them as infants whom you are afraid to trust without nurses; and I as adults whom I freely leave to self-government."
—TJ to Dupont de Nemours, April 24, 1816

An advocate of natural rights and limited government, Jefferson qua advocate for liberty has traditionally been placed squarely in a Lockean frame. Jefferson is a deep-dyed liberal who is committed foremost to the notions that democratic societies are best and that true democratic societies are those in which citizens embrace toleration of various views of the good life as a progressive ideal.[1] One writer goes so far as to say that, when it came to liberty, "Jefferson copied Locke."[2]

This view of Jefferson's liberalism is outdated and untenable. Jefferson's liberalism is not an atomic ideal in which governments exist solely to protect the interests of their citizens, who are free to do as they want to do. Jefferson's liberalism is tethered, as it were, by a communitarian strain in his thinking that allows for various levels of interdependency among citizens of a community, state, and nation.

This chapter is a critical analysis of Jefferson's liberalism. I begin with an analysis of Jefferson's republican schema through his critique of three forms of government. I turn then to four notions of "liberty" that can be disentangled from his writings. Next, I examine the political thinking of his political adversaries—Adams and Hamilton. I end with some thoughts on the friendship between Jefferson and Madison, and the similarities and differences of their republican visions.

THREE TYPES OF GOVERNMENT

In a letter to James Madison (January 30, 1787), Jefferson lists three "sufficiently distinguishable" societies. "Societies exist under three forms sufficiently distinguishable. 1. Without government, as among our Indians. 2. Under governments wherein the will of every one has a just influence, as is the case in England in a slight degree, and in our states, in a great one. 3. Under governments of force: as is the case in all other monarchies and in most of the other republics." Two of the three have merit. The third, a government of "wolves over sheep," he quickly dismisses, as it is inconsistent with liberty. The first enjoys perfect liberty, but it is inconsistent with "any great degree of population," so it has limited applicability. The second enjoys substantial freedom, as "the mass of mankind under that enjoys a precious degree of liberty & happiness," but it is subject to turbulence[3]—that is, insurrections. Still, turbulence is better than oppression. Jefferson writes, *"Malo periculosam libertatem quam quietam servitutem."*[4] Moreover, turbulence is a boon. "It prevents the degeneracy of government, and nourishes a general attention to the public affairs."[5]

In a letter to Virginia statesman Edward Carrington two weeks earlier (January 16, 1787), Jefferson elaborates on the first sort of government through the same tripartite distinction. Persons who live in a society without government—and here again he has Native Americans in mind—enjoy an "infinitely greater degree of happiness" than those who live anywhere in Europe. Yet we are led to believe that such persons are happy in an unstructured and barbarous manner—a sentiment confirmed by his account of the imperfection of Native American societies, namely, societies without laws, in Query XI of his *Notes on the State of Virginia.*[6] The Native Americans have no laws but are governed by shame and pride in the forms of public opinion and moral restraint. Though they are free, they wallow in freedom, and, thus, they do not and cannot enjoy the numerous technological benefits and moral advances of civilized societies. In contrast, European governments are mired in laws and such laws create class structure between "wolves & sheep"—that is, the rich and impoverished—in which the wolves enjoy the comforts of life at the expense of the sheep. "Experience declares that man is the only animal which devours his own kind," Jefferson adds sharply, "for I can apply no milder term to the governments of Europe, and to the general prey of the rich on the poor."

The possible dangers of autocratic governments, the third type of political society and typically kingships, are underscored sufficiently by Jefferson in the monarchical abuses of King George III limned in Jefferson's Summary View on the Rights of British America as well as his Declaration of Independence. To John Langdon (March 5, 1810), however, Jefferson gives a biological reason for the abuses of kings over the centuries: Kings tend to marry only into families of other kings, which are equally as slothful. That method of succession is a form of breeding that allows only for nincompoops, not morally responsible, clearheaded monarchs. He appeals to the science of breeding:

> Now, take any race of animals, confine them in idleness and inaction, whether in a stye, a stable, or a state room, pamper them with high diet, gratify all their sexual appetites, immerse them in sensualities, nourish their passions, let every thing bend before them, and banish whatever might lead them to think, and in a few generations they become all body and no mind: and this, too, by a law of nature, by that very law by which we are in the constant practice of changing the characters and propensities of the animals we raise for our own purposes. Such is the regimen in raising Kings, and in this way they have gone on for centuries.

Jefferson's critique of the three forms of government—coercive governments, lawless governments, and republic governments—shows that his republican experiment, a mean between lawlessness and superfluity of laws, is driven at least as much by the acknowledged encumbrances, harms, and affronts of coercive government as it is by the acknowledged benefits, merits, and advantages of government by the people.[7] It also shows that liberty, for any degree of social organization, must always be taken in political context: Liberty, unconstrained by human laws, is not an alternative. The number and severity of laws are signposts of political degeneration.

Liberty certainly takes pride of place in Jefferson's political thinking. Yet for him, freedom is inescapably conjoined to and a needed condition for human thriving, not an end. Following ancient eudaemonists such as Aristotle and the Greek and Roman Stoics, happiness is the human end. Thus, questions concerning the best schema of political ordering are always answerable to questions concerning human happiness.[8] *Liberty*, then, is chiefly a moral term and only derivatively a political term for Jefferson—a point that does not go unnoticed by some scholars.[9]

Jefferson underscores the normative function of liberty in a letter to fellow republican Isaac Tiffany (April 4, 1819), in which he distinguishes between *liberty* and *rightful liberty*: "Of liberty then I would say, that, in the whole plenitude of its extent, it is unobstructed action according to our will, but rightful liberty is unobstructed action according to our will within limits drawn around us by the equal rights of others. I do not add 'within the limits of the law,' because law is often the tyrant's will, and is always so when it violates the right of an individual." The sentiment of those definitions is responsible free activity—that is, the freedom to do what one wants so long as one does not contravene the rights of others to do what they want to do.

Jefferson's description, however, seems to allow much under the umbrella of concern for life, liberty, and the pursuit of happiness. Such rights are not merely political rights but are derivable from his notion of nature, which is normative—as is the case with Scottish philosopher Francis Hutcheson,[10] "right" is derivable from "good." Rights are part and parcel of Jefferson's purchase of eudaemonism—his notion of the happy or good life. The "pursuit of happiness" in his Declaration of Independence, thus, is idiosyncratic. It is up to each to decide for himself what makes him happy. Governments that essay to impose a vision of a happy life overstep their bounds and tend to do much to ensure that their citizens will never attain happiness. They establish a fixed ideal that is not subject to change over time with advances in human intellect and moral discernment. It is, therefore, the job of a properly structured society to allow its citizens the opportunity to set their own paths to happiness. That is not because there is no one-size-fits-all version of a happy life—for Jefferson, like Plato, Aristotle, and the Stoics, thinks that virtuous activity is chiefly responsible for men's happiness—but because freedom is an essential part of what it means to be happy. Happiness cannot be written into law.

Thus, we must guard against the notion that Jefferson is advocating a sort of anything-goes approach to happiness. For Jefferson, humans are progressive beings, both intellectually and morally, and true happiness can only be had in societies that are advancing both technologically and morally. Science, following the discoveries of Enlightenment science—for example, Boyle's law, Galileo's law of falling bodies, Newton's law of gravity and three laws of motion, and Jenner's vaccine for smallpox—is moving increasingly toward an understanding of the physical universe. Morality is moving toward the ideal of politically framed self-sufficiency, characterized, inter alia, by agrestic simplicity, the self-regard of ancient philosophers, and the benevolent other-regard preached by Jesus the Nazarene. That Native Americans enjoy an "infinitely greater degree of happiness" than do Europeans is anything but advocacy of such a lifestyle. Native Americans, whose lifestyle is preferable to that of the Europeans in that it is nonoppressive, enjoy merely a barbaric, unconstrained sort of freedom through neglect of science and moral advance, and because of bigoted filial piety.[11] Being loosely social, they enjoy merely a gossamery sort of social unity that is inadequate for true happiness, given humankind's social nature.

JEFFERSON ON LIBERTY

Though his reference to three sorts of government is helpful, what Jefferson means by *liberty* is a matter of considerable debate among scholars.[12] One can, I think, tease out at least four senses of *liberty* for Jefferson. First, there is what is today commonly called *negative liberty*. It is the capacity to live as one wants to live, without the intervention of others—especially meddlesome governors—in one's personal affairs.[13] Second, there is what today called *positive liberty*—the sort of liberty that occurs when one lives in a political body that allows for numerous outlets for self-fulfillment. It entails some measure of governmental involvement in defining the good life and some measure of political participation on the part of the citizenry. Third, there is what might be called *voluntary liberty*—the freedom to make and act on choices. Voluntary liberty involves human creativity and ingenuity as well as human rationality. It is the capacity to recognize different paths of potential activity and to deliberate on and choose among them. Finally, there is what might be called *moral liberty*. It is the capacity to recognize right action as right action and act on account of that recognition, or refuse to act or act otherwise in spite of that recognition.

Negative Liberty

The most prominent feature of Jefferson's liberalism is his attachment to negative liberty—a freedom from external constraints so as to live one's life as one wishes to live it. Advocating natural rights and limited government, Jefferson's conception of liberty is a code of restraint on sovereignty, exercised by a few or many. Freed from potential abuses through political intervention in their affairs, citizens are at liberty to manage their own affairs as they see fit to do so.

So prominent is this strain in Jefferson's political philosophy that numerous scholars, as we have already seen, tend to view Jefferson's commitment to negative liberty as the whole or most prominent part of his commitment to liberty. According to this view, Jefferson is a liberal atomist. Each citizen is committed to himself foremost and only committed to each other insofar as such a commitment ultimately has self-beneficial consequences. Thus, a community of persons is a loose-knit collection of persons, each of whom is out for his own best interest. Obedience to law occurs only because citizens recognize it is in their best interest to obey the laws. I offer some illustrations below.

One scholar says, "Government itself, the very framework of outer accommodation, indeed exists primarily to protect (not to promote . . .) the privacy of the individual. This privacy is the very seedbed in which ideals germinate and in which alone they can securely grow and proliferate." Most sacred among the human rights is the right to be left alone.[14] Another scholar posits that freedom, not happiness, is Jefferson's aim. "For Jefferson, Freedom is the going and the goal. Even happiness is not so elemental. For happiness is not an unalienable right; only the *pursuit* of happiness is."[15] A third scholar says Jefferson's liberalism is predominantly atomistic and progressive. Jefferson places the private interests ahead of concern for public utility. The influence of ancient communitarian thought on Jefferson's political thinking, if it exists, is negligible.[16] A fourth scholar states that Jefferson's "commitment to liberty reflects a Machiavellian moment, an encouragement of civic prickliness, rather than civic friendship, with the anticipated result of political conflict conducive to change and progress." Liberty for Jefferson is the right to withdraw.[17] Finally, a fifth scholar proffers the radical thesis that Jefferson's vision of liberty was irresponsibly negative, at least for some stretch of time. "Jefferson was in the grip of a fanatical cult of liberty [between the years 1787 and 1793], which was seen as an absolute to which it would be blasphemous to assign limits." He adds, "The liberty that Jefferson adored is . . . a wild liberty, absolute, untrammeled, universal, the liberty of great revolutionary manifesto: the Declaration of Independence."[18]

According to the liberal-atomism view of Jefferson's liberalism, citizens grudgingly give their service to their state in a socially responsible manner only to earn time to themselves—namely, time to be left alone. The guarantee of governmental noninterference requires some amount of political participation. What citizens do when they are not politically involved neither concerns the state nor concerns anyone else, so long as in their actions bring no discernible harm to others. Evidence of this thesis in Jefferson's writings exists in abundance. For example, there are numerous explicit references to his execration of political service and his willingness to exchange it for retirement to his own affairs.[19]

That view, however attractive it might seem at first, is indefensible. It fails to accommodate numerous other references to *liberty* that are manifestly non-atomistic. Moreover, it fails to do justice to the inescapable normative dimension of Jefferson's political philosophy—a point to which I return later.

What is generally missed by scholars is that Jefferson was a eudaemonist in some sense of the word.[20] Advocacy of rights, social order, and political efficiency promoted human flourishing. He believed in liberty not for its own sake but because liberty was needed for happiness. He believed in political participation on behalf of all citizens to the extent that each could participate because humans, following Aristotle, were social animals. "Man was destined for society," he wrote to nephew Peter Carr (August 10, 1787). "His morality therefore was to be transformed to this object."

Thus, there is a noticeable communitarian strain in Jefferson's political philosophy. Happiness demands political participation in a morally responsible manner and disallows a separation of one's public persona and one's private persona (disallows inauthenticity)—what customarily occurs in certain consequentialist lines of morality. "I know but one code of morality for men," he says in a letter to James Madison (August 28, 1789) concerning authenticity, "whether acting singly or collectively. He who says I will be a rogue when I act in company with a hundred others, but an honest man when I act alone, will be believed in the former assertion, but not in the latter." Later, he writes to Judge Noah Woodward (April 3, 1825) concerning political participation, "Withdrawn by age from all other public services and attentions to public things, I am closing the last scenes of life by fashioning and fostering an establishment for the instruction of those who are to come after us. I hope its influence in their virtue, freedom, fame and happiness, will be salutary and permanent." Participation in the affairs of one's fellow citizens, construed parochially and globally, is deemed necessary for one's happiness.

Recognition of a communitarian strain in Jefferson's political philosophy is not to categorize Jefferson as a communitarian or to posit stupefaction on

Jefferson's part—errors made by another group of writers.[21] Jefferson is not a communitarian in any strict sense of the term, for he never places the state above the collection of people in it at a given time—thereby awarding it axiological priority of some sort. For Jefferson, the state exists for the sake of it citizens; citizens do not exist for the sake of the state.[22] Moreover, Jefferson is not stupefied. Positive liberty and negative liberty are not mutually exclusive.

Jefferson's purchase of negative liberty is well illustrated by his commitment to free presses. Though he was scandalized and harassed by presses that catered to gossip more than to useful information—"Were I to undertake to answer the calumnies of the newspapers," he writes to Maryland politician Samuel Smith (August 22, 1798), "while I should be answering one, twenty new ones would be invented"—he always openly advocated the free expression of information. "It is so difficult to draw a clear line of separation between the abuse and the wholesome use of the press," he writes to Professor Picket (February 5, 1803), "that as yet we have found it better to trust the public judgment, rather than the magistrate, with the discrimination between truth and falsehood." In a letter to newspaper editor John Norvell (June 14, 1807), written at the apex of his disdain for sensationalist or scandalous journalism, Jefferson notes that a newspaper, constrained by facts and principles, would find few subscribers, so contaminated and wedded to sensationalism have the papers become: "Nothing can now be believed which is seen in a newspaper. Truth itself becomes suspicious by being put into that polluted vehicle." Those letters show that Jefferson was concerned about the great potential damage that presses, under governmental influence, could do. Nonetheless, he consistently supported a free press, in spite of its capacity for ill. "Were it left to me," he said famously to statesman Edward Carrington (January 16, 1787), "to decide whether we should have a government without newspapers or newspapers without a government, I should not hesitate a moment to prefer the latter." He believed that free presses, notwithstanding their abuses, were necessary for orderly, republican government. "Nature has given to man no other means of sifting out the truth either in religion, law, or politics," he writes to President George Washington (September 9, 1792).[23]

The importance of negative liberty for human happiness was certainly concretized by his reading of ancient history—namely, ancient cities like Athens and Rome that thrived not in spite of their toleration of eccentricities of thought but because of their toleration of eccentricities of thought. "Commonplacing" the Earl of Shaftesbury, Jefferson writes: "As the Antients tolerated visionaries and enthusiasts of all kinds so they permitted a free scope to philosophy as a balance. As the Pythagoreans and latter Platonists joined with the superstition of their times the Epicureans and Academicks were allowed all the use of wit and raillery against it. . . . Superstition and enthusiasm thus let alone never raged to bloodshed, persecution &c."[24]

Embrace of negative liberty betrayed hatred or, at least, fear of the corruptive effects of power on those governing. To philosopher A. L. C. Destutt, Comte de Tracy (January 26, 1811), Jefferson writes: "I know that I have never been so well pleased, as when I could shift power from my own, on the shoulders of others; nor have I ever been able to conceive how any rational being could propose happiness to himself from the exercise of power over others."[25] He says to geographer and mapmaker John Melish (January 13, 1813), "An honest man can feel no pleasure in the exercise of power over his fellow citizens." Then he continues:

And considering as the only offices of power those conferred by the people directly, that is to say, the executive and legislative functions of the General and State governments, the common refusal of these and multiplied resignations, are proofs sufficient that power is not alluring to pure minds, and is not, with them, the primary principle of contest. This is my belief of it; it is that on which I have acted; and had it been a mere contest who should be permitted to administer the government according to its genuine republican principles, there has never been a moment of my life in which I should have relinquished for it the enjoyments of my family, my farm, my friends and books.

To statesman Edward Livingston (April 4, 1824), he writes in response to Livingston's speech on national improvement: "In one sentiment of the speech I particularly concur. 'If we have a doubt relative to any power, we ought not to exercise it.'" The antitoxin for the corruptions of strong, centralized government was weak, decentralized government in the hands of the citizenry.

Advocacy of weak, decentralized government notwithstanding, one might argue as numerous scholars have, that Jefferson as president exhibited considerable muscle and influence and made decisions that displayed anything but disdain of power. The Louisiana Purchase, in contravention of his strict constructionism apropos of the Constitution, is an oft-used illustration. Yet I think it can be safely asserted that he generally did so not to advance his own situation but the well-being of the citizenry. He was of halcyon—not

tyrannical—disposition, tended to eschew cronyism, and labored toward conciliation of political differences with political opponents not vengeance for
past grievances.[26] His First Inaugural Address is an excellent illustration of
his conciliatory character.[27] Moreover, he was drawn to strict constructionism
because free interpretation of the Constitution was a gateway for abusive government. For Jefferson, laws and constitutions were not sacrosanct but were
mere shields against tyranny.[28]

Positive Liberty

The notion of positive liberty—the capacity for self-determination by having
access to numerous outlets for fruitful human activity—is also noticeable in
Jefferson's writings. It is not sufficient for happiness that one is left alone. It
is, for Jefferson, in some measure the task of government to secure citizens'
happiness through allowing the creation of social settings in which citizens
can thrive. I offer several illustrations.

In his 1776 Draft Constitution for Virginia, Jefferson proposes that
every person of full age and without property should be given fifty acres
of land. Those owning property in deficiency of fifty acres will be given
property to bring them to fifty acres.[29] The clear implications are that there
is a material side to freedom and that some governmental incentives ought
to be in place to allow for human thriving—that is, negative liberty without
some measure of positive liberty is not liberty. It also shows that the right
to property is not for Jefferson an end in itself but is instead needed for the
sake of human flourishing. A man confined to a prison cell but told he can
do whatever he wishes to do is not free—at least, not in any fully human
sense. In 1786, Jefferson asks James Monroe (July 9), "How may the territories of the union be disposed of so as to produce the greatest degree of
happiness to their inhabitants?" The suggestion here is that cities, towns,
and land in general ought to be zonated in a manner best suited to promote
human thriving. To Virginian David Campbell (March 27, 1792), Jefferson
writes, "That [government] is calculated to produce general happiness,
when administered in it's true republican spirit, I am thoroughly persuaded."
In his Sixth Annual Message as president, Jefferson speaks of a surplus of
governmental revenue and suggests spending that money on public education, roads, rivers, canals and "such other objects of public improvement as it may be thought proper to add to the constitutional enumeration

of federal powers." The aim is "new channels of [interstate] communication" so that "lines of separation will disappear, [states'] interests will be
identified, and their union cemented by new and indissoluble ties."[30]

In short, the government must sometimes intervene in citizens' affairs
to allow for full expression of humans' capacities, and thereby allow for the
possibility of human thriving. To minister and patriot Francis Adrian van der
Kemp (March 22, 1812), Jefferson states, "The only orthodox object of the
institution of government is to secure the greatest degree of happiness possible
to the general mass of those associated under it." As is the case with Plato in
The Republic,[31] it is not the function of a thriving republic to guarantee the
happiness of all persons in it but the greatest amount of happiness of those in
it. For Jefferson, however, it is only the task of government to allow for the
possibility of human thriving—the pursuit of human happiness—not for happiness itself. To James Madison (February 17, 1826), he writes:

> It has also been a great solace to me, to believe that you are engaged in vin-
> dicating to posterity the course we have pursued for preserving to them, in
> all their purity, the blessings of self-government, which we had assisted too
> in acquiring for them. If ever the earth has beheld a system of administration
> conducted with a single and steadfast eye to the general interest and happi-
> ness of those committed to it, one which, protected by truth, can never know
> reproach, it is that to which our lives have been devoted.

Rest assured that Jefferson has in mind here the Bill of Rights.

These passages show—and there are numerous more than can be mar-
shaled—that it is in some measure the function of government to secure happiness by certain "mild interventions" in citizens' affairs—that is, government is
willy-nilly in the human-welfare business. Government ought to act to promote
happiness, but such promotion, the various passages show, involves enhancement of human autonomy, not encroachment on it. Citizens are to be ensured
that government will not be tempted to intervene in the affairs of its citizens
and promote some one-size-fits-all conception of the human good—hence the
need of separation of church and state. All "interventions" must be designed
with long-term aim of promoting human flourishing through assuring human
progress and championing science, while honestly safeguarding autonomy.
To assure such things, government must act, but its actions must be citizens-
directed, not self-directed. Government must make general education accessible

to all citizens and higher education accessible to the natural best. Government must remove the privileges of wealth and birth and reward hard work, honest dealings, and ingenuity. Government must not fall into debt. Government must work toward the elimination of slavery. Government must make land readily available to all citizens needing land. Finally, government must patronize the practical sciences—for example, learn about America's land and resources and about the potential for continental expansion.

Jefferson did not see such "welfarism" as intrusion in the rights of citizens to live their lives as they best saw fit to live them, as numerous critics harshly claim. He was not dictating a manner of living. He was merely creating a milieu in which all citizens could act freely and responsibly, and could thrive, because he realized that liberty was not the human end, but an ineliminable means to that end.

Voluntary Liberty

Voluntary liberty, the freedom to make and act on choices, assumes that humans are in some sense free-choosing organisms that can deliberate on possible courses of action and decide among them. The capacity to deliberate on and choose among possible courses of action means little, however, without knowledge and some degree of imagination. This is what Jefferson had in mind in his defense of slave Samuel Howell in April, 1770. "Under the law of nature, all men are born free, every one comes into the world with a right to his own person, which includes the liberty of moving and using it at his own will. This is what is called personal liberty, and is given him by the author of nature, because necessary for his own sustenance."[32]

Voluntary liberty without knowledge is bootless. To enable persons to make worthwhile voluntary choices, education and meaningful life experiences are needed. Jefferson's efforts vis-à-vis promoting meaningful life experiences are covered above in the section on positive liberty. Jefferson's efforts vis-à-vis promoting general and higher education are the topics of the final three chapters.

Imagination is an ally of knowledge. Humans possess the inborn capacity to imagine the world as it might be. As I mention in the preface, Jefferson, because of his unstinted belief in human advance, was continually in the business of imagining the world as it might be. As gardener, he was a plotter of esculent, medicinal, and ornamental plants in an aesthetically pleasing manner.

As architect, he was a designer of buildings that accommodated, inspired, and educated people. As inventor, he was a creator of technological devices to improve human efficiency. As scientist, he was a deviser of hypotheses to be tested by experience. As philologist, he tinkered with proper formation of neologisms by enhancing the structural capacities of the English language. As political philosopher, he proposed both a basic schema for republican government and offered several suggestions on instantiations of that schema through his ideas on constitutional reforms.

Human creativity and ingenuity are answerable to human rationality, and human rationality, ultimately to the moral sense (the topic of chapters 5 through 7), so the depiction here is incomplete without expatiation on moral liberty.

Moral Liberty

Moral liberty, which might be provisionally grasped as a capacity to recognize right action as right action and act on it because of that, is strictly speaking a species of voluntary liberty, as moral activity is a species of voluntary action. Under voluntary liberty, we can list adiaphorous actions (actions, like counting stars, unrelated to morality) and moral actions.

Not all activities, for Jefferson, are moral activities. Some are adiaphorous. The engagements of science—for example, squaring the circle, tracing the orbit of a comet, or investigating the arch of greatest strength or the solid of least resistance, as he says in his Head-and-Heart letter to Maria Cosway (October 12, 1786)—are not moral activities but strictly affairs of reason, though they certainly might have moral implications in circumstances.[33] Boondoggling—for example, counting the number of limes on a tree or the number of freckles on a face to pass the time—is also not a moral action so long as one is not boondoggling to eschew moral action.

Many other activities—the lion's share of them, for few human activities have no moral implications—are moral actions for Jefferson. Again from his letter to Cosway, Jefferson's decision to bypass a "poor weathered soldier," who pleaded to be taken up on Jefferson's coach at Chickahominy was, he admits, a moral failing—a judgment of reason against the moral sense. His purchase of the Louisiana territories and work on the University of Virginia, were moral accomplishments.

For Jefferson, discernment of correct moral action is in the main, as we shall see in the chapters on morality, independent of reason. Rationality and moral sensibility are separate faculties. "When nature assigned us the same habitation, she gave us over it a divided empire," Jefferson says to Cosway. "[Reason or Head was] allotted the field of science; [Heart or the moral sense] that of morals." Discernment of morally correct action is visceral and immediate, not ratiocinative. Says Heart to Head in the same letter, "I do not know that I ever did a good thing on your suggestion, or a dirty one without it. I do forever then disclaim your interference in my province." Following philosopher Lord Kames, whose work on morality greatly influenced Jefferson, moral discernment occurs intuitively, by ignoring reason.[34] For Kames, through intuitive perception—"the faculty of perception, working silently, and without effort" or a sort of immediate grasp of some truth or convenience[35] that is guided by sensory data—we come immediately to see our moral duties.[36] It is the same with Jefferson.[37] The intrusion of reason is not only unneeded, it is also morally injurious.

Though each person is free to obey or disobey the judgment of the moral sense and follow, say, the urgings of more bestial passions, it is difficult to see how one with perfect moral regard can be free. Kames calls the moral sense "the voice of God within us which commands our strictest obedience."[38] Jefferson would not disagree. Thus, though all are free to disobey the moral sense, it is difficult to see how anyone with moral regard—and almost all persons (with few exceptions, like Napoleon[39]) are born with a moral sense—would disobey.

Yet, one might say, is not each person free to choose to disregard moral law? Did not Jefferson himself, in a letter to grandson Thomas Jefferson Randolph (November 24, 1808), mention a choice between hedonic and honorable lifestyles early in his life, when he found himself drifting toward a life of self-serving pleasure?

If such a course of reasoning is applicable to Jefferson, then one is at liberty to choose a moral life or otherwise, but each is in some sense a life of constraint. To choose a moral life is to be morally free insofar as one is constrained to live in pursuance of moral law. To choose otherwise is to be free from morality insofar as one is constrained to live in pursuance of bestial passions.[40] So, either way, humans are constrained, though they are at liberty to choose among constraints—among two possible paths of life.

That seems overstated. Choosing does not seem to be the issue. For Jefferson, since all are born with a moral sense, moral discernment comes naturally to humans. Thus, it is hard to see how anyone would "choose" to act against the moral sense, which is comparable to choosing not to use one's eyes to see or one's hands to grasp, which would be acting against nature. Anyone acting against his internal moral monitor would likely not be choosing vice as a way of life but would be beguiled by the entrapments and occlusions of reason, which often argues against moral discernment and in favor of self-interest, or overwhelmed by bestial passions. Reason gone awry can readily lead astray a person to think that egoistic action is right action, another natural impulse for Jefferson. Passions overstimulated by overindulgence can readily overwhelm the moral sense.[41]

While it is difficult to apprehend how anyone could choose not to use his eyes to see and not to use his hands to grasp, it is not difficult to see how someone could choose to see only certain things or see things in a certain way, instead of how they are, or choose to grasp only certain things to the exclusion of others. Such is the case when one, like Napoleon, is born without a moral sense; when reason, overstrong, habitually oversteps its bounds and intrudes on matters of morality; or when the moral sense, overweak, falls prey to hebetude or sensual depravity through long exposure to either. While the former scenario is rare for Jefferson, the latter two scenarios unfortunately are far too common.

REPUBLICANISM VERSUS FEDERALISM

In a passage from a letter to Dr. Benjamin Rush (January 16, 1811), which begins the introduction to this book, Jefferson writes of a conversation at a dinner engagement at Monticello involving himself and Federalists Alexander Hamilton and John Adams. (Recall, I adopt the convention throughout of using "Federalism" as a party movement and "federalism" as a political philosophy; the same with "Republicanism" and "republicanism.") The three dined and then, with wine in hand, they sat to converse. The discussion turned to the British constitution. Two events that day shed considerable light on the differences between Adams's and Hamilton's federalism as well as Adams the man and Hamilton the man.

First, Adams asserted that the British system of government would be the most perfect system of government, if some of its "defects and abuses" were corrected.[42] Hamilton countered that it was the most perfect form of government with its vices, as any correction would render it impracticable.

The second point I leave in Jefferson's own unexampled words: "The room being hung around with a collection of the portraits of remarkable men, among them were those of Bacon, Newton and Locke, Hamilton asked me who they were. I told him they were my trinity of the three greatest men the world had ever produced, naming them. He paused for some time: 'the greatest man,' said he, 'that ever lived, was Julius Caesar.'"[43] Jefferson sums, "Mr. Adams was honest as a politician, as well as a man;[44] Hamilton honest as a man, but, as a politician, believing in the necessity of either force or corruption to govern men."[45]

The two examples serve as illustrations to Jefferson's view of the differences between Adams and Hamilton as well as Jefferson's republicanism and perhaps two different versions of federalism. In the first example, Adams's view seems to be that the vices of the British constitution should be altered to ensure good government. Hamilton's reply is revelatory in two senses. First, his belief that the British constitution is perfect as is indicates a view that humans are corrupt and self-interested, and government must do some ill to check destructive human passions. His choice of Caesar, a conqueror and autocrat, as the greatest person who ever lived speaks volumes of his personal ambition and autocratic tendencies. Second, it shows that Hamilton has little interest in science and philosophy, as it is astonishing that he could not have recognized portraits of three of the most recognizable pundits of the world at the time. Failure to recognize Newton, for instance, perhaps would be comparable today to failure of a prominent American political figure to recognize a portrait of Einstein, and that is unimaginable. Overall, Jefferson's admiration of his "trinity" betrays a political vision that is at once a philosophical vision.

What precisely were the differences between Jefferson's political vision and that of Hamilton?

The period after the Declaration of Independence was a time of great philosophical debate—a debate between federalism, defined and defended much by Hamilton and actualized in some measure in Adams's tenure as president, and republicanism, defined and defended much by Jefferson, mostly in response to federalism. There is considerable critical discussion today vis-à-vis the nature of the debate—that is, whether it was chiefly political, economic, or philosophical.

On the political side, according to one writer, Federalists advocated that

political power should be in the hands of an elite group of citizens—an educated minority of landowners, an aristocracy—that could unify the varied
interests of manufacturers, merchants, and tradesmen of mostly urban areas.
In such a manner, the country could avoid the pitfalls of involvement of the
hoi polloi, who in their eyes were essaying to secure public goods for personal
interests without contributing to public well-being. Thus, urbanization and
manufacture were critical for political unity. Republicans accepted the notion
of potential for political abuse through self-interest but maintained that it was
not the hoi polloi whose ambitions needed to be kept in check but those of the
urbanized aristocrats. The political corrective for Jefferson was agrarianism,
which was valuable not because it was in itself virtuous activity but because it
happened to lead to independence, self-reliance, and the common good—each
democratic and political interests.[46]

On the economic side, Jefferson's republicanism, according to another
scholar, was chiefly motivated by a form of protocapitalism. Acknowledging the force of the classical-republican objections to staunch liberals,
early America was friendly both to liberalism and capitalism, and it was the
freedom of opportunity offered by liberalism and nascent capitalism—with
opportunities for achievement and advancement, free movement of ideas, and
rewards for hard work and creativity independent of social status—that moved
Jefferson as well as early Americans. For Jefferson, big government and big
capital could not be segregated.[47] According to another scholar, Jefferson's
republicanism was an economic-driven commitment to agriculturalism—an
attempt for America, with a superabundance of arable land, to meet European
demands for food. The disagreement between Jefferson and Hamilton was
not over agrarianism and commercialism as competing social ideologies, but
it was a disagreement about different modes of commercial development—
farming versus commerce.[48]

On the philosophical side, one writer argues that Jefferson's republicanism
and Hamilton's federalism were merely or chiefly different moral visions of
social institutions. For Hamilton, social institutions comprising a ruling aristocracy were a moral corrective to the impetuosity of the masses, which were
incapable of productive, rational activity. For Jefferson, social institutions were
an encumbrance to moral development. They quashed human autonomy and
human thriving by keeping uninformed and uninvolved the general citizenry.[49]
Evidence against the federalist notion that aristocracy and institutionalization
were needed to instill some form of morality on the masses came with Jeffer-

son's observations of Native Americans, who had no government but had a sense of society through recognition of moral correctness and incorrectness.[50]

All three views add something to the overall explanation of Jefferson's motivations for his actions as statesman. None should be pretermitted. Yet perusal of his writings, I have been arguing all along, indicates baldly that his political philosophy is grounded normatively—that is, it aims at all citizens being as happy as possible. Yet it is not the function of government to make citizens flourish by promoting any one vision of the good life, but merely to allow citizens abundant space to pursue their own course to happiness. In essence, Jeffersonian republicanism is a political schema that allows for government for and of the people through elected and recallable representatives, utmost political participation by all citizens, and morally sensitive governorship through strictest possible conformity to constitutional principles.

Yet Jeffersonian republicanism is not a commitment to any particular political constitution. So complete is his purchase of human moral and intellectual advance that he can neither be chained, nor chain a people, to one constitution. A constitution is needed, but it is not the immutable, sacrosanct political framework that regulates the interactions of the federal government, the states, and their citizens. Instead, for Jefferson, they are chiefly a reflection of the rightful and reasonable intellectual, political, and especially moral climate of a people at a given time. Consequently, they are alterable and must be altered so that they do not shackle a people to their past and prevent them from a better future. Human happiness is a progressive, not an inertial, ideal.

Thus, the key difference between Jeffersonian republicanism and Hamiltonian federalism, at least in Jefferson's eyes, lay in the philosophy undergirding their political principles. Jefferson's republicanism is principally ethical—a forward-looking vision of human flourishing. Thus, it is a philosophical, not a political, movement that looks ahead to a "new order for the ages, a federal republican regime that would preserve peace (in the world, among states), sustain republican government (in the states), and secure liberty and natural rights of individual citizens."[51] Hamiltonian "federalism" is political, mundane, and backhanded. It draws from the past to show that humans are in the main inescapably bestial and unthinking. Federalism for him is a matter of strong, forceful government to direct the affairs of the state and the masses, which are incapable of self-direction. For Jefferson the argument is philosophical; for Hamilton, political—a point with which biographer Henry Adams would likely agree.[52]

Jefferson believed in the overall good judgment of the masses. The people themselves, if generally educated, could conduct their own affairs. Governments were needed primarily to see that no one part of a people impose their vision of the good life on another part—a point made elliptically in a letter as president to Dr. Benjamin Rush (June 13, 1805): "I am but a machine," he writes, "erected by the Constitution for the performance of certain acts according to laws of action laid down for me." Jefferson advocated complete but translucent government that was predominantly bottom-up driven.[53] He believed that people, given a modicum of education, could govern themselves and watch over those persons elected to govern the affairs of nation. He encouraged participation in governmental affairs at various levels, pursuant to talents and virtue. He advocated the relative independence of the three branches of government.[54]

In contrast, Hamilton had a profound distrust in the masses. He wanted strong, centralized government to direct the affairs of the citizenry, as allowing people to govern their own affairs would result in chaos.[55] One might say his view of democracy was Platonic. As Plato says in *The Republic*, democracy parades around as the "finest and most beautiful of the constitutions, for, like a coat embroidered with every kind of ornament, this city, embroidered with every kind of character type, would seem to be the most beautiful."[56] It is like something multicolored that is judged beautiful by women and children, but behind the veneer of beauty there lurks ataxia through mobocracy. In short, Hamilton preached democracy but underhandedly sought to instantiate oligarchy.

The disparate philosophical visions of Jefferson and Hamilton concerning the general citizenry—doubtless the result of acute differences in demeanor: Jefferson trusting and optimistic, Hamilton distrustful and unphilosophical—resulted in disparate political views of government and the executive as well as foreign policy, which Hamilton influenced much more than a secretary of treasury should have influenced.[57] Hamilton aimed for loose construction of the Constitution or implied powers to allow for strong government and swift, heavy-handed executive action. He writes, "Every power vested in a government is in its nature sovereign, and includes by force of the term a right to employ all the means requisite and fairly applicable to the attainment of the ends of such power, and which are not precluded by restrictions and exceptions specified in the Constitution, or not immoral, or not contrary to the essential ends of political society."[58] He sought firm ties and free commercial exchange with England. Jefferson aimed for strict construction of the Constitution as a preventive of oppressive government and for a strong, independent executive, not dizzied with power and mindful of his obligations to the general citizenry. He sought firm ties and free commercial exchange with nations—commercial exchange only insofar as it was needed—but wished for strict noninvolvement in the political wrangling of such nations.[59]

Jefferson's view, drawing from the lessons of the past and of the present to provide impetus for the future, was labile and embraced intellectual and moral advance. In Jefferson's eyes, Hamilton's view, drawing from the one lesson of the past—that the people could not be trusted—was filiopietistic and fixed. Jefferson writes to John Adams (June 15, 1813) vis-à-vis federalism and republicanism:

> On one of the questions you know on which our parties took different sides, was on the improvability of the human mind, in science, in ethics, in government etc. Those who advocated reformation of institutions, pari passu, with the progress of science, maintained that no definite limits could be assigned to that progress. The enemies of reform, on the other hand, denied improvement, and advocated steady adherence to the principles, practices and institutions of our fathers, which they represented as the consummation of wisdom, and akmé of excellence, beyond which the human mind could never advance.

As Jefferson saw things, republicanism was wedded to science, broadly construed, and forward-looking; Hamilton's Federalism was pococurante concerning science and backward-looking.[60]

Believing that people could not be trusted, Hamilton maintained that government should be centralized, take-charge, and economically secure. He aimed to secure such goals by appeal to human self-interest. Jefferson writes of Hamilton's thinking in "The Anas": "It had two objects. 1st as a puzzle, to exclude popular understanding & inquiry. 2dly, as a machine for the corruption of the legislature; for he avowed the opinion that man could be governed by one of two motives only, force or [self-]interest: force he observed, in this country was out of the question; and the interests therefore of the members must be laid hold of, to keep the legislature in unison with the Executive."[61] With grief and shame, he adds, some members were "sordid enough to bend their duty to their interests." Hamilton also believed, pursuant to self-interest, that a good executive should govern for life. Cozenage and deception were always options.

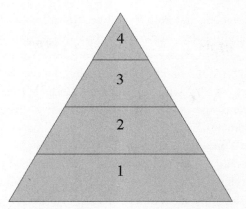

**Figure 3.1. Jefferson's Republicanism
Instantiated.** The various numbers in the
pyramid represent, respectively, Jefferson's
ward (1), county (2), state (3), and federal
(4) governments. Ward governments, at the
bottom, are the foundation of the nation.

It is a mistake, however, to categorize Jefferson's opposition to Hamilton as one of extreme liberalism versus extreme conservatism. As Jefferson's divide-and-divide-again ward-system policy shows, Jeffersonian republicanism aims at mediation—a middle path between the extreme centralism of Hamilton and the extreme view of states' rights of Patrick Henry.[62] Citizens would live in wards, which would measure some six square miles and which would have a great amount of political independence from each other (see figure 3.1).[63] Wards would be parts of counties—each "of such size as that every citizen can attend, when called on, and act in person."[64] Counties would be parts of states, which would concern themselves with legislation and administration of its citizens. Finally, states would be part of the nation, whose chief roles would be to secure human rights and represent the various states in foreign affairs as a unified nation. "The elementary republics of the wards, the county republics, the State republics, and the republic of Union," he writes to politician Joseph C. Cabell (February 2, 1816), "would form a gradation of authorities, standing each on the basis of law, holding every one its delegated share of powers, and constituting truly a system of fundamental balances and checks for the government."

On such a medialist view, state government would not be subordinate to the federal government, but both would be "co-ordinate departments of one simple and integral whole," he writes to political reformist John Cartwright (June 5, 1824). Jefferson's aim was to give each level its proper sphere of control. "To make us one nation as to foreign concern, and keep us distinct in Domestic ones," writes Jefferson to James Madison (December 16, 1786), "gives the outline of the proper division of powers between the general and particular governments."

As Jefferson's one-many schema shows, mediation, not partisanship, was his intent. "If I could not go to heaven but with a party," he writes to Francis Hopkinson (March 13, 1789), fellow signer of the Declaration, "I would not go there at all." Republicanism as a political party was formed gradually over time as a panacea to the impertinencies of High Federalists through sensationalist presses and underhanded Federalist actions during Adams's administration, such as the XYZ Affair and the Alien and Sedition Acts.[65]

Though he trusted the sound judgment of the people, Jefferson deeply distrusted persons in positions of power. Of one thing he was sure: power corrupts. Thus, the legislative, executive, and judiciary were to be kept separate to guard against any one branch controlling the others or any branch, like the judiciary, having the final word.[66] Legislators in the lower house were to be chosen by the people, whose judgment on their character was deemed sufficient. Yet legislators in the senate were not to be chosen by the people. "I have ever observed that a choice by the people themselves is not generally distinguished for it's wisdom," he writes to Virginian politician Edmund Pendleton (August 26, 1776). "This first secretion from them is usually crude & heterogeneous." Thus, legislators in the upper house were to be chosen by the representatives. Senators were not to hold office for life. Were they capable of being continually reelected, they would likely cast their eyes to future, curry favor with their electors, and thereby lose their independence. Knowing they will return to the "mass of the people," they might "keep alive that regard to the public good."

Laws should be few and mild—not restrictive of peoples' liberties—and clearly articulated. Fewness of laws is indicative of nonoppressive governing. Mild laws reflect a policy of leniency and mercifulness for transgressors.[67] Clearly articulated laws keep judges from their continued and often arbitrary interpretation of them. He sums in his letter to Pendleton: "Let mercy be the character of the lawgiver, but let the judge be a mere machine."

HOBBES VERSUS LOCKE

Hamilton and Adams, in effect, were Hobbesians. In *Leviathan*, Hobbes asserts that human life, in the state of nature, was anarchic. Humans were ceaselessly at war and their lives were "nasty, brutish, and short." For security and peace, they moved to civil society and took umbrage under a strong, tyrannical individual. In short, the transition from nature to civil society was the transition from anarchy to tyranny—a decided improvement. Speaking of himself in the second person, Hamilton[68] says in "The Farmer Refuted" about a certain the similarity of his own views to them of Hobbes:[69]

> There is so strong a similitude between your political principles and those maintained by Mr. Hobbes, that, in judging from them, a person might very easily *mistake* you for a disciple of his. His opinion was exactly coincident with yours, relative to man in a state of nature. He held, as you do, that he was then perfectly free from all restraint of *law* and *government*. Moral obligation, according to him, is derived from the introduction of civil society; and there is no virtue but what is purely artificial, the mere contrivance of politicians for the maintenance of social intercourse.[70]

Adams too was a Hobbesian. He writes in this letter to Jefferson (October 9, 1787): "I have long been settled in my own opinion, that neither Philosophy, nor Religion, nor Morality, nor Wisdom, nor Interest, will ever govern nations or Parties, against their Vanity, their Pride, their Resentment or Revenge, or their Avarice or Ambition. Nothing but Force and Power and Strength can restrain them." In short, the social state was contractarian. Individuals agreed to be governed by a strong sovereign, even a tyrant, to keep them from being harmed by others in the state of nature. For both statesmen, harm was the stuff of the cosmos, but there was less of it in a social state.

In contrast to Hamilton and Adams, Jefferson, as we have seen in his letter to Melish, believed in force—especially excessive force—only in dire circumstances and as a last resort. Otherwise, a political leader should behave machinelike. Jefferson did not grasp how a man could find happiness in the subjugation of and the exercise of control over another, especially through mendacity. Jefferson was disposed and pleased to share power with others, and as president, to invoke the opinions of competent, morally sensitive statesmen as advisors.[71]

As I note in the prior chapter, Jefferson's republicanism was heavily, though not exclusively, influenced by Locke.[72] Jefferson was a Lockean in many respects. He believed that natural rights—rights to life, liberty, and the pursuit of happiness—belonged to humans by nature and were independent of human's choice of manner of living.[73] He believed that humans ought to be governed by reason, not force. He believed that government ought to interfere in individuals' personal affairs only when individuals interfere with peace and social order. He believed that truth, if unimpeded, would ultimately prevail over untruth. He believed that the people themselves were fair judges of how government was acting, but they could not involve themselves in everyday political affairs without bias—that is, they needed to be governed.[74] I expand on some of these points, and others unstated, below.

First, believing that nature was law-governed—here following in the footsteps of Newton's great discoveries of the physical universe—Jefferson maintained that humans too were in some sense law-governed animals and those "laws" were in nature and discoverable by reason. Each human was born, experience showed, with certain natural capacities and the varying talents and courses of their upbringing dictated their different paths. Reasoning backward, the state of nature was not then garrulous but rather precarious, because of human ignorance, and civil society helped to reduce that precariousness and eradicate human ignorance through the advances of science.

What brought things together for Locke, the second commonality, was the existence of natural rights, which belonged by nature to humans—independently of their manner of living. These rights included foremost the rights to life, individual liberty, and property (pursuit of happiness, not property, for Jefferson[75]), and such laws were continually transgressed by the strong in the state of nature. Thus, civil society was also a way to guarantee that each person, regardless of capacities, would be guaranteed his civil rights through a "social contract." When a government violated the rights of any of its citizens, whether the majority or a certain minority, the citizens had a right to nullify the social contract and rise up in revolt against the government.

Third, there is Locke's belief, incorporated by Jefferson, that persons are rational, equal, and free. "Nothing is more evident," writes Locke, "that Creatures of the same species and rank promiscuously born to all the same advantages of Nature, and the use of the same faculties, should also be equal one amongst another without Subordination or Subjection."[76] Jefferson echoes the sentiment in a letter to Roger Weightman (June 24, 1826), mayor of Washington, DC, "The mass of mankind has not been born with saddles on their backs, nor a favored few booted and spurred, ready to ride them legitimately, by the grace of God." Government, thus, can legitimately govern only by consent of the governed.

Fourth, there is the effect of Locke's religious thought on Jefferson. Locke sanctioned religious toleration, but he did not take the extra step, as did Jefferson, of separation of church and state.[77] In *The Reasonableness of Christianity*, Locke maintains that Christians and atheists ought not to have the patronage of the British Constitution: Christians, because they pledge allegiance to a foreign prince; atheists, because their atheism is anarchical. All other religions ought to be tolerated, which assumes that what they profess is in error but is politically harmless.[78] Jefferson, in contrast to Locke, was for toleration of divergent religious beliefs, but he was also for free expression of divergent beliefs. His argument, contained in his *Notes on the State of Virginia*, is similar to that of Locke: "It does me no injury for my neighbor to say there are twenty gods, or no God. It neither picks my pocket nor breaks my leg."[79] Yet the real issue for Jefferson is not physical injury but mental coercion. The state has no business to dictate one's innermost beliefs.

Fifth, Jefferson bought into some measure of Lockean distrust of persons, concerning their own affairs, when those affairs were not self-contained—that is, when they had an effect on others. Locke thought that the law of nature was "plain and intelligible" to all rational beings, but humans were in the main biased in its application and "not apt to allow of it as a Law binding to them in the application of it to their particular Cases." In short, in a case where some offense has taken place and each of two involved accuse the other of that offense, only one standing outside of the disagreement can generally judge with discernment and accuracy which of the two is at fault, or mostly so. When one is one of the disputants, self-interest prejudices one's judgment.[80]

Locke's view of property and its influence on Jefferson is covered in the next chapter.

JEFFERSON AND MADISON

It is today well-known that Jefferson and James Madison formed a deep and lasting friendship almost from the time they first met. Said John Quincy Adams of the bond between the two, "Mr. Madison was the intimate, confidential, and devoted friend to Mr. Jefferson, and the mutual influence of these two mighty minds upon each other is a phenomenon, like the invisible and mysterious movements of the magnet in the physical world, and in which the sagacity of the future historian may discover the solution of much of our national history not otherwise easily accountable."[81]

Jefferson historian Merrill D. Peterson writes that while Madison had a "more penetrating mind, sharp, probing, and persistent," Jefferson was the "bolder thinker, more inventive, more talented in generalization and synthesis, and easily caught up in any idea that promised improvement to mankind." While Madison was more of a political realist, Jefferson was a political idealist.[82]

James Morton Smith, editor of the correspondence between Jefferson and Madison,[83] which lasted fifty years, has this to say of the two men:

> Jefferson was the more speculative, inventive, and theoretical, gifted at coining generalization and powerful metaphors and writing felicitous prose. Madison as tougher-minded, more analytical, and the more persistent student of politics, the harder-headed thinker of the art of the possible. . . . Jefferson was the eternal optimist, thinking always in terms of human happiness. Madison was the occasional pessimist, constantly aware of the power of human selfishness. In balancing the elements of liberty and power in a republican system, Jefferson, the author of the Declaration of Independence, tended to emphasize the first, fearing governmental power as a threat to liberty, while Madison, the father of the Constitution, tended to stress the second, viewing the new and more powerful government under the Constitution as a protector of liberty.[84]

What makes Jefferson's legacy a lasting one is the universality of his vision—its insistence on the equality of all people and the extension of rights, naturally founded, to them—and his unflagging optimism. James Madison was pivotal in bringing that vision to fruition. Republicanism, Madison writes in "Federalist 57," is "the vigilant, and manly spirit which activates the people of America—a spirit which nourishes freedom and is in return nourished by it." It was Madison's realism, manifest in the Constitution, that complemented Jefferson's idealism, exhibited in the Declaration of Independence.[85] The Declaration was more than a crystalized expression of a people's right to revolt against unrepresentative government. It was Jefferson's depiction at the time of a philosophical vision of government being accountable to its citizens. That vision included inalienable rights[86] and self-evident truths. Says one writer: "The principles of the Declaration were not only an expression of the American mind . . . but an expression of the mind of the time; it reflected the intellectual climate in which lived all the liberal thinkers of the period. What was new was the fact that these principles had been proclaimed in an official document and signed by men who were the duly elected representatives and spokesmen of a new nation."[87] Another writer speaks of the Declaration as a paradox. On the one hand, it is a bullish statement of national identity. On the other hand, that bullish statement entails a "weakly articulated national *government*."[88]

Madison's Constitution[89] eleven years later was some attempt at an instantiation of that vision. Through its several articles, it laid out the duties of the three branches of government along with the role of states.[90] Yet Jefferson insisted in a letter to Madison (December 20, 1787) that a bill of rights ought to be amended to the Constitution, for no just government should be without one, and without one, a government "rest[s] on inferences."[91] Madison initially resisted, but one year later, he remarked to Jefferson (October 17, 1788) that such a bill might be useful and "could not be of disservice," properly put into practice. The Bill of Rights was eventually added to the Constitution. Jefferson also objected that there was no clause in the Constitution that restricted the eligibility of the president from reelection over time. That allowed for the possibility of a perpetual president—a short step to dictatorial leadership.[92]

Though sure friends and political allies, one must not think that the political views of Jefferson and Madison were identical, or nearly so. The political ideologies of Madison and Jefferson on several issues were often remarkably different. Madison was frequently more in line with conservative Federalists than Jeffersonian liberalism. Says one scholar, "James Madison was both more market-oriented and more antidemocratic than is generally realized; ideologically, he stood closer to Alexander Hamilton than to Thomas Jefferson" when it came to his conceptions of property, man, government, and society.[93] Madison did not see an inverse correlation between governmental power and citizens' liberties.[94] While Jefferson feared too much government, Madison the realist bought into Hamiltonian self-interest. He recognized the potential dangers of government in the hands of the few or the many—that is, power could easy corrupt the many as well as the few. Moreover, Madison and Hamilton collaborated on the Constitution and, along with Jay, on *The Federalist*, while Jefferson was in Paris.[95]

Overall, the federalist policies and abuses of the Adams's administration—for example, loyalty to England and hostility toward France, building up of the army and navy, and the Alien and Sedition Acts—helped align politically Jefferson with Madison, and through works like the Kentucky Resolutions and Virginia Resolutions, helped define Republicanism as a political party in opposition to the Federalism of Hamilton and Adams. Factionalism was no one's intention at the outset. For instance, the earliest version of the Constitution provided for the most capable politician to become president and the second most capable politician to become vice president. It was designed in some measure to prevent, not to foster, factionalism. There was no anticipation of significant future political friction through bipartisanship.[96] That explains Jefferson's comment to Francis Hopkinson (March 13, 1789) that he would prefer not to go to heaven, if he should have to go as a political-party affiliate.

Republicanism, however, was always more of a political philosophy with an ethical undergirding for Jefferson than it was a party. He detested partisanship but saw it as an inevitable fact of human nature. "The division between whig and tory is founded in the nature of men, the weakly and nerveless, the rich and the corrupt seeing more safety and accessibility in a strong executive,"[97] he writes to politician Joel Barlow (May 3, 1802), "the healthy, firm and virtuous feeling confidence in their physical and moral resources, and willing to part with only so much power as is necessary for their good government, and therefore to retain the rest in the hands of the many."[98] The issue according to Jefferson was obscurantist government based on the lessons of history in line with the interests of a privileged few versus progressive government in line with the sentiments of the people and the advances of knowledge.

CHAPTER 4

"THE EARTH BELONGS . . . TO THE LIVING"

Jefferson on Revolution and Political Renewal

> *"Man, like the fruit he eats, has his period of ripeness. Like that, too, if he continues longer hanging to the stem, it is but an useless and unsightly appendage."*
>
> —TJ to General Henry Dearborn,
> August 17, 1821

robably having the French Revolution in mind, Jefferson in reply to a letter of John Adams (September 4, 1823), addresses the issue of the difficulties of revolutions. "The generation which commences a revolution can rarely compleat it. Habituated from their infancy to passive submission of body and mind to their kings and priests," he says, "they are not qualified, when called on, to think and provide for themselves, and their inexperience, their ignorance and bigotry make them instruments often, in the hands of the Bonapartes and Iturbides to defeat their own rights and purposes." The notion is that not all revolutions can establish a workable government of representatives of the people. The first few revolutions might fail, but as a "younger, and more instructed race comes on, the sentiment becomes more and more intuitive, and a 4th. a 5th. or some subsequent one of the ever renewed attempts will ultimately succeed." Overall, for a revolution to succeed, he adds, the "middling classes" need to be educated.

"All Europe," Jefferson goes on to say, "will [in time] attain republican government, more or less perfect." For that to happen, "rivers of blood must yet flow, and years of desolation pass over. Yet the object is worth rivers of blood, and years of desolation for what inheritance so valuable can man leave to posterity."

Jefferson is often reproached for such ultraist comments on revolutions. Some reproaches are aimed at his putative purchase of a sort of consequentialism in which the end of liberty justifies the means of bloody violence, whatever the score. More extreme reproaches concern a perceived commitment to a form of anarchic liberty—liberty for its own sake—in which violence is a mere upshot of the right to do whatever one wants to do, whenever one wants to do it.

This chapter is an examination of Jefferson's thoughts on political revolutions in the context of his theoretical commitment to republicanism as a general schema of good government. I begin with Jefferson's early thoughts on the need of periodic revolutions. I then turn to a critical examination of two prominent objections to Jefferson's views on revolutions. Next, I address his notions of usufruct and constitutional renewal in a well-known letter to James Madison. I end with some thoughts on revolution and constitutional renewal within the context of Jefferson's purchase of progressivism and his references to the Saxon constitution.

THE "NATURAL MANURE" OF LIBERTY

On January 30, 1787, Jefferson writes to James Madison about the recent troubles in the "Eastern states"—namely, Shays' Rebellion.[1] The channels of commerce have been stopped, money has been rendered scarce, and the scarcity of money has made people uneasy. Their uneasiness has produced acts "absolutely unjustifiable," but Jefferson's hope is that such acts will not trigger severe recriminations and punishments. He avers that one must guard against the notion that "nature has formed man insusceptible of any other government but that of force, a conclusion not founded in truth, nor experience." Perilous liberty, he adds, is preferable to quiet servitude. Rebellion in the service of liberty is a needed evil, as it prevents governors from serving their own interests and it keeps governors aware that they govern for the people. He adds in a passage now famous: "I hold that a little rebellion now and then is a good thing, & as necessary in the political world as storms in the physical. Unsuccessful rebellions indeed generally establish the encroachments on the rights of the people which have produced them. An observation of this truth should render honest republican governors so mild in their punishments of rebellions, as not to discourage them too much. It is a medicine necessary for the sound health of government."

Ten months later, Jefferson addresses British propaganda concerning the presumed continued state of anarchy in America in a letter to revolutionist William Smith (November 13, 1787), husband of John Adams's daughter "Nabby." The lies have spread across the globe and they have had such an effect that even Americans have come to believe them. Yet the anarchy is reducible to "the single instance of Massachusetts." He adds: "And can history produce an instance of rebellion so honourably conducted. I say nothing of its motives. They were founded in ignorance, not wickedness. God forbid we should ever be 20 years without such a rebellion. The people cannot be all, & always, well informed. The part which is wrong will be discontented in proportion to the importance of the facts they misconceive. If they remain quiet under such misconceptions it is a lethargy, the forerunner of death to the public liberty." There are thirteen states in the eleven years of American liberty and only one rebellion in that span of time, Jefferson says. That makes for one rebellion in some 150 years and that is probably insufficient for the preservation of liberty. "What signify a few lives lost in a century or two? The tree of liberty must be refreshed from time to time with the blood of patriots & tyrants. It is it's natural manure."

One month later, Jefferson refers to Shays' Rebellion in another letter to Madison (December 20, 1787). His reasoning is identical to that in his letter to Smith. "The late rebellion in Massachusetts has given more alarm than I think it should have done. Calculate that one rebellion in 13 states in the course of 11 years, is but one for each state in a century & a half. No country should be so long without one." Jefferson adds, "The will of the majority should always prevail." Perhaps anticipating the Madisonian objection that the majority too can be corrupt—"Wherever the real power in a Government lies, there is the danger of oppression"[2]—Jefferson then asserts that states' governments will be virtuous so long as America is chiefly an agrarian country and the common people receive an education proportioned to their needs. Agrarianism and education are checks against the corruption of the people.

Several years later, Jefferson returns to the issue of revolution vis-à-vis the French Revolution in a letter to his former secretary William Short (January 3, 1793). "The liberty of the whole earth was depending on the issue of the contest, and was ever such a prize won with so little innocent blood? My own affections have been deeply wounded by some of the martyrs to this cause, but rather than it should have failed, I would have seen half the earth desolated. Were there but an Adam & and Eve left in every country, & left free, it would be better than as it now is."

To some, such passages give unambiguous evidence that Jefferson is an anarchist or an in-the-clouds liberal without concern the particulars of reality and with little concern for the value of human lives. I offer the critiques of Conor Cruise O'Brien and Michael Hardt as illustrations.

JEFFERSON'S "CULT OF LIBERTY"

Conor Cruise O'Brien writes that Jefferson, between the years of 1787 and 1793 was "in the grip of a fanatical cult of liberty, which was seen as an absolute to which it would be blasphemous to assign limits." He adds, "The liberty that Jefferson adored is . . . a wild liberty, absolute, untrammeled, universal, the liberty of a great revolutionary manifesto: the Declaration of Independence."[3]

O'Brien offers as evidence Jefferson's written response to Shays' Rebellion in his letter to William Smith and Jefferson's Adam-and-Eve letter to William Short.

The letter to Smith, O'Brien says, is an attempt to justify the violence of Shays' Rebellion. He quotes Jefferson, "God forbid we should ever be 20 years without such a revolution. . . . The tree of liberty must be refreshed from time to time with the blood of patriots & tyrants. It is it's natural manure." O'Brien then asks rhetorically, "That is something very like a Jeffersonian charter for the most militant segment of the modern American militias, is it not?" He has in mind the antigovernment actions of the Michigan militia at the time of his writing. O'Brien notes that the Oklahoma City bombing was inspired by Jefferson, since McVeigh was wearing a T-shirt on which was printed Jefferson's tree-of-liberty quote.

There are several difficulties here. First, there is O'Brien's presumed rhetorical question, "That is something very like a Jeffersonian charter for the most militant segment of the modern American militias, is it not?" The phrasing of the question—"something very like"—is so irreparably vague and greasy that it perhaps amounts to a loaded question in which any conceivable answer incriminates the answerer. Moreover, Jefferson is writing a personal letter to a correspondent. To suggest that a few sentences of the letter make the letter a gory manifesto and Jefferson a blood-thirsty revolutionist is absurd. Weighed against numerous other references to "liberty" in Jefferson's writings—and I have broken down Jefferson's various meanings of *liberty* in the previous chapter—the argument is sapless and is uncogent. Furthermore, O'Brien emphasizes that the charter is written not for any revolutionaries, but only for the "most militant" of modern American militias. That suggests Jefferson was an unbending proponent of anarchic liberalism, anarchy come what may, which is unsustainable, given what we have seen of Jefferson's conception of liberty in the prior chapter. Finally, the statement that Jefferson should somehow be held accountable for McVeigh's actions is outlandish. Overall, the suggestion that the letter is a charter for anarchic militias is unsupportable.

Drawing from the letter to William Short, O'Brien makes much of Jefferson's statement that it is preferable for half the earth to be martyred in a successful cause than for the cause to fail. "Were there but an Adam and Eve, left in every country, and left free, it would be better than it now is." Refusing to see the sentence as, in Dumas Malone's words, an "isolated flash of hyperbole," O'Brien writes, "Short should accept that there was no limit (except the sparing of two persons per nation) to the slaughter that might legitimately be perpetrated in the holy cause of freedom."[4] As evidence O'Brien cites one other reference, Jefferson's "Notes of a Conversation with Washington on French Affairs," in which Jefferson describes the French Revolution as his "polar star."

It is absurd to take the letter to Short as proof positive that Jefferson was advocating a lawless, anarchistic cult of liberty. One has only to reconsider his critique of the Native American system of government (chapter 3). That Jefferson believes Native American lawlessness is preferable to tyrannical oppression is not evidence of the perfection of and preference for lawlessness but evidence of the turpitude linked with tyranny and oppression. Jefferson also believes that Native Americans' lawlessness is inferior to republican government, as humans can flourish only in social settings of a specific sort— that is, where laws and governors are few and in place to respect and defend natural human rights, and where the social setting allows for scientific and moral advance.

Jefferson was much under the spell of liberty during his stay in France, but neither then did he embrace and nor ever did he embrace liberty for its own sake—anarchic liberty. The reasons are many.

First, in his letter to William Smith, Jefferson writes of the British exaggerations concerning American anarchy and cites Shays' Rebellion as the sole incident. That is scarcely an unqualified endorsement of the rebellion. In a letter to James Madison (January 30, 1787), he says the acts of violence in the rebellion are "absolutely unjustifiable"—something that escapes O'Brien's selective attention. In 1795, he writes to Jean Nicolas Démeunier (April 29), "Being myself a warm zealot for the attainment and enjoyment by all mankind of as much liberty, as each may exercise without injury to the equal liberty of his fellow citizens, I have lamented that in France the endeavours to obtain his have been attended with the diffusion of so much blood."

Second, Jefferson qua anarchist did not practice what O'Brien asserts he preached. There is no better illustration that his response as vice president to the Alien and Sedition Acts. His and James Madison's responses to the "unconstitutional laws" were the Kentucky and Virginia Resolutions, which essayed to bypass debate with Hard Federalists and appeal to popular opinion. "Firmness on our part, but passive firmness, is the true course," he states to Madison (January 30, 1799). "Keep away all show of force, and they [the people] will bear down the evil propensities of the government, by the constitutional means of election and petition." In short, Jefferson's actions showed a profound belief in the ability of the people to recognize corruption, if given access in print to the truth, and to remedy it through peaceable, constitutional means.

Third, even a cursory inspection of Jefferson's writings shows that he recognized varied senses of *liberty*. In chapter 3, I argue for four distinct senses: negative, positive, voluntary, and moral liberty. Other scholars argue for different categories. Nevertheless, nearly all Jeffersonian scholars who examine the issue are in agreement that Jefferson's concept of liberty was not monolithic. To argue that Jefferson ever—even at one particular point in his political career—gave aegis to one and only one category of liberty, liberty for its own sake, is to paralogize.

Fourth, O'Brien suggests a wholesale commitment by Jefferson to a sort of "negative liberty" that amounts to freedom from governmental intervention in any activities whatsoever. Jefferson's embrace of negative liberty is emphatically freedom from the encroachments and corruptions of government—freedom from the tyranny of one or some group of humans with power over others without or with lesser power. "Of liberty then I would say, that, in the whole plenitude of its extent," he writes to politician Isaac Tiffany (April 4, 1817), "it is unobstructed action according to our will, but rightful liberty is unobstructed action according to our will within limits drawn around us by the equal rights of others. I do not add 'within the limits of the law,' because law is often the tyrant's will, and is always so when it violates the right of an individual." Again, as he says in the early 1787 letter to Madison, perilous liberty is preferable to quiet servitude. In other words, autonomy is so much a part of the human constitution that humans who are not beaten down will always prefer death to political suffocation. That is not advocacy of anarchism but instead recognition of human rights.[5] That sentiment O'Brien ignores.

Fifth, Jefferson is not committed to liberty per se, but liberty in the service of intellectual and moral advance—liberty in the service of human betterment. As noted Jeffersonian scholar Dumas Malone writes, the danger Jefferson perceived was inertia—that is, listlessness and complacency—for inertia was a signal of despotism.[6] As Jefferson says in a letter to Dr. Joseph Willard (March 24, 1789), clergyman and president of Harvard University: "We have spent the prime of our lives in procuring [the American youth] the precious blessing of liberty. Let them spend theirs in showing that it is the great parent of science and of virtue; and that that a nation will be great in both, always in proportion as it is free."[7] This letter, it should be noted, was written in 1789, when Jefferson was in Paris—during those years especially when he was supposedly blindly attached to the cult of liberty.

Against the background of everything Jefferson has written on liberty, to place two letters at the forefront of Jefferson's thinking on liberty is misguided. One expects a scholar to finecomb Jefferson's writings apropos of "liberty" and then to show the development of his thinking over time on the topic, or at least, offer a complete study of Jefferson's use of the concept in the years O'Brien profiles—Jefferson's years of avowed fanatic cultism. Were O'Brien to do that, his thesis would implode.

In building his straw man, O'Brien commits throughout his essay what I elsewhere call the *fallacy of historical anachronism*.[8] Here one (1) forms a judgment of a historical figure (or event) by using contemporary standards that were not in place during the epoch of that figure (or event) or (2) forms a judgment of a contemporary figure (or event) by recourse to the standards of the past that are no longer in place. O'Brien is guilty of the first. I list a few examples.

First, O'Brien argues that Jefferson was not an American nationalist, but a "Virginia Firster." Proof sits on his gravestone, he asserts, which fails to mention that he was president of the United States.[9]

There are several difficulties here.

To begin, in Jefferson's time, the nation was merely a loose confederation of states, each more or less self-sufficient, not a strongly centralized nation with unified interests. Thus, to state that Jefferson put the interests of his state ahead of the confederation of states would not have been unexpected.

Nonetheless, Jefferson was uncommonly dedicated to the burgeoning nation. He was "notable among his countrymen for his devotion to the cause of the feeble Union."[10] His letters during his presidency show plainly that he generally placed the interests of the nation even ahead of his own family.[11] So wedded to duty was he that he waited till Congress adjourned on March 27, 1804, before he rushed back to Monticello to try to convalesce his moribund daughter Maria. Furthermore, Jefferson always advocated states' compliance with legitimate federal policies—especially policies intended to maintain peace and public safety.[12]

Next, Jefferson's political ideology, though mostly bottom-up driven, was more of an organic ideal than is traditionally recognized. Wards were parts of counties; counties were parts of states; states were parts of the nation. There is here unity—though a loose sort of unity—that is constitutionally secured insofar as constitutions are "binding" documents—a point O'Brien seems to overpass.

In addition, it is true that Jefferson did not want the epithet "president of the United States" on his gravestone, but he also did not want "governor of Virginia"—something a "Virginia Firster" would have had proudly engraved on his stone. The reason Jefferson shunned both epithets was likely his express disdain of politics. Politicians sought outright victories in policies, but Jefferson recognized the natural differences in men and the need for political policy to be conciliatory.[13]

Second, O'Brien anachronistically castigates Jefferson for the behavior of the Michigan-militia rebels and the anarchic behavior of the Oklahoma bomber. As was previously mentioned, McVeigh, after all, was wearing a T-shirt with Jefferson's tree-of-liberty quote on it when the bombing occurred.[14] Thus, because certain entrepreneurs, with an eye to money-making and not to historical integrity, have taken a Jefferson quote out of context and placed it on a T-shirt, and because McVeigh used the out-of-context quote as motivation for his misdeed, Jefferson ought to be held accountable.

Third, Jefferson's liberalism, O'Brien asserts, had an inescapably racist dimension. He might be called father of the KKK. Why? Populist leader Tom Watson of Georgia put out a magazine titled *The Jeffersonian*—a magazine that spread the parochial racism of the South to future generations. "*The Jeffersonian* . . . propagated in crude emotive forms ideas to which *the master* [italics added] had given discreet and *overtly unemotional* expression. And in the southern states in the years after the Civil War the whites who most practiced what *The Jeffersonian* was preaching were members of the Ku Klux Klan."[15] O'Brien's concludes, "The Ku Klux Klan was ideologically descended from Thomas Jefferson."[16] That misleadingly and falsely suggests direct causal succession of events from Jefferson to the formation of the KKK. That also suggests Jefferson was an outright racist. The syllogism, put into its most charitable form, goes as follows:

1. *The Jeffersonian* gave explicit expression to racist sentiments like those underexpressed or unexpressed by Jefferson.
2. Post–Civil War KKK members practiced the racism that *The Jeffersonian* preached.
3. So, Jefferson is the father of the KKK.

Further comment on the ill-formed premises and the "tightness" of the syllogism is unneeded.

Overall, even if it were fair to assess Jefferson by the standards in place today, Jefferson would think it untoward. He was an above-board progressivist.[17] As such, he was confident that each successive generation would make not only intellectual advances but also moral advances over the preceding generation. Consequently, he did not hold the Constitution, viewed by many today as a document to guide America's political interests for all time—as inviolable. Jefferson's embrace of the need of some spilt blood over the generations was just to guarantee steady advance—movement away from oppression. As one scholar puts it, "He did not actually *like* rebellion, but he most feared repression," so he put his trust in the people.[18] For him, a constitution was a living document that needed alterations, and presumably every so often, substantive changes by a constitutional convention, at which the changes suggested could be confirmed by the citizenry.[19] The thread that held together a constitution was the notion that the government it reflected would be a government progressive and for and of the people.

JEFFERSON'S "CELEBRATION OF REBELLION"

In "Jefferson and Democracy," literary theorist and political thinker Michael Hardt claims boldly that Jefferson's liberalism can "only be seen" as advocacy of anarchy. He too makes much of the letters to Smith and Short.

Hardt reconstructs Jefferson's thinking in his letter to William Smith thus. First, for Jefferson, revolutions are legitimate even if they are the result false or confused motives. Quietude, even when one is ignorant, is "death to the public liberty." Second, Jefferson believes that regular revolutions are desirable. Hardt quotes Jefferson, "God forbid we should ever be 20 years without such a rebellion." Third, Jefferson states that revolutions are needed to maintain freedom. The blood of patriots and tyrants is the "natural manure" of liberty. Hardt writes in a manner that rules out any nonpolitical aims of Jefferson: "Liberty and freedom mean simply for Jefferson that the multitude is autonomous and thus able to exert its priority over government. This has little to do with individualist notions of the freedom to do as one pleases in the course of everyday life. Freedom for Jefferson is the right of the multitude constantly to exert its power over and determine the actions of government."[20]

Hardt's conclusion that Jefferson's "celebration of rebellion and his apology for political violence can only be seen as a recipe for anarchy" is too strong and unwarranted. Nonetheless, his arguments are more nuanced than those of O'Brien. I offer a critique of his reconstruction of Jefferson's three arguments.

Jefferson's first argument might be fleshed out from the conditional claim "rebellions are legitimate even when they are based on false or confused motives" so long as agents, even if ignorant, are not wicked. Hardt says, "His point is that since people cannot always be well informed, they should act on the basis of the knowledge they have," for quietness is lethargy—in Jefferson's own words, "the forerunner of death to the public liberty."[21]

One difficulty here is a sort of fallacy of false quantifier. Hardt assumes Jefferson is committed to the quantifier "all" in front of "rebellions are legitimate" and that is nowise obvious. Jefferson's point cannot be that anarchic rebellion—that is, rebellion for the sake of rebellion—is justifiable, for his concept of "liberty," as his writings show, is polysemous, not monolithic. Liberty, I have shown, is not the liberty to do whatever one wants without fear of governmental reprisal. It is the liberty to do whatever one wants without fear of governmental reprisal so long as one's actions do not encroach on the liberties of others—foremost among those liberties is perhaps the pursuit of happiness. Moreover, there is the communitarian strain in Jefferson's thinking, which shows that liberty entails more than the requirement that actions not be socially harmful. Thus, to assume the quantified "all" is to assume too much. Jefferson would have granted "some," but never "all," and never before any proposition that asserted rebellion for its own sake.

Another difficulty is Hardt's assumption that, for Jefferson, political action is always preferable to political inaction, irrespective of one's knowledge. Again, there is a fallacy of false quantifier. Jefferson's point is that liberty needs vitality, and true vitality is a matter of action in the direction of human intellectual and moral progress. Rebellious action for its own sake is something Jefferson never advocated and thus could not have championed. Moreover, Jefferson often viewed political inaction as preferable to action. Elsewhere[22] I show Jefferson's foursquare commitment to *kairos*—things happening at the opportune moment. It was critical for Jefferson for actions to be at the right time, otherwise mistimed actions could result in more ill than good. For illustration, Jefferson refused to act on the issue of slavery in his days of retirement because of his belief that to act then would be to act before the time was ripe for appropriate action. Action on slavery at the wrong time might result in more harm—that is, separation of the union—than good.

That Jefferson excuses the agents of Shays' Rebellion because they acted "in ignorance, not wickedness" is not a blanket statement that all good-hearted, misinformed actions are justifiable. It is a statement that actions with an eye to preservation of liberty and removal of political corruption ought to be judged with utmost leniency. Jefferson writes to Madison (December 20, 1787): "The part which is wrong will be discontented in proportion to *the importance of the facts* they misconceive. If they remain quiet *under such misconceptions* it is a lethargy, the forerunner of death to the public liberty" (my italics). Jefferson is saying that lethargy *on important issues* and, implicitly, *at critical times* is the death knell of liberty. That is not sanction of rebellion for its own sake. The year 1786 was still a time of great volatility for the fledgling nation— hence my inclusion of "at critical times"—and Shays' Rebellion, a rebellion of farmers, was likely excusable for Jefferson because it was a rebellion of farmers.[23] Jefferson, it is well known, was through-and-through anti-city. As he says in his letter to Madison, one way to ensure the incorruptibility of the masses is to keep America chiefly agrarian.

Jefferson's second argument and third argument can be taken together. His second argument, according to Hardt, is that Shays' Rebellion is excusable because of its infrequency. "Jefferson notes that such rebellions have not been frequent—this is the only significant rebellion during the eleven years since independence—and indeed that regular rebellions are desirable."[24] Jefferson's third argument, which includes his "most dramatic statements," is about the need for rebellion to sustain freedom. Hardt says, "He considers that a few lives lost periodically are insignificant compared to the beliefs of rebellion."[25]

"Jefferson's celebration of rebellion and his apology for political violence can only be seen as a recipe for anarchy," states Hardt. To see that, Hardt takes us to a distinction between primacy-of-sovereignty and primacy-of-resistance political stances. In the primacy of sovereignty, rebellions are sometimes justifiable when they serve as a check to governmental abuses of power, but rebellions must never threaten monarchical power and its primary status. In the primacy of resistance—Jefferson's view, according to Hardt—rebellions are the means by which sovereignty is reminded of its own secondary status—that is, of the primacy of the power of the people. Hardt writes, "What is most important for [Jefferson] is not the justness of the specific rebellion but the political relation that all such rebellions reaffirm: the multitude is primary and sovereign power merely a shadow or reflection of it."[26] Rebellion and the concomitant political violence remind governors that they are subservient to the people and that government must change periodically to "bring it in line with the current desires and composition of the multitude." Hardt sums Jefferson's attitude toward liberty: "Liberty and freedom mean simply for Jefferson that the multitude is autonomous and thus able to exert its priority over government. This has little to do with individualist notions of the freedom to do as one pleases in the course of everyday life. Freedom for Jefferson is the right of the multitude constantly to exert its power over and determine the actions of government."[27]

Hardt's view is attractive and has much prima facie luster as well as a certain amount of textual succor. If true, it does make Jefferson a political anarchist, insofar as appeal to the "desires and composition" of the hoi polloi is a matter of government in the service of the wants of the many—a commitment to deciding political issues by a crass appeal to the uncultivated interests of the masses.

Like many other political interpretations of Jefferson's liberalism, Hardt's critique fails to take note of Jefferson's purchase of progressivism. That is at least part of what Jefferson meant in his First Inaugural Address when he stated that the will of the majority, if rightful, must be reasonable.[28] Thus, Jefferson was not advocating anarchy because he was inflexibly committed to liberty for the sake of progress. So wedded was he to progress that he could not envisage one generation enslaving the next to its state of ignorance—hence the need of periodic constitutional renewal in keeping with usufruct.

Jefferson's system of wards, never instantiated, was an attempt to provide a minimal structure of bottom-up, participatory government.[29] By dividing each county into roughly one hundred wards, each with its own school, each ward would be somewhat self-sufficient and invite full participation of its citizens apropos of local issues. Yet citizens would also indirectly participate in county issues by sending representative delegates to their county. There were as well representative delegates of the state and representative delegates of the federal government. Though bottom-up driven, there is, as I have argued above, at least a gauzy organic structure to the whole picture that cannot be overpassed.

Hardt has something to say about wards too, as he addresses a perceived problem of representative government—"dialectical negation." He writes: "Jefferson's proposal for these elementary republics . . . undermines the representational schema at the heart of the Constitution by operating a kind of dialectical negation, playing on the dual role of representation, to connect and to separate. The wards . . . aim to make representation complete, absolute (in linking multitude to power) and thereby destroy representation (as a mechanism of separation). When the connective function of representation is pushed to its extreme, it undermines representation's function of separation." Unbeknown to Jefferson, representation is not at the heart of, but an obstacle to, republicanism—"a government in which the multitude directly rules itself or in which there is a small as possible gap between the rulers and the ruled."[30]

Hardt's critique of Jefferson's divide-and-divide-again policy has bite. It might be that his system, if implemented, would not have had the sort of effects Jefferson envisaged: It might not allow representatives to act autonomously and to serve the interests of the people. For Hardt, that is a self-contradiction. As he sees things, separation is a function of government because representative governors act at levels that the people cannot act and thus are distinct from the people they represent. Separation is also an obstacle to good government because representative governors are beholden to the people and consequently do not have the sort of autonomy they need to function distinctly and, presumably, effectively.

Does Jefferson's divide-and-divide-again policy negate itself? I think not. Jefferson is clear that "the will of the majority should always prevail."[31] On Hardt's interpretation of Jefferson, however, elected representatives, because of their dependency on their electors, are mere pawns in the hands of their electors, and representatives become at least ineffective, if not superfluous.

That is not Jefferson's view of representation. Governors are elected on account of their capabilities and their virtue, and they are elected precisely because citizens—and Jefferson, especially early on, has principally in mind communities of farmers—have neither the time nor the talents to function at the higher levels of governing. Citizens can take care of their own affairs at the ward level, but there are important county-level, state-level, and federal-level affairs in which they cannot participate. For Jefferson, representatives in many instances are at liberty to do as they see fit so long as they have in mind the best interest of their constituency, taken as autonomous and progressive beings. Jefferson believes that citizens, as moral equals of those persons they elect, are suitable checks on the character of their representatives.[32]

Hardt's critique, I acknowledge, is considerably more subtle and nuanced than that of O'Brien, who seems out to get Jefferson in whatever manner whatsoever. Yet Hardt's critique also fails. Jefferson is not pococurante about the justness of rebellious actions, and rebellious actions are warranted only when they are just—when there is a history of governmental abuse. For him, revolution with the aim of removal of corrupt governors is a just revolution. That is why he much fretted over the framing of a constitution after the American Revolution. "Should a bad government be instituted for us in the future it had as well to have accepted at first the bad one offered to us from beyond the water without the risk and expence of contest."[33] Rebellion is a normative issue for Jefferson, and rebellions are warranted only when both human rights are violated and there is little reason to think any acts of diplomacy will be effective in the restoration of those rights. Since Hardt's thesis overlooks the normative dimension of Jefferson's political thinking, it is unsustainable.

The presumed inconsistencies that O'Brien and Hardt spot in key Jeffersonian writings are perhaps best explicable by Jeffersonian ambivalence, driven by his dual role as both philosopher and statesman. As political philosopher, he was devoted to practical principles—for example, freedom and the pursuit of happiness—which he considers universal. As philosophical statesman, he was aware that principles are not always neatly applied to the complexities of everyday-life circumstances.[34]

USUFRUCT AND RENEWAL

Though Jefferson owes much to philosopher John Locke, he goes beyond Locke in one key element—a right to rebellion. In the Declaration of Independence, Jefferson notes that when absolute despotism surfaces, "It is [the people's] right, it is their duty, to throw off such Government."[35] While Locke acknowledges a right to resist tyranny, "the exercise of power beyond right,"[36] Jefferson posits a right, if not a moral duty, to rebel against tyranny. When it fails to secure the rights of its citizens, a government loses any claim to legitimacy and its citizens ought to rise up in rebellion.

The right to rebellion is a consequence of Jefferson's naturalism. In that regard, the Declaration of Independence can also be viewed as a naturalistic argument for jus ad bellum.[37] It is, as one author says, the right of one to punish any other who would "violate his rights in the state of nature."[38] Yet that considers humans back in the state of nature, not in social settings, and for Jefferson, what was guaranteed humans in the state of nature was guaranteed humans in social settings. In social settings, however, the circumstances were much more complex. It is here worth iterating a point made in the previous chapter. Jefferson, following Locke, recognized that each person was a poor judge of applying the laws of nature to his own case, so there was need of judges to decide such affairs and a constitution to which judges could appeal to help adjudicate complex cases.

Yet constitutions, unlike the rights of men, were alterable, in conformance to the level of scientific, political, and moral progress of a state. Thus, constitutions were to be replaced, altered, or renewed pursuant to humans' intellectual, political, and moral progress. Jefferson writes to Samuel Kercheval (July 12, 1816), "I know also, that the laws and constitutions must go hand in hand with the progress of the human mind." Moreover, Jefferson was enough of a practicalist to recognize that even the most fundamental rights of men could be sacrificed when self-preservation of person or country was at stake. "A strict observance of the written law is doubtless *one* of the high duties of a good citizen, but it is not the *highest*," he tells fellow republican John B. Colvin (September 20, 1810). "The laws of necessity, of self-preservation, of saving our country by a scrupulous adherence to written law, would be to lose the law itself, with life, liberty, property and all those enjoying them with us; thus absurdly sacrificing the end to the means."[39]

The issue of constitutional renewal takes center stage in a famous letter to James Madison (September 6, 1789). Jefferson writes: "The question Whether one generation of men has a right to bind another seems never to have been started either on this or our side of the water. Yet it is a question of such consequences as not only to merit decision, but place also, among the fundamental principles of every government."[40]

Jefferson goes on to say that the obligations of one generation do not bind the next, which he justifies by the following self-evident proposition: "I set out on this ground which I suppose to be self evident, '*that the earth belongs in usufruct to the living*;' that the dead have neither powers nor rights over it." The principle he takes as sufficiently obvious, but it has heretofore unseen implications, when fully examined.

Jefferson considers land without occupancy. Assuming a society has no laws for the appropriation of its lands, the lands belong to those persons who first occupy and work it. When the owner of a parcel of land has passed, his land goes to his wife or children or to the legatee or creditor of the deceased. Yet that transfer occurs not by natural right, but by the laws of the deceased's society. "No man can by *natural right* oblige the lands he occupied, or the persons who succeed him in that occupation, to the payment of debts contracted by him. For if he could, he might during his own life, eat up the usufruct of the lands for several generations to come, and then the lands would belong to the dead, and not to the living, which would be reverse of our principle." He concludes, "What is true of every member of the society individually, is true of them all collectively, since the rights of the whole can be no more than the sum of the rights of individuals."

Jefferson assumes a scenario in which each person of one generation is born on the same day, will mature on the same day, and will die, at fifty-five years of age, on the same day. Upon maturation, say at the age of twenty-one, that generation will be succeeded by the next generation. "Then I say the earth belongs to each of these generations during it's course, fully, and in their own right." Usufruct entails no encumbrance of debt, upon transference of property, as transference of debt entails that the earth belongs to the dead and not the living. It follows that no generation can contract debts greater than can be paid during its lifespan. Upon maturation of twenty-one years, in its first year of self-dominion, each person of a generation can contract a debt for thirty-three years; in the tenth, twenty-four years; in the twentieth, fourteen years; and so on. As things stand legally, upon death, if a debt is not repaid in full, property will go to a creditor and not a child or any other. Nonetheless, that is not how nature intended things to be.

Jefferson's thought experiment assumes, for the sake of convenience, each generation comes and goes on a fixed day. That, of course, does not happen. Generations are not fixed. To solve the conundrum, Jefferson appeals to the mortuary table of Buffon in which the French scientist gives 23,994 deaths at varied ages. He supposes the existence of a society in which the number of people that are born each year is the same and whose people live to the ages in Buffon's table. That society, consisting of 617,703 persons at any time, will have, (1) at any point of time, one half of all persons dead in twenty-four years and eight months, (2) each year, 10,675 persons attain the age of twenty-one, (3) always, 348,417 persons over the age of twenty-one, and, (4) at any point of time, one half of them over twenty-one years dying in eighteen years and eight months or, roughly, nineteen years. "Then 19. years is the term beyond which neither the representatives of a nation," Jefferson sums, "nor even the whole nation itself assembled, can validly extend a debt."

Jefferson considers Genoan money lenders, doling out money to Louis XV on condition that no interest is to be paid until the end of nineteen years, at which time the money lenders will receive an annual interest of 12.5 percent. The king and his generation then squander the money in dissipative living. Why ought the next generation to inherit the debt?

While present debts will be a matter of honor and expediency, future debts will be constrained. To constrain future debts, it is wise for a constitution to stipulate that a nation can borrow no more than it can repay in the span of nineteen years. Here borrowers and lenders would be guarded, and borrowing would be constricted to its natural limits and that would "bridle the spirit of war."

It follows that "no society can make a perpetual constitution, or even a perpetual law." Each generation has a right to govern as it pleases. "Every constitution, then, and every law, naturally expires at the end of 19. years. If it be enforced longer, it is an act of force and not of right." In such a manner, one writer notes, "the absolutist metaphysical character of natural rights and social compact disappear; and a more practical ideal is evolved, which conceives the basic right to self-government . . . as a limited contract with the present members of society, formalized in a constitution."[41] Defects of constitutions are to be addressed at periodic constitutional conventions at which amendments can be made with philosophical sangfroid.[42] Viewed in this manner, Jefferson's republicanism was designed to circumvent revolution, as periodic constitutional renewal was itself a built-in mechanism set in place to forfend revolutions.[43]

Jefferson acknowledges difficulties in application, each of which concerns retroactive application. What of lands given to churches, hospitals, colleges, and orders of chivalry? What of ecclesiastical or feudal privileges affixed to lands? What of hereditary offices, authorities, and jurisdictions? What of perpetual monopolies in business and the arts and sciences? In such instances, reimbursement is nowise a question of right, but of generosity.

James Madison's objections to Jefferson's notion of usufruct come in a letter the following year (February 4, 1790), and are evidence sufficient that Madison was not blown away by Jefferson's discovery. They are, in keeping with Madison's bent, mostly of a practicable sort.

First, Madison objects that the frequent constitutional changes would lead to political instability and would engender "pernicious factions." He says, "The most violent struggles [would] be generated between those interested in reviving and those interested in new-modelling the former state of property." Property would depreciate in value. The consequent uncertainty would discourage industry and give "disproportionate advantage . . . to the sagacious and interprizing part of the Society."

Second, Madison notes, the state of nature and the civil state are significantly different. What is guaranteed man in the state of nature applies to man only in the state of nature.

Third, it is manifest that the deceased leave more than debts to the living. They also leave improvements, from which the living derive great benefit. Are persons, on the death of their benefactors, supposed to return things to an earlier state of affairs, when the benefits did not exist?

Fourth, many debts are beneficial, like the debt incurred when one nation repels the attempted conquest of another or the current debt of post-revolution America. Nineteen years is merely not long enough for repayment.

Madison sums: "There seems then to be a foundation in the nature of things, in the relation which one generation bears to another, for the *descent* of obligations from one to another. Equity requires it. Mutual good is promoted by it." He adds pragmatically, "All that is indispensable in adjusting the account between the dead and the living is to see that the debits against the latter do not exceed the advances made by the former." The only relief from the ill consequences of Jefferson's continual constitutional renewal is to infer "tacit assent" when there exists no positive dissent to a constitution over time.

Jefferson the idealist is stymied by Madison the realist. Jefferson unsurprisingly does not return to the topic with Madison again.

PROGRESSIVISM: JEFFERSON AS A PHILOSOPHER FOR PEACE

It is astonishing that Jefferson appears not to have anticipated any of Madison's objections. So intent was he on fleshing out the theoretical implications of his notion of usufruct and constitutional change that numerous and varied problems of practical application eluded him.

It is also worth repeating that in practice Jefferson was not a radical revolutionist.[44] When it came time to consider a constitution for Virginia pursuant to republican aims in 1776, Jefferson did not propose complete effacement and wholesale reconstruction but a substantial revision of the old laws.[45] When he took office as president in 1801, he proposed conciliation with the past Federalist administration, as "every difference of opinion is not a difference of principle." He added, "We are all Republicans, we are all Federalists."[46] In short, though he appeared to be a radicalist in theory, he was always a moderate in praxis. Slow but steady political progress through conciliation—everything in a timely manner—was his credo. "The ground of liberty is to be gained by inches," he tells Rev. Charles Clay (January 27, 1790), "that we must be contented to secure what we can get from time to time, and eternally press forward for what is yet to get. It takes time to persuade men to do even what is for their own good."

What prompted Jefferson's thinking on usufruct was his purchase of progressivism. He writes in a letter to John Adams (January 11, 1816): "[The eighteenth century] certainly witnessed the sciences and arts, manners and morals, advanced to a higher degree than the world had ever before seen. And might we not go back to the aera of the Borgias, by which time the barbarous ages had reduced national morality to it's lowest point of depravity, and observe that the arts and science, rising from that point, advanced gradually thro' al the 16th. 17th. and 18th. centuries, softening and correcting the manners and morals of man?" The advances of Galileo, Boyle, Rittenhouse, and Newton in science and of Priestley, Sterne, Kames, and Hutcheson in morality offer undeniable proof of progress. Politics, with the emergence of the notion of representative government, was no exception.

The "Gothic idea" that people ought to look backward for human improvement, he writes to Reverend Joseph Priestley (January 29, 1800), is absurd. That is a bigoted idea that serves the purpose of political conservatives that would have the ideals of one era serve as the ideals of every era.[47] In "Thoughts on Lotteries," he speaks of the "ineffable joy" of those persons in retirement on seeing "a grade of science beyond their own ken."[48] In a letter to economist and writer Pierre Samuel Dupont de Nemours (April 24, 1816), he grants that the human condition might never advance to such a state of perfection that all pain and vice will be eradicated. Nonetheless, "I believe it susceptible of much improvement, and most of all in matters of government and religion [i.e., morality]."

Jefferson was no relativist concerning constitutional adoption, as many make him out to be.[49] Though greatly under the spell of Montesquieu early in his life—his *Legal Commonplace Book* contains twenty-eight pages devoted to the French political theorist—he was condemnatory of the French philosopher's *Spirit of the Laws* later in life[50] and rejected many Montesquieuan postulates: the notion of republican effectiveness being related to smallness of size of a state, the impossibility of extreme equality in a thriving republic, efficacy of the British model, and, important for our purposes, political relativism.[51] In spite of his purchase of usufruct and its implication of periodic constitutional renewal, Jefferson held to the notion of an ideal form of government, what one writer calls "a limiting ideal toward which legislators, statesmen, and educators may look for inspiration and guidance."[52] Political progressivism, consistent with his view that science as a whole was progressing, demanded such an ideal. In that regard, his political philosophy was like his ethics, where the Stoicized teachings of Jesus were close to a limiting ideal for morally correct behavior.[53] That also explains fully Jefferson's eschewal of ancient political thinkers—for example, Plato in *The Republic* and Aristotle in *Politics*—for such thinkers never latched on to the notion of representative government, a decided advance over prior thinkers.[54]

Eschewing relativism, the progressivist element of his republicanism was scientific, construed broadly as it was in Jefferson's day. It was not any sort of rights-sensitive government that mattered, but one in which government was committed to the advances of science to promote human happiness. Scientific communities or societies, having the interests of the global community of people in mind, were necessarily cordial and cooperative. Ideas, discoveries, and often even inventions were readily shared between scientists of different nations. Thus, Jeffersonian republicanism, linking liberty to knowledge, presciently anticipated a global revolution, in which nations, at peace with each other, would freely exchange goods and ideas with each other to advance the global human condition. Peace was needed to ensure greater human flourishing.[55] As Jefferson scholar Merrill Peterson notes, Jefferson's animus was "against systems of energy, force, and command, whether fiscal or military," for they were "simply different faces of a statecraft at war with the liberties and happiness of the people." Republicanism was "a plan to reverse the natural tendency of every government toward power and aggrandizement." Europeans, noting the implications of Jefferson's republicanism, "rubbed their eyes in disbelief at the spectacle of a chief magistrate renouncing patronage and power."[56]

Jefferson's purchase of progressivism is perhaps no more evident than in his stance on neoterism in languages. "If dictionaries are to be arbiters of language," he writes to John Adams (August 15, 1820), "in which of them shall we find *neologism*. No matter. It is a good word, well sounding, obvious, and expresses an idea which would otherwise require circumlocution." He continues: "I am a friend to *neology*. It is the only way to give to a language copiousness and euphony. without it we should still be held to the vocabulary of Alfred or of Ulphilas; and held to their state of science also: for I am sure they had no words which could have conveyed the ideas of Oxigen, cotyledons, zoophytes, magnetism, electricity, hyaline, and thousands of others expressing ideas not then existing, nor of possible communication in the state of their language."[57] The implicit propositions are that language will inevitably advance with the progress of the human mind and that political conservatives,[58] who would have language conform to a once-and-for-all standard that is dictated by unbending rules and a dictionary, are themselves mossbacks and roadblocks of progress.[59]

With the constraints of primogeniture, entails, and state-sponsored religion removed, the mechanism of advance, Jefferson states in his First Inaugural Address, is that "the will of the majority is in all cases to prevail [and that] that will to be rightful must be reasonable."[60] That will is to be made reasonable by the "diffusion of knowledge among the people."[61] Education is the key to steady improvement. "I look to the diffusion of light and education," he writes to Dr. Cornelius Camden Blatchly (October 21, 1822), "as the resource most to be relied on for ameliorating the human condition, promoting virtue, and advancing the happiness of man."[62] To academician George Ticknor (November 25, 1817), he expresses a Baconian appreciation of education. "My hopes however are kept in check by the ordinary character of our state legislatures, the members of which do not generally possess information enough to perceive the important truths, that knolege is power, that knolege is safety, and that knolege is happiness." Not all cultures possess knowledge to the same degree and not all cultures have the same level of moral refinement. Thus, Jefferson, in keeping with his appropriation of *kairos* (timeliness), was wont to emphasize that people should not be democratized before they are ready to be democratized. As he writes in a letter to French correspondent and friend Madame La Comtesse de Tessé (March 20, 1787), "Should [the French revolutionaries] attempt more than the established habits of the people are ripe for, they may lose all, and retard indefinitely the ultimate object of their aim."

Education, at the lower levels, equips all citizens with the requisite intellectual tools to be self-sufficient. It readies each person for some level of political participation. Education, at the higher levels, equips the natural aristoi, the most moral and talented citizens, for morally sensitive participation in the highest levels of governmental affairs and in other disciplines, like the practice of science, deemed essential for the progress of the state.

Thus, happiness and liberty can be secured only through continued scientific advance—namely, continued intellectual and moral advancement. Such advancement, however, requires constitutional renewal, in keeping with intellectual and moral advances,[63] and educational reform in the direction of general, practical education.[64] Jefferson, as I show in the final three chapters of this book, had a schema for that too.

THE ANCIENT CONSTITUTION

I end this chapter with some words on Jefferson's take on the Ancient Constitution—that is, his purchase of Saxonism.

The Ancient Constitution was seen by British historians of Whiggish persuasion as a sort of golden age in British history. Prior to the epoch of British feudalism with monarchical tyranny, Saxon tribes were thought to live freely on the land, privately owned, and to decide for themselves their governmental policies, so the story goes. There was no government to dictate economic, religious, and political concerns. Persons were free. Persons were equal.

This "historical" account is apocryphal and factitious, invented by Whigs as historical leverage against Tories. Garrett Ward Sheldon sums neatly, "This notion of a prefeudal, Saxon constitution thus served the seventeenth-century parliamentarians, who invented it, by providing the essential substance of modern liberal doctrine with the advantage of beating the traditionalists at their own game by situating their historical claim to liberty in a period ante-dating the monarchy."[65]

Jefferson, I suspect, did not consider it fictive. He relied heavily on the notion of the Ancient Constitution in his Summary View of the Rights of British America. The Saxon ancestors of the British, he notes, left the wilds and removed themselves to the island of Britain, where they established laws most likely to produce happiness. Once there, the mother country, from which they left, made no claims of superiority or dependence on them. Jefferson writes of the similarity of the Saxon occupation of Britain with the British occupation of America, "And it is thought that no circumstance has occurred to distinguish materially the British from the Saxon emigration." The conquest of the new land was made not by the British public but by individuals who emigrated. Such individuals spilled their own blood and spent their own for-tunes. They have the same rights as their Saxon ancestors.[66]

Saxons, Jefferson believed, held their lands and personal property in abso-lute dominion, "disencumbered with any superior," until William the Norman introduced and imposed feudalism. The lands of the many that lost their lives in the Battle of Hastings were the lion's share of the kingdom. William the Norman then forced, via threats or persuasions, many other landholders to cede their lands to him. These lands were given to lords and thereafter they were subject to feudal duties. What was left in Saxon hands was subject to mil-itary duties, and the landowners were subject to other feudal burdens. Thus, William the Norman introduced this general principle: *All lands in England are held mediately or immediately by the crown.* That is the view, Jefferson indicates, that King George III, by his autocratic actions on behalf of the colo-nies in America, assumes as true.

The Saxon myth surfaces too in several of Jefferson's letters. I offer two illustrations: one early in life; one late. To Virginian politician Edmund Pend-leton (August 13, 1776), Jefferson asks, "Are we not the better for what we have hitherto abolished of the feudal system? Has not every restitution of the antient Saxon laws had happy effects? Is it not better now that we return at once into that happy system of our ancestors, the wisest & most perfect ever yet devised by wit of man, as it stood before the 8th century." Jefferson returns to the myth in a late-in-life letter to British political reformist John

Cartwright (June 5, 1825). The Saxons, having driven off the former inhabitants of England, doubtless had a constitution, though one that was not left to posterity. The constitution was "set to naught" by the Normans, but "force cannot change right," and a perpetual claim was kept up by the nation for a restoration of their Saxon laws. "In the pullings and haulings for these antient rights, between the nation, and its kings of the races of Plantagenets, Tudors and Stuarts, there was sometimes gain, and sometimes loss, until the final re-conquest of their rights from the Stuarts." Jefferson sums, "It has ever appeared to me, that the difference between the whig and the tory of England is, that the whig deduces his rights from the Anglo-Saxon source, and the tory from the Norman."

The American Revolution, Jefferson continues, did not need to appeal to "musty records," "royal parchments," or "a semi-barbarous ancestry." It appealed, as did the Saxons, to the laws of nature, etched in the hearts of the revolutionists, which demands natural rights. Most states' constitutions indicate that power and its exercise are in the people, that people have a right to bear arms, and that people are entitled to freedom of person, religion, property, and press.[67]

If we are to take such references by Jefferson of the Saxon origin of the American Revolution seriously, the Saxon myth seems to betray a retrogressive strain in Jefferson's thinking that is difficult to accommodate with his progressivism. One writer notes that Jefferson, in his "Autobiography,"[68] says that beginning a constitution from scratch would have been too difficult. What he opted for was a synthesis of the common-law tradition of Saxon England with liberal republicanism. "On the one hand, republican principles demand revision of the law to purge it of monarchical elements, while on the other, attributing principles of liberty to the common law suggests that liberal republicanism is not the complete and adequate source of political good."[69] Yet a commitment to progress need not imply a commitment to steady and consistent movement toward some political end, keenly in view. Though progress for Jefferson seems ultimately to be inevasible—it seems part of the divine scheme of humans over time—its path is anfractuous and sometimes even retrogressive, as reference to the Norman conquest shows. Yet the Saxons were, according to Jefferson, morally and politically far in advance of the Normans who conquered and subjugated them and of the Normanism of King George III.

Jefferson's references to the myth show that the Saxon laws "form the basis or groundwork of the common law, to prevail wheresoever the exceptions have not taken place"—a point iterated in a letter to Italian physician Philip Mazzei (November 1785). "The Common law is a written law the text of which is preserved from the beginning of the 13th century downwards, but what preceded that is lost. Its substance however has been retained in the memory of the people and committed to writing from time to time in the decisions of the judges and treatises of the jurists, insomuch that it is still considered as a lex scripta,[70] the letter of which is sufficiently known to guide the decisions of the courts." By implication, the Saxon laws, qua the common will of any people, are the naturalistic bedrock of the common laws in the New World[71] or the common laws of any community of persons. Thus, they represent a conservative strain in Jefferson's progressivist republican scheme to which any morally sensitive constitution will adhere.

PART 3

JEFFERSON ON MORALITY

CHAPTER 5

"NOT TO LEAN ON OTHERS"

Jefferson on Man and Morality

"In a world which furnishes so many employments which are useful, and so many which are amusing, it is our own fault if we ever know what ennui is."
—TJ to Martha Jefferson, May 21, 1787

As I have argued in chapter 1, Jefferson's view of nature is in keeping with Enlightenment deism, but it also betrays a debt to Greek and Roman antiquity—especially Stoicism and, to a lesser extent, Epicureanism. The cosmos is law-governed and knowable, principally by appeal to the senses. The cosmos bespeaks a good, caring deity that created and superintends it. Thus, the nature of "man," for Jefferson, is critically dependent on a thorough grasp of the nature of "nature."

In the last three chapters, I hope to have shown that Jefferson's republicanism is much richer, more nuanced, than it is customarily made out to be by most historians and political scientists. His political thinking is essentially normative, because Jefferson is a fundamentally a eudaemonist in some sense of the word. The best sort of political structure for a society is that which engenders, not checks, human progress, and thereby allows for human happiness. Liberty is a key component of that normative vision.

The next three chapters concern Jefferson's moral thinking. Any legitimate account of how humans ought to behave, the normative issue and the topics of the next two chapters, must first come to terms with the nature of humans, which is the descriptive issue and the topic of this chapter.

In this chapter, I flesh out Jefferson's account of "man," grasped universally. I then turn to Jefferson's account of "men," grasped parochially.

THE ANCIENT HERITAGE

Given the normative dimension of his republicanism, Jefferson's views on the nature of humans parallel his views on nature. He believes that humans, across the board, share certain generic features—rationality and the moral and aesthetic senses—but also that there are certain local idiosyncrasies that are explicable only by environmental causes. That tradition goes back to ancient Greek and Roman philosophy and medicine, with which Jefferson, like many others of his day, was amply acquainted.[1]

For Greek and Roman philosophers and physicians, it was commonly grasped that all human beings shared certain generic features essential to their being with all other human beings and that each human had certain idiosyncratic aspects of being that were not shared with all other humans. Aristotle of the fourth century BCE in his *Nicomachean Ethics* writes that one becomes virtuous by knowing that some actions are consistent with virtue and others are not, by choosing those actions consistent with virtue, and by acting, over time, from a firm and guileless state of character.[2] Therefore, knowledge, choice, and character are three needed conditions of virtuous activity. Cicero tells us that the Stoic Panaetius in the second century BCE states that what dictates one's capacity for moral character are these: first, a universal capacity for rational thought; second, certain idiosyncratic capacities that vary considerably from person to person; third, one's unique real-life circumstances; and, fourth, the choices one makes along the way.[3] Galen, the great second-century CE Roman physician, says that etiological disclosure in rational medical practice is the result of three "indications": the nature of the human body; the strength, age, and nature of a patient; and auxiliary factors such as climate, waters, occupation, foods, and habits.[4] The first indication is universal; the second and third are idiosyncratic.

What of Jefferson's conception of man? One scholar says that Jefferson's *man* is reducible to four notions: "Jefferson's notion of humanity can be reduced to four postulates: (1) humans are largely creatures of their environment; (2) they are innately social and endowed with a moral sense; (3) it is this moral sense of justice that makes all humans equal; (4) humans are developmental beings who are capable of ongoing human progress and grassroots, participatory democracy."[5]

The depiction is consistent with the general view of antiquity. The difference is that Jefferson emphasizes man as a progressive being, and *prog-*

ress can only be cashed out in Enlightenment terms of scientific and moral advances. Placed in a retrogressive or conservative milieu, as were the Germanic tribes in the time of the Roman republic or the Native Americans of Jefferson's day, humans are obtusely filiopietistic. They use the past as a rationalization for the malaise of the present. Placed in a stimulating and progressive milieu—as were Bacon, Locke, and Newton—humans are inquisitive, discontent with the present, and forward-looking. They will use the past to explore avenues of possible human existence that promote human flourishing through progress. That was Jefferson's belief and the motivation for his "political experiment."

UNIVERSAL MAN

To understand humans, for Jefferson, one has to understand nature. One author writes: "For Jefferson, any theory of society that ignored the fundamental character of man was doomed to failure. Natural law was the source of our knowledge of the true character of man." Founded on natural law, Jefferson's political experiment was a "rendezvous with the destiny of mankind. Jefferson believed this so thoroughly that he considered the American theory of government to be the discovery man had been searching for and felt that it would remain a model for governments because of the permanency of the principles of natural law on which it was grounded."[6]

Jefferson's Stoic Naturalism

Jefferson's views of *nature*, as I show in chapter 1, and *man* draw much more from the Stoics than has heretofore been recognized. For the Stoics, what dictates how men ought to act in social settings are the laws of nature. Thus, the Stoics speak of *nature* both normatively and descriptively. Normatively, they speak of nature as both cosmological and anthropological regulative forces.

For the Stoics, the aim of life, virtue, was to live in agreement with nature.[7] Chronicler Diogenes Laertius says of the Stoics: "This is why the end [of life] may be defined as 'life, following nature' or, again, '[living] in agreement with our own human nature as well as that of the universe.' In such a life, we refrain from every action forbidden by the law common to all things—by right reason that both pervades all things and is identical with Zeus, lord and ruler of all that is."[8]

What nature shows was that humans have two impulses: a self-concern impulse and other-concern impulse.[9] The primary human impulse, dictated by nature and evident at birth, is self-preservation. The Roman Stoic Seneca writes that all animals consult their own safety and shrink from what harms them: "Impulses toward useful objects and revulsion from the opposite are according to nature. Without any reflection to prompt the idea and without any advice, whatever nature has prescribed is done."[10] Yet humans also have a social impulse. Nature creates parental affection for one's children, and parental affection is the foundation of communal living. Parental affection leads to the mutual attraction that unites all human beings. In such a manner, people are by nature fitted to form unions, societies, and states, as well as fitted to integrate with the cosmos.[11] "Our relations with one another are like a stone arch that would collapse," states Seneca, "if the stones did not mutually support each other."[12] It is thus recognition of natural law, upon the maturation of humans' rational faculties, that enables humans to have a fuller, cosmic sense of justice.

Nature also guides moral progress by merging virtuous activity with knowing. For the Stoics, the universe, of which humans are a part, is itself a divine and rational animal, and the best human life is one that emulates divine activity, which acts always in the most rational, most efficient, and best manner. The aim of human activity is to emulate deity by optimizing rationality, efficiency of action, and goodness. Sagacity is acting in complete agreement with nature or deity—what the Stoics called *homologia*.[13]

How is *homologia* achieved? First, humans begin, as do other living things, with the instinct of self-preservation. They soon come to value all such things that are in agreement with nature and avoid all such things that are contrary to nature, and they pattern their actions, through choice, thus. Next, progressors learn to choose by considering what is appropriate. Continued choice becomes fixed habit to do what is right—to act appropriately. Appropriate action[14] (Gr., kathekon; L., officium) does not imply that one's actions must have the right outcome, but only that one's actions must be properly motivated. Purity of intention is everything. Cicero gives an example of spear-throwing. One's purpose is to have true aim. It is desirable, not necessary, to hit the target.[15] When habit harmonizes perfectly with reason and duty, there is *homologia*—complete integration with divine or cosmic design. *Homologia* is sagacity. Human intention is perfectly in keeping with cosmic intention, action and outcome converge and all of one's actions now, as it were, hit the mark, because all of one's intentions are perfectly virtuous. Appropriate action now becomes perfect appropriate action or right action (Gr., katorthoma; L., recte factum).[16]

Having one's reason accord with the cosmic flow of events implies not cosmic indifference, as it is commonly said of the Stoics, but complete cosmic immersion or integration. The Stoic philosopher Hierocles explains how Stoic integration in the cosmos occurs through ten concentric circles that bind people locally and globally:

> The first and closest circle is one that a person has drawn as though around a center—his own mind. That circle encloses the body and anything taken for the sake of the body. It is virtually the smallest circle and it almost touches the center itself. Next, the second one, further removed from the center but enclosing the first circle, contains parents, siblings, wife, and children. The third one has in it uncles and aunts, grandparents, nephews, nieces, and cousins. The next circle (4) includes the other relatives, and that is followed by (5) the circle of local residents, then (6) the circle of fellow demes-men, next (7) that of fellow-citizens, and then (8) in the same way the circle of people from neighboring towns, and (9) the circle of fellow-countrymen. The outermost and largest circle (10), which encompasses all the rest, is that of the whole human race.[17]

Hierocles's circles allow for a sort of privileging of the individual, but, in the end, each person is not just a citizen of a *polis*, but also a citizen of the cosmos.[18]

A bedfellow of Stoic cosmopolitanism is Stoic egalitarianism, which was not always a popular feature of Stoicism in antiquity. Egalitarianism bars no one—slave or king—from aiming at the ethical archetype of Stoic invincibility. Each person has the same beginning; each has the same end.[19] Each person comes to virtue, as it were, unclothed. Seneca states, "Virtue shuts out no one. It is open to all, admits all, invites all—the freeborn and the freedman, the slave and the king, and the exile. Neither family nor fortune determines its choice. It is satisfied with a naked human being."[20]

Jefferson's thinking is often seen as antipodal to Stoic cosmopolitanism. It is mistakenly viewed as a form of liberal atomism—and we have seen two illustrations in the views of O'Brien and Hardt—that is normatively neutral, if only because his political thinking is often mistakenly viewed as a form of liberal atomism that is normatively neutral.

That depiction is mistaken for two chief reasons.

First, liberal atomism is not normatively neutral but has an on-the-quiet normative dimension:

> Liberal individualism [atomism] is liberalism . . . [in which] individuals are the basic units of political analysis and, thereby, are methodologically or metaphysically more fundamental than the communities and institutions to which they are conditionally bound. It asserts that people are autonomous and self-contained individuals, whose rights are prior to and independent of any conception of the good. . . . In prioritizing right over good, liberal individualism privileges political analysis, in that no conception of what is good must interfere with the fundamental rights, unconditionally guaranteed, of each individual.[21]

Liberal atomism, as a political code, champions autonomy as a value. What one does in one's solitude is one's own concern. It allows one to be a rascal, when alone, so long as the rascality nowise spills over into one's social activities and brings discernible harm to others. Championing autonomy as a value, however, it is not normatively neutral.

Second and most significant, liberal atomism is neither Jefferson's political view nor his moral view. People for Jefferson are essentially social creatures, not political atoms. "I am among those who think well of the human character generally," he writes to Virginian politician William Green Munford (June 18, 1799). "I consider man as formed for society, and endowed by nature with those dispositions which fit him for society." Again, "Man was created for social intercourse," he writes to Francis Butler eighteen years later (June 7, 1817). He was also born with a sense of justice to regulate his moral duties. Furthermore, Jefferson consistently speaks of duty to others as a critical component of morality. In his "Syllabus of the Estimate of the Merit of the Doctrines of Jesus," he writes: "In developing our duties to others, [the ancients] were short and defective. They embraced . . . the circles of kindred & friends, and inculcated patriotism, or the love of our country in the aggregate, as a primary obligation: toward our neighbors & countrymen they taught justice, but scarcely viewed them as within the circle of benevolence. Still less have they inculcated peace, charity & love to our fellow men, or embraced with benevolence the whole family of mankind."[22]

To lawyer Thomas Law (June 13, 1814), Jefferson says love of deity is one of the branches of morality, as morality comprises duty to deity and duty to fellow humans. Concerning the latter, Jefferson writes to Professor John S. Vater, "I have long considered the filiation of languages as the best proof we can ever obtain of the filiation of nations."[23] Duty to love others and deity suggests mental alignment with Stoic sympathy (Gr., *sympatheia*)— a sort of cosmic connectedness and belonging. Moreover, Jefferson inflexibly advocates authenticity—that is, consistency of moral action in the public and private realms. He does not allow for any divide between one's personal and social activities, as even one's most personal actions are moral actions as well. Jefferson tells Peter Carr (August 19, 1785) to act always and in all circumstances as if everyone in the world were looking at him—the suggestion being never to do wrong, even if no one is watching, which is a starkly Stoic notion[24] that also found its way into the Scottish empirical philosophy of Jefferson's day.[25] "I know but one code of morality for men, whether acting singly or collectively," Jefferson writes to James Madison (August 28, 1789). "He who says I will be a rogue when I act in company with a hundred others, but an honest man when I act alone, will be believed in the former assertion, but not in the latter." "When tempted to do any thing in secret, ask yourself if you would do it in public," Jefferson says to grandson Francis Wayles Eppes (May 21, 1816). Finally, for Jefferson, the duties that regulate human morality in the state of nature are the duties that regulate both each human in any social setting and the behavior of each nation toward all others. "The Moral duties which exist between individual and individual in a state of nature, accompany them into a state of society," he writes in "Opinion on the French Treaties."[26] Consequently, like the Stoics, Jefferson too has a view of human nature conceptually distinct from cosmic nature but in alignment with it.

There is a second similarity. For both the Stoics and Jefferson, human nature is fixed, yet both are in some sense progressivist vis-à-vis knowledge.

For Jefferson, humans are both intellectually and morally progressive beings. The notion is Kamesian.[27] Here there is recognition by Jefferson that past moral codes are no longer deemed acceptable, not because of a capricious shift of moral interests over time, but because an improvement in moral discernment of right actions. Morally accepted practices in the past are now adjudged atrocious. Killing captives of war was standard practice among barbarians but is now considered opprobrious and is no longer practiced. The same can be said of the Greek practice of the perpetual enslavement of war captives. "But is an enemy so execrable that tho in captivity his wishes and comforts are to be disregarded and even crossed?" Jefferson rhetorically asks Patrick Henry (March 27, 1779), governor of Virginia. "I think not. It is for the benefit of mankind to mitigate the horrors of war as much as possible."[28]

The moral (and intellectual) progress of the species is evident in microcosm in the North American continent of Jefferson's day. A "philosophic observer" who commences a journey from the Rocky Mountains to the eastern seacoast would notice these changes, he writes to politician William Ludlow (September 6, 1824). First, he would see savage Indians, clothing themselves with the flesh and skins of wild beasts, who live under only the law of nature. Next, he would see pastoral frontiersmen that domesticate animals for food. Third, he would see the "semi-barbarous citizens"—"pioneers of the advance of civilization." Finally, he would reach man in his most advanced state in the seaport town. "This . . . is equivalent to a survey, in time, of the progress of man from the infancy of creation to the present day." He adds, "Barbarism has . . . been receding before the steady step of amelioration; and will in time . . . disappear from the earth." In each stage, moral progress ensues apace with intellectual progress.

Jefferson's progressivism prima facie seems inconsistent with that of the Stoics. Moral improvement for Stoics is a matter of individuals realizing fully their human capacities, implanted by nature. A person, drawn toward virtue, progresses toward virtue by performing actions that are consistent with virtue. At day's end, there is the potential for complete virtue and perfect living through right actions. Jefferson, however, seems to have a richer view of moral improvement—what we might dub "moral advance"—as he speaks of the improvement of the human species over time, not just of certain individuals, committed to virtuous living.

Yet Jefferson's view of moral advance is not so dissimilar. Jeffersonian moral advance is not a matter of the species converging toward some as-yet-unseen ideal. The moral ideal toward which humans are and ought to be converging is roughly that of a Stoicized Jesus of Nazareth (see chapter 7), who has preached the purest moral code, stripped of the falsities of corrupters, and who, qua mortal man, seems for Jefferson to have come closer to perfect human living than has anyone else. It follows, given the fixity of the human species and the limits of human abilities for both, there is a fixed ideal toward which each human ought to aim—for the Stoics, a completely veridical ideal in which knowledge is sufficient for virtue and happiness; for Jefferson, full integration of the teachings of Jesus, epitomized by loving oneself, others, and deity with all one's heart—a notion captured as well by the Scottish philosopher Francis Hutcheson.[29]

In sum, both assume that human nature is fixed. Both assume humans are radical underachievers. Both assume a limit to correct human living. For both, concern for self, others, and deity is the recipe for human flourishing.

"A Divided Empire"

In chapter 3, I argued that there are at least four senses of "liberty" that Jefferson employs. The first three senses—negative, positive, and voluntary—depict humans as pleasure-seeking organisms with a rational capacity for deciding among alternatives to optimize their happiness pursuant to their wants. The last sense of liberty, moral liberty, I described as the nonrational capacity to "sense" right action and act on account of that sensing.

These meanings bespeak of two of the three faculties common to all humans that have a bearing on philosophical discernment: reason, the moral sense, and taste. All three are innate and underdeveloped at birth and so each must be exercised to gain its fullest capacity. I focus on reason and the moral sense below.

The rational faculty and moral sense Jefferson describes in his memorable love letter to Maria Cosway (October 21, 1786), which takes the form of a dialogue between Heart (morality) and Head (reason). The rational and moral faculties, Jefferson writes, have their own empires—science and morality, respectively. Writes Heart, "When the circle is to be squared, or the orbit of a comet to be traced; when the arch of greatest strength, or the solid of least resistance is to be investigated, take up the problem; it is yours; nature has given me no cognizance of it." It is much different for Heart. "In denying you [Head] the feelings of sympathy, of benevolence, of gratitude, of justice, of love, of friendship, [nature] has adopted the mechanism of the heart. Morals were too essential to the happiness of man to be risked on the incertain combinations of the Head. She laid their foundation therefore in sentiment, not in science."

Head might pretend command of all conduct and has "grave saws and maxims" to guide moral conduct, but that is pretense. Jefferson then gives three illustrations of instances in which Head dictated one course of action, Heart another. First, there was the time, when his coach drove through Chickahominy and passed a "poor weathered soldier," with a pack on his back, who begged to be let up on the chariot. Head calculated that the soldier was merely one of many, that all could not be taken up, and to take up one would lead to greater distress of the others, so Jefferson's carriage passed by the soldier. Heart, realizing that "tho we cannot relieve all the distressed we should relieve as many as we can," knew better. Jefferson turned back for the solider, but the soldier was not to be found and thus, Jefferson was filled with regret for failure to act on morally correct sentiment. Second, there was the time when a woman in Philadelphia asked for charity and Head took the women for a drunkard and refused. Heart, again regretful, sought out the woman and gave the woman one-half dollar, which she immediately used, not for a bout at the ale house, but to place her child at school. Finally, there was the American Revolution. "You [Head] began to calculate & to compare wealth and numbers: we threw up a few pulsations of our warmest blood; we supplied enthusiasm against wealth and numbers; we put our existence to the hazard when the hazard seemed against us, and we saved our country." Heart sums, "I do not know that I ever did a good thing on your suggestion, or a dirty one without it."[30]

The implication is that Head, when it comes to moral decision making, is burked by calculation, which, given Jefferson's examples, seems to decide in terms of what is easiest and least inconvenient for one to do in a specific scenario. Head is guarded, as it wishes to have all available information before one puts out oneself to help another for fear that the one, needing help, is merely taking advantage of the other, offering it. In doing so, it often offers nothing but reasons for disengagement in the affairs of others.

In contrast, Heart, disregarding inferences from appearance, is brash. It makes its "decisions" immediately. Nonetheless, its choices seem always to be correct. One must acknowledge that moral decision making does not always accommodate rational calculation, as immediacy is often needed. When a house is burning and a young child screams for help, one has not the time to assess all the particulars before acting. Delay can spell doom for the child. And so, Heart, unlike Head, is not suffocated by amaranthine calculation. It merely acts.

Overall, Jefferson says that each rules in a "divided empire": Head, the intellectual parcel; Heart, the moral parcel. I shall say more about the faculty of reason below, but I leave further discussion of the moral sense for the next chapter.

There is, however, a reason for seeing Jefferson's reference to a "divided empire" as misleading, as it suggests two faculties of equal strength that rule over equal, but different, empires. Yet for Jefferson, reason is a petty tyrant, as it is ultimately beholden to passion—at least, passion of the right sort—hence,

Jefferson's preoccupation with practical science, that is, science in the service of vital human needs.

In that, Jefferson nowise differs from empiricists such as Bacon, Hobbes, Bolingbroke, Kames, and Hume—each of whom tied moral assertions to some form of "hedonism" (that is, passions, appetites, desires, and/or affections), with reason at the service of passion.[31] The most influential of them has been David Hume, an elaboration of whose thoughts on morality might prove profitable for grasping Jefferson. Hume is by far the greatest of the Scottish empiricists.

Consistent with the Scottish empiricism of his day, Hume begins his critique of moral thinking with a plea that it be founded on experience, not conjecture.

> The other scientifical method [i.e., Newton's method] where a general abstract principle is first established, and is afterwards branched out into a variety of inferences and conclusions, may be more perfect in itself, but suits less the imperfections of human nature, and is a common source of illusion and mistake in this as well as in other subjects. Men are now cured of their passion for hypotheses and systems in natural philosophy, and will hearken to no arguments but those which are derived from experience. It is full time they should attempt a like reformation in all moral disquisitions; and reject every system of ethics, however subtle or ingenious, which is not founded on fact and observation.[32]

Having rejected reason,[33] Hume's grounding of morality is feeling[34]—a social or moral sentiment of all human beings to act in socially beneficial ways. To the normatively packed question "Why ought we to act kindly toward others?" comes the descriptively blunt answer "Because, over time, we in fact tend to act kindly toward others." That is another way of saying that the normative question is meaningless.

Hume believes that grounding moral judgments in social sentiment is a suitable grounding of morality—the best for which one can hope by an empirical approach. As he sees things, the alternative is to scrap ethical considerations altogether, which he is not inclined to do.[35]

On human agency, Hume says famously, "Reason is, and ought only to be the slave of the passions, and can never pretend to any other office than to serve and obey them."[36] Human agency for Hume is reduced to a mere causal event, triggered by passion, in which reason acts instrumentally at the behest of want:

> Reason is the discovery of truth and falsehood. Truth and falsehood consists in an agreement or disagreement either to the real relations of ideas, or to real existence and matter of fact. . . . Now 'tis evident our passions, volitions, and actions, are not susceptible of any such agreement or disagreement; being original facts and realities, compleat in themselves, and implying no reference to other passions, volitions, and actions. 'Tis impossible, therefore, they can be pronounced either true or false, and be either contrary or conformable to reason.[37]

As such, judgments on actions, as products of passions that are "compleat in themselves," cannot be "pronounced either true or false." This, of course, applies equally to judgments on ethical actions. Thus, we find in Hume the first steps toward moral noncognitivism.

Just how are we to cash out Hume's noncognitivism to shed light on Jefferson's moral-sense theory? Philosopher Simon Blackburn has attempted to clear up obfuscation in interpretations of Hume's moral thinking as they relate to the interplay of reason and moral sentiment. Blackburn writes:

> Reason can inform us of the facts of the case, features of the situations in which we have to act. And it can inform us which actions are likely to cause which upshots. But beyond that, it is silent. The imprudent person, or the person of unbridled lust, malevolence, or sloth is bad, of course. We may even call them unreasonable, but in a sense that Hume considers improper. For, more accurately, it is not their reason that is at fault, but their passions. Even the person who apparently fails to adapt means to ends is not necessarily unreasonable.[38]

Imprudence, Blackburn goes on to say, is not a matter of limiting reasoning to a bureaucratic or instrumental function; it is for Hume and Blackburn a defect of passion.

> Reason's office is to represent the world to us as it is. How we react to that situation, and that includes how we react to it ethically, is another matter. It is a matter of a dynamic response—the formation of passions, attitudes, policies, or intentions—and the most clear-sighted apprehension of the situation is no guarantee that this side is functioning well. The nature of our dynamic response shows our passionate nature, or sensibility. We typically express this structure by voicing ethical remarks, saying what is to be done, or felt, or avoided.[39]

Moral activity, like other forms of human activities, is for Blackburn a matter of acting reasonably—where "reasonable" does not imply that the motivation or grounds for one's behavior is reason, instead of passion or sentiment. It is rather freedom from various incapacities—ignorance, lack of understanding, shortsightedness, and unconcern. By having of the right sorts of passions, directed by sentiment, we engage in morally appropriate behavior.[40]

In such a manner, though the self is in large part constituted by desires and inclinations, it is not a heteronomous bundle of desires and inclination that gets "blown around by the winds of passion." The self is not passive when it contends for a say in its direction. It is also not something that sits above the passions and directs them. To effect such a separation is, in outcome, to effect a separation of passions and intellect—the Kantian ruse of separating the noumenal self from the phenomenal self.[41]

Humans, Blackburn states, deliberate about goals, but these are not fixed by reason but rather by the type of person we are. When we make desires the object of deliberation, we mistakenly posit an inner deliberator and this takes us back to Kant's noumenal, transcendental self—a person of this world, but somehow and at the same time above it. There is no second-order standing back and assessing the moral weight of the deliberative process by some "controlling Captain." Moral deliberation, like deliberation on all types of human activity, is entirely first-order. "Deliberation is an active engagement with the world, not a process of introspecting our own consciousness of it." No one deliberates from above this world. It is, in effect, when we criticize ourselves morally or philosophize about passions that things fall apart. Our passions then appear arbitrary, fickle, and unmanageable. Yet when we recognize that our desires are properly related to our normal concerns, the panic dissipates.[42]

Is this view of moral agency too normatively undemanding? Blackburn thinks it is not. He states that Kantian morality—with its stock of moral imperatives grounded in universal reason—has no lock on categorical imperatives. "The sentimental tradition," he says, "can be as demandingly categorical as possible."[43] That, however, seems a strange normative defense. Yet, then again, Blackburn admits that it is an illusion to think that there is such a thing as an aboveboard normative question.

Yet no more can be expected of morality for Hume, for whom moral principles are "in continual flux and revolution."[44] Hume states: "Human life is more governed by fortune than by reason; is to be regarded more as a dull pastime than as a serious occupation; and is more influenced by particular humour, than by general principles. . . . While we are reasoning concerning life, life is gone; and death . . . treats alike the fool and the philosopher. To reduce life to exact rule and method, is commonly a painful, oft a fruitless occupation: And is it not also a proof, that we overvalue the prized for which we contend?"[45]

Jefferson's First-Order Eudaemonism

Blackburn's defense and critique of Hume sheds light on Hume. Reason is no controlling captain that oversees all human operations, morality included. Reason merely sheds light on the way the world is and on the likely consequences of possible courses of action. What humans do with that information is not reason's province.

For Blackburn, however, there is no divided empire. Passions control reason and passions dictate morality in a first-order manner. That does not mean that human behavior is arbitrary. Human passions are in large measure homogenous, not heteronomous. It is when humans allow the vagaries of circumstances or the intrusions of reason to have an influence on human sentiment that humans go astray.

Blackburn's analysis of Hume also sheds light on Jefferson, for Jefferson is clear that the moral sense acts relatively independent of reason, that reason is a capable but not fleckless faculty, and that the moral sense is axiologically superior to reason.[46] It suggests that Jefferson's reference to "a divided empire" is misleading. For Jefferson, as for Hume, passions rule. How, then, can Jefferson be a eudaemonist as I categorize him, given that the ancient eudaemonists posited moral stability as rational control of a human organism?

Happiness or human thriving is the end of human activity for Jefferson, and political processes are beholden to that moral aim. Consequently, reason is in a sense subordinate and, ultimately, answerable to the moral sense in the manner specified fully in the next chapter. It follows that the two parts of the empire are only geographically divided in the manner that the Virgin Islands are divided from the United States: Strictly speaking, Head's parcel of land is a satellite of Heart. As Jefferson says to nephew Peter Carr (August 19, 1785), "I can assure you, that the possession of [science] is, what (next to an honest heart) will above all things render you dear to your friends, and give you fame and promotion in your own country." In short, for Jefferson, as is the case for Hume, Heart rules.

Subservience and answerability to Heart does not mean that passion is second-order. Here the divided-empire analogy is helpful. For Jefferson, passion does not sit above reason and guide it; it sits beside reason and guides it in the sense suggested by the analogy above—that of a satellite sitting beside its mother country.[47]

It follows that Jefferson, as a eudaemonist, is not a eudaemonist in the traditional sense—for example, like Plato or Aristotle, for whom morally correct activity is a function of the rational faculty and for whom rationality is the ruling faculty.[48] Sentiment, for Jefferson, rules the moral domain.

Key features of Jefferson's eudaemonism are liberty, equality, virtue and industry, agrarianism, and political participation. I expatiate below on each of those—liberty excepting, as I have already covered it sufficiently in chapter 3.

Equality

The Declaration of Independence, Abraham Lincoln says, is "a standard maxim for free society . . . constantly looked to, constantly labored for, and even though never perfectly attained, constantly approximated."[49] That standard—comprising life, liberty, and the pursuit of happiness—is the received view of the document today. Nonetheless, it is not the view that Jefferson or any of the forefathers had in mind when the Declaration of Independence was framed and signed. Consider, for example, what Jefferson says of the motivation behind the document in a letter to General Henry Lee (May 8, 1825).

> When forced, therefore, to resort to arms for redress, an appeal to the tribunal of the world was deemed proper for our justification. This was the object of the Declaration of Independence. Not to find out new principles, or new arguments, never before thought of, not merely to say things which had never been said before; but to place before mankind the common sense of the subject, in terms so plain and firm as to command their assent, and to justify ourselves in the independent stand we are compelled to take. Neither aiming at originality of principle or sentiment, nor yet copied from any particular and previous writing, it was intended to be an expression of the American mind, and to give to that expression the proper tone and spirit called for by the occasion. All its authority rests then on the harmonizing sentiments of the day, whether expressed in conversation, in letters, printed essays, or in the elementary books of public right, as Aristotle, Cicero, Locke, Sidney, &c.

Lincoln's view, that the Declaration of Independence was a declaration of independence, is wrongheaded. As one writer eloquently indicates, it was not a "declaration of independence"—for as a declaration of independence, by a people who already considered themselves free of British yoke, it would have been redundant—so much as it was a "declaration by independents"— an exhaustive compilation of reasons for America's newfound independence. The Declaration of Independence was about dissolving, not building, connections; it performed no action but merely rationalized and publicized, "The Declaration was the publication of the resolution for independence, not the assertion of independence itself." Focus on the "self-evident truths" was a radical interpretation of the text in order to address and contest nineteenth-century inequalities.[50]

That qualification grasped, there are two chief self-evident truths in the Declaration of Independence: the equality of all people and existence of unalienable rights of all people.[51] As the latter has been covered in chapter 3, only the first will be addressed in this section.

In its most generic sense, the equality of all people signifies that no person is by nature an authority over any other[52] and that each person is not only capable of but responsible for forging his own path in life. Thus, it can be taken to mean roughly that everyone in America is approximately on "square one"—no one has a privileged starting position over any other person. In short, inequalities that might arise are due to differences in capacities and ambition, or differences due to happenstance. That is precisely the idea behind Jefferson's conception of a natural aristoi in a well-known letter to John Adams (October 28, 1813)—the subject of chapter 7. Experience and talent, not wealth or heredity, are to be the difference makers in a Jeffersonian republic, and virtue ensures that those best suited for governing, once elected, will govern well.

"Equality" can be cashed out in two different senses: equality of opportunity and moral equality.[53] Equality of opportunity recognizes the differences between persons—for example, talents, prior social status, education, wealth—and seeks to level the playing field, as it were, inasmuch as it can be leveled. Moral equality recognizes that each human, considered as a moral equal, is deserving of equal status in personhood and citizenship. In a letter to James Monroe (January 8, 1804), Jefferson writes, "The principle of society, as well as of government . . . is the equality of the individuals composing it." The laws are designed, he writes in "Thoughts on Lotteries" (1826), with the notions of liberty and equality in mind. Primogeniture and entails needed to be abolished and freedom of religious expression needed to be established so no one religious sect could predominate politically and subordinate citizens who practiced another religion.

Jefferson also realized that inequality of property was an important obstacle to equality of opportunity and the cause of "numberless instances of wretchedness."[54] He says to James Madison (October 28, 1785) apropos of the inequality that exists in France, "The consequences of this enormous inequality producing so much misery to the bulk of mankind, legislators cannot invent too many devices for subdividing property, only taking care to let their subdivisions go hand in hand with the natural affections of the human mind." As I note in chapter 3, he advocates, in his Draft Constitution for Virginia in 1776, fifty acres of property—for Jefferson, property and wealth were equivalent—to every male Virginian or that measure added for a Virginian owning property to equal fifty acres. His aim is clearly agrarian. He sums in the letter to Madison: "The earth is given as a common stock for man to labour and live on. If, for the encouragement of industry we allow it to be appropriated, we must take care that other employment be furnished to those excluded from the appropriation. If we do not the fundamental right to labour the earth returns to the unemployed."

Equalitarianism as well as Stoic disregard for ostentation spilled over into Jefferson's political practice and rules of etiquette. When matters were left to a vote among members of his cabinet, himself included, he counted himself no more than one. Next, when entertaining visitors as president, he adopted two basic rules, from which other rules of etiquette could be derived. First, when foreign or domestic visitors would come, the first visit would be granted to strangers at a first-comers-first rule. Only then would visits be granted to others, in keeping with first-comers-first rule. Foreign ministers would have to make their first visit to American ministers. Thereafter, that visit would be returned. Second, no one—whether foreign or domestic, titled or untitled—brought together in American society was to be treated superior to any other person.[55] In keeping with his rules of etiquette, he did what he could to avoid displays of ostentation—especially at his inaugurations. For Jefferson, the president of the United States was to be no Triton among minnows, but merely primus inter pares.[56]

Virtue and Industry

In a letter to friend and physician Benjamin Rush (April 21, 1803), Jefferson attaches his "Syllabus of an Estimate of the Merit of the Doctrines of Jesus, Compared with Those of Others." The "Syllabus" shows three great contributions to the discipline of ethics.[57] The philosophers—and here he lists Pythagoras, Socrates, Epicurus, Cicero, Epictetus, and Antoninus—handed down precepts to help persons govern their passions, but they failed to help regulate one's relationships with others. The Jews handed down the system of deism—that is, belief in one god—but they mischaracterized deity and they left behind a grossly imperfect (repulsive and antisocial) morality. Finally, "inculcating universal philanthropy . . . to all mankind," Jesus, as man and not god, arrived and handed down the most wholesome and sublime morality ever devised by correcting the defects of the philosophers and Jews. In short, Jesus made the greatest contribution to moral advance.

Jefferson's "Syllabus" and his own version of the Bible—that is, Jesus's life, stripped of supernature (see chapter 7) greatly helps us grasp the significance of what he often lists as twin conditions of a happy life—virtue and industry. Following the philosophers, virtue is important in attaining equanimity. Yet virtue for Jefferson is more than equanimity. It involves industry, which might be cashed out more than recognition that in a thriving, happy life, one must be busy. In its moral sense, industry is recognition of duties to others or "universal philanthropy"—namely, what Jesus meant by benevolence.[58] Thus, industry for Jefferson can be understood as keeping oneself busy in ways to benefit oneself and one's fellow men.

Jesus's principles of benevolence are evident where one might best expect to find them—in Jefferson's letters to his daughters Martha and Mary and, later, his grandchildren, while he is away from Monticello. His consistent message is pursuit of virtue and industry. He advises Martha (December 11, 1783), his oldest daughter, never to say or do any bad thing as the surest preparation for death. His comfort is in seeing his daughter "developing daily those principles of virtue and goodness" because virtue and goodness render one happy and valuable to others. He adds in another letter to her (May 21, 1787) that she should acquire talents and that degree of science that protects her from ennui—"the most dangerous poison of life." The remedy is employment—industry. "Determine never to be idle. . . . It is wonderful how much may be done if we are always doing" (May 5, 1787). Industry, for Jefferson, is more than eschewal of idleness. He tells Martha, "A mind always employed is always happy" and, thus, allows one always to be serviceable to others.[59] He bids Martha to teach young Mary to be good, to be true, never to be angry, and to be industrious. Goodness allows one to be valued by others and oneself. Want of truth is the meanest vice and useless. Anger leads to self-torment and diverts and alienates oneself from others. Industry makes one happy and, being serviceable to others, it makes one precious to others.[60] Genius—that is, intelligence—pales in comparison with virtue. It is more important to be a good person, an industrious farmer, and to be beloved by neighbors than to be talented or intellectual.[61]

Jefferson links virtue to industry because happiness has an ineliminable social component, involving not just right actions but benevolently motivated right actions. To his daughter Mary (March 3, 1802), Jefferson as president writes that happiness demands that we "continue to mix with the world" and keep up with it as it moves forward. He adds that, while retired from 1793 to 1797, he kept to his own affairs and saw only those persons who came to visit him. Withdrawal had a deleterious effect on his mind. It rendered him "unfit for society" and "uneasy when . . . engaged in it." He became antisocial and misanthropic, which were punishment sufficient. Again, in a letter to Martha (February 11, 1800), he considers purchase of a Forte piano, not only because of its fineness and quality, but also because he wishes to help its inventor, an "ingenious, modest and poor young man." Finally, there is Jefferson's generous involvement as mentor to aspiring young men of his day. "A part of my occupation," Jefferson tells Polish General Thaddeus Kościuszko (February 26, 1810), "and by no means the least pleasing, is the direction of the studies of such young man as they ask it."[62]

Virtue and industry require friendship, and no one can be a friend to another without forgiving the faults of that other. In a 1790 letter to Martha (July 17), Jefferson writes: "All we can do is to make the best of our friends: love and cherish what is good in them, and keep out of the way of what is bad: but no more think of rejecting them for [what is bad in them] than of throwing away a piece of music for a flat passage or two." No one is perfect. All have considerable good in them. He says, "And your own happiness will be the greater as you percieve you promote that of others." In sum, virtue requires industry, and industry requires friendship. As friendship is desirable, rational society is even more desirable. "It informs the mind, sweetens the temper, chears our spirits, and promotes health," he writes James Madison (February 20, 1784). The sentiment is, once again, Stoical.[63]

Moreover, virtue and industry require Stoic resolve and resignation. "When we see ourselves in a situation which must be endured and gone through," he advises Mary (January 7, 1798), "it is best to make up our minds to meet it. Meet it with firmness and accomodate every thing to it in the best way practicable. This lessens the evil, while fretting and fuming only serves to increase our own torment." Thus, others' mistakes and misfortunes can be a school of instruction.

Agrarianism

Agrarianism was for Jefferson not a provincial ideal—that is, what promotes human flourishing for Americans, given America's surfeit of land and want of persons—but a catholic ideal—that is, what promotes human flourishing for all persons anywhere and at any time.[64] That is not to say Jefferson does not recognize other forms of human livelihood or the need for manufacture in a progressive country, in which independence is critical. He does. He merely posits that agrarianism is uniquely suited for human happiness. A farmer's labor, he believes, decuples its yield. That is not the case with manufacture or commerce. Moreover, only those persons who labor the earth can love the earth, and thus, will fight to defend it. Again, that is not the case with manufacture or commerce.

Jefferson greatly values the labor and production of farmers. "The greatest service which can be rendered any country is," Jefferson writes in a memorandum, "to add an useful plant to its culture; especially, a bread grain; next in value to bread is oil."[65] In "Travelling Notes for Mr. Rutledge and Mr. Shippen," Jefferson lists eight "objects of attention for Americans" abroad. Agriculture tops the list. "Everything belonging to this art, and whatever has a near relation to it. Useful or agreeable animals which might be transported to America. Species of plants for the farmer's garden, according to the climate of the different states."[66]

Jefferson's love of farming is unquestionably a consequence of his view of property, which was, in the main, anthropocentric and Lockean. In *Second Treatise on Government*, John Locke writes:

> Though the earth, and all inferior creatures be common to all men, yet every man has a *property* in his own *person*: this no body has the right to but himself. The *labour* of his body, and the work of his hands, we may say,

are properly his. Whatsoever then he removes out of the state that nature hath provided, and left in, he hath mixed his *labour* with, and joined to it something that is his own, and thereby makes it his *property*. It being by him removed from the common state nature placed it in, it hath by this *labour* something annexed to it, that excludes the common right of other Men.[67]

For Locke, land uncultivated and "wholly left to Nature" was valueless—mere "waste"—if it proves to be of no benefit to humans.[68] Humans, because they owned their own labor, had a right to property for their self-preservation. The right was not unconditioned.[69] Every person has a duty not to harm others in their "life, health, liberty, or possessions," and the yardsticks of harm were super-sufficiency and spoilage.[70] If one were to take so much land that his appropriation led to others being incapable of having their own land, he would be harming those others. Likewise, if one were to appropriate land that spoiled, he would be harming others. Locke says, "as much land as man tills, plants, improves, cultivates, and can use the product of, so much is his property."[71]

Jefferson writes on *property* in a chapter of his *Commonplace Book*. He argues that one cares for property that is fitfully one's own. "A man who has bestowed labor in preparing and improving a field, contracts an affection for a spot."[72] The notion of affection is crucial. A man who loves his land will care for it and protect it in times of turmoil. The relation that a person has toward his property is the relation he ought to have in general toward nature. One is obliged to use well the resources nature has given one and to leave it better than it was to future generations. That is the notion of "usufruct."[73]

Getting by an "Angry Bull"

Jefferson's disdain of politics is well-known and comes out preeminently in his letters to his daughter Martha and numerous other letters on duty and retirement.[74] Politics is a discipline where "envy, hatred, malice, revenge, and all the worse passions of men are marshalled to make one another as miserable as possible," he writes (February 8, 1798). Over a month later, he says (May 17, 1798), "Politics and party hatreds destroy the happiness of every being here"—even women. Over a year later (February 11, 1800) Jefferson states, "Politics are such a torment that I would advise everyone I love not to mix with them." Jefferson adds that he has changed his circle of associates. He has abandoned the parties and dinners of the rich and now associates wholly with the "class of science." So great is the discord between the parties, he states to Martha (January 16, 1801), that that one feels oneself "in an enemy's country" when among Federalists. "Worn down here with pursuits in which I take no delight, surrounded by enemies and spies, catching and perverting every word which falls from my lips or flows from my pen, and inventing where facts fail them," he again writes to Martha weeks later (February 5, 1801), "I pant for that society where all is peace and harmony, where we love and are loved by every object we see." In 1807, during his second term as president, he states (January 13) to Congressman William Dickinson, "I am tired of a life of contention, and of being the personal object for the hatred of every man, who hates the present state of things."

Jefferson's detestation of politics is the result of his detestation of pointless disputation, blandishment, and the sort of boastfulness and catachresis he came to detest in Virginian politician Patrick Henry. His detestation of disputation is never better spelled out than in a letter to his eponymous grandson (November 24, 1808). He advises "Jeff" never to enter into argument with another. Argument, he adds, is futile. No one has ever convinced another by it, but harm—in the forms of anger, rudeness, and even death—is often the result.

There are two classes of disputants to avoid, Jefferson adds. First, there are the young students who have just entered the threshold of science. Having much energy but merely a taste of science, they spend their time in argument. Second, there are the rude and ill-tempered men. Having swagger and a passion for politics, they tend toward bravado and use words any which way for persuasion. Both groups are as harmful as persons infected with yellow fever or pestilence. Yet politicians are the worst. They are selective of facts and inflexible in position. The advice suggests Stoic-like stances to avoid anger at all costs and to eschew argument with persons incapable of rationality. Concerning the former, he tells daughter Mary (April 1, 1790), "Never be angry with any body, nor speak harm of them, try to let every body's faults be forgotten, as you would wish yours to be." Many years later, he writes to grandson Francis Wayles Eppes (21 May 1816): "Whenever you feel a warmth of temper rising," he tells Eppes, "check it at once, and suppress it, recollecting it will make you unhappy within yourself, and disliked by others." That has its advantages. He adds, "Nothing gives one person so great advantage over another, as to remain always cool and unruffled under all circumstances." That sentiment is repeated in a political context in a story Jefferson relates in his "The Anas." "I told [British Minister Erskine] it [writing and speaking strongly] was an unhappy talent, that nothing enabled a man to get along in business so well as a smooth temper and smooth style."[75]

PARTICULAR MAN

"The substances [that] compose the body are, both nominally and essentially, always the same and unchanging; in youth as well as in age, in cold weather as well as in warm," says the Hippocratic author of *The Nature of Man*.[76] To study medicine aright, writes the Hippocratic author of *Airs, Waters, and Places*, a student of medicine needs to study the following. "First, he must consider the effect of each of the seasons of the year and the differences between them. Secondly, he must study the warm and the cold winds, both those which are common to every country and those peculiar to a particular locality. Lastly, the effect of water on the health must not be forgotten. Just as it varies in taste and when weighed, so does its effect on the body vary as well." He must study as well the habits of the inhabitants: Do they edaciously englut their food and drink with the effect of laziness or, with a mind to work and exercise, do they eat and drink moderately?[77]

In *Politics*, Aristotle writes of the influence of climate on people, and thus, the sort of constitution they might adopt, given their climate. Cold regions produce persons full of spirit (*thumos*) but without intelligence (*dianoia*) and without technical ability (*technē*). They are free, but cannot rule over their neighbors due to their dullness and lack of skills. Asians, living in warm regions, are intelligent and skilled, but spiritless. Lack of spirit readily makes them slaves. Greeks are intermediately located apropos of geography, so they are spirited, skilled, and intelligent. "Thus, [the Greek race] continues to be free and to have the best political institutions and to be capable of ruling all other peoples, if it has constitutional unity." Both spirit and intelligence must be naturally in a people, capable of being "easily guided to virtue by the lawgiver."[78] Consequently, chance factors in ponderously for virtue and happiness.

Similarly, it was believed in Jefferson's day that climate had a profound influence on health and character—Hume and writer John Bristed being notable exceptions.[79] Members of the American Philosophical Society, in anticipation of favorable results concerning the soil and climate on inhabitants, anxiously awaited the results of the 1800 census. They expected it to show—pace Buffon, Raynal, De Pauw, Robertson, and Volney, each of whom denigrated the New World—"that the duration of human life in this portion of the earth will be found at least equal to what it is in any other, and that its population increases with a rapidity unequalled in all others."[80] Jefferson mirrored that view, as he envisaged the population of the United States many years hence at 1.2 billion.[81] Comte de Volney, in his *View of the Soil and Climate of the United States of America* (1804), challenged that view. He argued that coughing, catarrhs, and other respiratory problems; tooth decay; "autumnal intermittents"; and yellow fever were prevalent in America.[82] Jefferson wrote Volney after the count published his book. In his letter (February 8, 1805), Jefferson compares three aspects of the climate of Europe with that of America: the fluctuations of hot and cold, the amount of sunlight, and the fluctuations of wet and dry. Overall, America has greater fluctuations of hot and cold, much more sunlight, and less fluctuations of wet and dry than does Europe.[83] He concludes that the climate of America is "more cheerful," and therefore, preferable. He adds: "Still I do not wonder that an European should prefer his grey to our azure sky. Habit decides our taste in this, as in most other cases."

The debate over the suitability of the American climate was in some part political, as arguments in favor of America's climate were designed to encourage immigration and increase America's population, while arguments against America's climate were designed to discourage immigration. Nonetheless, climate was seen by Jefferson and others as a significant factor for intellectual and moral development, or their lack. A "pure state of the atmosphere must have a considerable effect upon the temper and genius of the inhabitants," writes Dr. Hugh Williamson.[84] Jefferson writes to scientist and explorer William Dunbar (January 12, 1801) of the toll of immoderate climate—especially cold—on humans over a lifetime. To Volney (February 8, 1805), he writes of the effect of cloudlessness on mood. To scientist and physician Lewis M. Beck (July 16, 1824), he concerns himself with the effect of "clearing [of foliage] and culture" on changes in climate.

Jefferson did believe that climate was critical to intellectual and moral improvement. In reply to another letter to the Marquis de Chastellux (September 2, 1785) concerning his fellow Virginians, Jefferson essays to explain certain regional variations in the characters of Americans, which are presumed to be the result of climate. The reply lists the variations between northerners and southerners.[85] The nine character traits (see table 4.1 below) are each contraries, with the exception of one—the middle trait, which is independence of spirit. "These characteristics grow weaker and weaker by gradation from North to South and South to North," writes Jefferson in Aristotelian fashion, "insomuch that an observing traveler, without the aid of the quadrant may always know his latitude by the character of the people among whom he finds himself." Pennsylvania, being situation neatly between north and south, forms a people "free from the extremes of both vice and virtue."[86]

TABLE 4.1. CHARACTER TRAITS OF NORTHERNERS AND SOUTHERNERS COMPARED

Northerners	Southerners
cool	fiery
sober	voluptuary
laborious	indolent
persevering	unsteady
independent	*independent*
jealous of own liberties, and just to those of others	zealous of own liberties, but trampling on those of others
interested	generous
chicaning	candid
superstitious and hypocritical in religion	without attachment or pretensions to any religion but that of the heart

Charles Miller maintains that independence is the feature that distinguishes human nature in America from human nature in the rest of the world.[87] That seems reasonable, given that Jefferson mentions that he is listing variable character traits, not invariant attributes of humans. Yet what is it about American soil and climate that makes independence a variant, but stable characteristic of American people irrespective of location? Would one transported, say, from France to America, upon acclimatization to American soil, become independent in time?

Miller's reply has a distinct Aristotelian flair. Not everyone is suited by nature for independence. Only they whose governing faculty is in command of the lesser parts of the soul and of the body are independent.[88] Thus, there must be something about America's climate that conduces them to rationality and independence.

That answer cannot be correct, if only because, for Jefferson, it is the moral-sense faculty that guides, or ought to guide, human activity. Reason, we have seen, subserves the moral sense, and even in its most polished form, is anything but infallible.[89] For Aristotle, in contrast, the rational soul rules over the passions.

The correct answer, consistent with the liberalism of Enlightenment thought and the overall tenor of Jefferson's writings, is that independence of spirit is not a character trait that varies from region to region, because independence is not a character trait shaped by air and climate. It is, instead, a fixed part of the human constitution. For Jefferson, one of sobriety, labor, and perseverance can readily become one of sensuality, indolence, and unsteadiness through a change of climate. Yet every person, independent by nature, will remain independent in any climate. Climate cannot alter independence; only culture in some sense can.

David Hume offers a helpful distinction between characteristics that result from physical causes and those that occur from moral causes. Physical causes, qualities of air and climate, "are supposed to work insensibly on the temper, by altering the tone and habit of the body, and giving it a particular complexion."[90] Moral causes act on the mind as motives or reasons, and "render a peculiar set of manners habitual to us." For Hume, moral character is relatively independent of physical causes, and "the character of a nation will much depend on *moral* causes," not physical causes.

Thus, one might think that liberty for Jefferson is a moral characteristic, in that it is climate-independent, while the other characteristics are physical and climate-dependent. Yet there are problems with that posit.

First, though Hume considers industry, knowledge, and civility to be of universal use, moral character varies much from culture to culture.[91] Still, independent of their employments, one cannot say that industry, knowledge, and civility for Hume are needed for human happiness or thriving—that they are part of the fabric of the human organism. Yet that is just what Jefferson wishes to say about independence. Independence might be an observable universal characteristic of Americans and it might be seen lacking in Europeans, but that is not to say for Jefferson that Europeans do not by nature yearn for independence.

Second, all of the characteristics that Jefferson lists would be moral characteristics for Hume, and it is difficult to think that they would not be so for Jefferson. For Hume, such moral characteristics are relatively climate-independent; for Jefferson, "these characteristics grow weaker and weaker by gradation from North to South and South to North," so that one traveling could know his quadrant by observing the people. On this reading, morality is prodigiously influenced by climate for Jefferson—an unsavory consequence.

However one interprets the lists of characteristics, there are foreseeable problems. I can only presume that Jefferson did not think through the implications of his list.

What can be salvaged from the perspective of understanding Jefferson? One must presume that, of moral characteristics, independence has an irrefragability that others lack, and there is something about American culture that allows it to thrive, independent of extremes of climactic conditions, which other cultures lack.

Independence was for Jefferson a fundamental virtue—the most important for happiness and social thriving. Thus, Jefferson gave wholehearted support of the French Revolution and those revolutions of other countries in Europe—Spain, Portugal, Italy, Prussia, Germany, and Greece—as well Spanish America.[92] Thus, Jefferson backed abolitionism and proposed removal of slaves over time to colonies where they could cultivate and enjoy their independence. The urgent push toward independence through natural rights, guaranteed by representative democracies, was for Jefferson a necessary global phenomenon. Revolutions were in the service of human rights and of integrating all willing nations into one "great family of nations."[93]

Difficulties with the distinction between northerners and southerners notwithstanding, Jefferson often writes as if the two basal "climate-conditioned" types of character are needed for good governing. He writes to fellow Republican John Taylor (June 1, 1798): "In every free and deliberating society, there must, from the nature of man, be opposite parties and violent dissensions and discords; and one of these, for the most part, must prevail over the other for a longer or shorter time. Perhaps this party division is necessary to induce each to watch and relate to the people the proceedings of the other."[94] To John Cartwright (June 5, 1824), Jefferson writes that the difference between the Whig and the Tory is that the Whig "deduces his rights from the Anglo-Saxon source, and the Tory from the Norman." One cannot help but think of the history between Jefferson and Federalist John Adams as a perfect illustration—their early friendship as framers of and participants in the American Revolution, their split due to climate-conditioned political differences founded perhaps on natural temperamental inclinations, their eventual rapprochement in spite of temperamental and philosophical differences, and their meaty correspondence thereafter. In storybook fashion, their eventual deaths on July 4, 1826, and Adams's putative last words, articulated rhetorically—"Thomas Jefferson survives"—helped to give birth to a picture of antipodal men reconciling differences and fusing interests for the common good of their fledgling nation and as exemplars for all people of all nations.

Nonetheless, Jefferson did think that America, with its abundance of arable land and mostly moderate climate, was ideally suited to nurture independence through agrarianism as a moral ideal to be approximated as fully as possible.[95] In contrast, the entrenched, unnatural aristocracies of France and England as well as their overall lack of arable land made them unsuited for independence—a sizable obstacle for moral improvement. Jefferson writes to Charles Bellini, an émigré living in Virginia (September 30, 1785), that France, where "every man . . . must be either the hammer or the anvil," displays an unhealthy class division between the rich and the impoverished. The great mass suffers tremendous "physical and moral oppression." Still the French as a people are never rude, unite temperance with good taste in eating etiquette, avoid drunkenness, and shine in architecture, sculpture, painting, and music. To fellow Virginian John Banister Jr. (October 15, 1785), he says that the British notion of education is tantamount to "drinking, horse-racing, and boxing." To friend and lawyer George Wythe (August 13, 1786), he notes that the British worship "nobility, wealth & pomp." Under the spell of kings, nobles, and priests, they are not free-minded. The educated are too few and overwrought by prejudices.

The list in the 1785 letter to the Marquis de Chastellux is evidence of what scholar James Morton Smith calls Jefferson's preference for "simple dichotomy." In his excellent commentary on the correspondence between Jefferson and Madison, he contrasts the two great patriots. Jefferson was theoretical, imaginative, speculative, of fluent pen, and an "eternal optimist." Madison was realistic, analytical, down-to-earth, and an "occasional pessimist." Smith adds that Jefferson, on account of his "philosophical intellectuality" and using the "vigor of simple dichotomy," tended to categorize men and issues in terms of "conflicting opposites"—for example, wolves and sheep, the hammer and the anvil, Head and Heart, and Republicans and Federalists.[96]

Consistent with his preference for simple dichotomy, Jefferson acknowledges in a letter to republican and diplomat Joel Barlow (May 3, 1802) that "the division between whig and tory is founded in the nature of men." The weakly, nerveless, rich, and corrupt seek safety and accessibility in a strong executive. The healthy, firm, and virtuous trust their own physical and moral capabilities and grant the executive only such powers as they must for good government. That is a sentiment he repeats many years later to Henry Lee (August 10, 1824). The account, however, shows that biological consider-ations are not the whole account. Circumstances play a part. To John Adams (June 27, 1813), Jefferson says that both a person's circumstances and his con-stitution dictate whether he sides with the many or the few.[97]

What, then, of the Native American, whom Buffon held as proof of the inferiority of the American continents? Jefferson glossed over apparent deficiencies in their cultural and moral development not by positing innate deficiencies of character and intellect but by positing regional variations and, especially, retardation of development, due to their "bigoted venera-tion for the supposed superlative wisdom of their fathers"—namely, their filiopiety.[98] Exposure to and integration in white American culture would expedite moral and intellectual development, as did exposure to Roman culture expedite the moral and intellectual development of the Germanic tribes, claimed Jefferson.[99]

The problem with African American slaves was less byzantine, because, for Jefferson, less was on the line, so to speak. African Americans were not natives to the continent, and thus their avowed moral and intellectual infe-riority—they were said to be innately the moral equals of all other men but innately intellectually inferior to all other men—could offer no proof of the inferiority of the American continent.[100]

In Jefferson's eyes, African Americans had the advantage of exposure to European culture that Native Americans did not have, and though given that advantage, they showed no signs of being able to assimilate to that culture. Thus, Jefferson considered blacks intellectually inferior and incapable of the sort of rapid advancement of which Native Americans were capable. African Americans were deserving of freedom, but miscegenation with white Ameri-cans would result in the intellectual degeneration of offspring. Hence, he saw no alternative other than expatriation—an inordinately costly alternative. Overall, his belief in black intellectual inferiority posed a significant problem for Jefferson's view of the natural equality of all persons.[101]

Other variant character traits, endemic to all Americans through their culture, are resolve and resourcefulness. To daughter Martha (March 28, 1787), who was having difficulty mastering Livy in Latin, Jefferson writes, "It is part of the American character to consider nothing as desperate; to surmount every difficulty by resolution and contrivance." Europe, he adds, has a shop for every want. Thus, Europeans have no idea that their wants can be furnished otherwise. Americans are "obliged to invent and execute," and to find means within themselves, "not to lean on others."

CHAPTER 6

"THIS FAITHFUL, INTERNAL MONITOR"

Jefferson on the Moral Sense

"When we consider the lights that have been acquired, it would doubtless be a disgrace to the human race, to have measured the distance between the sun and the earth, to have weighed the heavenly orbs, and not to have discovered those simple and efficacious laws by which mankind should be discovered."
—Louis-Sébastien Mercier, *L'An 2440*

Jefferson's moral-sense ethics, it is well known, is highly indebted to Scottish empiricists. The most immediate influence was William Small, who was the only Scotsman at William and Mary, a school otherwise composed of Anglican ministers. Other prominent moral-sense Scots were Lord Kames, Francis Hutcheson, Lord Bolingbroke, Adam Smith, and David Hume. Yet Jefferson is also greatly indebted to ancient Greek and Roman ethical thought—namely, Cicero; Epicurus; the Stoics Seneca, Panaetius, and Epictetus; Aristotle; and even Plato, whom he expressly detested.[1] Some work has been done on the influence of such philosophers on Jefferson's views.[2] Precious little has been done that carefully examines Jefferson's ethical views and his moral sense through perusal of his own writings.[3] This chapter is an attempt to remedy those defects.

A SIXTH SENSE

With their friendship rekindled, John Adams (March 2, 1816) writes Jefferson and asks, "Would you go back to your Cradle and live over again Your 70

Years?" Adams himself is uncertain of an answer, as "the question involves so many considerations of Metaphysicks and Physicks, of Theology and Ethicks of Phylosophy and History, of Experience and Romance, of Tragedy Comedy and Farce" that he would have to write a "Volume" in response.

Jefferson, in reply (April 8, 1816), cuts through Adams's philosophical muck. He does not need a "Volume." A measured paragraph in a single letter suffices. "I think with you that it is a good world on the whole, that it has been framed on a principle of benevolence, and more pleasure than pain dealt out to us." To the gloomy and hypochondriac naysayers, disgusted with the present and despairing of the future, he says Stoically, "How much pain have cost us the evils which have never happened?"[4] Jefferson adds, "I steer my bark with Hope in the head, leaving Fear astern."

Jefferson acknowledges the existence of "terrible convulsions"—"heavy set-offs against the opposite page of the account"—even in the happiest life. They give him pause for reflection and reason to question the benevolent intentions of deity. Given that both pains and pleasures are meted out to humans, human perfectibility comes not with apathy but with affective equilibrium. "The perfection of the moral character is, not in a Stoical apathy, so hypocritically vaunted, and so untruly too, because impossible," he asserts, "but in a just equilibrium of all the passions."

Though Jefferson has unquestioned Stoical leanings, his reply owes more to Aristotle than to the Stoics. For the Stoics, the human soul is monolithic and rational. There is no irrational (or irrational part of the) soul,[5] as there is for Plato and Aristotle. The Stoics maintain that all emotions—being mistakes of reasoning and thus diseases of the soul—need to be extirpated, not tamed. The Roman Stoic Seneca says, "The question has often been raised whether it is better to have moderate emotions or not at all. We Stoics reject the emotions; the Peripatetics keep them in check. I do not grasp how any halfway disease [L., mediocritas morbi] can be wholesome or helpful."[6] Emotions, qua diseases of the soul, impede its proper rational functioning and, thereby, lead to vice. For Aristotle, humans are rational and emotional animals, as Aristotle's soul has both rational and irrational components.[7] Thus, some amount of emotional outlet is needed for proper ethical functioning, and that varies according to one's stage of life.[8] In *Nicomachean Ethics*, some of the virtues (Gr., aretai) that Aristotle catalogs expressly require emotional outlet—for example, bravery (Gr., andreia), a mean activity in situations regarding fear and confidence; and indignation (Gr., praotēs), a mean activity in situations regarding anger.[9] Jefferson's view, aimed at a "just equilibrium of passions," is in keeping with Aristotle's views, not the Stoics. Yet, as I have shown in the previous chapter, that need not imply reason, for Jefferson intervenes to establish that equilibrium.

In a letter to lawyer Thomas Law (June 13, 1814), Jefferson considers truth, the love of God, the aesthetic sense, and egoism as candidates for the grounding of morality.[10] Truth cannot be a foundation for morality, though it is one of its branches. "The thief who steals your guinea does wrong only inasmuch as he acts a lie in using your guinea as if it were his own." Love of God cannot be a foundation for morality, for atheists too have a sense of morality. Yet love of God too is one of its branches, he adds Stoically, as morality comprises other-concern—that is, duty to God and duty to fellow humans. The aesthetic sense, founded on taste, cannot be a foundation for morality, because taste is a separate faculty. Finally, egoism, pace the philosopher Lord Bolingbroke,[11] cannot be the foundation for morality because each stands with himself "on the ground of identity, not of relation," and morality fundamentally comprises relations with others. As targets of egoism, he has in mind especially the ancient philosophers—Pythagoras, Socrates, Epicurus, Cicero, Epictetus, Seneca, and Aurelius.[12] Jefferson writes, "To ourselves, in strict language, we can owe no duties, obligation requiring also two parties." The remaining alternative is that humans have innate social dispositions, which are pleasant when people act on them. "The Creator would indeed have been a bungling artist," he sums, "had he intended man for a social animal, without planting in him social dispositions."

The moral sense is not planted in everyone, for all rules have exceptions.[13] He appeals to sensory organs. Some persons, for instance, are born without organs of sight or hearing; others, without hands. Moreover, not all persons are given the same "perfection" of moral sensitivity. "The want or imperfection of the moral sense in some men, like the want or imperfection of the senses of sight and hearing in others, is no proof that it is a general characteristic of the species." Imperfection of the moral sense can be rectified by education, appeals to reason, and the presentation of motives to do good, such as love, and motives to avoid evil, such as social rejection.[14] Here one might envisage an underdeveloped, nonfunctioning arm that gains some degree of functionality over time through focused exercise, designed specifically to strengthen the arm.

What precisely is the moral sense? In a 1785 letter to Peter Carr (August

19), Jefferson says that the moral sense is as much a part of a person's nature, at birth, as are his senses of hearing and seeing. "I believe," Jefferson writes years later to John Adams (October 14, 1816), "that it is instinct, and innate, that the moral sense is as much a part of our constitution as that of feeling, seeing, or hearing; as a wise creator must have seen to be necessary in an animal destined to live in society: that every human mind feels pleasure in doing good to another." From comparisons to hearing and sight, the moral sense is a sensorylike faculty that might be tied to a specific bodily organ, which he says is the heart.[15]

We are perhaps invited to take the comparison with our senses as more than a simile. Consider the sight of an infant. At first, the infant is bombarded by a jumbled mess of sensory perceptions. In time, as the child acts on and is acted on by the nearest objects of perception, he begins to disambiguate between them. Eventually the jumbled mess becomes mother, father, and sister Persephone; the cats Zebulon, Lord Nigel, and Roosevelt; and a playpen, rattle, and picture booklet. The right amount of visual stimulation promotes the fastest, healthiest visual progress. Overstimulation or understimulation as well as improper guidance during maturation can significantly hinder vision and impede disambiguation of sensory data.

Jefferson in the letter to Carr compares the moral sense to a limb. Like a limb, it is given to each person in a greater or lesser degree, and like a limb, it can be "atrophied" or "hypertrophied" through exercise or inactivity, for as the philosopher Lord Kames says, "passions, as they gather strength by indulgence, so they decay by want of exercise."[16] Exercise of the moral sense is no mere desideratum; it is needed, especially early in life, as exercise makes a habit of morally correct action. The comparison with a limb is also given to emphasize the notion of moral accountability. One can fault a valetudinarian, if his perpetual illness is ultimately the result of voluntary faineance or disengagement. Likewise, one who is morally impotent through, say, acquisition of bad habits can be faulted if his moral impotency is ultimately the result of voluntary disengagement.

Not only is the moral sense capable of improvement with use, it is also perfectible over time in the species. Marginalia in his copy of Kames's *Essays on Morality and Religion* contains Jefferson's express agreement with Kames's notion that the "law of nature, which is the law of our nature [i.e., the moral sense], cannot be stationary. It must vary with the nature of man, and, consequently, refine gradually as human nature refines."[17] Jefferson made purchase not only of intellectual progress of the species over time, but also its moral progress.[18] "I fear, from the experience of the last twenty-five years that morals do not of necessity advance hand in hand with the sciences," he writes to the abbot José Francisco Correia da Serra (June 28, 1815). That indicates that the progressive moral march need not be steady. World events, like the war between France and England that began during Jefferson's presidency, were symptomatic of retrogression. Jefferson's own experiment of an embargo with England, instead of war, was likely evidence of American employment of more humane means than war as a way of retaliatory justice for the unprovoked attack of the British on the USS *Chesapeake* on June 22, 1807.[19] Jefferson also made purchase of some moral standard of human perfection, or near perfection, to which all humans ought to strive. That standard is best exemplified by a Stoicized Jesus (see chapter 7), who corrected the Jews on deity and reformed morality to "the standard of reason, justice & philanthropy."[20] In that regard, Jesus was a cynosure, who preached a morality that was centuries ahead of its time.

A SUREFIRE GUIDE

As chapter 1 shows, Jefferson's deity is an intelligent material creator, preserver, and in some sense regenerator of the cosmos. Deity created humans as social animals and gave them freedom to determine, in large measure, their own affairs, to make them responsible for their own happiness. It was not his role to make humans happy, but to make them of such a nature that they, if suitably nurtured, could find happiness by themselves.

Jefferson, however, was not naively sanguine. He recognized, we have seen, the existence of "terrible convulsions." As with the Stoics, Jefferson believed that people had the capacity to endure such convulsions. As with the Stoics, Jefferson believed that people often hyperbolized difficulties by fretting over anticipated ills as if they were inevitabilities. "How much pain have cost us the things which have never happened," he writes to namesake Thomas Jefferson Smith (February 21, 1825) as one of his ten canons of conduct.

How does the moral sense work? A letter to his daughter Martha (December 11, 1783) offers an illustration that suggests it works spontaneously, without the input of reason.

If ever you are about to say any thing amiss or to do any thing wrong, consider before hand. You will feel something within you which will tell you it is wrong and ought not to be said or done: this is your conscience, and be sure to obey it. Our maker has given us all, this faithful internal Monitor, and if you always obey it, you will always be prepared for the end of the world: or for a much more certain event which is death. This must happen to all: it puts an end to the world as to us, and the way to be ready for it is never to do a wrong act.[21]

That is also consistent with philosopher Francis Hutcheson's view of the moral sense. "Virtue it self, or good Dispositions of Mind, are not directly taught, or produc'd by Instruction; they must be originally implanted in our Nature, by its great Author; and afterwards strengthen'd and confirm'd by our own Cultivation."[22] This view is similar to that of Aristotle, who writes of the soul being not naturally virtuous, but naturally of such a nature to become virtuous. The difference, of course, is that Aristotle refers to the rational soul for moral activity, whereas Hutcheson refers to an irrational faculty.

Nonetheless, there is always the temptation not to do what is morally advised by the moral sense. How can one stay away from vice? Jefferson says that one ought to resist the temptation to act viciously in circumstances when vice will not be detected. He tells Peter Carr (August 19, 1785) to act always and in all circumstances as if everyone in the world were looking at him. Grandson Thomas Jefferson Randolph (November 24, 1808) he asks to appeal to moral exemplars before acting. "Under temptations and difficulties, I would ask myself what would Dr. Small, Mr. Wythe, Peyton Randolph do in this situation? What course in it will insure me their approbation?" he answers, "I am certain that this mode of deciding on my conduct, tended more to correctness than any reasoning powers I possessed." The intimation in both letters is that one can use the moral sense unerringly, or relatively so, if one disregards the advice of reason and assumes that all of one's actions are under the scrutiny of all persons—that is, the interests of special groups will be countervailed and there will be no temptation to act under the pressure of peers.

In a later letter to Carr (August 10, 1787), Jefferson disadvises his nephew to attend lectures on moral philosophy and again appeals counterfactually to a ham-handed creator. "He who made us would have been a pitiful bungler if he had made the rules of our moral conduct a matter of science."[23] Morally correct action, then, is not the result of deliberation about circumstances. It is decided by feeling.

Here again a comparison with Aristotle is helpful. "Ethical excellence" or "virtue" (*ethikē aretē*) is derived from "habit" (*ethos*). It follows that "none of the [particular] ethical excellences [virtues][24] is in us by nature, as none of the things that exist by nature can become otherwise by habituation." A stone, by nature, moves to the center of the cosmos due to its heaviness. No person, through habituation, can get it to be something that naturally moves upward, even by tossing it upward ten thousand times. It is the same with ethical excellence. No one is by nature virtuous, insofar as no one acts virtuous from the moment he is born. Nonetheless, all persons are of such sort by nature to become virtuous through habituation. Humans have by nature the capacity to acquire virtue, though they are not born virtuous. It is habituation to right actions through habit, early in life, and exposure to useful rational directives that lead to knowledge and choosing, later in life, that prompts virtue.[25]

Jefferson's view is otherwise. People are born with a capacity for right action that does not require the cultivation of reason—at least, not in any significant sense. People, when placed in situations that require the exercise of the moral sense, just know what to do. Reason, as his famous love letter to Cosway (October 12, 1786) states, seems mostly to prevent right action. "So invariably do the laws of nature create our duties and interests," Jefferson writes to French economist Jean Baptiste Say (February 1, 1804), "that when they seem to be at variance, we ought to suspect some fallacy in our reasonings." Again, that explains why Jefferson disadvises his nephew Carr to take classes in ethics. Driven by reason, they are likely to do more harm than good.

Finally, the function of reason, he says in his 1787 letter to Carr, is "in some degree" to oversee the exercise of the moral faculty, "but it is a small stock which is required for this." Jefferson unfortunately says nothing about how, when, and to what extent reason is supposed to do that. That is the subject of a later section of this chapter.

HEAD VERSUS HEART

In a letter to religionist James Fishback (September 27, 1809), which was written in reply to a missive of Fishback on Christian revelation (June 5, 1809), Jefferson says, "The practice of morality being necessary for the well-being of society, [deity] has taken care to impress it's precepts so indelibly on our hearts that they shall not be effaced by the subtleties of our brain." Jefferson's

1814 letter to Thomas Law states that the care of the creator was necessary in making the moral sense "so much a part of our constitution as that no errors of reasoning or of speculation might lead us astray from it's observance in practice." He adds that want of the moral sense—some do not possess it just as some do not possess eyes for seeing—can be rectified to some extent by education and employment of rational calculation, but the sentiment is that such educative remedies are mere blandishments not aimed to encourage morally correct action, which is impossible without a moral sense, but to discourage morally incorrect action. Such and other references show that the moral sense is a faculty distinct from reason that functions independently of reason.

Then there is Jefferson's impassioned letter to Maria Cosway—his famous dialogue between his Head and his Heart. That each refers to the other as "friend" suggests that the relationship between Head and Heart is amicable, though contrary.

Jefferson has Heart explicate the different empires of the two: science and morality: "When nature assigned us the same habitation, she gave us over it a divided empire. To you she allotted the field of science; to me that of morals." Head functions by nature to square a circle, trace the orbit of a comet, test the arch of greatest strength, or investigate the solid of least resistance. In contrast, Heart functions in feelings of sympathy, benevolence, gratitude, justice, love, and friendship. "Morals were too essential to the happiness of man to be risked on the incertain combinations of the head," Jefferson asserts. "She laid their foundation therefore in sentiment, not in science."

Head, in the dialogue, represents Epicurean moral philosophy, with which Jefferson is often mistakenly said to have aligned himself.[26] It begins by admonishing Heart about an unreserved investment of affection in "objects you must soon lose"—that is, Cosway. "Everything in the world is a matter of calculation," he adds. One must advance only with a balance in one hand to measure the immediate gain of pleasure by the anticipated pain to be had later. "Do not bite at the bait of pleasure," it warns, "until you know there is no hook beneath it [as] the art of life is the art of avoiding pain."

Head next suggests retirement into oneself and contemplation of "truth & nature, matter & motion, the laws that bind up their existence, & that eternal being who made & bound them up by those laws" as the best means of avoiding the pitfalls of pain. Enjoining retreat as a buffer to pain is starkly Epicurean, as are enjoining contemplation of truth, nature, matter, and motion. Consequently, friendship, "another name for an alliance with the follies & the misfortunes of others," ought to be avoided,[27] not cultivated. Each person has his own share of misfortunes without taking on the misfortunes of others.

The reply of Heart is unnecessarily prolonged—more than twice the length as that of Head—and begins with an appeal to the beauty of friendship. Heart turns to an assessment of Head's "mathematical balance." It begins not by considering the burden of helping others in need, but by considering oneself being such person in need. The comforts of sharing one's pain when aggrieved are inestimable. Heart then turns to the argument from retirement. Each person is perpetually exposed to want and accident, and appealing queerly to principle, Heart adds, "Nobody will care for him who cares for nobody." Retirement and lassitude are foolish.

Jefferson's optimism chimes in. Heart adds, "Friendship is precious not only in the shade but in the sunshine of life; & thanks to the benevolent arrangement of things, the greater part of life is sunshine." Heart then appeals to the time Jefferson had spent recently with Cosway and the gaiety and beauty of it. "Let the sublimated philosopher grasp visionary happiness while pursuing phantoms dressed in the garb of truth! Their supreme wisdom is supreme folly; & they mistake for happiness the mere absence of pain. Had they ever felt the solid pleasure of one generous spasm of the heart, they would exchange for it all the frigid speculations of their lives."

Heart proposes to prove that nature has not organized Head for moral counsel. Recall the three illustrations of the previous chapter where Head, through deliberation on ends, makes morally wrong decisions: the tired and weathered soldier who sought a ride on Jefferson's wagon, the poor "drunkard" who asked for charity, and the American Revolution. In each instance, Head, with starched and unmalleable precepts, led astray Jefferson. Head's moral advice is empty, even harmful.

Jefferson's dialogue between Head and Heart strongly suggests that morally correct action is wholly, as it were, a visceral matter. Thinking through circumstances leads astray an agent. Head is made for science, not ethics.[28] To see moral judgments as products of deliberation on possible ends is a mistake made by scholars who wish to see Jefferson as a sort of deontologist in the process of disclosing the laws of morality in the manner Newton disclosed the laws of nature.[29]

The notion of a divided empire, dealt with in the prior chapter, suggests a problem. One might argue, as does one author,[30] that there is a sort of confusion in Jefferson's insistence on unalienable rights, guaranteed by nature and presumably with normative force, and his purchase of the moral sense, which functions independently. Hume, for instance, appeals to the moral sense precisely because he believes that there can be no successful appeal to universal moral principles, among them natural rights, to dictate moral behavior and guide politically correct action.

Ari Helo essays to settle the tension. He argues that natural rights comprise a naturalistic, not a normative category. "This right [i.e., self-government] appears to have been naturalistic rather than moral in character, derived from historically valid experience and political practice rather than from any assumed universal moral truth, such as human equality. . . . In essence, Jefferson's naturalist conception of self-government entailed viewing some political ordering of society as a basic necessity of human life."[31]

Helo is correct to assert that "some political ordering of society" is needed for human life, but that is an understatement. Yet pace Helo, it is not living at which Jefferson aims, but good living—that is, human happiness. Moreover, nature for Jefferson, as it is for the Stoics and Hutcheson and Kames, is a normative force, so there can be no severance of nature and normativity, even when considering rights. What is right is natural and what is natural is right. That does not mean Jefferson's warrant for "unalienable" rights founded in nature is a priori. His discovery of moral "truths," given the aegis of nature, was empirical, in the manner that Newton's discovery of the laws of motion was empirical: All experience speaks for it; nothing speaks against it.

ACTING SINGLY OR COLLECTIVELY

The subject of the relation of rights and morality invites further discussion. Moreover, what was the relationship of Jefferson's moral sense to his notion of political justice? Hume maintained that morally correct action was a matter of following moral sentiment. Justice, based on utility, was the sole exception.[32] Locke maintained that morally correct actions was rights-driven—a derivative of the social contract.[33] What was Jefferson's view?

Jefferson's writes syllogistically in a letter to lawyer Francis Walker Gilmer[34] (June 7, 1817). "Man was created for social intercourse; but social intercourse cannot be maintained without a sense of justice; then man must have been created with a sense of justice." To James Madison (August 28, 1789), he writes: "I know but one code of morality for men, whether acting singly or collectively. . . . If the morality of one man produces a just line of conduct in him, acting individually, why should not the morality of one hundred men produce a just line of conduct in them, acting together?" Thus, justice, for Jefferson, depends on the moral sense. To Reverend William Green Munford (June 18, 1799), he adds: "I am among those who think well of the human character generally. I consider man as formed for society, and endowed by nature with those dispositions which fit him for society." To Thomas Law (June 13, 1814), he says deity has implanted in men "social dispositions"— that is, a moral sense—to complement their egoism.

Scholar Tadashige Shimizu believes such passages commit Jefferson to a "communitarian or organic view of society," because the moral sense works toward the good of the community and does not allow for "individualistic ideas." Thus, the "rights and interests of the community must be more important than those of the individual." Moreover, no one can rebel against a community or act contrary to the decisions of the majority.[35]

Jefferson has communitarian leanings, which keep him from being a political atomist, but he is no communitarian. Government exists for the sake of the collection of individuals, but the individuals are significant, not the collection. For communitarians like Plato, the city-state, with its form of government or constitution (Gr., politeia) is something greater, more stable than the collection of individuals comprising it at any time. Individuals come and go, but the city-state endures, and it does so on account of its constitution.

That is not the case for Jefferson. The state endures for the sake of its individuals, not the individuals for the sake of the state. It is undeniable that individuals have political roles to play, for Jefferson. Yet the state is not something above and beyond its collection of individuals at any given time. Jefferson's emphasis is always on individuals—yet individuals construed as social beings. That he, like many other statesmen, should have spent much of his life in service to his fellow countrymen as well as to the citizens of the progressive world is a measure of his willingness to fulfill selflessly a moral role in pursuance of his abilities as a politician for the sake of human progress. It is a measure of his commitment to and care for others. That is not pure selflessness, however. As with communitarianism, a well-run community, state, or nation benefits all citizens so long as each does his part for the benefit of himself and all others.

Shimizu makes two more points about Jefferson's moral sense and his communitarianism.

First, because of Jefferson's presumed commitment to communitarianism, "the conception of a 'moral sense' idealizes minimal government" which leans toward political anarchy. He cites Query XI of Jefferson's *Notes on the State of Virginia*, where Jefferson contrasts the lifestyle of Native Americans with that of Europeans. For Native Americans, lawlessness is lex terrae[36]; for Europeans, there is excess of law. Jefferson's preference for the former, he asserts, "with its flavor of anarchy—can be said to be the logical conclusion of moral sense philosophy," which "repels everything artificial and attaches primary importance to human nature."[37]

Against Shimizu, preference for the Native American lifestyle, with its paucity of laws and its incapacity to accommodate large groupings of people, is not the logical outcome of moral-sense theory, which is fundamentally other-concerned. Jefferson is clear in a great number of places that minimal government can work only if a certain schema, bottom-up driven, is put in place that prompts participation in governmental affairs, if only parochially. Each citizen, given a modicum of education, is fully capable of governing himself. That is not a slide into anarchy.

Second, the moral sense, Shimizu adds, embraces a monistic worldview that is not value-pluralism friendly. The moral sense is uniform and generally distributed. Thus, it "presupposes a universal standard of value" that is intolerant of "conflicts or differences of opinion."[38]

Shimizu is correct to state that Jefferson does not embrace value-pluralism, but one ought not to infer that he does not allow for differences of opinion on moral issues. Nowhere does Jefferson say that the moral sense, acting independently of reason, is an infallible judge of morally correct action. That he considers it a sensory or quasi-sensory faculty suggests it needs to be kept in proper working order. A healthy eye deteriorates through overstimulation or overuse. A healthy limb suffers muscular atrophy if it is insufficiently exercised and is at risk of injury if overused. Moreover, moral scenarios are at least sometimes sufficiently labyrinthine to beguile the moral sense and entice it to appeal to reason, if only to have correct "perception" of particulars. Finally, the seeming embrace of different values in different cultures, which I address fully below, is an added difficulty. These difficulties notwithstanding, the people of a town, state, or nation, or even globally can, like individuals, generally decide moral issues correctly if the majority of them allow their moral sense spontaneous, guileless expression.[39]

In "Opinion on the French Treaties," Jefferson expatiates on the line of thought in his sense-of-justice syllogism in his later letter to Gilmer by showing how the "Law of nations" is derived from the "Moral duties" that exist between individuals and why the former is just as binding as the latter.

> The Moral duties which exist between individual and individual in a state of nature, accompany them into a state of society & the aggregate of the duties of all the individuals composing the society constitutes the duties of that society towards any other [i.e., the "Law of nations"]; so that between society & society the same moral duties exist as did between the individuals composing them while in an unassociated state, their maker not having released them from those duties on their forming themselves into a nation. Compacts then between nation & nation are obligatory on them by the same moral law which obliges individual to observe their compacts.[40]

Jefferson's political thinking, thus, is underpinned by his moral thinking. Political theory is fundamentally a branch of morality.[41]

Given the existence of the moral sense, the subsumption of political theory under moral theory, and Jefferson's insistence on inalienable rights, granted by nature to all persons and grounded in moral sentiment, it follows that there are distinct limits to the function and powers of government. Thick government is no option. It will interfere with each person's correct use of the moral sense and with individual rights.

FOREMOST AN ETHICIAN

Tadashige Shimizu also argues for the following differences between the rational and moral faculties. First, they are independent of each other. For proof, he appeals, as I have done, to Jefferson's 1787 letter to Carr and his celebrated 1786 letter to Cosway. Second, the moral sense is a "more prevalent endowment than reason." This too is a sensible claim, as it exists equally in all persons, though it is unexercised in some and unrefined in others. Last, it "can give sure and more reliable judgment than reason" which is often undependable by comparison.

In support of the last claim Shimizu cites Jefferson's letter to Fishback, which says, "The practice of morality being necessary for the well-being of society, he [i.e., the creator] has taken care to impress its precepts so indelibly

on our hearts that they shall not be effaced by the subtleties of our brains."
He cites also Jefferson's 1785 letter to Carr in which Jefferson's moral is,
"An honest heart being the first blessing, a knowing head is the second."
Finally, he cites the roguish nature of the learned in France (qua robbers) and
in England (qua pirates).[42] There is nothing in those citations to demonstrate
any unreliability of reason, that the moral sense "can give sure and more reliable judgment than reason," when reason is used properly, given the qualification that reason is used for the purposes of science, broadly construed, and
not morality. If anything, what Shimizu shows is the axiological priority of
morality apropos of science. For Jefferson, science is practiced for the sake
of human flourishing, therefore the aims of science are ultimately the aims of
morality. Human flourishing or happiness is autotelic; science is heterotelic.
Jefferson is, above all else, a moralist. Jefferson is fundamentally a philosopher; only secondarily, a statesmen.

The same can be said of politics, which for Jefferson is part of his scientific curriculum. Politics is heterotelic: Its excellence lies in its contribution to
human happiness.[43] Thus, though consistency with political policies is important for Jefferson—the "knowing-head" part of the equation—it is secondary,
when compared to an "honest heart."

In such a manner, Jefferson justifies his breach with political policy concerning the Louisiana Purchase in a letter to Virginia politician John Breckinridge (August 12, 1803). "The constitution has made no provision for our
holding foreign territory, still less for incorporating foreign nations into our
Union." Therefore, purchase of the Louisiana territories, he acknowledges, is
an act that is neither sanctioned nor forbidden by the Constitution. To republican John B. Colvin, Jefferson shows there is one political principle he held
in some sense inviolable—the preservation of the nation. "A strict observance
of the written laws is doubtless *one* of the high duties of a good citizen: but
it is not the *highest*. The laws of necessity, of self-preservation, of saving our
country when in danger, are of higher obligation. . . . The *salus populi* [is]
supreme over the written law" (September 20, 1810). The second statement
betrays a naturalistic slant. The final statement betrays moral obligation: An
honest politician's first duty is the well-being of the citizenry.[44]

Jefferson's breach of strict constructionism in the Louisiana Purchase,
being fodder for his adversaries and numerous historians today, is not to be
judged or justified by his head, but by his heart, as there are no inviolable rules
of morally correct action,[45] and the Louisiana Purchase is at least a political

decision with moral implications, if not chiefly a moral decision. What bothered Jefferson was that the decision, without constitutional sanction, might be construed as the paternalistic act of a strong executive. Yet he was ineluctably convinced that the purchase was in the best interest of the nation. Morality trumps politics. The right thing to do is the right thing to do. To Breckinridge, he compares the Louisiana Purchase to a guardian's investment of the money of his ward by purchasing an "important adjacent territory." When the boy comes of age, he might disavow his guardian, but the guardian, consistent with his role as guardian, will reply, "I did this for your good. . . . I thought it my duty to risk myself for you." Jefferson here is not rationalizing a morally dubious decision. Instead, he willfully takes on anticipated censure for the sake of the well-being of his country. He is readied for the reproaches of Federalists, who grudgingly, but generally, recognized the decision was in the best interest of the country.

A SMALL STOCK

Jefferson's letter to Cosway suggests a strictly antithetical relationship between reason and morality, which is in keeping with Lord Kames's notion that the moral sense as a guide to morally correct action is action on intuitive perception without premeditation.[46] Yet Jefferson also states that morally correct action is in some slight measure guided by reason. Jefferson's 1785 letter to Peter Carr states, "This sense is submitted indeed in some degree to the guidance of reason; but it is a small stock which is required for this: even less one than what we call common sense." He fails unfortunately to elaborate, but merely adds, as if to muddy waters that are already dirty, "State a moral case to a ploughman and a professor, the former will decide it as well, and often better than the latter, because he has not been led astray by artificial rules."[47] Just what is this "small stock"? Why will the ploughman decide moral cases "often better than the [professor]"? We must look elsewhere to answer those questions.

Jefferson's reference to a small stock of reason might be taken as evidence that the moral sense does not function spontaneously and independently of reason.

That is harefooted induction, for it is easy to explain Jefferson's curious addendum without assuming a relationship of dependency between reason and the moral sense, when confronted with moral decision making. Reason might have as many as seven functions vis-à-vis the moral sense. It might function to encourage or reinforce morally correct action, to keep the moral sense vital and vigorous, to instill the first elements of morality in children through exposure to moral exemplars in history, to allow for a sort of cultural sensitivity to morally retarded cultures, to ensure the continual advance of morality through charting the course of moral progress through reading history as adults, to encourage the moral adjustments of men by making plain their rights (especially derivative rights), and to encourage the moral improvement of the species over time through sexual selection apropos of moral discernment. As I have already covered these in great detail in *Dutiful Correspondent*, I merely summarize those findings here.

First, reason functions to encourage and reinforce morally correct action. Jefferson writes in an early letter to lifelong friend Robert Skipwith (August 3, 1771) that acts of charity or of gratitude presented to sight or imagination impress in humans "a strong desire in [them] of doing charitable and grateful acts also." It is the opposite with acts of dereliction. Of virtuous actions, he adds: "Now every emotion of this kind is an exercise of our virtuous dispositions, and dispositions of the mind, like limbs of the body acquire strength by exercise. But exercise produces habit, and in the instance of which we speak the exercise being of the moral feelings produces a habit of thinking and acting virtuously." In sum, virtuous acts, whether observed or imagined, are contagious; vicious acts are repulsive. He tells Peter Carr (August 10, 1787) to read good books because "they will encourage as well as direct your [moral] feelings." That is advice he himself was wont to follow. "I never go to bed without an hour, or half hour's previous reading of something moral," he writes his physician Dr. Vine Utley (March 21, 1819) "whereon to ruminate in the intervals of sleep."

Second, reason watches over the moral sense to keep it strong, vigorous, and adaptable to varying circumstances. Since the moral sense is strengthened with use and enfeebled with disuse, reason functions to maintain or improve the strength of the moral sense and perhaps even refine its use. That is why Jefferson likens the moral sense to a limb in his letter to Carr (August 10, 1787). To some extent, any limb is made more dexterous with practice at certain types of activity—imagine a carpenter's skilled use of his hammer—and so right use of the moral sense over time makes it stronger.

Third, reason can allow for cultural sensitivity to morally retarded or regressive cultures. In such instances, as in the letters to Adams and Law, reason, with the help of the moral sense, can recognize moral lag, as in the case of the Native Americans, or moral decline, as in the case of large European nations in the last part of the eighteenth century. It can convince the moral sense to withhold its correct judgment of moral indignation or moral condemnation and offer instead moral guidance, in the case of Native Americans, or moral remediation, as in the case of retrogressive European nations. Thus, it is reason's role to see to it that the moral sense, forming immediate judgments, does not always express its judgments immediately, but that it uses resourcefulness and tact.

Fourth, reason enables children, whose moral-sense faculty—here, more like a limb than an eye—is still maturing, to overcome prejudices and social biases. Children, through study of history, can store what is "most useful" from history and acquire the "first elements of morality." They might learn that wealth and good birth are mere cultural biases and that good conscience, good health, good occupation, and freedom in all just pursuits enable persons to rise above the condition of life in which chance has placed them.[48]

Fifth, by reading and assimilation of history, reason can reflect on the barbaric and hedonic practices of earlier times that were given moral sanction, compare them with later advances, and work toward still further advances. "It is the happiness of modern times," writes Jefferson in a manner to mark moral improvement of humans over time, "that the evils of necessary war are softened by the refinement of manners & sentiments and that an enemy is an object of vengeance, in arms, & in the field only."[49] Recall Jefferson's marginal comments in Lord Kames's *On the Principles of Morality and Natural Religion* concerning the moral treatment of prisoners of war. The cumulative effect of such study is rational enculturation the sort Kames mentions. "Refinement in taste and manners," writes Kames, "operating by communication upon the moral sense, occasions a stronger perception of immorality in every vitious action, than what would arise before such refinement."[50]

Sixth, and here I add to the list in *Dutiful Correspondent*, reason can help to make plain for the purposes of social justice the rights of men. It can help the moral sense flesh out humans' most substratal and derivative rights. For illustration, concerning derivative rights, one can acknowledge, following Francis Hutcheson, that misers have an "external Right" to hoard their possessions, for coercing the rich to share their wealth does overall greater harm than good. It makes the "Industrious . . . constant Prey to the Slothful" and, by reducing generosity to a tax on wealth, invalidates generosity. In sum, reason aids the "moral Sense, by a little Reflection upon the tendencys of actions, [to] adjust the Rights of Mankind."[51]

Last, reason can facilitate moral improvement through promoting breeding for moral advance. In his natural-aristoi letter to John Adams, Jefferson argues for the possibility of moral improvement of humans through the creation of a "natural aristocracy," founded on virtue and talent. Like sheep and other animals that are bred for physical or behavioral characteristics, "the moral and physical qualities of man, whether good or evil, are transmissible in a certain degree from father to son" (October 28, 1813). The implication here is that reason is needed in order to breed selectively virtuous persons. Yet Jefferson acknowledges that breeding for moral improvement would be anathema to "the equal rights of man"—that is, the masses would adjudge it repugnant.

It follows that Jefferson's mysterious statement about reason assisting the moral sense—expressed without expatiation—can readily be accommodated to the view that the moral sense functions, in forming its judgments, independently of reason, or relatively so.

INTENSION VERSUS OUTCOME

Jefferson says in a letter to Thomas Law, "Men living in different countries, under different circumstances, different habits and regimens, may have different utilities; the same act, therefore, may be useful, and consequently virtuous in one country which is injurious and vicious in another differently circumstanced" (June 13, 1814). Again, in a letter to John Adams (October 14, 1816) two years later, he writes:

> The non-existence of justice is not to be inferred from the fact that the same act is deemed virtuous and right in one society, which is held vicious and wrong in another; because as the circumstances and opinions of different societies vary, so the acts which may do them right or wrong must vary also: for virtue does not consist in the act we do, but in the end it is to effect. If it is to effect the happiness of him to whom it is directed, it is virtuous, while in a society under different circumstances and opinions, the same act might produce pain, and would be vicious. The essence of virtue is in doing good to others.

These passages pose a problem for the view of the moral sense heretofore expressed. They suggest cultural relativism with a utilitarian twist. They show that the moral sense in different social settings is a disobliging and aidless guide to morally correct action. Morally correct action, it seems, varies from culture to culture, since what is useful or right varies from culture to culture, and reason must be employed by an alien to ascertain the moral codes when visiting another culture. The measuring stick of morally correct action is rational calculation of utility—that is, the production of pleasure or absence of pain. Jefferson, then, is very much an Epicurean, of whom in a letter to William Short (October 31, 1819), he claims to be a disciple.

That is the view, it seems, of Jeffersonian scholar Gilbert Chinard, who touches on the issue in his version of Jefferson's *Literary Bible*. Early in life, writes Chinard, Jefferson favored Stoicism. Later in life, he "transferred his moral allegiance to Epicurus," for whom rational calculation to maximize pleasure in avoidance of pain was key.[52]

That is also the view of historian Robert Booth Fowler, who maintains that to see Jefferson as merely a political philosopher without seeing him as an Epicurean is to see only one side, perhaps the lesser side, of Jefferson. Jefferson lived his life as an Epicurean. He practiced withdrawal, cultivated friends, privacy, and pursuit of personal pleasure. The germ of his Epicureanism was utilitarian.[53]

Historian Adrienne Koch too defends the view that Jefferson was a sort of Epicurean utilitarian. Jefferson's ethics, she argues, was an unsavory salmagundi of Epicureanism, Jesus's precepts, and moral-sense intuitionism. The salmagundi became savory, it seems, only with the late addition of utilitarianism. "Only utilitarianism could be relied on to cut the suggestion of absolutism out of these more single-valued philosophies, making room for that variability of moral judgement which Jefferson's historic sense made him acknowledge as one segment in the development of man in society." What was lacking was the social element, which made up for the defects of Christian idealism, and thereby allowed for a context to moral scenarios.[54]

The shirt of Nessus for Jefferson was that he aimed to reconcile happiness as the aim of life, in the egoistic sense of the ancients, with utility as the "test of virtue." Koch appeals, of course, to Jefferson's letters to Law and to Adams. Because people have different utilities, the letters show, the same act might have a different utility, and thus, be virtuous in one country and vicious in another. In adopting utility as the test of virtue, Jefferson becomes a moral utilitarian/relativist.

For Koch, the addition of utility as the standard of virtue and sensitivity to the richness of varying circumstances marks a maturity in Jefferson's ethical thinking. Moral action for him is action, first, that is based on correct perception of particular circumstances, and then, that is judged to maximize human happiness. Here reason is needed both to disentangle the complexity of circumstances in difference moral scenarios and to decide on correct action.[55] How precisely does utility tie up the loose, eclectic strands of Jefferson's prior moral thinking? On that, Koch is silent.

One wishes Koch would have preferred expatiation to silence. Utility is not a way of reconciling moral-sense theory, the teachings of Jesus, and virtue ethics, as Koch thinks it is. Instead, it is manifestly inconsistent with the moral-sense view expressed in his 1786 Head-and-Heart letter to Maria Cosway (October 12, 1786)—a view Jefferson never abandoned.[56] It is also inconsistent with his take of Jesus, whose precepts were based on selfless beneficence and spontaneous activity, not social utility and context sensitivity.[57]

Jean Yarbrough, in "The Moral Sense, Character Formation, and Virtue," adopts a similar take on Jefferson's moral thinking. For her, Jefferson's embrace of utility is not a matter of tying up loose ends, but instead of allowing for moral action in complex scenarios. She believes that Jefferson recognized that the moral sense was "too weak and diffuse" to adjudge right action in different circumstances—especially in different societies—so reason was needed to lead one through that Gordian complexity and allow for right action, after deliberation.[58]

Against Koch, Yarbrough observes a difficulty in essaying to reconcile Jefferson's appeal to utility in late letters with his early view that the moral sense works independently of reason and is a matter of right intentions, not results. She merely adds somewhat unmindfully that Jefferson's aim in these late letters is to "defend the existence of the moral sense while accounting for the variety of different moral codes in different cultures." Humans' social nature, she says, demands that they must "sometimes do the right thing for the wrong reasons."[59]

Yarborough's view too is disobliging. Appeal to utility as arbiter in complex scenarios is inconsistent with the view that the moral sense functions independently of reason, when forming moral judgments. It is also, as she renders it, inconsistent with the view that right moral action is objective. Her view is tantamount to saying that the moral sense is an unaccommodating faculty in complex scenarios. Jefferson was eclectic and inconsistently so.

We are left with a messy, Byzantine imbroglio, or are we?

MORAL PROGRESS

The imbroglio is neither as messy nor as Byzantine as it might seem. There is a way to reconcile the tension that Yarbrough notes. To do that, one must grasp that Jefferson was fundamentally and always a progressivist apropos of science, in the broad eighteenth- and nineteenth-century sense, and he was fundamentally and always a progressivist with respect to morality and political systems.

A child of the Enlightenment and a lifelong patron and practitioner of science, Jefferson was an empiricist and steadfast progressivist. He resented the ultraconservatism of many Federalists because their stance was unscientific, antediluvial, obscurantist, and treadmill. To scientist and religionist Joseph Priestley, he writes (January 27, 1800) of a certain Gothicism of politics, religion, and science. "The Gothic idea that we were to look backwards instead of forwards for the improvement of the human mind, and to recur to the annals of our ancestors for what is most perfect in government, in religion and in learning, is worthy of those bigots in religion and government, by whom it has been recommended, and whose purposes it would answer." To John Adams (June 15, 1813), Jefferson acknowledges that Federalist and Republican Party differences, during their years in public service, were, in part, due to different positions on the significance of science. Here again he refers to science and politics, but now ethics takes the place of religion. There are the reformists—who make purchase of the illimitable "improvability of the human mind in science, in ethics, in government"—and the "enemies of reform"—who "denied improvement, and advocated steady adherence to the principles, practices and institutions of our fathers, which they represented as the consummation of wisdom, and acme of excellence, beyond which the human mind could never advance."

What is the relationship of political advance to that of science in general? In a letter to Virginian and lawyer Samuel Kercheval (July 12, 1816), Jefferson suggests that political systems lag behind general advances in science. "Laws and institutions must go hand in hand with the progress of the human mind," he asserts. "As . . . new discoveries are made, new truths disclosed, and manners and opinions change with the change of circumstances, institutions must advance also, and keep pace with the times." He adds that it is as absurd for a political institution to remain the same while science advances as it is for a man to wear the coat that fitted him as a boy.

Jefferson also makes purchase of moral progress, which he believed was observable over time.[60] As we have seen, progress in morality is not inevasible insofar as retrogression is always possible. The seemingly interminable tension between England and France in Jefferson's later years was to him evidence of that. Still, he gives evidence that such moral retrogressions, considered overall, are like planetary retrogradations—temporary setbacks— than genuine moral regressions. In a letter to Adams (August 1, 1816), he writes that the Americas will show Europe the path to moral advance. "We are destined to be a barrier against the returns of ignorance and barbarism. Old Europe will have to lean on our shoulders, and to hobble along by our side, under the monkish trammels of priest and kings, as she can. What a Colossus shall we be when the southern continent comes up to our mark!" To physician and professor Benjamin Waterhouse two years later (March 3, 1818), he writes: "When I contemplate the immense advances in science and discoveries in the arts which have been made within the period of my life, I look forward with confidence to equal advances by the present generation, and have no doubt they will consequently be as much wiser than we have been as we than our fathers were, and they than the burners of witches."[61] The implied keys to the continuation of such rapid progress he cashes out in numerous places elsewhere as augmented liberty and respect for humans' rights.

Jefferson made purchase of moral progress, yet what did he mean by "moral progress"?

There were unquestioned advances, to which I allude in prior chapters, in the sciences in or before Jefferson's day through discoveries. William Harvey's work *De Motu Cordis* (1628) in anatomy showed that blood moved circularly in the body. Galileo Galilei, during his life (d. 1642), discovered that bodies fall *in vacuo* independently of their weight and gave an equation of their rate of fall: $d = kt^2$. He also discovered four moons around Jupiter, sunspots, and the rings of Saturn. Robert Boyle (1662) formulated the ideal gas law, which showed an inverse relationship between pressure and volume: $pV = k$. Isaac Newton (1687) discovered the three laws of planetary motion and the universal law of gravitation, $F = Mm/r^2$, which gave an equation for the tug each body exerted on any other body, given the mass of each and the distance between them. Paleontologists at the time were finding bones of extinct animals—some of ponderous size. Overall, scientists, through careful observation and experimentation, were learning the secrets of the cosmos and supplanting the Aristotelian *Weltanschauung*, the result more of metempirical posits than hard-fought empirical advances. The findings of such scientists were movements toward the correct view of how the cosmos worked. Thus, one might say that *scientific progress*, for Jefferson, denotes those movements.

Yet Jefferson used *progress* also for political and moral movements. It would be pointless to assume that he equivocated while using the term—that is, that progress apropos of science meant one thing, while progress apropos of politics and morality meant another thing. Scrutiny of the passages listed above, for instance, gives no reason to assume polysemy. If in science, Jefferson took *progress* to mean movement toward some sort of aim or telos—namely, in the most general sense, correct understanding of just how the cosmos works—he unquestionably had something similar in mind for moral progress.[62] His moral telos is happiness through human flourishing—an ideal that admixes virtue ethics, Christian beneficence, and moral-sense ethics, within a social-political frame. As human happiness is impossible without certain political ends being met—for example, liberty, equality, rule by merit, and government of and for the people, and so on—political systems that can best accommodate those ideals in a manner that best facilitates human happiness are progressive. Thus, moral aims are inseparable from political aims.

Overall, Jefferson's take on moral progress, which never wavered over the course of his life, makes it improbable, if not impossible, that he was a moral relativist or even a political relativist. Relativism can make no sense of movement toward some end or aim—an individual's or the species's convergence toward a moral ideal. Thus, the relativist interpretation of his letters to Adams and Law is untenable.

As I have argued previously, Jefferson had a Panaetian take on morally correct action.[63] What was morally good was useful and what was useful was morally good—namely, moral goodness and utility were mutually entailing. That explains Jefferson's references to utility as the standard of moral goodness, without narrowly painting him a utilitarian, because for Jefferson, as for Panaetius, moral goodness is also the standard for utility. Intention counts as much as outcome counts. Note carefully what Jefferson says in his letter to Thomas Law, which is taken as evidence for moral relativism. "Virtue does not consist in the act we do, but in the end it is to effect. If it is to effect the happiness of him to whom it is directed, it is virtuous." Here he does not say virtue is measured by its effect, but by "the end it is to effect." It is, as Kames says, decided by the end which the actor has in mind, not by the end simpliciter. Intention is critical. Consider too what moral-sense philosopher Lord

Kames says on intention and outcome. "By the [moral sense] certain actions are perceived to be right, and are approved accordingly as virtuous. The most illiterate rustic would [know] that to be honest or to be grateful is right; and there he would stop, never having thought of their useful tendency."[64] Note too in his letter to Law that Jefferson appeals to education, "appeals to reason and calculation," love, hatred, and rejection as motivations to incite virtuous action, *when the morals sense is wanting*. One can, it seems, blandish action consistent with virtue by rational coaxing.

CHAPTER 7

"THE MOST PRECIOUS GIFT OF NATURE"

Jefferson on the "Natural Aristoi"

> *"I shall not die without a hope that light and liberty are on steady advance."*
>
> —TJ to John Adams, September 12, 1821

Jefferson believed that all persons, irrespective of color of skin, were deemed equal insofar as they were deserving of the same fundamental rights and that they had the same capacity for morally correct action. Desert of the same fundamental rights was more of a moral imperative, as it were, than a political expedient, for desert of fundamental rights could be justified only by the existence in each person of a moral sense—a faculty implanted in each person by deity and possessed by each person (roughly) the same, and a faculty through which the judgments of a ploughman were equal to, and often better than, a professor.[1]

Beyond the existence of the moral sense, Jefferson recognized different degrees of moral attainment in, and different degrees of aptitude and skill possessed by, each person. For instance, after complimenting astronomer David Rittenhouse (July 19, 1778) for his contribution to the welfare of Pennsylvania and noting that all able persons have a duty to participate in governmental affairs, he adds:

> I am also satisfied there is an order of geniuses above that obligation, & therefore exempted from it [and] nobody can conceive that nature ever intended to throw away a Newton upon the occupation of a crown. It would have been a prodigality for which even the conduct of providence might have been arraigned, had he been by birth annexed to what was so far below him.

> Cooperating with nature in her ordinary economy we should dispose of and employ the geniuses of men according to their several orders and degrees.

Thus, desert of the same fundamental rights did not qualify everyone equally for governmental office any more than did desert of the same fundamental rights qualify everyone to be a blacksmith, a merchant, or sailor. In short, being qualified for governmental office did not mean that every qualified person should govern. In Jefferson's political schema, only the best and most virtuous by nature could secure the health and functional unity needed for a republic to run smoothly, and only the people, endowed with a moral faculty and sufficient reason, could decide who were the best and most virtuous. In effect, his republicanism aimed to steer clear of the toxic effects of traditional aristocracies, based on heredity or wealth, and the leveling influence of radical egalitarian populist democracy, which at least theoretically saw no differences between men and were impracticable.

THE STEWARDSHIP MODEL

It is in a letter to John Adams (October 28, 1813) that Jefferson's moral vision for his political schema comes best into focus.[2] The letter is a reply to prior letters by Adams on Adams's sense of aristoi[3]—a sense radically different from that of Jefferson. The different takes that Adams and Jefferson have on aristoi are expressions of their different approaches to politics and, perhaps, are in some measure the difference between Federalists and Republicans.[4] Adams's take is realistic and fatalistic. Drawing from experience, he maintains that there is little reason to believe that humans will ever be anything other than what they have already been. Jefferson's take is idealistic and sanguine. Drawing too from experience, he maintains that there is every reason to believe that humans are progressing morally, politically, and scientifically, and there is no reason to think such progress will discontinue.

On July 9, 1813, Adams begins by noting a request of Jefferson of some thirty years ago for him to write something on aristocracy. Since that request, Adams has been "writing Upon that Subject ever since," without being understood by readers.[5] "Birth and Wealth together," experience teaches, "have prevailed over Virtue and Talents in all ages."

Subsequent letters show that the topic of the aristoi is one that Adams cannot let aside, perhaps because of the negative responses of his readers. On July 13, 1813, Adams states, "Whig and Torey belong to Natural History, as the ancient Greeks wrote of the continual quarrels of the two Ladies *Aristokratia* and *demokatia*." He adds in a passage that starkly reveals the differences between the two friends on their views of human nature:

> Inequalities of Mind and Body are so established by God Almighty in his constitution of Human Nature that no Art or policy can ever plain them down to a Level. I have never read Reasoning more absurd, Sophistry more gross, in proof of the Athanasian Creed, or Transubstantiation, than the subtle labours of Helvetius and Rouseau to demonstrate the natural Equality of Mankind. Jus cuique [i.e., justice for each]; the golden rule; do as you would be done by; is all the Equality that can be supported or defended by reason, or reconciled to common Sense.

Adams returns to the topic of aristoi on July 15, August 14, September 2, and September 15 of the same year. He is antsy to get a response from Jefferson on the issue. In the second of those letters, he appeals to the authority of the ancient Greek poet Theognis,[6] who argues that wealth and birth are, in Adams's own words, two "Monsters" in the "Constitution of human nature, and wrought into the Fabrick of the Universe" that cannot be eliminated, only subdued. "The five Pillars of Aristocracy," he adds on September 2, "are Beauty Wealth, Birth, Genius and Virtues. Any one of the three first, can at any time over bear any one or both of the last two." The consistent sentiment is that there cannot be a ruling aristoi based on talent and virtue, as men have always chosen and will always choose wealth, birth, and even beauty in preference to them. Adams is, of course, making psychological, not normative, points.

With an express focus on Adams's letters of August 14 and September 2, Jefferson offers a lengthy reply on October 28, 1813. He begins by noting that the passage by Theognis is a moral exhortation (Gr., parainesis), a reproof, to the effect that procreation ought not to be for the sake of pleasure, but for the sake of children. Yet nature, Jefferson objects, does not trust the moral motive. It seems to make the procreation of children not the object, but the effect of sexual excitation and activity. The sexual impulse carries away persons to such an extent that scarcely a thought is given to the beauty, healthiness, understanding, and virtue of those engaged in the act of intercourse. Yet selectivity, as done with animals and recommended by Theognis, would doubtless improve the human species and produce a race of aristoi, "for experience proves that the moral and physical qualities of man, whether good or evil, are transmissible in a certain degree from father to son." In such a way, it is possible to generate a natural aristocracy of humans, based on virtue and talents, in place of the "accidental aristoi" of the "fortuitous concourse of breeders"— that is, the offspring of a man and his wife, as they come together in keeping with social conventions.

At this point, Jefferson takes himself to be in agreement with Adams on the existence of a natural aristoi. He differs from Adams on its nature. For Adams, the [natural] aristoi comprise the beautiful, wealthy, wellborn, the talented, and the virtuous, or, as he says playfully in a follow-up letter (November 15, 1813), a person who can carry more than his own vote. For Jefferson, only the talented and virtuous are by nature aristoi. The other categories listed by Adams—and here Jefferson specifically singles out ambition and wealth—make up an "artificial aristocracy," which is currently in place in governmental institutions. Jefferson elaborates:

> There is . . . an artificial aristocracy founded on wealth and birth, without either virtue or talents; for with these it would belong to the first class. The natural aristocracy I consider as the most precious gift of nature for the instruction, the trusts, and government of society. And indeed it would have been inconsistent in creation to have formed man for the social state, and not to have provided virtue and wisdom enough to manage the concerns of the society. May we not even say that that form of government is the best which provides the most effectually for a pure selection of these natural aristoi into the offices of government? The artificial aristocracy is a mischievous ingredient in government, and provision should be made to prevent it's ascendency.

Key here is the adscription of "without either virtue or talent" to the category of aristoi, based on wealth and birth. That shows Jefferson thought, pace Adams and Theognis, that wealth and birth contribute nothing to the category of aristoi, properly (i.e., naturally) grasped.

Moreover, the rhetorical question near the end of the passage is crucial to grasping Jefferson's political experiment. Following Aristotle, it is not so much the form of government that matters—whether it is a government directed by one, a few, or a large number—but whether the social structure makes it probable that the true best will govern, and do so in the best interests of the citizenry, of which they are a part. The many, though equally deserving of rights and in equal possession of a moral sense, cannot be the best.[7]

The only way to allow for the best to govern is to leave governmental offices in the hands of the people, equal in moral sensitivity and deserving of natural rights. They, when given the benefit of general education, are best suited to choose the natural aristoi. Jefferson himself played a direct role in political reforms, aimed to pave the way from the natural aristoi: for example, abolition of primogeniture and entails, to allow for social equality, and freedom of religious expression, to sever the link between religiosity and rule. When the natural aristoi govern, all benefit.[8]

One scholar describes Jefferson's program as turning Aristotle upside down. For Jefferson, there are no natural slaves, only natural aristoi, as everyone meets a certain moral minimum and only a few rise above that minimum.[9] What vitiates the comparison is that Aristotle has both natural slaves and natural aristoi. He too has a moral minimum, but one that is not applicable to all persons—only to them who are Greek and free. Only among Greeks can virtue be cultivated and the path to virtue is long and arduous. The great majority of people, as non-Greeks, are hopeless moral causes.

For Jefferson, there was always the threat of the concentration of wealth and political power in the hands of a few, governing through birth or elected for life, and its concomitant degenerative effect, observed throughout history. Jefferson preferred independent and politically active citizens.[10] He thus moved to abolishing primogeniture and entails to put "the axe to the root of Pseudo-aristocracy."[11] Wishing all able persons to have access to property, he allowed for them to lose it also. As Dumas Malone aptly puts it, "The way must be left open for the fit to rise, and, by unavoidable implication, for the unfit to fall."[12]

Overall, Jefferson did not wish to leave any room in government for the artificial aristoi—even such room to prevent them from doing mischief. To give them any function in governing affairs was to invite disaster. "*I* think the best remedy is exactly that provided by all our constitutions," he writes to Adams (October 28, 1813), "to leave to the citizens the free election and separation of the aristoi from the pseudo-aristoi, of the wheat from the chaff. In general they will elect the real good and wise. In some instances, wealth may corrupt, and birth blind them; but not in sufficient degree to endanger the society."[13]

The sentiments expressed are the mature extension of sentiments shared with M. L'Abbé Arnoux decades earlier (July 19, 1789). To Arnoux, Jefferson says that the safest, most honest, and best form of government is that in which the American people can participate to their fullest capacity. The American people are not qualified to preside over the country—it is just too large—but they are qualified to elect the president; they are not qualified to legislate, but are qualified to choose legislators; they not qualified to judge matters of law, but are qualified to form juries and judge matters of fact.

Jefferson was clear that the elected officials were to be true representatives of those persons who elected them. Thus, they were not free to act in any manner whatsoever, but only as representatives. For example, in keeping with the mechanization of the times, he was fond of speaking of government as a "machine"[14]—the implication being that a time's people and the established laws, not the governors, move forward things. Governors, in effect, merely superintend the machine. In a letter to physician Benjamin Rush (January 15, 1811), Jefferson writes of a conversation with John Adams in which Jefferson said: "Were we both to die to-day, to-morrow two other names would be in the place of ours; without any change in the motion of the machinery. Its motion is from its principle, not from you or myself." Adams agreed. Again, as president, he was unceremonious—exaggeratedly so, as many scholars assert—but his unceremoniousness was not duplicity, but consistent with the sort of stewardship model of representative leadership he advocated.

With the ascendency of Enlightenment thinking in Europe, Jefferson argues toward the end of his lengthy letter on aristoi that a change is taking place.

> Science had liberated the ideas of those who read and reflect, and the American example had kindled feelings of right in the people. An insurrection has consequently begun, of science, talents and courage against rank and birth, which have fallen into contempt. It has failed in its first effort, because the mobs of the cities, the instrument used for its accomplishment, debased by ignorance, poverty and vice, could not be restrained to rational action. But the world will recover from the panic of this first catastrophe. Science is progressive, and talents and enterprise on the alert.

This scientific liberation—and here he undoubtedly has in mind contributions of his triad without equal of empiricists Bacon, Locke, and Newton—would have the result of freeing the people to recognize that those fit to govern are the natural aristoi and that "rank and birth, and tinsel-aristocracy will finally shrink into insignificance even there [in Europe]."[15]

Jefferson's political experiment, as shown by his exchange with Adams on aristoi, is truly revolutionary. He is proposing government of the best—elected by and beholden to the people. Adams, the realist and conservative, cannot do other than see things as they have been. For Adams, history shows that humans are incapable of escaping their past. They are destined by their nature to relive it. Jefferson, the idealist and progressivist, cannot do other than see things as they might be. For Jefferson, history is a guide to future avenues of potential human exploration. As he says in late-life letter to Adams (September 12, 1821), "The flames kindled on the 4th. of July 1776. have spread over too much of the globe to be extinguished by the feeble engines of despotism. On the contrary they will consume those engines, and all who work for them."

JESUS AS NATURAL ARISTOS

As I have shown in chapter 5, Jefferson offers a simple recipe for a happy, good life in several letters to his daughters. He advises daughter Martha (December 11, 1783) that the best preparation for death is a good life. Virtue and goodness render one happy and valuable to others. Talents and science too are important, as they protect persons from "the most dangerous poison of life"—boredom. "A mind always employed," he writes years later to her (May 21, 1787), "is always happy." He bids Martha to inculcate habits of goodness, truth, equipoise, and industry.[16]

In such letters, Jefferson's recipe seems to be taken from some archetype or moral exemplar. That archetype, I have stated in the previous chapter, is Jesus.[17]

In his mature years, Jefferson tended to equate *morality* with *religion*, grasped in its *true* naturalistic sense. In a letter to Robert Skipwith (August 3, 1771), brother-in-law of Jefferson's soon-to-be wife, he recommends Locke, Xenophon, Epictetus, Antoninus, Seneca, Cicero, Bolingbroke, Hume, Kames, and Sterne, among others, as persons worth reading under the rubric of "religion."[18] Years later (August 10, 1787), he recommends the Bible to Peter Carr on a par with Livy and Tacitus, and advises his nephew against accepting any biblical claims that seem to transgress the laws of nature without due examination. Some twenty years later, after acquaintance with the likes of the Unitarian minister Richard Price and Unitarian theologian Joseph Priestley, Jefferson becomes preoccupied with the persona of Jesus, whom he labels in a later letter the "greatest of all [moral] Reformers."[19]

From what we can gather of his early life, Jefferson's interest in Jesus begins in his *Literary Commonplace Book*. Jefferson copies or paraphrases over fifty passages from Lord Bolingbroke's *Philosophical Works*, where Bolingbroke rejects the miracles and divinity of Christ, divine inspiration, the fall of man, and the sacrifice of Christ for the sins of man.[20] Those passages almost certainly reflect Jefferson's early views on Christianity, which focus on what is false concerning the Christianity of his day.[21] In 1793 or shortly thereafter, Jefferson reads Priestley's *An History of the Corruption of Christianity*, which talks of the corruption of Jesus's teachings by apostles and early dignitaries of the church and influences Jefferson's own thoughts significantly. Jefferson writes his "Syllabus of an Estimate of the Merit of the Doctrines of Jesus, compared with Those of Others,"[22] which is included in his letter to Benjamin Rush on April 21, 1803. He then composes *The Philosophy of Jesus*[23] one year later—no known copy survives—and finally *The Life and Morals of Jesus of Nazareth* (a.k.a., *The Jefferson Bible*) around 1819[24]—each of which is a compilation of biblical extracts. He sums, "To the corruptions of Christianity, I am indeed opposed; but not the genuine precepts of Jesus himself." He considers himself a Christian in the sense that he is firmly committed to the true, uncontaminated precepts of Jesus.

Just what are those true precepts of Jesus and how are they to be found?

The Stripping Process

In a letter to William Short (August 4, 1820), he writes of the entanglement of the fictions of the Christian "biographers" of Jesus with "aphorisms and precepts of the purest morality":

> We find in the writings of his biographers matter of two distinct descriptions. First, a groundwork of vulgar ignorance, of things impossible, of superstitions, fanaticisms and fabrications. Intermixed with these, again, are sublime ideas of the Supreme Being, aphorisms and precepts of the purest morality and benevolence, sanctioned by a life of humility, innocence and simplicity of manners, neglect of riches, absence of worldly ambition and honors, with an eloquence and persuasiveness which have not been surpassed.

The teachings of Jesus, it seems, were intentionally poisoned with fictions.

What was the point of such profanations? He writes Adams (July 5, 1814) that the corruptors, though acknowledging the teachings of Jesus, were moved by desire of wealth and power, not truth. They built up an artificial system of principles and rules to "admit everlasting control, given employment for their order, and introduce it to profit, power and pre-eminence," because Jesus's teachings threatened their power.[25] They faced a dilemma: Obfuscate their message of moral equality and remain in power or acknowledge their moral equality and remove themselves from positions of power. They chose the former. Jefferson adds, "Rational men not being able to swallow their impious heresies, in order to force them down their throats," Jefferson writes to Samuel Kercheval (January 19, 1810), "they raise the hue and cry of infidelity, while themselves are the greatest obstacles to the advancements of the real doctrines of Jesus, and do in fact constitute the real Anti-Christ." Thus, the doctrines that have come down to us are often unintelligibly mutilated and have been further disfigured by "schismatisers,"[26] whom he identifies, in letters to Adams (August 22, 1813), as Platonists.[27] "Sweep away their gossamer fabric of factitious religion, and they would catch no more flies."

Jefferson sums his overall view succinctly in a letter to his former secretary William Short (August 4, 1820). If one takes the New Testament literally, then Jesus is a scapegrace, which Jefferson thinks is not the case. If one takes it nonliterally, then anything goes, which Jefferson is not inclined to accept. There is to his thinking only one alternative, and a reasonable one. Jefferson opts for taking it literally, once it is stripped of its scandalous untruths—its supernaturalism, falsification, and hyperboles.

Jefferson admits to Benjamin Rush (April 21, 1803) that he himself has been eager to embark on such a program of stripping away fictions from fact in the New Testament. "At the short intervals since these conversations, when I could justifiably abstract my mind from public affairs, the subject has been under my contemplation." The presidency has gotten in the way.

How precisely is this stripping to be done to preserve the true nature of Jesus and his teachings? It is simply through the "free exercise of reason," Jefferson explains in his 1820 letter to Short:

> When Livy or Siculus . . . tell us things which coincide with our experience
> of the order of nature, we credit them on their word, and place their narra-
> tions among the records of credible history. But when they tell us of calves

> speaking, of statues sweating blood, and other things against the course of nature, we reject these as fables, not belonging to history. In like manner, when an historian, speaking of a character well known and established on satisfactory testimony imputes to it things incompatible with that character, we reject them without hesitation, and assent to that only of which we have better evidence. . . . This free exercise of reason is all I ask for the vindication of the character of Jesus.

Once stripped of its falsifications, one is left with a tableau vivant of the life of Jesus insofar as we can know of the life of Jesus insofar as we can know of the life of Jesus from the sources available.

When such an appeal-to-experience test is applied to the New Testament, he continues to Short, one strips away testimony—based on vulgar ignorance, things impossible, superstitions, fanaticism, and fabrications—and is left with sublime ideas of a supreme being, aphorisms and precepts of purest morality, a life of humility, innocence, honors, and a personage of eloquence and persuasiveness. In sum, testimony of a particular character must be consistent with the laws of nature, and it must be consistent with other reports of that character.[28]

In addition to Bolingbroke's critique of Christianity, it is without question that Jefferson has maverick clergyman Conyers Middleton's book on miracles[29]—he cites him in a letter to Adams (August 22, 1813)—and perhaps also David Hume's essay "On Miracles" as his measuring sticks. Both sensibly and soberly argue, apropos of any reported miracle, which is essentially a violation of a law of nature, that it is always much more probable that one's testimony of the "miracle" is erroneous, rather than that a law of nature has been transgressed.[30]

Overall, the project, Jefferson boasts to Adams (October 12, 1813), is as easy as distinguishing "diamonds in a dunghill."[31] He expands on that in a letter to patriot and Philadelphian Charles Thomson (January 9, 1816). "I . . . have made a wee-little book from the same materials [i.e., from the Bible], which I call the Philosophy of Jesus; it is a paradigma of his doctrines, made by cutting the texts out of the book, and arranging them on the pages of a blank book, in a certain order of time or subject."

Jefferson's aims are, thus, historical and normative. First, he wishes to rescue the character of Jesus from political opportunists. Second, he wishes, through success in his historical aim, to preserve for posterity, as he writes in 1820 to Short, "the outlines of a system of the most sublime morality which has ever fallen from the lips of man." It follows that Jefferson is undertaking a project of sweeping, prodigious consequence. Historically, he aims to clean up the falsities and obfuscations of opportunistic and politically motivated "Platonizers" and present the real Jesus. Normatively, given the success of the stripping project, Jefferson aims to leave humanity with a précis of the greatest system of morality. Christ is, to Jefferson, a historical figure, not son of a god, and he and his teachings are matters for historians and ethicians, not opportunistic theologians.[32]

Jefferson sums in a letter to John Adams (October 12, 1813) the results of his stripping project: "The principle of . . . the Christian [is] the love of God."

Jesus and His Doctrines

When he turned to the New Testament, Jefferson did not expect to find a complete system of moral beliefs, given his belief that Jesus died before reaching intellectual maturity.[33] He writes to William Short (October 31, 1819):

> The greatest of all the reformers of the depraved religion of his own country, was Jesus of Nazareth. Abstracting what is really his from the rubbish in which it is buried, easily distinguished by its luster from the dross of his biographers, and as separable from that as the diamond from the dunghill, we have the outlines of a system of the most sublime morality which has ever fallen from the lips of man; outlines which it is lamentable he did not live to fill up. Epictetus and Epicurus give laws for governing ourselves, Jesus as supplement of the duties and charities we owe to others.

Jefferson expatiates on the last point in an earlier letter to Benjamin Rush (April 21, 1803). The ancient philosophers, especially Epicurus and the Stoics, taught us how to act in matters purely self-regarding, but Jesus taught us how to act purely and perfectly in other-regarding matters.[34] First, his teachings went much beyond the ancient philosophers and Jews by "inculcating universal philanthropy, not only to kindred and friends, to neighbors and countrymen, but to all mankind, gathering all into one family, under the bonds of love, charity, peace, common wants and common aids." Next, he moved morality to the heart of man, so to speak, as he showed that actions alone were not the province of morality. One's thoughts too dictated the sort of person one was. Finally, he preached of a life beyond the grave.

Jesus's teaching, Jefferson asserts, aimed at all men, but mostly the Jews. "[Jesus] was the herald of truths reformatory of the religions of mankind in general," writes Jefferson to statesman and lawyer George Thatcher (January 26, 1824), "but more immediately of that of his own countrymen, impressing them with more sublime and more worthy ideas of the Supreme being, teaching them the doctrine of a future state of rewards and punishments, and inculcating the love of mankind, instead of the anti-social spirit with which the Jews viewed all other nations."

One of Jefferson's most revealing passages occurs in a letter to Bishop James Madison[35] (January 31, 1800). In this letter, he shows that Jesus's moral teachings have laid the groundwork for liberality and self-government through his teachings of self-love and, especially, benevolence-guided other-love. Following the philosopher Adam Weishaupt, Jefferson asserts that Jesus's object was to "promote this perfection of the human character."

> That his intention was simply to reinstate natural religion, & by diffusing the light of his morality, to teach us to govern ourselves. His precepts are the love of god and the love of our neighbor. And by teaching innocence of conduct, he expected to place men in their natural state of liberty & equality. Wishaupt [*sic*] says, no one ever laid a surer foundation for liberty than our grand master, Jesus of Nazareth. He believes that the free masons were originally possessed of the true principles & objects of Christianity, & have still preserved some of them by tradition, but much disfigured. The means he proposes to effect this improvement of human nature are "to enlighten men, to correct their morals & inspire them with benevolence. Secure of our success, sais he, we abstain from violent commotions. To have foreseen the happiness of posterity & to have prepared it by irreproachable means, suffices for out felicity. The tranquility of our consciences is not troubled by the reproach of aiming at the ruin or overthrow of states or thrones."

One must be cautious here. The letter is composed in 1800 and the subject, Jefferson admits, is new to him at the time. So, one cannot assume that he uptakes entirely Weishaupt's views. Nonetheless, Weishaupt has given him much over which to mull.

What Weishaupt asserted that resonated most with Jefferson, likely because it affirmed his own suspicions on Jesus's teachings, is that there can be no correct notion of morally appropriate action without benevolence. Here it is profitable to distinguish *benevolence* (well-wishing) from *beneficence* (well-doing). On the one hand, strictly speaking, one can act beneficently without acting benevolently—when one does the right thing for the wrong reason, for example, helping out a needy person only to extract some information from that person. On the other hand, one can be benevolent and disengaged—for example, as when, as Aristotle says, a virtuously inclined person sleeps all the time.[36] When Jefferson lauds Jesus for preaching benevolence, he is at once lauding benevolently motivated activities—beneficence incited by benevolence. Intention matters. So too does action.

Benevolence was also a significant element in the moral-sense ethics of the philosophers Hutcheson, Hume, and Kames.[37] For Francis Hutcheson, benevolence was foundational—the basis of virtuous activity: "All Actions suppos'd to flow from such Affections, appear morally Good, if while they are benevolent toward some Persons, they be not pernicious to others."[38] David Hume writes: "Nothing can bestow more merit on any human creature than the sentiment of benevolence in an eminent degree; and *that* a *part*, at least of its merit arises from its tendency to promote the interests of our species, and bestow happiness on human society."[39] For Lord Kames, benevolence is not foundational—a part of justice—but merely supererogatory: "Benevolent and generous actions are not objects of this peculiar sense [of justice]. Hence, such actions, though considered as *fit* and *right* to be done, are not however considered to be our *duty*, but as virtuous actions beyond what is strictly our duty."[40]

Benevolence, Jefferson's critique of the ancient ethicians shows, plays a significant role in his ethics. They were deficient not in that they failed to recognize other-concern in ethical action, but in that they failed to recognize benevolently motivated other-concern in ethical action. Given the weight Jefferson places on benevolence in his critique of ancient ethicians, it is reasonable to conclude that it was foundational, not supererogatory for him. Jefferson's castigation of the ancients, then, aims at their notion of other-concern, which was fundamentally important because it led to an agent's psychical equanimity through virtuous activity.

Jefferson offers a précis of Jesus's teaching in a letter to physician Benjamin Waterhouse (June 26, 1822), cofounder of Harvard's Medical School. He compares the doctrines of Jesus, which he lists as three, to those of John Calvin, which he lists as five. On the "great points" on which he tried to reform the religion of the Jews, Jefferson writes. Jesus has taught:

1. That there is one only God, and he all perfect.
2. That there is a future state of rewards and punishments.
3. That to love God with all thy heart and thy neighbor as thyself, is the sum of religion.[41]

Calvin and Athanasius have taught:

1. That there are three Gods.
2. That good works, or the love of our neighbor, are nothing.
3. That faith is every thing, and the more incomprehensible the proposition, the more merit in its faith.
4. That reason in religion is of unlawful use.
5. That God, from the beginning, elected certain individuals to be saved, and certain others to be damned; and that no crimes of the former can damn them; no virtues of the latter save.

What Jefferson found most disobliging about Calvinism were its trinitarianism and its predestinationism. To Pennsylvania delegate James Smith (December 8, 1822), Jefferson objects that deity as trinity is a "hocus-pocus phantasm of a god like another Cerberus, with one body and three heads."[42] He continues to Benjamin Waterhouse (June 26, 1822), "Had the doctrines of Jesus been preached always as pure as they came from his lips, the whole civilized world would now have been Christian." In America, "this blessed country of free inquiry and belief," Unitarianism is on the move. "I trust that there is not a *young man* now living in the United States who will not die a Unitarian."[43] The emphasis on "young man" is key. The older generations of men, ensconced in the skeins of tradition, must either die off or fade away, so that truth can come to light.[44] To fellow Virginian Thomas Parker, Jefferson objects to predestinationism by asserting that good deeds, not foreordained luck, make a man. "Were I to be the founder of a new sect I would call them Apriarians, and, after the example of the bee, advise them to extract the honey of every sect. My fundamental principle would be the reverse of Calvin's, that we are to be saved by our good works which are within our power, and not by our faith which is not within our power" (May 15, 1819).

Overall, Jefferson's embrace of Christianity is a commitment to Jesus's principles of "equal and exact justice to all men." That is Jesus's message, in a nutshell and stripped of its corruptions. Nonetheless Jefferson is not committed to everything Jesus said. "It is not to be understood that I am with [Jesus] in all of his doctrines," he tells William Short (April 13, 1820). "I am a Materialist; he takes the side of Spiritualism; he preaches the efficacy of repentance towards forgiveness of sin; I require a counterpoise of good works to redeem it, etc., etc." Here Jefferson shows the influence of ancient moralists—the materialism of Aristotle, the Stoics, and Epicurus and rejection of the Christian notion that repentance alone is sufficient for redemption.[45]

Jefferson sums his commitment to Christianity in a letter to Vermont politician Moses Robinson (March 23, 1801) and reveals what might be taken as a political agenda. "The Christian religion, when divested of the rages in which they have enveloped it, and brought it to the original purity and simplicity of its benevolent institutor, is a religion of all others most friendly to liberty, science, and the freest expansion of the human mind." The statement is, however, not propagandist. Jefferson, we have seen, is an out-and-out progressivist concerning politics, science, and morality. He clearly believes representative government—founded on liberty, science, and freedom of expression—is an improvement over ancient notions of democracy. To assert that Christianity best aligns itself with such republicanism is, then, merely to assert that advances in morality must accompany advances in government. Christianity, as preached by the pure teachings of Christ, countenances the liberty needed for such advances.

The character of Jesus is a much more snarled issue than his teachings, for too little is known of Jesus. To Dr. Benjamin Rush (April 22, 1803), Jefferson says, "[Jesus's] parentage was obscure; his condition poor; his education null; his natural endowments great; his life correct and innocent: he was meek, benevolent, patient, firm, disinterested, & of the sublimest eloquence." He goes on to add that Jesus wrote nothing and had no prominent disciple to write for him. Put to death in his prime and after only about three years of preaching, there was no occasion "for developing a complete system of morals." To William Short (August 4, 1820), Jefferson acknowledges Jesus's own belief in his divine nature. "That Jesus did not mean to impose himself on mankind as the son of God, physically speaking, I have been convinced by the writings of men more learned than myself in that lore. But that he might conscientiously believe himself inspired from above, is very possible." Though he might have spoken of himself of the son of God, he meant nothing more than that he was god-inspired.

In all, Jefferson esteemed Jesus's teachings above those of the ancients and far above those of the Jews. Though he knew little of Jesus the man, it is still reasonable to conclude that Jesus was, for Jefferson, le beau ideal of a natural aristos—the model moralist of Jefferson's ideal republic.

JEFFERSONIAN TARTUFFERY?

In spite of stating he is an Epicurean,[46] that Jesus's "system of morality was the most benevolent & sublime probably that has ever been taught,"[47] and Stoic perfectionism is untenable because a "just equilibrium of the passions" is impossible,[48] Jefferson's ethical views owe more to Stoicism than to Epicurus or even to Jesus. In this final section, I explain that it is this sort of intellectual "Tartuffery" that has made him a favorite target for many overly critical historians today.

Jefferson's Stoic-like thinking on nature and human nature significantly influenced his manner of living—much more so than did the teachings of Jesus or Epicurus. For some, hostile criticism is a matter of evening out the depiction of the saintly Jefferson, characteristic of early and mid-twentieth-century historians. For others, belittling Jefferson has become a way of life. The issue is almost always Tartuffery—the great divide between his words and manner of living. I cite merely three of numerous illustrations. Robert Dawidoff calls Jefferson a "limousine liberal" insofar as Jefferson's avowed egalitarian liberalism did not influence his lavish personal life.[49] Howard Temperly says that Jefferson was a hypocrite on key matters—for example, slavery, acquisitiveness, and self-sufficiency—perhaps more than any other major American figure.[50] Peter Onuf calls Jefferson a "monster of self-deception."[51]

One way to justify the hypocrisy is to say Jefferson appropriated the teachings of Jesus for political reasons—that is, he had a political agenda. Bitter party conflicts between Federalists and Republicans throughout his political career did much to stain Jefferson's name and character. Federalists charged Jefferson with being a "narrow-minded agrarianist" who eschewed commerce and industry, a Francophile, and one indifferent to religion or an atheist with a personal war against religion.[52] That is the stance of one author, who writes of the political agenda behind his moral reformations and his newfound embrace of Christianity:

> Jefferson was motivated by more than just a simple wish to rebut those who were assailing his character on religious grounds. He was also responding to another problem that was of deep concern to him: how to guarantee the per-

petuation of republican government in the United States at a time when, as it seems to him, political factionalism and social disharmony were threatening to undermine its basic foundations. Jefferson's solution to this problem was an effort to foster the social harmony that he considered essential for the survival of American's republican experiment by formulating a moralistic version of Christianity on which all men of good will could agree.[53]

Thus, his "Syllabus" and *The Philosophy of Jesus*, one could argue, were tailored to his republican principles.

That is to put the cart before the horse, however. It was Jefferson's cosmological thinking, which was in large part Stoical, that fashioned his thinking on human flourishing and the duties men had to themselves, others, and deity. His mature political thinking was the result of his normative naturalism—central components of which were Christian piety and benevolence. For Jefferson, liberal republicanism, which was government for and of the people, was not the prompting for his moral vision, but the result of his mature thinking on Stoicized, egalitarian Christianity.[54] Jefferson writes to James Fishback (September 27, 1809), "The interests of society require the observation of those moral precepts only in which all religions agree, (for all forbid us to murder, steal, plunder, or bear false witness) and that we should not intermeddle with the particular dogmas in which all religions differ, and which are totally unconnected with morality."

Also one might also argue that Jefferson's presumed Tartuffery was the result of his intellectualism. He had an intellectualist's curiosity to theological and moral issues. Like many professors of religious studies and philosophy today who are chiefly, if not wholly, interested in, say, what precisely were Priestley's views on deity or Bolingbroke's views on morality, Jefferson, in his letters pertaining to his "Syllabus" and two works on Jesus, was more interested in discovering Jesus's true views—that is, the true morality of the man—than in incorporating those views into his life in a consistent manner. Tartuffery, thus, is explicable by and excusable because of his intellectualism. Consequently, as he was motivated by the intellectual process of discovery, he should not be held responsible for failing to live up to those beliefs discovered.

Jefferson was plainly an intellectualist and he had an intellectualist's approach to numerous issues throughout his life. Slavery is a prominent example. That is because he approached nature as did a scientist, and that required coolness and emotional distancing.

Still more needs to be said. Jefferson was genuinely drawn to Jesus's teachings. They attracted him due to their simplicity and their emphasis on beneficence. There they had every advantage over abstruse and recondite moral treatises—like, say, Cicero's *Tusculan Disputations*. Simplicity was significant, because Jesus's teachings could readily be assimilated and instantiated and because morality for Jefferson was a matter of the heart, not of the head.[55] Stripped of their corruptions, they were comprehensible, accessible, and agreeable to every person. "We all agree in the obligation of the moral precepts of Jesus," he tells Fishback in the 1809 letter.

In short, Jesus's teachings, because of their simplicity and emphasis on benevolence, squared perfectly with Jefferson's view of an innate moral sense. They were accessible to both professor and plowman,[56] and they were reinforcements of everything everyone already knew. In short, when stripped of the corruptions of power-hungry exegetes, the doctrines of Jesus coincided neatly with the precepts innately implanted in the human heart by deity. Those precepts were to be at the bottom of any society, constructed with the aim of human well-being.

In sum, if Jefferson can be accused of Tartuffery, it is because he preached the naturalized doctrines of Jesus, though he lived pursuant to the moral principles of a Stoicized Jesus. Like the Stoics and pace Jesus, Jefferson was fanatical about the pursuit and acquisition of practical knowledge. Like the Stoics and pace Jesus, Jefferson did not give up his wealth and station in life. Like the Stoics and pace Jesus, Jefferson believed that the good life was a life in agreement with nature—belonging only to this, not another, world. Of course, Jefferson never said that the Jesus's doctrines comprised the whole of morality, but only the purest part, relating to duties to others.

Thus, Jefferson's avowed Tartuffery is best explicated by his Stoicism. Jefferson made full purchase of Stoic authenticity and made a lifelong effort to be the same person in public as in private—that is, to be uncontaminated by the jobbery of his peers. We recall that the Stoic Panaetius mentions, among his four personae, one's real-life circumstances.[57] One born into extreme poverty is penurious and ought to accept his penury. One born into wealth is wealthy and ought to accept his wealth. That is not to say that neither can work to improve his station throughout life—the former, by improving his wealth; the latter, by sharing it—so long as in doing either, neither person harms himself or others along the way.[58] The Christian notion that wealth was an obstacle to the possibility of salvation did not enter into Jefferson's formula for a life well lived.

Jefferson was certainly wellborn. He never denied that. Yet he viewed it as a part of him like a pug nose was a part of Socrates. His wellborn status was not something to lament and not something to celebrate. He just happened to be born into wealth and status. Though such things were mere accidents—as Aristotle would say, goods external to him, but goods nonetheless—these real-life circumstances were, as Panaetius stated, as much of the person Thomas Jefferson was as were, say, the choices he had made throughout his life. In short, what appears to be Tartuffery is authenticity of the Panaetian sort.

Scottish philosopher Francis Hutcheson, an early age-mate of Jefferson and whose works were studied by Jefferson, agrees. He argues that a person's wealth can contribute to his happiness and need not be a bane to others. Moreover, people have an external right to wealth, he argues, for even if it can be shown that one wealthy person, hoarding money, is detrimental to society, the denial of wealth to all men does more harm than good: "The external Right of the Miser to his useless Hoards, is founded also on this, that allowing Persons by Violence, or without Consent of the Acquirer, to take the Use of his Acquisitions, would discourage Industry, and take away all the Pleasures of Generosity, Honour, Charity, which cease when Men can be forc'd to these Actions."[59] The argument is persuasive. Forced generosity is not generosity, and the wealth of one person can be a great boon to social betterment and the good of many. Jefferson used his wealth to great benefit of his fellow men, and eventually and unfortunately to his own detriment. That possession of wealth is no cause for moral upbraiding—"'twas from heaven, and could be no reproach"—is a point also made by Jefferson's favorite novelist, Reverend Laurence Sterne. In "The Parable of the Rich Man and Lazarus," Sterne writes, "Riches are not the cause of dissipation, but the corrupt calculation of the world, in making riches the balance for honour, for virtue, and for every thing that is great and good."[60]

If Jefferson is to be accused of hypocrisy, let him be accused of hypocrisy because he expressed allegiance with Epicurus and greatest praise for the uncorrupted teachings of Jesus, while he lived life mostly as a Stoic.

Nonetheless, what is far too frequently neglected by caustic and stiff critics is Jefferson's generosity and magnanimity—other staples of Stoic thinking. Jefferson was generous and magnanimous. Giving, without concern of a return, was a way of life for him. Though often massively in debt much of the time, Jefferson gave often and freely to others.[61] He allowed unexpected visitors to Monticello to stay beyond a reasonable welcome. He sold his personal library to the Library of Congress, after the British burned its library in 1814. He frequently introduced new plants and animals into America—seeds of Malta grass, cork-oak acorns, rice to South Carolina, olive trees to southern states, and Merino sheep.[62] He believed in sharing, not hording, ideas. For instance, he refused to patent his innovatively improved plow mold board, his dry dock, or his hemp machine.[63] He was a lifelong patron of the useful sciences and a lifelong member of the American Philosophical Society, since becoming a member in 1780. He labored in drafting numerous bills over his lifetime. He mentored young men who wished to advance themselves through learning, and he made his library freely available to them. He spent his final years overseeing construction of the University of Virginia in an effort to set the standard for American secular education. Finally, though he frequently complained of political ostentation, double-dealings, and boastfulness, he devoted his salad days in service to his state and nation at expense of his personal life.[64] Those persons who rashly dub Jefferson a hypocrite because of his manner of living always seem, and conveniently so, to disacknowledge his generosity and magnanimity.

Jefferson was morally precocious—perhaps because he lost his father early in life. In a letter to grandson Thomas Jefferson Randolph (November 24, 1808), Jefferson states some of the difficulties he had faced in his early life that led him to reflect on the choice of a life of achievement or a life honesty and goodness, perhaps not unlike Hercules's choice in Greek mythology.[65] It was Jefferson's fate to have been exposed early on to horse racers, card players, foxhunters, scientists, professionals, and dignified men. Often, after the death of a fox, the victory of a horse, or an eloquent debate at the bar in the council of the nation, he would ask himself whether he was better off as a horse jockey, foxhunter, orator, or honest advocate of his country's rights. "These little returns into ourselves," he tells his grandson, "this self-catechising habit, is not trifling, nor useless, but leads to the prudent selection and steady pursuits of what is right."[66] Self-catechizing too was a staple of Stoic thinking.[67]

Jefferson, it seems, had no misgivings about his manner of living. Some eighteen years later and months before his death, he related to his grandson Thomas Jefferson Randolph (February 8, 1826)—who was then involved in a lottery to help his grandfather free himself from his massive debt (over $100,000 worth in his day)—that he has had a long life "with fewer circumstances of affliction than most men." He has had good health, a competence for reasonable wants, usefulness to fellow citizens and the esteem of most of them, no complaint against the world, and a family that has blessed him.

Consequently, Jefferson not only adopted views of nature and man that were Stoical, he also lived his life as a Stoic—in pursuit of practical knowledge and in acceptance, not rejection, of the gifts nature had bestowed on him. As he related to his grandson, he used those gifts throughout his life to the best of his capacity to advance the situation of his fellow human beings.

PART 4

JEFFERSON ON EDUCATION

CHAPTER 8

"UNITING MERIT WITH . . . LEARNING"

Jefferson's Philosophy of Education[1]

*"Enlighten the people generally, and tyranny and oppressions of
body and mind will vanish like evil spirits at the dawn of day."*
—TJ to P. S. Dupont de Nemours,
April 24, 1816

efferson's republicanism was critically dependent on general education for the general citizenry and higher education for those who would
govern. Only in such a manner could tyranny be forestalled. "Every government degenerates when trusted to the rulers of the people alone. The people
themselves therefore are its only safe depositories. And to render even them
safe, their minds must be improved to a certain degree."[2] This is not the general
Rousseauian view of the natural goodness of all persons but instead a general
observation—driven by scrutinizing history and prodded by reading works
such as philosophers Lord Kames's *Essays on the Principles of Morality and
Natural Religion* and A. L. C. Destutt de Tracy's *Commentaire sur l'esprit
des lois de Montesquieu*—that a structure must be put into place to guarantee,
insofar as such things can be guaranteed, that natural rights will be preserved
and that humans can flourish.

I have been arguing throughout that Jefferson's republicanism was a
people-first, mostly bottom-up political vision with a moral underpinning. His
purchase of Scottish moral-sense philosophy showed that all persons were
morally equal in that all persons were endowed with a moral sensory faculty
that allowed each to be equally capable of morally correct decisions. His purchase of ancient eudaemonism showed that those best fitted to the highest
offices of governance were among those who most distinguished themselves

211

through virtue and talent—that is, the natural aristoi. The teachings of Jesus, a true natural aristos, emphasized that other-concern must be motivated by unalloyed benevolence, and Jesus himself proved to be a shining and easily accessed exemplar of moral rectitude.

Political reform was insufficient for moral advance. Educational reform too was needed.[3]

In the final three chapters of this book, I examine Jefferson's educational views. This chapter contains an analysis of his general philosophy of education by enumerating some of its most fundamental principles, applicable to both elementary and higher education. I then turn to certain other issues, related to education, under the rubric *collectanea*. In the last two chapters, I examine Jefferson's views of general education (chapter 9) and higher education (chapter 10).

GENERAL AIMS OF EDUCATION

In an 1814 letter to John Adams (July 5), Jefferson tells of the lamentable state of education in America at the time. The postrevolutionary youth "acquire all learning in their mother's womb." They no longer need books. Experience is deplored or neglected; all knowledge is deemed innate. Petty academies are sprouting up in every neighborhood, "where one or two men, possessing Latin, and sometimes Greek, a knolege of the globes, and the first six books of Euclid, imagine and communicate this as the sum of science." Their pupils are exposed to "the theatre of the world" with learning sufficient to alienate them from serious pursuits and insufficient to make a contribution to science. "Every folly must run it's round," he concludes.

Jefferson's complaint is roughly that students are given a finishing-school education and then deem themselves educated and ready for the world. Education, for Jefferson, is broad and visceral—it caters to the whole person and involves the whole community. Most significant, it is ongoing.

Jefferson's educational views are spelled out neatly in several bills, a report, and selected correspondence: four bills, which were begun in spirit in 1776 and proposed a few years later to the General Assembly of Virginia (1779), Jefferson's "Bill for Establishing a System of Public Education" (1817), his "Rockfish Gap Report" (1818), and selected letters to correspondents—for example, Carr, Banister, Munford, Adams, Cabell, Burwell, Brazier, and Breckinridge.

Late in 1776, Jefferson began work on a committee—comprising Thomas Ludwell Lee, George Mason, Edmund Pendleton, George Wythe, and Jefferson—to revise the laws of Virginia. Lee died shortly thereafter and Mason asked to be excused, due to insufficient competence in legal matters, so all the work fell on the remaining three. Jefferson certainly did more than his share of the work. The three lawyers, working independently most of the time, drafted 126 bills for the General Assembly to consider.[4]

Four of the bills, Bills 79 to 82, were drafted by Jefferson to have a noticeable effect on educational reform for participatory republicanism; specifically, Bills 79 through 81 aimed directly at educational reform. Jefferson writes in his "Autobiography," "I consider four of these bills, passed or reported as forming a system by which every fibre would be eradicated of ancient or future aristocracy; and a foundation laid for a government truly republican." He adds:

> The first bill proposed to lay off every county into Hundreds or Wards, of a proper size and population for a school, in which reading, writing, and common arithmetic should be taught; and that the whole state should be divided into 24 districts, in each of which should be a school for classical learning, grammar, geography, and the higher branches of numerical arithmetic. The second bill proposed to amend the constitution of Wm. & Mary College, to enlarge it's sphere of science, and to make it in fact an University. The third was for the establishment of a library.[5]

"A Bill for the More General Diffusion of Knowledge" (Bill 79)—the most significant bill for pedagogy, "the most important bill of our whole code," and the surest "foundation . . . for the preservation of freedom and happiness"[6]— was drafted by Jefferson in the fall of 1778, and it contained the rudiments of a philosophy of education as well as a full-scale plan of implementation of that philosophy.[7] "A Bill for Amending the Constitution of the College of William and Mary" (Bill 80) was intended to upgrade the curriculum of the college, make it a state university of the highest rank, and financially stabilize it—the last being the work of Pendleton. "A Bill for Establishing a Public Library" (Bill 81) was intended to establish a library for scholars, elected officials, and talented citizens. None of those three bills, directly aiming at educational reform, passed as originally drafted. "A Bill for Establishing Religious Freedom" (Bill 82) did pass in 1786 and was called "The Statute of Virginia for Religious Freedom" on Jefferson's tombstone. It set a precedent for secular education by disestablishing the link between the state and any particular religious affiliation. Of these bills, Jefferson scholar Gilbert Chinard writes, "One may state here without fear of contradiction that no system so complete, so logically constructed and so well articulated had ever been proposed in any country in the world."[8]

Jefferson, it is clear, thought long and hard throughout his life on education. In its most general aim, educational reform toward public education, like political reform, served the role of promoting human flourishing.[9] In his "Rockfish Gap Report" of 1818, Jefferson lists the aims of elementary education and then the aims of higher education, yet nowhere does he give an exhaustive list of the general aims of education.

In a letter to Senator Joseph C. Cabell (September 9, 1817), Jefferson outlines six features of education, some of which express pedagogical aims.

1) Basic education should be available to all.
2) Education should be tax-supported.
3) Education should be free from religious dictation.
4) The educational system should be controlled at the local level.
5) The upper levels of education should feature free inquiry.
6) The mentally proficient should be enabled to pursue education to the highest levels at public expense.

In a letter to future son-in-law Thomas Mann Randolph Jr. (August 27, 1786), Jefferson he advises the young man to educate himself in four ways. Randolph should begin with languages and mathematics, for languages exercise youthful memory and prevent "habits of idleness" and mathematics "stores the mind with truths" that are useful in other sciences. Next, he should attend lectures in astronomy, natural philosophy, natural history, anatomy, botany, and chemistry and focus on any of them that most fascinates him. Third, he should read history in his spare time, after dinner, for the mind too needs its rest and history exercises mostly the memory, so it is ideal after dinner. Last he should keep fit his body through simple diet and rigorous walking, for "it is of little consequence to store the mind with science if the body be permitted to become debilitated."

Tyranny and the Rights of Men

Jefferson trusted the people, suitably educated, to govern themselves. "Wherever the people are well-informed, they can be trusted with their own government," he writes to philosopher Richard Price (January 8, 1789). "Whenever things got so far wrong as to attract their notice, they may be relied on to set them to rights."

Yet the addendum "wherever the people are well-informed" is critical. It is more than a commitment to educate all so that each can self-sufficiently fill his needs. In spite of numerous passages in which Jefferson writes of his faith in the people,[10] Jefferson's trust in the people was, for the most part, not unconditional, but it might be grasped syllogistically: One must trust the people or the governors; one cannot trust the governors; therefore, one must trust the people. He writes to Baron F. H. Alexander von Humboldt (June 13, 1817): "The first principle of republicanism is, that the *lex-majoris partis* is the fundamental law of every society of individuals of equal rights; to consider the will of the society enounced by the majority of a single vote, as sacred as if unanimous, is the first of all lessons in importance, yet the last which is thoroughly learnt. This law once disregarded, no other remains but that of force, which ends necessarily in military despotism." In *Notes on the State of Virginia*, Jefferson says that nothing is more important than rendering the people "the safe . . . [and] the ultimate, guardians of their own liberty." Their safety is best secured by the study of history, for "by apprising them of the past will enable them to judge of the future," and making them fit judges of ambition, history will fashion them fit judges of their governors. "Every government degenerates when trusted to the rulers of the people alone. The people themselves therefore are its only safe depositories. And to render even them safe their minds must be improved to a certain degree."[11] The notion is iterated in Section 1 of "A Bill for the More General Diffusion of Knowledge." Jefferson writes: "Whereas it appeareth that however certain forms of government are better calculated than others to protect individuals in the free exercise of their natural rights, and are at the same time themselves better guarded against degeneracy, yet experience hath shewn, that even under the best forms, those entrusted with power have, in time and by slow operations, perverted it into tyranny."[12]

The passages are gravid with implications. Jefferson acknowledges that political power is not merely insidious, but, in time, invidious. Irrespective of the type of government, there must be some check on political ambition. That check can only be the people themselves.

The passages also clearly illustrate why Jefferson's republicanism is an "experiment," as he was wont to call it.[13] He is in no position to assert categorically that government for and of the people must, or even can, work. Yet experience has shown that governments in which officials are not elected by and beholden to the people do not work—because they are ultimately unresponsive to the needs of the people. If citizens' rights are to be respected and defended and if governors are not to govern in their own best interest, something new must be tried.

Though his republicanism was mostly founded through eliminative induction—he could trust the people or the wealthy and wellborn, and the wealthy and wellborn have shown over time that they govern merely to suit their own interests—Jefferson did not share John Adams's pessimism apropos of the human condition. Instead, he adhered to the unflagging optimism of many Enlightenment thinkers, as he trusted that each generation of humans was advancing, intellectually and morally, beyond the generation prior to it. What prompted the rapid progress of humans in the seventeenth and eighteenth centuries, he was sure, was their unflinching belief that liberty was the bedfellow of progress.

In a letter to lawyer and mentor George Wythe (August 13, 1786), Jefferson states emphatically that the masses need to be educated to be capable of recognizing and preventing political decay:

> I think by far the most important bill in our whole code is that for the diffusion of knowledge among the people. No other sure foundation can be devised, for the preservation of freedom and happiness. . . . Preach, my dear Sir, a crusade against ignorance; establish & improve the law for educating the common people. Let our countrymen know that the people alone can protect us against these evils, and that the tax which will be paid for this purpose is not more than the thousandth part of what will be paid to kings, priests & nobles who will rise up among us if we leave the people in ignorance.

General diffusion of knowledge functions in accordance with the principle that each person should be educated to his needs. Only when all citizens have some measure of education and a large degree of independence can a republic be assured that legislators and administrators will do their best to protect the rights and liberties of their fellow citizens. He writes in Baconian fashion to academician George Ticknor (November 25, 1817):

> I am now entirely absorbed in endeavors to effect the establishment of a general system of education in my native state . . . [having] elementary schools . . . collegiate institutions . . . [and a] university. . . . My hopes however are kept in check by the ordinary character of our state legislatures, the members of which do not generally possess information enough to perceive the important truths, that knowledge is power, that knowledge is safety, and that knowledge is happiness.

In brief letter to politician Ebenezer Hazard (February 18, 1781), Jefferson congratulates his correspondent for his efforts in putting to press the historical and State papers he has collected. Jefferson mourns the loss of those papers that were casualties of the war but applauds Hazard's efforts to preserve what remains, not by lock and chain, but by multiplying their number and making them accessible to the public. The public availability of such information is a significant gift to future generations—additional evidence of Jefferson's beneficence and regard for truth—and itself a check against future corruption.

Each According to His Needs

Thomas Jefferson never wavered on his view that general education was the key to thriving, participatory republicanism. Enlighten only the well-to-do, and there will be no check on their appetites. "Enlighten the people generally," he writes to his friend Pierre Samuel Dupont de Nemours (April 24, 1816), "and tyranny and oppressions of body and mind will vanish like evil spirits at the dawn of day." To George Washington (January 4, 1786), he says, "It is an axiom in my mind that our liberty can never be safe but in the hands of the people themselves, and that too of the people with a certain degree of education."

As we have seen, Jeffersonian republicanism is "government by its citizens in mass, acting directly and personally, according to rules established by the majority." He adds in a manner that shows republicanism is an ideal to be approximated—not attained—"Every . . . government is more or less republican, in proportion as it has in its composition more or less of this ingredient of the direct action of its citizens."[14] For republican government to function well, its citizens need to be happy, well-rounded, politically active, and especially free. Human thriving, thus, is not merely a matter of economic prosperity, as it seems to be for Americans today, but requires political liberty.[15] The aim was not filling up—namely, putting knowledge into bodies lacking it—but sallying forth. Writes scholar James Carpenter: "For Jefferson, the finished product—the student venturing into the real world—was the ultimate goal of education. The practical application for republican citizens was their ability to function in the body politic."[16]

Jefferson here recognizes two classes of citizens, the laborers and the learned, and two levels of education to accommodate them.[17] The laborers are the majority and are divided roughly into husbandmen, manufacturers, and craftsmen. They need to conduct business to sustain and improve their domestic affairs. For that, they need to have full access to primary education. The learned are those destined to higher education—comprising college-level and university-level education—only the latter being readied to conduct the affairs of the nation or to contribute to the advances of science.

Needs are not all personal. People are, for Jefferson as they are for Aristotle, "political animals," and thus they have political duties. To fit and function in a stable, thriving democracy, each citizen is expected to know and assume a participatory role to the best of his capacity. That requires some degree of self-understanding, and self-understanding is best facilitated through education. In an 1814 letter to Peter Carr (September 7), Jefferson writes, "It is the duty of [our country's] functionaries, to provide that every citizen in it should receive an education proportioned to the conditions and pursuits of his life."

In all, education functions to gratify the idiosyncratic needs of all citizens as private persons, to ready all citizens for some level of participation in governmental affairs, and to prepare the elite for participation in the high-level governing or in science.[18]

Education and Progress

"If the condition of man is to be progressively ameliorated, as we fondly hope and believe," writes Jefferson to the French revolutionary Marc Antoine Jullien (October 6, 1818), "education is to be the chief instrument in effecting it."

Jefferson recognizes two senses of progress. There is the improvement that individuals make when they work assiduously over time at something, such as knowledge of Latin grammar through the study of Latin or physical strength through daily physical exertion. There is also the improvement that the collection of individuals makes when people push themselves over the course of human history in a particular direction, such as moral advance or accumulated scientific knowledge.

Though he bought into the improvement of the human species over time, Jefferson was nonetheless an essentialist concerning the human organism. Humans had a particular nature and that nature was not changeable over time. Yet experience undeniably showed that humans had advanced both intellectually and morally throughout history. That showed that human capacities were massively underdeveloped.[19] Consequently, one of the chief goals of education was to encourage that developmental process through tapping into untapped human potential in morally responsible ways:

> We should be far, too, from the discouraging persuasion that man is fixed, by the law of his nature, at a given point; that his improvement is a chimera, and the hope delusive of rendering ourselves wiser, happier or better than our forefathers were. As well might it be urged that the wild and uncultivated tree, hitherto yielding sour and bitter fruit only, can never be made to yield better; yet we know that the grafting art implants a new tree on the savage stock, producing what is most estimable both in kind and degree. Education, in like manner, engrafts a new man on the native stock, and improves what in his nature was vicious and perverse into qualities of virtue and social worth.[20]

Consequently, progress for Jefferson related to the degree to which the human mind was perfectible and, judged by the standard of history, there was a considerable amount of perfecting for humans yet to do.

One scholar states that one of Jefferson's novelties apropos of education—and he seems to be referring to both lower and higher education—is the notion that "schools should be so arranged as to maximize academic competition" through "pitting . . . each student against all others in an academic free-for-all." The aim was the survival of "the few truly fit scholars" through "keen academic competition."[21] Yet to say in rewarding talent and work Jefferson was aiming directly at keen academic competition—a sort of Darwinian survival of the fittest—is overstated. The educative system was a means of segregating the natural aristoi from the artificial aristoi and securing the higher levels of government functioning and other significant occupations only for the former. In that regard, each was merely finding his own level of competency. Selection of character—the moral dimension—was not to be neglected.

Overall, Jefferson's view of progress through education is straightforwardly forward-directed, liberal, and practical: Education aims to promote effective, participatory republicanism through allowing all citizens to be educated to their capacity, in accordance with their will, and for the sake of political stability and future, progressive change. Intellectual advance without moral advance is nugatory.

Moral Improvement

Referring to moral education, Jefferson writes Peter Carr (August 10, 1787), "I think it lost time to attend lectures in this branch. He who made us would have been a pitiful bungler if he had made the rules of our moral conduct a matter of science." Given the stricture that one ought not to attend lectures on morality, it might be surprising to find that Jefferson in his *Notes on the State of Virginia* has a role, though a small one, for education in moral development. The first stage of education, he says, is decisive. It is not the time to encourage critical engagement with material like the Bible, for human rationality is not sufficiently developed, but instead a time when children should store historical facts to be used critically later in life. He adds that here also the "elements of morality" can be instilled. Such elements teach children that "their own greatest happiness . . . does not depend on their condition in life in which chance has placed them, but is always the result of a good conscience, good health, occupation [i.e., industry], and freedom in all just pursuits."[22] The quote, minus the suggestion that good health is needed for happiness, is once again in keeping with Panaetian Stoicism. It also shows that learning the elements of morality is not a matter of ingesting and digesting moral principles to apply to circumstances, but a matter of unlearning, as it were—that is, placing faith in the capacity of one's moral sense to decide the right course of action without the corruptive influence of reason or peer pressure. It shows also that knowledge is truly liberating: Anyone, irrespective of their "condition in life," is capable of achieving happiness.[23]

The passage is important in another respect. It suggests that it is one thing to "know" morally correct actions; it is another to do them and to live happily. As is the case for Aristotle and versus Socrates, knowledge of happiness is not sufficient. Aristotle writes, and here he has Socrates as his critical target: "On the contrary, the aim of studies about action, as we say, is surely not to study and know about a given thing, but rather to act on our knowledge. Hence knowing about virtue is not enough, but we must also try to possess and exercise virtue, or become good in any other way."[24] Moreover, a good life is a life comprising virtuous actions as well as some other things—for example, consider Jefferson's list comprising good conscience, fine health, occupation, and freedom in just pursuits. Here education is aidful.

As I have stated in chapter 5, doing what is right comes naturally to the mature moral-sense faculty. What about the immature moral-sense faculty? Reason is needed to help the faculty mature through encouraging virtuous activity. One does not always do what one knows is the right thing to do. In youths, since both faculties are underdeveloped, peer pressure can be an impediment, and so some moral encouragement early on needs to occur through education. History here is invaluable.

In the main, proper education is in the business of promoting love of virtue—doing what is right. Jefferson writes to Cornelius Blatchly (October 21, 1822), "I look to the diffusion of light and education as the resource most to be relied on for ameliorating the human condition, promoting virtue, and advancing the happiness of man." Yet there is no reason to take these three as distinct ends. We need only to grasp that virtue, properly apprehended (i.e., pace the ancients) requires benevolence-motivated other-concern. In his "Rockfish Gap Report," Jefferson speaks of the primacy of the moral aspect of education in contrast to its political and economical aspects. "They are sensible that the advantages of well-directed education, moral, political and economical, are truly above all estimate. Education generates habits of application, of order, and the love of virtue; and controls, by the force of habit, any innate obliquities in our moral organization."[25] He also considers and rejects fear as a corrective to the tendency to vice.

> It may be well questioned whether *fear* after a certain age, is a motive to which we should have ordinary recourse. The human character is susceptible of other incitements to correct conduct, more worthy of employ, and of better effect. Pride of character, laudable ambition, and moral dispositions are innate corrective of the indiscretions of that lively age; and when strengthened by habitual appeal and exercise, have a happier effect on future character than the degrading motive of fear. Hardening them to disgrace, to corporal punishments, and servile humiliation cannot be the best process for producing erect character.[26]

The sense here is that there is a natural tendency for youths to behave indiscreetly—to follow the boisterous and cantankerous activities of other youths—and so the natural inclinations of the moral sense need to be reinforced. That is the sense of "unlearning" I allude to earlier. In modern parlance, reason needs to convince itself that there is nothing wrong in doing the right thing.

With the maturation of the moral sense and rationality, Jefferson advises grandson Francis Wayles Eppes (May 21, 1816) that it is important to court the favor of others. That cannot occur without honesty, disinterest, and good nature—indispensable ingredients of a happy life. The sentiment is that authentic goodness is crucial. Industry, without virtue, does no one good.

> But while you endeavor, by a good store of learning, to prepare yourself to become an useful and distinguished member of your country you must remember that this can never be, without uniting merit with your learning. Honesty, disinterestedness, and good nature are indispensable to procure the esteem and confidence of those with whom we live, and on whose esteem our happiness depends.

The addition of disinterestedness is, of course, Stoical. One cannot know what is in the interest of others without putting aside one's own interests. The moral is that education without virtue is vain.

As Jefferson did not consider ethics and religion, rightly construed as separate disciplines—he often said the principles on which all religions agree are merely those principles innate to the moral sense—here one might ask: How did religion fit into Jefferson's views of education? Jefferson was quick to realize that organized religion, because of its extra-ethical political dimension, would be not merely an encumbrance to liberty; it would burke liberty. State sanction of any particular religion would be tantamount to state sanction of one particular politicized formula for the good life and the refusal to acknowledge other possibilities. He recognized that liberty required toleration, so all forms of nonharmful religious expressions would have to be sanctioned as well as atheism and agnosticism. Inquiry in theological matters, as he said to Peter Carr (August 10, 1787), might lead to belief or disbelief in deity. The former does not close the door to virtue. The latter allows for greater mental comfort. The most important incentive, he told Carr, is nonprejudicial inquiry into the matter, and that is more to be lauded than the outcome of one's deliberations. Once again, we have an appeal to authenticity—being the same person in all inquiries or walks of life. Overall, there can be no state sanction of any religion in state-sponsored educational institutions.

Creation of Natural Aristocracy

That education was needed for intellectual advance follows from Jefferson's progressivism. In his letter to John Adams (October 28, 1813) apropos of a natural aristocracy, covered fully in the prior chapter, he says:

> Science had liberated the ideas of those who read and reflect, and the American example had kindled feelings of right in the people. An insurrection has consequently begun, of science, talents and courage against rank and birth, which have fallen into contempt. It has failed in it's first effort, because the mobs of the cities, the instrument used for it's accomplishment, debased by ignorance, poverty and vice, could not be restrained to rational action. But the world will recover from the panic of this first catastrophe. Science is progressive, and talents and enterprise on the alert.

Jefferson here advocates an egalitarianist objection to the artificial aristoi, based on rank and birth (and wealth), which resulted in the first catastrophe.[27]

Yet the liberation of the people, through science, is not a liberation based on recognition of moral equality. Instead, it is one based on recognition that those naturally superior by nature—the natural aristoi, who are superior in knowledge and talents and who have a fully cultivated moral sense—ought to oversee the political machinery. That he shows earlier in the same letter, when he sketches his aims for educational reform:

> ["A Bill for the More General Diffusion of Knowledge"] proposed to divide every county into wards of 5. or 6. miles square . . . ; to establish in each ward a free school for reading, writing and common arithmetic; to provide for the annual selection of the best subjects from these schools who might receive at the public expence a higher degree of education at a district school; and from these district schools to select a certain number of the most promising subjects to be completed at an University, where all the useful sciences should be taught. Worth and genius would thus have been sought out from every condition of life, and completely prepared by education for defeating the competition of wealth and birth for public trusts.

The final sentence in particular shows that one of Jefferson's aims in educational reform is the creation of a natural aristocracy to displace the artificial aristocracy. The right sort of educational system will allow not only genius, but also worth—namely, character or virtue—to rise to the top. Education not only allows for intellectual betterment but also promotes moral sensitivity.

His law for religious freedom has the same aim. Jefferson writes in his natural aristoi letter to Adams:

> The law for religious freedom, which made part of this system, having put down the aristocracy of the clergy, and restored to the citizen the freedom of the mind, and those of entails and descents nurturing an equality of condition among them, this on Education would have raised the mass of the people to the high ground of moral respectability necessary to their own safety, and to orderly government; and would have compleated the great object of qualifying them to select the veritable aristoi, for the trusts of government, to the exclusion of the Pseudalists.

It is worth underscoring that it is not only the intelligent who should rule, but also the virtuous—that is, intellect without character is worthless—and that education has as its aim the advance of intellect and the cultivation of virtue. That is a point neglected by the majority of scholars because they ignore the normative dimension of Jefferson's thought. American education today, in contrast, aims to promote learning, and though mission statements of colleges and universities expressly acknowledge the significance of morality, such acknowledgement is mere mouth honor, at best. Educational institutions increasingly treat students as consumers, and change their curricula, which are morally neutral, to accommodate the ever-changing demands of their students. Jefferson certainly would have lamented this sad state of affairs.

The result of Jefferson's purchase of a natural aristocracy is in some sense, as political scientist Robert Faulkner writes, undemocratic.

> The famous Jeffersonian plans for public education made education democratically general but also aristocratically hierarchical. . . . In general, Jefferson sought a natural aristocracy of enlightened talent as well as a democracy enlightened to be a republican citizenry. The mixture shows the extent to which an orientation by useful truth, and the prominence of its propagators and bearers, made Jefferson liberal democracy in important ways liberal but undemocratic.[28]

We recall that Jefferson suggests, in his natural-aristoi letter, breeding for moral sensitivity. That might seem strange to us today. Any suggestion of selective human breeding is always met with unabashed disdain by some segment of the human population today, in spite of the facts that selectivity occurs always in sperm or egg donation as well as in adoption of children, among other things. Thus, there is uncontestable resistance to the morality of breeding, let alone the breeding of morality, but resistance is no sure sign that there is nothing to the breeding of morality. The question redounds: Can one breed for moral temperament? In other words, can one breed for particular virtues such as honesty, kindness, generosity, and friendliness?

The question is intriguing. Animal breeders freely admit to a capacity to breed for an animal's temperament. Like breeding for anything else, it is generally a matter of probabilities, not certainties. Animal breeders can breed, for instance, for friendliness, but that is not a moral disposition, say, in the Peripatetic or Stoic sense. To breed successfully for a certain sort of amiability in a dog, for instance, is to breed for a disposition toward behaving in an amicable way, but that disposition is not moral, because it is not given the aegis of rationality. Moral dispositions are essentially rational for Aristotle and the Stoics. For Aristotle, an action is moral only if the following criteria are met: one knows that it is right, one chooses it because it is right, and one acts from a stable disposition, cultivated over time.[29] The Stoic view is similar. To breed a person who behaves "friendly" in all circumstances is not to breed a person who behaves friendly in a moral sense, as Aristotle's first two conditions of moral activity are not met.

For Jefferson, the question is more intriguing than it is for the ancient eudaemonists, since Jefferson's moral sense is not a rational faculty but some sort of sensual faculty. If my depiction of Jefferson's moral sense in chapter 6 is correct or even nearly so, there is no reason to think that one could not breed for moral sensitivity in the sense specified by Jefferson. Jefferson acknowledges that all are equals in moral capacity, but only inasmuch as all are equals in other sensual capacities—for example, olfaction, vision, or tactility. "The want or imperfection of the moral sense in some men," He writes to Thomas Law (June 13, 1814), "like the want or imperfection of the senses of sight and hearing in others, is no proof that it [i.e., the want or imperfection] is a general characteristic of the species." It is beyond doubt that some are born with better vision, olfaction, or tactility than others. Jefferson also acknowledges in his aristoi letter that one can breed for traits—among them moral sensitivity: "Experience proves that the moral and physical qualities of man, whether good or evil, are transmissible in a certain degree from father to son."

There is some evidence of something like Jefferson's moral-sense faculty in moral decision-making scenarios. In *Moral Minds*, Harvard professor of psychology Marc Hauser argues that evolution has hardwired into the neural circuits of people a certain "universal moral grammar," which is a "toolkit for building specific moral systems." The need for rapidity is fashioned by the need for quick decisions in vital situations, in which one has no time for rational reflection. Writes Hauser:

> [Humans] evolved a moral instinct, a capacity that naturally grows within each child, designed to generate rapid judgments about what is morally right or wrong based on an unconscious grammar of action. Part of this machinery was designed by the blind hand of Darwinian selection millions of years before our species evolved: other parts were added or upgraded over the evolutionary history of our species, and are unique both to humans and to our moral psychology. These ideas draw on insights from another instinct: language.[30]

The process, he adds, is not like learning about virtue and vice in Sunday school, but like growing a limb. There is no explicit access to underlying principles—that is, consciousness is not involved. Moreover, "moral instincts are immune to the explicitly articulate commandments handed down by religions and governments."[31]

Hauser illustrates through two scenarios of a greedy uncle who stands to inherit much money upon the death of his nephew. In scenario one, the uncle, intending to drown his nephew in the bathtub, walks into the bathroom and does just that. In scenario two, the uncle, intending to drown his nephew in the bathtub, walks into the bathroom, finds his nephew already drowning, and does nothing to save him. The difference is accomplishing some end τ through direct action versus accomplishing τ through nonintervention, though the results are the same. To Hauser, a jury that found the uncle guilty in scenario one and not guilty in scenario two would be countermanding everyone's moral intuitions.[32]

Inculcation of Liberty

I have been arguing that in spite of Jefferson's avowed alignment with the moral doctrines of Jesus, he is actually more in moral alignment with the Stoics—Panaetius especially—than with Jesus. One of the key tenets of Stoicism was the pursuit of knowledge as the means of securing virtue—a tenet absent in the teachings of Jesus.

Jefferson, it is fair to say, was obsessed with acquisition of knowledge—practical knowledge especially. Recall his letter to Ticknor (November 25, 1817), in which Jefferson recognizes the "important truth" that "knolege is power, . . . knolege is safety, and . . . knolege is happiness." To Joseph C. Cabell (January 22, 1820), he states that Massachusetts, though one-tenth the size of Virginia, exceeds it and all other states in political power, because of "her attention to education." To Professor Thomas Cooper (August 25, 1814), he says of Bacon's take on useful knowledge: "But what are the sciences useful to us . . . or to anybody? A glance over Bacon's *arbor scientiae* will show the foundation for this question, and how many of his ramifications of science are now lopt off as nugatory?"

Yet Baconian knowledge was not autotelic. Education was valued because of its benefits, one of which for Jefferson was liberty. "Liberty was a social idea, again reflecting the ideas of Locke, and an educational system provided a form of contract between the state and the individual," state two scholars.[33] There is a communitarian strain in Jefferson's thinking, the strain exists for the sake of maximizing human independence and happiness. In that regard, he was a pupil of Enlightenment thinking.

There is also the influence of French thinking on Jefferson's pedagogy. From the French, Jefferson would have learned that education ought to be nationalistic, equalitarian, secular, and philosophically founded. Yet nationalism was not his aim. Education was in the service of enabling people to know their rights, oversee their government, and preserve their liberties.[34] Such aims were global, not nationalistic. He likely studied the works of M. J. A. Nicolas de Caritat (a.k.a., Condorcet), Louis-René de Caradeuc de la Chalotais, Denis Diderot, Pierre Charron, and Anne-Robert-Jacques, among others. Turgot and was influenced by men such as the Marquis de Lafayette, J. Correia da Serra, George Cuvier, Comte de Buffon, Alexander von Humboldt, and Jean Baptiste Say.

Advocacy of parochial control over institutions is evidence that he went substantially beyond the French pedagogues and consulted other authorities, both in America and overseas.[35] He corresponded with John Adams, Joseph Priestley, John Locke, Thomas Cooper, Marc-Auguste Pictet, Dugald Stewart, George Ticknor, Richard Price, William Small, George Wythe, Governor Fauquier, Peyton Randolph, and Patrick Henry, among others.

Parochial control over educational institutions is also in keeping with his decentralized political philosophy. Jefferson was a true libertarian. He feared strong, centralized government because he was concerned about the corruptive effects of power on persons with political power.[36] Scholar Charles Arrowood says, "Jefferson's distinctive contribution to the theory of education grew out of his most characteristic political doctrine," which entailed governmental nonintervention is citizens' affairs, distrust of political power, and government by the people.[37] The sentiment is somewhat misleading. Jefferson's educational thinking paralleled his political views; they did not grow out of them. Both his educational and political views, I have been arguing, were the result of his normative thinking on the nature of the cosmos and the nature of man. Education and politics were subordinate to and in the service of human happiness or thriving—an ethical ideal. Arrowood himself seems to acknowledge that, as he writes later, "Education is the business of the state because education is essential to the happiness, prosperity, and liberty of the people, and it is for the maintenance and promotion of these that the state exists."[38]

Thin Government

Thin government, a key feature of his political liberalism, is also a key feature of Jefferson's progressivist views of education. Jefferson's political liberalism is driven by the normative notion that no one ought to decide for another that other's best interest. That is not a commitment to a radical form of value-pluralism, but instead a commitment to the belief that each must find his own path to virtue—and the paths among different persons are many—and that that path must be taken voluntarily. Acting rightly through coercion or for the wrong reason is not acting virtuously.

Thin government is not Jeffersonian devotion to some sort of radical atomism, as many[39] would have it, or of extreme libertarianism. It is a structured commitment to a system of education that is chiefly bottom-up driven and that functions for the sake of all citizens, irrespective of wealth or birth. Thus, thin government is manifest in education in the dependency of universities and grammar schools on primary schools in the manner that the national government is dependent on smaller local governments.

Thin government was manifest at Jefferson's University of Virginia, in many respects, modeled in parallel with his republican principles.

First, the professors were autonomous.[40] Writes historian Jennings Wagoner:

> Jefferson wanted professors who, as experts in specific fields of knowledge, would lecture on subjects that, in his familiar words, were "useful to us at this day, and in their *highest degree*." He was aiming to create a university much more akin to modern graduate and professional schools than to the more limited collegiate institutions of the day. It is for this reason that the university did not offer bachelor's degrees until long after Jefferson's death. The diplomas he and the initial Board of Visitors authorized were of two grades, "the highest of doctor, the second of graduate."[41]

Second, students had no set curriculum. Education was elective.[42] Jefferson writes to George Ticknor (July 16, 1823):

> There is one [practice] from which we shall certainly vary, although it has been copied . . . by nearly every college and academy in the United States. That is, the holding the students all to one prescribed course of reading, and disallowing exclusive application to those branches only which are to qualify them for the particular vocations to which they are destined. We shall . . . allow them uncontrolled choice in the lectures they shall choose to attend, and requiring elementary qualification only, and sufficient age.

Useful Knowledge

A corollary of Jefferson's progressivism is the notion that knowledge ought to be useful. Two of the most general and significant aims of education are effective, participatory citizenry and political stability. Thus, though he is not averse to study for the sake of study, Jefferson emphasizes the practicality of knowledge, and that comes out plainly in numerous writings. In his natural-aristoi letter to John Adams, Jefferson emphasizes that his aim at the University of Virginia is to teach "all the useful sciences." Jefferson writes to American delegate John Banister (October 15, 1785) that there is no need to send an American youth to Europe because all the useful sciences are taught just as well in America. Jefferson writes Colonel William Green Munford (June 18, 1799) to advise him on the branches of mathematics that might be most useful to him. To son-in-law Thomas Mann Randolph, Jr. (August 27, 1786), Jefferson states that languages and mathematics should be studied earlier in life to be useful guides for other sciences.

Jefferson always insisted on the practicality of education because of his Baconian take on knowledge. Writes historian Lucia Stanton:

> Jefferson pursued the improvement of the human condition as a passionate Baconian, gathering information with the aid of his watch, ruler, and scales. He applied his measuring mind to plantation projects in a search for economy and efficiency. He enveloped his unwieldy operations in the consoling security of mathematical truths. . . . His many monumental earth-moving projects, in particular, led to a lifetime of time-and-motion calculations. . . . At the same time that Jefferson applied a geometric grid of field boundaries to the irregular features of his mountain, he imposed Enlightenment ideals of economy and order on the people who lived there.[43]

In classifying subjects of study, he followed Bacon's *arbor scientiae*.[44] Upon selling books to Library of Congress, Jefferson arranged the books according to the Bacon's three faculties of mind: memory (civil and moral history), reason (moral and mathematical philosophy), and imagination (the fine arts, comprising architecture, gardening, painting, sculpture, music, poetry, and criticism). The classification was not driven by considerations of the nature of things, but utility, for, as we have seen, Jefferson was an express nominalist.

A fine example of emphasis on utility of knowledge comes with the praise Jefferson heaps on scientist and physician Edward Jenner (May 14, 1806) on behalf of the "whole human family" for his discovery of a vaccine for small pox. "Medecine has never before produced any single improvement of such ability. Harvey's discovery of the circulation of the blood was a beautiful addition to our knowledge of the animal economy, but on a review of the practice of medicine before & since that epoch, I do not see any great amelioration which has been derived from that discovery, you have erased from the Calendar of human afflictions one of it's greatest. Yours is the comfortable reflection that mankind can never forget that you have lived." For Jefferson, Harvey's discovery of the circulation of blood, considered by historians of science to be one of the greatest medical discoveries, pales in comparison to Jenner's vaccine because it seems to be nothing other than a bit of knowledge for its own sake. Yet every scientific discovery is potentially fruitful. As he writes to former soldier Robert Patterson four years earlier (April 17, 1803), "No discovery is barren; it always serves as a step to something else."

Another example of Jefferson's emphasis on utility is in a letter to a young friend, Bernard Moore,[45] who wishes to become a lawyer. Jefferson advises that Moore lay "sufficient groundwork" through the study of Latin and French and that he then turn to mathematics and natural philosophy, because they are "so useful in the most familiar occurrences of life." In addition to their utility, they are "so peculiarly engaging & delightful as would induce every person to wish an acquaintance with them."

Nonetheless, we must acknowledge that Jefferson's conception of "useful" is broad, not strictly utilitarian. "A complete education should produce men who were in all ways useful to society—useful because intelligent, cultured, well-informed, technically competent, moral (this particularly), capable of earning a living, happy, and fitted for political and social leadership." Jefferson promoted himself as an illustration of his "utilitarian demands."[46] That he devoted such great time to and found such pleasure in reading ancient Greek and Latin authors in the original language shows that Jefferson believed the ancient languages were indispensable for a happy, tranquil life.

Lifelong Learning

"I was a hard student until I entered on the business of life," Jefferson writes to personal physician Dr. Vine Utley (March 21, 1819), "the duties of which leave no idle time to those disposed to fulfil them; and now, retired, and at the age of seventy-six, I am again a hard student. Indeed, my fondness for reading and study revolts me from the drudgery of letter writing." The sentiment expresses a revivification, due to newfound time for his beloved books. It also expresses an unending commitment to learning.

Jefferson, we have seen, was no solitarian who was committed only to his own comfort and best interest, as certain scholars state.[47] Even in retirement, he was thoroughly immersed in the world around him and a consummate empirical investigator of it.[48] His daily activities afforded him numerous opportunities to formulate hypotheses on gardening, manufacture, natural history, and politics, among other things, and to test them through experience. So long as blood coursed through the arteries of his body, Jefferson was moved to broaden his familiarity with and deepen his grasp of the world around him.

Why was Jefferson such an indurated, incurable lifelong learner? Science was irretrievably on the move, he thought, and he wished to be a vital part of that movement forward. "It is impossible for a man who takes a survey of what is already known," he writes to William Green Munford (June 18, 1799), "not to see what an immensity in every branch of science yet remains to be discovered, & that too of articles to which our faculties seem adequate."[49]

The aim of education was to give persons the tools they would need to make them involved, free, and happy. As one scholar notes: "To Thomas Jefferson, school would never be a 'finishing' agency. From each stage, man would have to move on in a never ending process of self-education, deliberately using the tools he had acquired. The narrow professional who had but a technical knowledge of his little vocational area was a curse to him. Education had to be broad in order to assure the freedom and happiness of man."[50]

For that to occur, persons needed to be motivated to be self-educators—the laborers, to advance personal and local affairs; the learned, to advance affairs of science, state, and nation. As scholar Karl Lehmann notes, "[Social progress] depended entirely upon the natural, self-responsible desire of the individual for self-education and upon its fulfillment."[51] Citizens in the true sense of the term would participate in election, and if needed, recall of political officials, jury service, constitutional conventions, military service, and local political affairs, among other things. Thus, liberty for Jefferson did not mean, as certain radicalists state, the opportunity to do as one pleases whenever one pleases. Liberty entailed fullest participation of the citizens of a nation in the affairs of the nation, inasmuch as their time allowed. In that regard, Jefferson's (roughly) 40 years of political service to his state and nation, his devotion to writing letters not only to family and friends but also to correspondents unknown, seeking information, all of his life, and his tireless work vis-à-vis the founding of the University of Virginia are illustrations of Jefferson's profound generosity and active commitment to participatory republicanism.

There were limits to the advance of science, Jefferson recognized. In a letter to Pierre Samuel Dupont de Nemours (April 24, 1816), he writes: "Although I do not, with some enthusiasts, believe that the human condition will ever advance to such a state of perfection as that there shall no longer be pain or vice in the world, yet I believe it susceptible of much improvement, and most of all in matters of government and religion; and that the diffusion of knowledge among the people is to be the instrument by which it is to be effected."

COLLECTANEA

This final section is a sort of hodge-podge of Jefferson's thoughts on education: his preference for American education, his thoughts on educating women, and, finally, his views on education as they relate to Native Americans and African Americans.

American Education and Human Nature

In a letter to John Banister (October 15, 1785), Jefferson replies to a paragraph in a previous letter of Banister (September 19) on European education. Jefferson states that his reply has been retarded by his need to "make inquiries on the subject." His inquiries have indicated that an education in Rome or Geneva is best. Each is affordable and each has its own advantages.

"But why send an American youth to Europe for education?" Jefferson asks. The objects of "an useful American education" are classical knowledge, modern language, mathematics, natural philosophy, natural history, civil history, and ethics. Each, except for modern languages, can be learned equally as well at William and Mary as they can at any European institution.

Moreover, there are notable disadvantages of matriculating in Europe. A European student acquires a fondness for luxury and dissipation, contempt for simplicity, a sense of privilege, an abhorrence of equality, a love of wealth and birth, thin friendships, a distaste of fidelity, and appetency for harlots. He sums: "It appears to me, then, that an American coming to Europe for education, loses in his knowledge, in his morals, in his health, in his habits, and in his happiness. I had entertained only doubts on this head, before I came to Europe: what I see and hear, since I came here, proves more than I had ever suspected."

In contrast, American education for Jefferson is congruent with the moral ideals of agrarianism, simplicity of living, and full participatory government. Americans, he adds, are those person whose "manners, morals and habits, are perfectly homogeneous with those of [their] country." That notion is congruent with Plato's notion in *The Republic* of the homomorphic relationship between the virtue of a well-run polis and the virtue of a good citizen.[52]

Jefferson's letter to Banister also strongly suggests that American education, like American agrarianism,[53] is not merely a countrified standard that is suited to the American temperament, given acclimatization to American soil and American ways. European cultural standards are corrupt because they are at variance with human nature. Thus, Jefferson, through his systemic educational reforms, is essaying to set the bar for an education, both scientific and moral, that is best suited for all persons—an education in touch with human nature.

Female Education

Jefferson's systemic reforms for American education did include elementary-level education for females, for his bill in 1779 included three years of state-supported education for females. He did not anticipate any need for women to be educated beyond this most fundamental level. In a word, he was no visionary vis-à-vis the talents and potential contribution of females to social improvement beyond their traditional domestic roles. That is not to say that he did not have much to say about the important function of women in American, or any, society. As Brian Steele (2008) shows, Jefferson viewed women as natural equals of men. Jefferson merely thought, as his critique of the backwardness of Native American culture and excesses and effeminacy of the gentry of French culture indicates, they were naturally suited for domesticity, while men were suited for hardier work and political affairs.

Jefferson's only sustained discussion of female education occurs in letter to Virginian Nathaniel Burwell (March 14, 1818). "A plan of female education has never been a subject of systematic contemplation with me," he concedes. He has entertained the subject only insofar as it concerned his own daughters. They required an education that would enable them, once mothers, to educate their own daughters and even sons, in the event of the death or incapacity of their father.[54]

One of the largest obstacles to female education is the passion for reading novels, which is lost time, which could have been employed for useful chores. Jefferson says to fellow Virginian Colonel Nathanial Burwell (March 14, 1818): "When this poison infects the mind, it destroys its tone and revolts it against wholesome reading. Reason and fact, plain and unadorned, are rejected. Nothing can engage attention unless dressed in all the figments of fancy, and nothing so bedecked comes amiss. The result is a bloated imagination, sickly judgment, and disgust towards all the real business of life." One can surely guess what Jefferson would say about the tendency today of children to play video games, immerse themselves in plotless and amoral action-adventure movies, and gab and text-message on their own cell phones.

Jefferson does not categorically rule out reading novels. There are many fictitious narratives—for example, Maromontel's new tales and the works of Miss Edgeworth and Madame Genlis—which base their narratives on real life and thereby are "useful vehicles of sound morality." Pope, Dryden, Thompson, Shakespeare, Molière, Racine, and the Corneilles can be aidful in forming style and taste. He said in a letter to Peter Carr (August 10, 1787), "The writings of Sterne, particularly, form the best course of morality that ever was written."

Outside of salubrious novels, he continues to Burwell, there were other items important for female education. First, the French language was indispensable for females' education. For ornament, there were dancing, drawing, and music. Next, dancing was healthy, and its practice allowed for participation in "circles of festivity" without gawkiness. Drawing was innocent, engaging, and often useful. Music was a "delightful recreation for the hours of respite from the cares of the day," but should only be attempted by those with an ear, as it were. Otherwise, it might bring shame to the avowed musician. Most significant, there was household economy. "Diligence and dexterity in all its processes are inestimable treasures. The order and economy of a house are as honorable to the mistress as those of the farm to the master, and if ether be neglected, ruin follows, and children destitute of the means of living." The statement—that household economy is to be divided between husband and wife, with husband assuming order outside of the house and wife, inside of the house—is starkly Aristotelian.[55]

Beyond the letter to Burwell, we only have glimpses of Jefferson's thinking on female education. When Jefferson arrives in Annapolis from Philadelphia, he writes to his daughter Martha (November 28, 1783) and advises her on the following course of daily activity, subject to the approbation of her chief tutor Mrs. Hopkinson.

8-10 a.m.: practice music
10 a.m. to 1 p.m.: dance one day, draw another day
1-2 p.m.: draw on the dancing day and write on the drawing day
3-4 p.m.: read French
4-5 p.m.: exercise yourself in music
5 p.m.-bedtime: read English, write &c.

Overall, Jefferson's "schedule"—note the gap between 2 and 3 p.m.—might suggest haste, as it shows neither much imagination nor much thought, as if the matter clearly did not much concern him. It does, however, illustrate Jefferson's nearly neurotic attachment to order and symmetry. He wishes to make sure that Martha's time is well spent, that there is regularity to her life, that there is a certain balance to the activities she pursues each day, and that those activities lead to a fulsome life. Two points are worth noting. First, all pursuits relate to Bacon's category of imagination. Memory and reason are left out of the picture apropos of female education. That says much about Jefferson's vision of women. Second, what is missing—and it is an important part of a young person's day—is the opportunity for spontaneous activity or even some amount of misadventure—that is, some time in which she can decide for herself how best to spend her time. Martha was eleven at the time, but of course the times were different.

Native Americans and African Americans

In his Second Inaugural Address, Jefferson considers the plight of Native Americans: "Endowed with the faculties and the rights of men, breathing an ardent love of liberty and independence, and occupying a country which left them no desire but to be undisturbed," he writes, "the stream of overflowing population from other regions directed itself on these shores; without power to divert, or habits to contend against, they have been overwhelmed by the current, or driven before it." There is no longer space for hunting, so they must be taught agriculture and the domestic arts and be readied for that society which cultivates intellectual and moral advance and adds to bodily comforts— that is, white American society.

There are, before education for integration, sizable obstacles to overcome: habits long-standing both of body and, especially, mind. Concerning the latter, he says: "[Native Americans] inculcate a sanctimonious reverence for the customs of their ancestors; that whatsoever they did, must be done all through time; that reason is a false guide, and to advance under its counsel, in their physical, moral, or political condition, is perilous innovation; that their duty is to remain as their Creator made them, ignorance being safety, and knowledge full of danger."[56] With undue respect for the bigotry of their ancestors, Native Americans suffer from filiopiety.

Jefferson here and elsewhere generally expresses a good amount of sympathy for Native Americans, but he is only modestly empathic. He speaks of the invasion of whites as an overwhelming current, as if to excuse culpability with inevitability. The metaphor of a current is illustrative. Without capacities to divert or contend against the overpowering current, the implicit conclusion is that Native Americans must either learn to swim—that is, integrate fully in white society—or drown—that is, be destroyed by whites. Never does Jefferson give thought to the notion that the overwhelming current of white culture is genocidal. Never does he give evidence of thought to what it might be like to be a Native American. That thought, had it been entertained, would have been horrific—for him, a voluntary state of imposed barbarism.[57]

Jefferson addresses the question of black intelligence most directly in Query XIV of his *Notes on the State of Virginia*. He hypothesizes that blacks are intellectually inferior but exercises guardedness:

> The opinion, that they are inferior in the faculties of reason and imagination, must be hazarded with great diffidence. To justify a general conclusion, requires many observations, even where the subject may be submitted to the Anatomical knife, to Optical glasses, to analysis by fire, or by substance, we are examining; where it eludes the research of fall the senses; where the conditions of its existence are various and variously combined; where the effects of those which are present or absent bid defiance to calculation; let me add too, as a circumstance of great tenderness, where our conclusion would degrade a whole race of men from the rank in the scale of being which their Creator may perhaps given them.

Education of African Americans was a more labyrinthine issue than that of Native Americans, because Jefferson tended to think of African Americans as intellectually inferior to other humans, though morally as competent. Unlike Native Americans, they have had considerable exposure to white society, which is scientific and progressive, without showing in his eyes any promise of assimilation of that culture. He did not think that failure of assimilation might be due to the particular sort of exposure to white culture that Americanized Africans had—that is, exposure as slaves and inferiors. The diminishing effect of continued degradation can and often does have the effect, over time, of belief in inferiority.[58] In that regard, however, he differed little from most of the learned of his day.

As with Native Americans, Jefferson shows in his writings considerable sympathy for blacks, but little empathy, and sympathy occurs mostly at the level of generality. He sympathizes with African Americans, considered as a people.

Freedom is part and parcel of the human condition, and all people need to be free, so blacks need to be free. Yet he has difficulty seeing the plight of any particular black person. Only once does he consider how he would have felt if he had been a black man, a slave, or even someone perceived to be inferior, and that occurs when he explains blacks' disposition to thievery as the result of the degrading state of enslavement. That thought too, I suspect, would have been horrific—to his thinking, a state of perpetual childlike naïveté and ignorance. For failure to be empathic, Jefferson ought to be faulted. Nonetheless, there is no reason to believe he thought blacks were an exception to the general rule that each person ought to be educated according to his means and that blacks of his day were incapable of any considerable degree of education. Moreover, there is every reason to believe, were he alive today, that he would have had an antipodean change of mind.

CHAPTER 9

"AN UTOPIAN DREAM"

Jefferson on Primary Education
for Enlightened Democracy

"As Cato then concluded every speech with the words 'Carthago delenda est,' so do I every opinion with the injunction 'divide the counties into wards.'"

—TJ to Joseph C. Cabell, February 2, 1816

Jefferson, in a letter to Virginian John Tyler (May 26, 1810), gives two great measures of a thriving republic—general education, whose chief aim is "to enable every man to judge for himself what will secure or endanger his freedom," and wards, which are deemed a complement to and are needed for general education and political stability. Here, as elsewhere, a key aspect of Jefferson's liberalism shows itself: It aims to allow each citizen a large measure of freedom to decide for himself his own path in life.[1]

Jefferson believed that each person was the most suitable judge of what was best for himself and that the most effective participatory democracy was libertarian: In the main, the less government intervened in each person's life, the better off each person and the state would be. For the success of his republican system, the citizens needed to be educated generally and the political system needed to be established so that all, not only the wealthy, would be educated. Privileged education only for the wellborn was the means of sustaining the pseudo-aristocratic injustices that have been perpetuated and rationalized for centuries.

In championing the need for general education in a republican government, Jefferson was indebted to others—Montesquieu especially[2]—but, though he drew inspiration from still others, he went significantly beyond them. Thus, he was a beacon for the foggy times. As one author states:

Any summary of Thomas Jefferson's educational legacy must thus take into account the context of the times and the negative as well as positive judgments that might be made by those of our own and succeeding generations. While Jefferson was in some ways a product of his time, he was most significantly the prophet of later times. His labors on behalf of the education of citizens showed him to be far in advance of the thinking of his day.[3]

Education in Jefferson's Virginia was generally not considered something to which all citizens ought to have some access, but only the privileged.[4] Considered as an entitlement only of the privileged, the political abuses of the privileged were perpetuated from generation to generation, for the general citizenry, being kept ignorant of abuses, had no recourse to effective and corrective action.

Jeffersonian republicanism was intended to correct the abuses of government of privilege by placing the political power ultimately in the hands of the citizenry. Government for and, in an indirect sense, of the people, he recognized, required some basal measure of education for the general citizenry.

ATOMISM OR ORGANICISM

"The laws of education are the first impressions we receive," political philosopher Montesquieu writes in *The Spirit of Laws*, "and as they prepare us for civil life, every private family ought to be governed by the plan of that great household which comprehends them all." It is in republican government especially, he adds, that "the whole power of education is required."[5]

Montesquieu's notion is echoed by A. L. C. Destutt de Tracy: "This form of government requires the general diffusion of the most correct and useful knowledge; information should be promulgated constantly, and error exposed and dissipated; popular and moral writers should be rewarded, not by engagement, but by such means as may be devised for exciting a general emulation, without rendering the reward of virtue a business of intrigue on the one hand, or of patronage on the other."[6]

Jefferson knew well Montesquieu's *The Spirit of Laws*—a work to which he was early on very much attracted—and he patronized and translated Tracy's critique of the book many years later as he became more critical of Montesquieu. Yet all realized that government for and of the people, through representatives chosen by them, was impossible without a certain level of education among the populace. Jefferson writes to statesman and Virginian Edward Carrington (January 16, 1787), "The basis of our government being the opinion of the people, the very first object should be to keep that right." He then considers "a government without newspapers or newspapers without a government" and adds, without hesitation, that the latter is preferable so long as—and this is a significant addendum—every person receiving those papers should be capable of reading them. That declaration seems remarkable, if only because of Jefferson's express disdain at times of newspapers, due to their preference for sensationalized stories and fabrications, especially at his expense. "The man who never looks into a newspaper is better informed than he who reads them," he tells newspaper editor John Norvell (June 14, 1807), "inasmuch as he who knows nothing is nearer to truth than he whose mind is filled with falsehoods & errors." It is unremarkable, however—merely a measure of his unwavering belief that freedom and truth are bedfellows, and truth, even if obscured by a sea of falsehoods in newspapers, will be recognized by an educated citizenry.

It is often thought that Jefferson had a preference for higher education because of his involvement with the University of Virginia and because of his nonsuccess in instantiating his ward system with ward schools in Virginia. That is a misconception. The educational reforms he proposed through his bills of 1779 and 1817 were substantial, not cosmetic, and would have amounted to a systematic overhaul of the Virginian educational system, from bottom to top, if eventually adopted. Jefferson's bills were not to his thinking to be taken in part, but completely. To General James Breckinridge (February 15, 1821), he writes: "I have never proposed a sacrifice of the primary to the ultimate grade of instruction. Let us keep our eye steadily on the whole system. If we cannot do every thing at once, let us do one at a time."

Jefferson was proposing wholesale reform not merely of Virginia's educational system but also of the American educational system. Evidence for that is the philosophical vision—undergirded morally and in keeping with the tenor with his proposed republican schema—beneath the reforms. His philosophy of education, thus, is laid out to engender the proposed reforms needed for sustainable, responsible republican government.

As with his political thinking, there are atomistic and communitarian strains in Jefferson's philosophy of education. Was he then an educative atomist or communitarian, or neither?

The general tendency in the literature is to see Jefferson's philosophy of education as atomistic, because of the tendency to see his political philosophy as atomistic—namely, he championed individual rights and governmental nonintervention in individuals' affairs.

One scholar, however, maintains that the overall educative scheme for all early American educational reformists—foremost among them being Jefferson—was not so much atomistic in any vital sense, but communitarian:

> While they hoped that the general diffusion of knowledge would maximize happiness and assist able and deserving young men to attain positions of influence in society and government, they were in actuality much more concerned about the future of the nation than with the rise of individuals. These essayists, along with Jefferson, were searching for a system of education that would be suitable for coming generations of free and independent citizens intent on maintaining a republican society. They sought educational arrangements that would unite Americans as a people and as an expanding union of republics bound together by ties of interest, affection, and mutual consent.[7]

Early reformists were motivated by organic more than by atomistic ideals. They wished to instantiate an educational system that would not only promote republican liberal ideals, but also preserve the unity of the nation as well as their individuality.

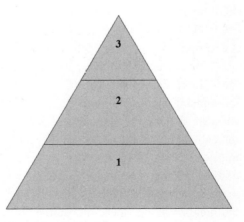

Figure 9.1. Jefferson's Educational System. The various numbers in the pyramid represent, respectively, Jefferson's (1) ward-level, (2) college-level, and (3) university-level education. As in the case with his republicanism (see figure 3.1), his education reforms are systemic and ought to be taken as a structured, holistic scheme.

It is correct to say that there is both an organic strain in Jefferson's thinking as well as an atomistic strain. Though I said in chapter 2 that Jefferson's political scheme was chiefly bottom-up—that is correct more methodologically than axiologically—it is, strictly speaking, neither atomism nor organicism at which Jefferson aimed, but medism. On the one hand, Jefferson believed that individuals ought to be granted fullest expression of their individuality through recognition of certain fundamental and inalienable rights, guaranteed by nature. On the other hand, Jefferson believed, as did Aristotle and the Stoics in antiquity, that humans were fundamentally social creatures whose happiness could not be had in isolation from other human beings. Thus, Jefferson went beyond Montesquieu, since he believed that education was not merely in the service of political ideals that could be reasonably instantiated. Educative and political aims were reducible to an ethical aim—happiness or human thriving—grounded in sense or sentiment, not reason.

In a letter to politician Littleton Waller Tazewell (January 5, 1805), Jefferson stresses the significance of two tiers of education for the preservation of liberty—general and higher education:

> Convinced that the people are the only safe depositories of their own liberty, & that they are not safe unless enlightened to a certain degree, I have looked on our present state of liberty as a short-lived possession unless the mass of the people could be informed to a certain degree. This requires two grades of education. First some institution where science in all it's branches is taught, and in the highest degree to which the human mind has carried it. This would prepare a few subjects in every State, to whom nature has given minds of the first order. Secondly such a degree of learning given to every member of the society as will enable him to read, to judge & to vote understandingly on what is passing.

What is at stake is the actualization of liberty through participatory republicanism and representative government. Through tripartitioning the educational system, Jefferson was striving for—as he did through his tripartitioning of nation into ward, county, and state—sundry levels of educational participation to connect with the needs of the sundry levels of citizenry and to ensure some measure of functional political organicism.[8] A nation as large as the United States, which would to his thinking eventually span North America, needed a sense of identity to make it a unity. The divide-and-divide-again proposal would allow for idiosyncrasies at the levels of wards and states, and to Jefferson's thinking, the strongest possible sense of unity—unity through citizens' recognition that the federal government's chief occupation was to see to it that their rights were secured.[9]

Since the reforms were to be taken and evaluated in toto, as a philosophical system, it is perhaps unfair to give either educational tier axiological priority. That is not to say that Jefferson did not have educative priorities. Jefferson recognized the indispensability of primary education for the sorts of normative-based political reforms he was aiming to make. There was immediate need of such ground-based educational reform. Moreover, higher education without full access of citizens to primary education had been practiced historically and the benefits derived were only for those persons educated. Higher education without the education of the general citizenry was merely a way disallowing the general citizenry any access to political participation, thereby ignoring citizens' rights. Thus, had it been a choice between competing alternatives, Jefferson would have been willing to give up the University of Virginia for instantiation of his ward system of education. "Were it necessary to give up either the Primaries or the University," he wrote to Senator Joseph C. Cabell (January 13, 1823), "I would rather abandon the last, because it is safer to have a whole people respectably enlightened, than a few in a high state of science, and the many in ignorance. This last is the most dangerous state in which a nation can be." That sentiment is in keeping with P. S. Dupont de Nemours's advice to Jefferson on education: "All knowledge readily and daily usable, all practical sciences, all laborious activities, all the common sense, all the correct ideas, all the morality, all the virtue, all the courage, all the prosperity, all the happiness of a nation and particularly of a Republic must spring from the primary schools or Petites Écoles."[10]

THE AIMS OF PRIMARY EDUCATION

What are the aims of primary education? In his 1818 "Rockfish Gap Report," Jefferson lists the following as aims:

> To give every citizen the information he needs for the transaction of his own business;
> To enable him to calculate for himself, and to express and preserve his ideas, his contract and accounts, in writing;

To improve, by reading, his morals and faculties;

To understand his duties to his neighbors and country, and do discharge with competence the functions confided to him by either;

To know his rights;

To exercise with order and justice those he retains;

To choose with discretion the fiduciary of those he delegates; and to notice their conduct with diligence, with candor, and judgment;

And, in general, to observe with intelligence and faithfulness all the social relations under which he shall be placed.[11]

In what follows, I flesh out each of these aims, some grouped together for expediency.

Promotion of Domestic Affairs

Jefferson believed that one of the general aims of education was to ensure that each citizen could be educated to his own means. Both the laboring and the learned would need general education—the first, for "their [parochial] pursuits and duties"; the second, as "foundation for further acquirements."[12] The parochial pursuits and duties include the transaction of personal business, the preservation of one's ideas, and the calculation of contracts, accounts, and ideas, among other things.

We take it for granted today that some degree of education is needed for citizens to conduct their personal affairs. In Jefferson's day, personal-business transactions, say for a farmer, would include purchasing agricultural supplies, having farming equipment fixed, selling produce in the market, and purchasing other needed goods (for example, a new plow mold board, some sheep, an ox, or a work horse, or clothes). What Jefferson calls "preservation of ideas" probably means things such as inventions or ideas for increased efficiency as well as preservation of family history and affairs through letters, biography, or autobiography. The calculation of accounts, contracts, and ideas likely refers to the deliberation that goes into preparation for daily transactions, which were greatly negotiable and often occurred by barter, due to lack of readily available currency in Jefferson's state. This was in accord with Jefferson's principle of education pursuant to the needs of each citizen. Since Jefferson envisaged Americans as principally agrarian, the needs of most citizens, he thought, were not to be ignored. Self-sufficiency was the goal.

Promotion of Morality, Improvement of Other Faculties

Under this rubric, I include the need of education for the improvement of the moral faculty; enhancement of one's memory, reason, and imagination; the facilitation of industry; and observation of social relations.

As I showed in chapter 6, Jefferson was clear that the moral sense functioned independently of rationality, or relatively so. Following moral-sense thinkers like Hume—"'Tis not contrary to reason to prefer the destruction of the whole world to the scratching of my finger"[13]—he gave sufficient reason to think that encroachment of rationality in moral scenarios—for example, his Head-and-Heart letter to Maria Cosway—helped nowise and generally led to the wrong decision. Nonetheless, Jefferson was clear that reason was needed to some degree to promote the interests of morality. While there was no need for courses on morality—right action for one whose moral sense was properly developed was not a matter of deliberating on alternative courses of action but instead a matter of relatively spontaneous activity in keeping with moral feeling—there was great need to study history and read works that promoted morally correct activity. History through education would show students how humans have progressed morally over time, and, thus would promote continued progress over time. Good literature, like Cicero's *Tusculan Disputations* or Laurence Sterne's *Tristram Shandy*, would help actualize morally correct action by overriding moral slaggardliness.

Jefferson also believed elementary education would promote industry and subserve social relations. Industry, as I have shown in chapter 5, is the bedfellow of virtue. Virtue in the ancient sense, for Jefferson, is a matter of acting to promote self-interest by seeking equanimity. Industry is a matter of avoiding sloth and keeping busy in a manner that promotes morality and social acceptance—the two being inseparable. For Jefferson, we recall, it was important that industrious acts always be benevolently motivated, otherwise they are self-serving. That some amount of general education was needed to enhance social relations betrays Jefferson's Hieroclesian understanding that one's moral duties to others cannot be fulfilling without first fulfilling one's "duties" to oneself.[14] As Jefferson asserts in a letter to James Monroe (May 20, 1782), "If we are made in some degree for others, yet in a greater are we made for ourselves."

That education was a means to improve memory, reason, and imagination is too obvious to need explication.

To those things, we might add education for the sake of encouraging local political participation—namely, that thriving republicanism is full-participatory republicanism. "Where every man is a sharer in the direction of his ward republic, or of some of the higher ones," he writes to Joseph C. Cabell (February 2, 1816), "and feels that he is a participator in the government of affairs not merely at an election one day in the year, but every day; when there shall not be a man in the State who will not be a member of some one of it's councils, great or small, he will let the heart be torn out of his body, sooner than his power be wrested from him by a Caesar or a Bonaparte." To Virginia lawyer Samuel Kercheval in the same year, Jefferson adds, "By making every citizen an acting member of the government, and in the offices nearest and most interesting to him, [wards] will attach him by his strongest feeling, to the independence of his country, and its republican constitution" (July 12, 1816).

Knowing and Exercising Rights

Jefferson worried that in a country in which only one in ten has the right to vote, those inclined to buy their way to the assembly, "get nine-tenths of their price clear."[15] Thus, he was adamant that the American constitution, drafted to a large extent by James Madison, should include a bill of rights. Only a bill of rights could secure certain "fetters against evil," he writes to Virginia merchant Alexander Donald (February 7, 1788), which are "freedom of religion, freedom of the press, protection against standing armies, restriction against monopolies, the eternal & unremitting force of the habeas corpus laws, and trials by jury in all matters of fact triable by the laws of the land & not by the law of nations." It is not enough to assume that such rights are presumed in the constitution. "A bill of rights is what the people are entitled to against every government on earth, general or particular," he writes to James Madison (December 20, 1787) "& what no just government should refuse, or rest on inferences."[16] Over a year later (March 15, 1789), Jefferson responds to certain of Madison's demurs to inclusion of a bill of rights. To Madison's objection that not all rights would be obtained in due time, Jefferson replies, "Half a loaf is better than no bread." He also acknowledges with Madison that introduction of a bill of rights would "cramp government in it's useful exertions." Yet the inconveniency of cramped government is "short-lived, trivial & reparable." The inconveniency of untrammeled government is "permanent, afflicting & irreparable."[17]

Alexander Hamilton, in "Federalist 84," objected that a bill of rights would be redundant, even harmful. "Bills of rights, in the sense and in the extent in which they are contended for, are not only unnecessary in the proposed constitution, but would even be dangerous. They would contain various exceptions to powers which are not granted; and on this very account, would afford a colorable pretext to claim more than were granted. For why declare that things shall not be done which there is no power to do?"[18] Hamilton's concern here is, of course, an executive that acts as a mere machine. He wished for executive flexibility and, most significant, for executive power.

Jefferson wished for inclusion of a Bill of Rights as a means of checking a flexible and powerful president. He grasped that a bill of rights was superfluous if people had no knowledge or grasp of the meaning of those rights, and thus, were kept from acting on those rights. Education he saw as the proper corrective.

On September 25 of 1789, Congress proposed the Bill of Rights and most of its articles were ratified by 1792.

Choosing and Overseeing Governors

Jefferson scholar Dumas Malone states that two significant public purposes of general education stood out for Jefferson and each concerned liberty: guarding the freedom and happiness of citizens and ensuring freedom from tyranny. Freedom from tyranny, he says, was "prominent if not predominant in his thought."[19] Jefferson writes in a letter to fellow Virginian Mann Page (August 30, 1795):

> I do not believe with the Rochefoucaulds and Montaignes, that fourteen out of fifteen men are rogues; I believe a great abatement from that proportion may be made in favor of general honesty. But I have always found that rogues would be uppermost, and I do not know that the proportion is too strong for the higher orders, and for those who, rising above the swinish multitude, always contrive to nestle themselves into the places of power and profit. These rogues set out with stealing the people's good opinion, and then steal from them the right of withdrawing it, by contriving laws and associations against the power of the people themselves.[20]

The passage confirms Malone's point. It is not so much Jefferson's unswerving faith in the people that drives his republicanism—Jefferson had seen too little of what the people could do to have unswerving faith—but instead a historically founded fact that the wealthy and wellborn tend to govern in their own best interest at expense of the people. As A. L. C. Destutt de Tracy writes, "Laws should always endeavor to protect weakness; while too frequently they incline to favour power."[21] If a nation is in some sense—even if only in a loose sense—a unit and if that unit comprises all people equally, then government is equally for all people. Thus, the only faction whose judgment ought to be carried is that of the majority, suitably enlightened through education. For elected officials to exercise their judgments on the people without consent of the people is a baseless, unconscionable abuse of power. Thus, governors are to be chosen by the people, watched by the people, and if needed, recalled by the people.

PARADOX OF PUBLIC SERVICE

Jefferson's republicanism was in some sense a compromise between traditional aristocracy and direct-participation democracy. He recognized that governments ought to be for all the people—not just for them governing—and that governments could not be by the people—at least, not in any immediate sense, because people were incapable of directing political affairs, especially in large nations.

As members not only of communities, but also of states and a nation, most American citizens lacked the intellectual and financial resources to participate in high-level government functions. Yet even those citizens with intellectual and financial wherewithal sufficient to participate in high-level government functions often found out, as did Jefferson, that substantial and sustained participation in the affairs of their state or their country could be personally detrimental, even debilitating. It could lead to ruination, financial or otherwise, of their domestic affairs. Thus, public office for Jefferson, though a duty for those persons capable of it, was onerous. "In a virtuous government," Jefferson writes to Virginia statesman Richard Henry Lee (June 17, 1779), "public offices are, what they should be, burthens to those appointed to them, which it would be wrong to decline, though foreseen to bring with them intense labour, and great private loss." Who, then, of sober mind would wish to govern?[22]

Jefferson's concern was the same as that of Plato in *The Republic* over two thousand years before him. Jefferson recognized, as did Plato, that there was always a zealous pool of potential governors awaiting a suitable opportunity to govern on their own tyrannical terms. He also recognized, as did Plato, that those persons best suited to govern, those persons with foursquare and unimpeachable virtue, would be least motivated to govern. Power and celebrity would have no grip on them.

Plato acknowledges that the true aristoi, the complete guardians or rulers, are happiest, when not ruling their polis. What most suitably promotes their happiness is solitary, not political, activity—contemplating the metempirical Forms of the realm of things pure, unchanging, ungenerated, and eternal. What might induce them to rule? The true aristoi will merely recognize that their nurture and happiness are due to their polis, and grudgingly take to ruling "as to something compulsory . . . which is exactly the opposite of what's done by those who now rule in each city."[23]

Jefferson too acknowledges that the "natural aristoi," the most talented and virtuous, are happiest when not ruling. It is plain to them that a socially active domestic life is preferable to that of political service. Nonparochial governing means being rent from domestic tranquility, being forced to leave behind one's personal affairs to decay, and being tossed willy-nilly in the coliseum of nonstop political wrangling, most often to no fruitful end. Recall his letter, to Monroe (May 20, 1782), in which he writes humans must first manage their own concerns before they attempt to manage the concerns of others. That is not to denigrate the significance of benevolence in a virtuous life—Jefferson thought benevolent activity a mainstay of happiness—but merely recognition that benevolence, when taken to extreme, can be ruinously wasteful such that a "benefactor" might no longer be of benefit to another or to himself—a point made by Aristotle millennia ago.[24]

Thus, Jefferson qua political philosopher faced the same problem that Plato faced. How could a state be structured so that the wisest and most virtuous would be motivated to rule?[25]

Like Plato, the key for Jefferson was to encourage political participation of the intelligent and moral by setting up a minimal political structure in which intelligence and moral sensitivity would be rewarded or, at least, encouraged. Like Plato, the encouragement was to come through indirect rewards. The natural aristoi would realize that utmost political stability was incentive sufficient. In a stable state, all would be gainers. Yet for a stable state, all would have to contribute. Against Plato, ultimate political authority and responsibility for

Jefferson lay in the hands of the people, not the governors. "It is an axiom in my mind that our liberty can never be safe but in the hands of the people themselves, and that too of the people with a certain degree of instruction."[26] The natural aristoi had to rule both for the good of the state and to their personal detriment.

Jefferson's minimal political structure involved wards and general education. By establishing numerous political units in each state—that is, wards functioning as atoms—Jefferson could countenance a sort of organic unity through encouragement of parochial political participation. The key was inclusion of a primary school in each ward to give each citizen the minimum education needed for parochial political participation as well as management of his own affairs.

Citizens would also be responsible for electing officials to represent their interests in higher governmental affairs. Terms of office were not to be for life, and elected officials who were not responsive to their electors were recallable by those persons electing them. Limited terms were also to ensure, to a lesser extent, that no one governing would neglect his domestic life for an undue length of time.[27] Thus, the people would be happy because their governors would be virtuous, or as virtuous as possible, and thus, would be true representatives of their interests and of the advance of their nation. The governors would be happy, or as happy as possible, because they would be working toward the sort of political stability that was required of a progressive state. Failing to do so, they would suffer the pains of regret upon dereliction of duty. It is as Constantin François de Volney states in his utopian work *Les Ruins*, when the people speak to those persons whom they have elected to represent them (the translation from French is Jefferson's): "We raise you to-day above us, that you may better discover the whole of our relations, and be above the reach of our passions. But remember that you are our fellow-citizens; that the power we confer on you is our own; that we deposit it with you, but not as a property or heritage; that you must be the first to obey the laws you make; that to-morrow you redescend among us, and that you will have acquired no other right but that of our esteem and gratitude."[28]

THE WARD SYSTEM

As we have seen, the minimal political structure needed, a sort of blueprint for Jefferson's republicanism, was to be provided by establishing "hundreds," or wards. Writes one scholar: "Wards are units of local government, constructed to bring political management and administration straight to the people who are being 'represented.' They are the bulwark against all attempts to 'mining and sapping' the liberties of the people. As political machinery, they are the heart of pure republicanism, because through a system of wards the government keeps in touch with the needs of the people and is sensitive to their criticism."[29] Introduction of the ward system in Virginia would be a matter of introducing something comparable to New England's townships to give Virginians a greater sense of community and political involvement.[30] The key difficulties in instantiation of such a system would be the largeness of Virginia and the relative lack of population in certain sectors of land.

In "A Bill for the More General Diffusion of Knowledge," Jefferson writes of how wards are to be established in Virginia:

> The said Alderman . . . shall meet at the court-house of their county, and proceed to divide their said county into hundreds, bounding the same by water courses, mountains, or limits, to be run and marked, if they think necessary, by the county surveyor, and at the county expence, regulating the size of the said hundreds, according to the best of their discretion, so as that they may contain a convenient number of children to make up a school, and be of such convenient size that all the children within each hundred may daily attend the school to be established therein, and distinguishing each hundred by a particular name; which division, with the names of the several hundreds, shall be returned to the court of the county and be entered of record, and shall remain unaltered until the increase or decrease of inhabitants shall render an alteration necessary, in the opinion of any succeeding Alderman, and also in the opinion of the court of the county.[31]

Wards Jefferson construed as microrepublics, each functioning relatively independently of every other. He elaborates: "In each of these might be, first, an elementary school; second, a company of militia, with its officers; third, a justice of the peace and constable; fourth, each ward should take care of their own poor; fifth, their own roads; sixth, their own police; seventh, elect within themselves one or more jurors to attend the courts of justice; and eighth, give in at their folk-house, their votes for all functionaries reserved to their election."[32] The overall aim was to make individuals self-sufficient—to keep state and federal governments out of people's affairs and to have, in effect, the people govern themselves. Jefferson realized that any intrusion of high-level government in ward affairs, best intentions notwithstanding, could only be seen as quid pro quo. A county government, asked to supply monetary relief to the poor of a certain ward, might decide for that ward how it is best for it to alleviate poverty. A state government, allowed and commissioned to build roads in a particular ward, might wish to have a great deal to say about where those roads should be built and how they should be used. The national government, asked to determine justice for a particularly troublesome dispute between bitter disputants, might impose a standard of justice that fails to consider the circumstances of the dispute as well as local mores. In short, Jefferson was sufficiently savvy to recognize that not only people, but also governments, do not provide succor without asking for something in return. To invite any amount of nonparochial succor for something that could be handled locally was to invite encroachment on individual liberties and rights and to centralize and redouble political power.

To illustrate, in a letter to Joseph C. Cabell (February 2, 1816), Jefferson considers opposition to ward schools, which would to be funded chiefly by the wealthy in each ward. If it should be decided that it is up to the state and its governor to provide schools for each county, then it would be up to the governor and his council, the commissioners of the literary fund, or some other central authority to manage the schools. That a centralized authority can manage a ward's school better than the parents of that ward is a "belief against all experience." Jefferson continues:

> The way to have good and safe government, is not to trust it all to one; but to divide it among the many, distributing to every one exactly the functions he is competent to. Let the national government be entrusted with the defence of the nation and it's foreign and federal relations; the State governments with the civil rights; the Counties with the local concerns of the counties; and each Ward direct the interests within itself. It is by dividing and subdividing these republics from the great National one down thro' all its subordinations, until it ends in the administration of every man's farm and affairs by himself; by placing under everyone what his own eye may superintend, that all will be done for the best.

Beyond self-sufficiency, there were practical considerations, relevant early on for the fledgling country as well as later on for the developing and expanding country. First, because the new-formed federation of states was embryonic, the ward system, if universally adopted at some point in time, would be a way of establishing political stability from the ground up,[33] and thus, a greater probability of long-term survival. The scenario is in some sense comparable to an investor who diversifies his investments. While diversification makes negligible the likelihood of a great return on his investment, it buffers against loss of everything and makes probable a modest but secure return on an investment. Second, Jefferson's ward system was his way of ensuring that democratic ideals and political stability could survive in a country that was expanding territorially and progressing at a rapid technological and scientific pace.[34] Jefferson writes in 1816 to Governor Wilson C. Nicholas (April 2):

> My partiality for that division [into wards] is not founded in views of education solely, but infinitely more as the means of a better administration of our government, and the eternal preservation of its republican principles. The example of this most admirable of all human contrivances in government, is to be seen in our Eastern States; and its powerful effect in the order and economy of their internal affairs, and the momentum it gives them as a nation, is the single circumstance which distinguishes them so remarkably from every other national association.

Wards had an additional function. They were proposed by Jefferson as means of ridding state-sponsored religion—especially Anglicanism—and secularizing each state from the ground up. That would give states additional concerns, among them being education and care of the poor.[35]

The ward system was never instantiated, in some part because the well-to-do were uninterested in taxing themselves to educate the not-so-well-to-do in ward schools—namely, the evil that wards were meant to eradicate through general education was partly responsible for their rejection.[36] Nonetheless, that system reveals much about its author—his trust in the people and, especially, his distrust of people who are eager to wield political power. It also bespeaks an author with an expansive and consistent philosophical vision. As I mention in chapter 2, wards are a means of mediating between two antipodal philosophical views: the extreme nationalistic centrism of Alexander Hamilton and Patrick Henry's states'-rights view. Jefferson wanted nationalistic unity without centralization and without consolidation of power. He also wanted people to be freed from paternalistic government. The problem was intricate—one of attaining a strong sense of nationalistic unity, while preserving liberty and individuals' rights.[37]

That problem was decupled with the Louisiana Purchase, which added 828,800 square miles to United States in 1803. The purchase more than doubled the size of the nation's territories, and President Jefferson had to face directly the problem of preserving liberty and rights as well as a strong sense of nationalistic unity. Before evaluating Jefferson's justification of the purchase, it is gainful to see what Aristotle said millennia earlier about unity, human thriving, and size.

In VII.4 of his *Politics*, Aristotle writes:

> Yet this is clear also from circumstances that it is difficult, perhaps impossible, for what is over-populated to be well-governed. At any rate, among those poleis that seem to be well-governed, we see none without some restriction of its numbers. This is also plain through the force of reason. For law is a certain ordering (taxis), and good-government is necessarily good-ordering. But it is not possible to have order with an excessively large number of things, for that would be a task for a divine power, which holds together even this cosmos. But necessarily that polis is most beautiful whose limit (horos) is constrained by number, for indeed beauty is usually found in number and magnitude, but there is a proper boundary of magnitude for a polis as there is also for all other things—animals, plants, and tools. For when each of them is either too small or too large, it will lose its proper function (tēn autou dunamin); it will wholly forfeit its nature or, otherwise, be in poor condition.

Thus, if a polis is too small, it will not be self-sufficient; yet if a polis is too large, it will be self-sufficient in a loose sense, but "it will not be easy for it to possess a constitution."[38] Aristotle's point is that for any sort of political institution to have good order—and the good constitutions (politeiai) of which he speaks are polities, aristocracies, and kingships, or some admixture of them—it cannot exceed a certain size. The size, of course, varies with the type of constitution, the nature of the people, the location of the polis, and the climate of the location. If it exceeds its proper size, it is incapacitated. It fails to have good order and, thus, it ceases to be a functional unit.

Teleological language notwithstanding, Aristotle certainly makes some telling points—the most important of which is that a well-functioning political entity is recognizable, if not characterized, by its self-sufficiency. Too small of a political entity will not have even the capacity for self-sufficiency. Too large of a political entity will have the capacity for self-sufficiency, but that capacity will likely not be actualized because of the difficulty of keeping orderly something so large. His arguments are sensible.

In *The Spirit of Laws*, Montesquieu writes similarly, but his thoughts concern the nature of republics:

> It is natural for a republic to have only a small territory; otherwise it cannot long subsist. In an extensive republic there are men of large fortunes, and consequently of less moderation; there are trusts too considerable to be placed in any single subject; he has interests of his own; he soon begins to think that he may be happy and glorious by oppressing his fellow-citizens; and that he may raise himself to grandeur on the ruins of his country.
>
> In an extensive republic the public good is sacrificed to a thousand private views; it is subordinate to exceptions, and depends on accidents. In a small one the interest of the public is more obvious. better understood, and more within the reach of every citizen; abuses have less extent, and, of course, are less protected.[39]

Montesquieu goes on to say that a "despotic authority" is needed for a large empire. The prince must be the sole source of law and his decrees must shift in accordance with the caprices of the empire. The prince's resolutions must be quickly passed on to governors of territories and those governors must be kept loyal through fear.

The problems for Montesquieu are principally two. Large republics, having a large number of citizens, will doubtless have certain men of considerable fortune. Men of large fortune are men without moderation, and so such persons will look to prosper at expense of their fellow citizens. In doing so, the republic will degenerate into a plutocracy, or numerous plutocracies, in which chaos will abound. The sentiment is frighteningly prophetic. Second, in a large republic, the interests of the general public are subordinated to the interests of the thousand or so with wealth enough to be heard. No individual citizen will have a chance of being heard. There is only one way to preserve any sort of order in a republic of considerable size—that is, by rule of an autocrat—but then the republic ceases to be a republic.

In his Second Inaugural Address, Jefferson addresses the problem of preserving unity and liberty with the increase in size of the nation. He states:

> I know that the acquisition of Louisiana has been disapproved by some, from a candid apprehension that the enlargement of our territory would endanger its union. But who can limit the extent to which the federative principle may operate effectively? The larger our association, the less will it be shaken

by local passions, and in any view, is it not better that the opposite bank of the Mississippi should be settled by our own brethren and children, than by strangers of another family?[40]

The passage contains three arguments for justifying the purchase and expansion of the country, only two of which are relevant for our purposes.

In the first argument, the premise is given in the form of a rhetorical question. Fleshed out, the argument reads:

(1) No one knows the limit of effective federalist governing.
(2) So, it might work quite effectively on a large scale (2).
(3) So, the Louisiana Purchase is justifiable (3).

In this argument, claim 2 as a conclusion is strongly supported by claim 1 only because claim 2 is an especially weak claim and weak claims need little evidential support. Yet claim 2, as a premise for claim 3, the ultimate conclusion, is too weak to guarantee cogency. The argument, as a whole, fails.

The second argument, the argument from swamping,[41] can be fleshed out as follows:

(1) The effect of local passions on government is in inverse proportion to the size of a state.
(2) The Louisiana Purchase will greatly increase the size of the United States.
(3) So, the Louisiana Purchase will greatly diminish the effect of local passions on government (1 & 2).
(4) [Whatever diminishes the effect of local passions on government is something good for a nation.] [implied]
(5) So, the Louisiana Purchase is something good for a nation (3 & 4).
(6) So, the Louisiana Purchase is justifiable (5).

Here claim 1, derived from Montesquieu, seems reasonable and claim 2 is undeniable. The conclusion, claim 3, necessarily follows. Yet the ultimate conclusion, claim 6, does not seem to follow, because claim 4, which is implicit, is at best questionable. Thus, the modus-ponens argument to generate claim 5 is not sound. Of course, Jefferson might be assuming a proposition of nonuniversal scope for claim 4, instead of one with universal scope. Jefferson might be assuming something like *Whatever diminishes the effect of local passions on government is most often something good for a nation.* That weaker claim seems reasonable. In that case, claims 3 and 4 would be given as inductive evidence for claim 5 and the argument would be, I suspect, at least plausible.

The third argument, what might be called the argument from neighborhood,[42] is again given in the form of a rhetorical question. It does not address directly the problem of size, but it is not irrelevant. Its aim is relative; its force, pragmatic. Jefferson says that it is better for a republic to expand into the whole of the land into which it is situated so that its citizens will be bounded on all sides by "[one's] own brethren and children" rather than by strangers, whose political interests and views might not be similar to their own or might even be detrimental to their own. This argument, it is clear, does nothing to handle the objections of Aristotle that concern governing well any large state or those of Montesquieu that concern managing a thriving republic. It seems to be asserting that it is better to have a large, disordered, and incapable state without neighbors than a small, orderly, and self-sufficient state with potentially hostile neighbors.

One might object that Jefferson's attitude toward the problem of size is flippant. His arguments in favor of acquisition and assimilation of the new territory, in light of the problem of size, are overall not very persuasive. One suspects that he has not given the problem of size due consideration. Aristotle's statement that a state ceases to have any functional unity upon expanding beyond a certain limit seems to be given short shrift.

Jefferson's arguments, of course, are parts of an inaugural address, and inaugural addresses are meant to inspire confidence, hope, and trust in an administration. Thus, they are to be judged by their rhetorical merit more than by their cogency or soundness. As rhetorical devices, the arguments are successful.

That much is unquestionably true. Nonetheless, Jefferson uses the argument from swamping elsewhere.

In 1786, Jefferson writes to lawyer Archibald Stuart, "Our present federal limits are not too large for good government, nor will the increase of votes in Congress produce any ill effect. On the contrary, it will drown the little divisions at present existing there" (January 25, 1786).

To Vermont politician Nathaniel Niles, Jefferson says in 1801 not only that Montesquieu's doctrine is false but also that the reverse of it is true. "The later chapter of our history . . . furnishes a new proof of the falsehood of Montesquieu's doctrine, that a republic can be preserved only in a small territory. The reverse is the truth. Had our territory been even a third only of what it is, we were gone. But while frenzy and delusion, like an epidemic, gained certain part, the residue remained sound and untouched, and held on till their brethren could recover from the temporary delusion" (March 22). He iterates that sentiment in a letter to French politician François Barbé-Marbois in 1817: "I have much confidence that we shall proceed successfully for ages to come, and that, contrary to the principle of Montesquieu, it will be seen that the larger the extent of country, the more firm its republican structure, if founded, not on conquest, but in principles of compact and equality. My hope of its duration is built much on the enlargement of the resources of life going hand in hand with the enlargement of territory, and the belief that men are disposed to live honestly, if the means of doing so are open to them" (June 14, 1817). Here largeness is not a liability but an asset. Soundness of republican government is in proportion to size, granting a constitution of compact and equality.

On May 26, 1801, he speaks to the Rhode Island General Assembly: "While smaller governments are better adapted to the ordinary objects of a society, larger confederations more effectually secure independence, and the preservation of republican government." The argument here is that small governments are sensitive to the parochial wants and needs of their people, but that sensitivity and their smallness makes them fragile. Moreover, they can do little, on account of their small size, to secure for their citizens freedom and their rights.

To Robert Williams (November 1, 1801), governor of the Mississippi Territory, Jefferson writes:

> I have seen with regret, the violence of the dissensions in your quarter. We have the same in the territories of Louisiana and Michigan. It seems that the smaller the society the bitterer the dissensions into which it breaks. Perhaps this observation answers all the objections drawn by Mr. Adams from the small republics of Italy. I believe ours is to owe its permanence to its great extent, and the smaller portion comparatively, which can ever be convulsed at one time by local passions.

Here smallness is proportioned to bitter factionalist disputation. That notion is echoed in a letter to fellow republican Elbridge Gerry (June 11, 1812). Jefferson writes, "The extent of our territory secures it, I hope, from the vindictive passions of the petty incorporations of Greece." The implication is that the continual factionalism and warring among Greek poleis was due not only to commitments to heterogeneous constitutions among poleis, but also to their small size. He says much the same thing in letters to lawyer Horatio Gates Spafford (March 17, 1814) and politician Henry Dearborn (August 17, 1821).

In short, these letters, beginning in 1786, show that Jefferson considered largeness of a state to be an asset of republican government because in his estimation republican government thrives in proportion to its size so long as it is based on compact and equality. There is nothing metempirical in the argument from swamping. Jefferson's various employments in his writings show a decided appeal to experience.

Moreover, Jefferson was sanguine about the prospect of successful territorial expansion of the fledgling nation, because of his commitment to agrarianism as both an economic ideal and a moral ideal. In the New World, there was land aplenty but want of people to farm the land. That was not a concern for Jefferson. As Thomas Malthus had shown in his "new work,"[43] population increases rapidly, in geometric ratio, over time. With people to farm the arable land through western expansion, Jefferson added, food too, pace Malthus, would increase geometrically—at least, in the short term.[44]

It is especially significant to grasp that Jefferson's commitment to agrarianism cannot be divorced from his commitment to humans being social creatures. For Jefferson, humans are not atoms but rather are inescapably gregarious. Recall what he says to fellow Virginian Francis Gilmer (June 7, 1817), "Man was created for social intercourse" and, in him, there is implanted a sense of social justice. It follows that humans are not fully human unless they are part of some society of their fellow men.

Yet for Jefferson, humans qua social creatures are also rational and progressive beings. Thus, it is not any sort of society that is suited for human thriving or happiness, but one in which progressive thinking thrives. That is why he says to James Madison and statesman Edward Carrington that the Native Americans' form of government without laws, though preferable to coercive government, allows only for a mawkish form of happiness, based on pride, shame, and reverence of pastness.[45]

Human rationality and the concomitant yearning for progress fueled Jefferson's passion and preference for a large nation of states. Jefferson was somehow convinced that size was no impediment to liberty. "We should have such an empire for liberty as she has never surveyed since the creation," he writes to James Madison (April 27, 1809), "and I am persuaded no constitution was ever before so well calculated as ours for extensive empire and self-government."[46]

How could Jefferson be so optimistic about maintenance of political unity and thriving liberty in the expanding nation? In one obvious respect, the hope seems half-baked. As Aristotle sensibly noted, excessive size at some point is impossible to manage.

The answer is that Jefferson always held out hope for instantiation of the system of wards, which was to be the bedrock and mainstay of his republican schema. The hundreds, as little republics, "were to represent the first stage in self-government, as the free primary schools were to represent the first entities in public education."[47] These wards were to be anchored by responsible, participating citizens—enabled to be responsible and participating by general education.

From Jefferson's perspective, republican government would begin with the wards. A system of wards needed to be established before there could be a system of public education. "The truth is," Jefferson writes to Joseph C. Cabell (November 28, 1820), "that the want of common education with us is not from our poverty, but from the want of an orderly system [that is, wards]."[48] Education and order were inseparable for Jefferson. If order through wards could be instantiated and if wards should prove to be self-sufficient, then the country would be able to spread out across the whole continent, maintain a strong sense of functional unity, and preserve the fullest sense of human liberty, in keeping with humans' social nature. Wards and not individuals were, normatively speaking, the axiologically substratal parts of Jefferson's theoretical vision.[49] As he wrote to Joseph C. Cabell (January 13, 1823), "As Cato then concluded every speech with the words '*Carthago delenda est*,' so do I every opinion with the injunction 'divide the counties into wards.'"[50] That is also why he wrote to Cabell years later that he would rather give up the university before giving up elementary schools.

GENERAL EDUCATION

Jefferson's wards were to provide the political structure and order that characterized and undergirded county, state, and national politics from the bottom up and allowed for fullest expression of human liberty. Central to each ward in both literal and figurative senses was an elementary school, where all youths were to be educated generally.[51]

The general education of the masses was a radical suggestion for its time, and certainly egged on by invention of the printing press. Jefferson—against Plato, Thomas Hobbes, and certainly Federalists of his day—was claiming that all persons, given normal rational and moral faculties, were fully capable of making decisions concerning their own best interest—that is, their own happiness. He also thought that persons were capable of electing and overseeing elected officials, if given a modest education. For those tasks, both the rational faculty and the moral sense needed honing or exercise through education.

As we have seen, the aims of ward-school education were encouragement of morally appropriate conduct, just transactions in everyday commercial affairs, and effective citizenry, in both private and public domains, which allowed each citizen to know and act on his rights and suggested paths for participation in political affairs at the most basic level of government.[52] Jefferson sought to secularize education.[53]

In his "A Bill for the More General Diffusion of Knowledge" in 1779, Jefferson says ward schools are to be established as follows. Three aldermen— "three of the most honest and able men of their county"—are to be chosen through vote each year, by electors of each county. To begin, the aldermen in each county are to convene in their county's courthouse to divide their county into hundreds so that the school of each hundred might generally have the same number of children. Under the direction of the aldermen, electors will convene to decide on the site for each ward school. Aldermen of each county will choose each year an overseer—"eminent for his learning, integrity, and fidelity"—for every ten schools of each county, or roughly so. Every overseer will appoint a teacher for each ward school and be responsible for visiting each school to make sure that the "general plan of reading and instruction," proposed by the visitors of William and Mary College, is observed. Every teacher will have food and lodging provided for him and his washing done.[54]

Concerning the subjects of education, he writes succinctly:

> At every one of these schools shall be taught reading, writing, and common arithmetick, and the books which shall be used therein for instructing the children to read shall be such as will at the same time make them acquainted with Græcian, Roman, English, and American history. At these schools all the free children, male and female, resident within the respective hundred, shall be intitled to receive tuition gratis, for the term of three years, and as much longer, at their private expence, as their parents, guardians or friends, shall think proper.[55]

In his "Bill for Establishing a System of Public Education" in 1817, Jefferson says that a judge in every county will appoint three Visitors to divide the county into wards. They will designate a day for each ward in which all adult males will meet, along with one of the Visitors, and vote on the location, size, and structure of the ward school and house for the teacher as well as how it is to be constructed—that is, by the joint labor of the warders or by pecuniary contributions. They will also elect a warden to direct and superintend the buildings.[56]

The Visitors will be responsible also for designating in each ward "a person of good moral character," who will have a house and other accommodations and an annual salary to be determined by the warders. The teacher will teach reading, writing, numerical arithmetic, and geography. All persons will be entitled gratis to three years of education. No one, attaining fifteen years of age, who cannot read "readily in some tongue, native or acquired," will be considered a citizen. A Visitor will visit each school at least once each year and reward with "honorary marks and testimonies of approbation" those who excel in any subject to "excite industry and emulation."[57]

One striking difference between the two proposed bills, introduced some thirty-eight years apart, is the inclusion of geography as a course of study. That is a direct consequence of the expanding nation and the clamant need of all citizens to know not only their own property and its resources to maximize their liberty but also something about even the most distant parts of their country and its resources.

After his tenure as president, Jefferson's vision for the United States became continental. "Our confederacy must be viewed as the nest from which all America, North and South, is to be peopled," he writes to Archibald Stuart (January 25, 1786), Virginia lawyer, judge, and friend of Jefferson. Geography was a vital discipline—especially for a fledgling country with much unexplored land with resources unknown.[58]

As an obsessively orderly person throughout his life, Jefferson had an obsessively orderly vision for an expanding country that required knowledge of geometry as well as geography. On the one hand, geography would enable persons to get to know the layout of the land and its resources so that land could be put to use most effectively. On the other hand, geometry was the means of taming by framing that land.[59]

UPSHOT

Polish patriot Thaddeus Kościuszko writes to Jefferson on the pressing need for general education in Jefferson's republicanism. <<Qui me dira positivement que votre Gouvernement Rèpublicain durerat longtems [*sic*]; Si L'èducation de la jeunesse n'est pas établie sur la base fixe des principes Republicains sure La morale es La justice, et Surveillèe par Le Congrès même afin qu'aucun Professeur ne puisse s'en écarter. . . . Votre véritable force consiste dans les habitants de l'intèrieur ou il y a des moeurs des vertus sociales susceptibles de grandeur d'Ame et de génerosité si vous renforcez ces qualites par une éducation strictement surveillér alors votre but sera rempli, et vour vèrez sortir de votre Pays autant de Hèros que la Grece et plus sages que de Rome.>>[60]

Jefferson's comprehensive plan of education, fully spelled out in his bill of 1779 and modified in his bill of 1817, was never implemented. The bill of 1817 gained few votes. There was near unanimity on the need of a university, general agreement on the need for colleges or grammar schools, but disagreement on their number and location, and great disagreement on the need of primary schools in wards.[61] A large obstacle was that the self-sufficiency at which Jefferson aimed for wards came with a monetary price. The money was to come from within wards and each would have to pay a part. Many, especially the wealthy who would bear the lion's share of the burden—and in Jefferson's day only the wealthy were suitably educated—objected to Jefferson's plan to levy taxes in wards to pay for public education. An additional problem was its equalitarianism. The wealthy would be educated with, not separated from, the nonwealthy.

Jefferson had two criticisms to the objections. First, following the observable cycle of things, he noted that the descendants of the rich would become poor within three generations, and then their children would be recipients of education at the hands of the new class of wealthy citizens. One can see that that objection, articulated in a private letter to Joseph C. Cabell (January 14, 1818), would have nowise mollified the concerns of the wealthy. Second, the rich's refusal to pay for the education of the nonrich would merely perpetuate the problem Jefferson was aiming to solve: riddance of the artificial aristoi from governance. The extant system created and perpetuated an artificial aristocracy, based on wealth and birth, not on talent and virtue, and that artificial aristocracy predominated in governing. Only by educating all persons to some degree could the natural aristoi supplant the artificial aristoi and just governors supplant unjust governors.

Overall, Jefferson soberly noted that the cost of instantiating general education through wards was negligible in comparison with the cost of ignorance.[62] Yet Jefferson never lost his faith that his educational system and his vision of a thriving republic would best be secured by partitioning the counties into wards and establishing a primary school in each ward. To Joseph C. Cabell (January 14, 1818), he writes, "A system of general instruction, which shall reach every description of our children, from the richest to the poorest, as it was the earliest, so will it be the latest, of all public concerns in which I shall permit myself to take an interest."[63] In a paradisiacal letter to J. Correia da Serra (November 25, 1817), he sums, "Mine . . . may be an Utopian dream, but being innocent, I have thought I might indulge in it till I go to the land of dreams, and sleep there with the dreamers of all past and future times."

CHAPTER 10

"THE ABLEST . . . OR NONE AT ALL"

Jefferson on Secondary Education
for Sensitive Meritocracy

> *"Nobody can doubt my zeal for the general instruction of the*
> *people. Who first started that idea? I may surely say, myself."*
> —TJ to General James Breckenridge,
> February 15, 1821

Like Plato millennia before him, Jefferson believed in two classes of people: the laboring and learned. "The laboring will need the first grade of education to qualify them for their pursuits and duties; the learned will need it as a foundation for further acquirements."[1] Reference to "further acquirements" included further education to prepare individuals for governing at the levels of county, state, and country as well as for educating and doing science.

As a counterbalance to the egalitarianism at the primary tier, where the rich and poor would be educated together, college-level (the intermediate tier for Jefferson) and university-level education were to be put into place to select the intellectually and morally strong and to weed out the weak. Jefferson's aim was to differentiate the natural aristoi from the artificial aristoi and restrict governing for the former.

Higher education was, thus, a needed complement to general education in a thriving society. A thriving state was one in which there was political stability through a strong sense of unity and utmost regard for individuals' rights. However, a thriving state was also intellectually and morally progressive. Intellectual and moral progress could only be ensured by having the natural aristoi in place in the most significant positions in a state.

AN ARISTOCRAT WITH DEMOCRATIC SYMPATHIES

As vice president, Jefferson enlisted the advice of both scientist Joseph Priestley and celebrated French economist and diplomat Pierre Samuel Dupont de Nemours on a general plan of education. Priestley replied with "Hints concerning Public Education"; Dupont, with a book-length manuscript. As Priestley's "hints" likely had little influence on Jefferson, I focus on Dupont's treatise below.

After narrowly escaping the guillotine and enduring harassment at the hands of anarchic mobs in France, Dupont wrote to Jefferson about coming to live in the New World. "I am commissioned by the National Institute x to make a trip there [America], which has for its aim a report on my researches which may be of use to science; and it is my intention to prolong this trip to the end of my life. I wish to die in a country in which liberty does not exist only in the laws, always more or less well, more or less badly, carried out; but chiefly in the fixed habits of the nation."[2] In the 1770s, Dupont had counseled the Polish monarch on numerous issues, education being one of them. Consequently, two years after his letter to Jefferson, the newly elected president wrote Dupont (April 12, 1800) for the latter's thoughts on education.

> I do not mean to trouble you with writing a treatise; but only to state what are the branches of science which in the present state of man, and particularly with us, should be introduced into an academy, and to class them together in such groupes, as you think might be managed by one professor devoting his whole time to it. It is very interesting to us to reduce the important sciences to as few professorships as possible because of the narrowness of our resources. Therefore I should exclude those branches which can usually be learned with us in private schools, as Greek, Latin, common arithmetic, music, fencing, dancing, &c. I should also exclude those which are unimportant, as the Oriental languages &c. and those which may be acquired by reading alone, without the help of a master. such as Ethics, &c.
>
> A short note on each science, such as you might give without too much trouble would be thankfully received. Possessing yours & Dr. Priestley's ideas, we should form a little committee at home, and accommodate them to the state of our country, and dispositions of our fellow citizens, better known to us than to you. Our object would be, after settling the maximum of the effort to which we think our fellow citizens could be excited, to select the most valuable objects to which it could be directed.

Jefferson's request betrays his predilection for useful knowledge—knowledge in the service of his country's advance.

Dupont, happy to have made such a cordial and significant friend in America, wrote in reply:

> All instruction really of use in our daily life, all practical sciences, all physical activity, all good sense, all upright notions, all morality, all virtue, all courage, all prosperity, all the happiness of a nation, and especially of a republic, must begin with primary and elementary schools.
>
> Boarding schools, colleges, universities, learned and philosophical societies can and must serve only in the development of a small number of outstanding natures, which have only two actual uses themselves: first, the advancement of the sciences; second, the application of their results to the arts, which find a suitable place in common instruction and in those courses, taught without effort in the elementary schools.[3]

Dupont's reply must have considerably pleased Jefferson, as it was wholly in keeping with the latter's basic notion of educating the laborers pursuant to their needs and educating the aristoi pursuant to their fullest capacities for the betterment of the nation.

Dupont responded eventually to Jefferson's request with his manuscript *Sur l'education nationales dans les États Unis d'Amérique*. In it, he advocated two distinct school systems—one for the sons of laborers and one for the sons of the gentry—a dichotomy that betrayed an aristocratic bent and a general distrust of the masses—two themes pervasive in the manuscript.

Jefferson appreciated Dupont's insights but could not accept his wholesale distrust of the masses, for Jefferson's republicanist experiment gambled much on the well-being of all citizens and the good judgment of the general citizenry both in determining their own affairs and in minding their elected governors. His letter of April 24, 1816, to Dupont, in reply to Dupont's manuscript, is a précis of the philosophical undergirding of Jefferson's educational views. Though one of the learned, Jefferson had a strong belief in the capacities of the laborers. "Enlighten the people generally, and tyranny and oppressions of body and mind will vanish like evil spirits at the dawn of day." Diffusion of knowledge—education of the masses—will lead to "much improvement . . . in matters of government and religion."[4] Jefferson's reply indicates considerable trust in the powers of the people.

In a letter to the Marquis de Lafayette (April 24, 1816), Jefferson politi-cally distances himself from his correspondent by distinguishing between two sorts of love of the people. Jefferson avers that his love of the people is trustful, while Lafayette's love is distrustful. "You love them as infants whom you are afraid to trust without nurses; and I as adults whom I freely leave to self-government." Jefferson's love is sanguine—perhaps even panglossian. Lafayette's love is conditional and paternalistic. Where there is distrust in the scaffolding, there cannot be political stability in a republic.

In "A Bill for the More General Diffusion of Knowledge," Jefferson says, consistent with the paradox of public service, that it is the duty of the natural aristoi to serve the republic to the best of their abilities for the sake of public happiness:

> Whereas it is generally true that people will be happiest whose laws are best, and are best administered, and that laws will be wisely formed, and honestly administered, in proportion as those who form and administer them are wise and honest; whence it becomes expedient for promoting the public happi-ness that those persons, whom nature hath endowed with genius and virtue, should be rendered by liberal education worthy to receive and able to guard the sacred deposit of the rights and liberties of their fellow citizens, and that they should be called to that charge without regard to wealth, birth, or other accidental condition or circumstance.[5]

Such passages show higher education serves not so much the persons being educated, but public happiness and a thriving state. Jefferson is a natural aristos with strong democratic sympathies and leanings.

AIMS OF HIGHER EDUCATION

In his "Rockfish Gap Report" (1818), Jefferson lists the following as aims and expresses his mature view of the "higher branches of education."[6]

> To form the statesmen, legislators and judges, on whom public prosperity and individual happiness are so much to depend;
> To expound the principles and structure of government, the laws which regu-late the intercourse of nations, those formed municipally for our own government, and a sound spirit of legislation, which, banishing all arbi-

trary and unnecessary restraint on individual action, shall leave us free
to do whatever does not violate the equal rights of another;

To harmonize and promote the interests of agriculture, manufactures and
commerce, and by well informed views of political economy to give a
free scope to the public industry;

To develop the reasoning faculties of our youth, enlarge their minds, cultivate their morals, and instill into them the precepts of virtue and order;

To enlighten them with mathematical and physical sciences, which advance
the arts, and administer to the health, the subsistence, and comforts of
human life;

And, generally to form them to habits of reflection and correct action, rendering them examples of virtue to others, and of happiness within
themselves.[7]

Following the lead of the previous chapter, I expatiate on each aim in what
follows.

Form Just, Wise Political Leaders/Scientists

One of the chief aims of Bill 79 in 1779 and Jefferson's bill of 1817 was
to bring about stable government. Dumas Malone says, "His concern was to
broaden the educational base of society and, at the same time, to search out
and utilize for the public good the aristocracy of worth and genius which he
afterwards describes as 'the most precious gift of nature.'"[8]

Jefferson's most precious gift of nature was that of the natural aristoi to
the common people. With the natural aristoi assuming the most significant
functions of a thriving republic, due to their assimilation of a useful education
taught at the highest levels, all would be gainers. The state would benefit from
the assiduous work toward scientific advance. The laborers would benefit
from the state, which would be progressive and run by just governors. Even
the learned or natural aristoi would benefit, at least indirectly, from the political stability they were responsible for sustaining.

It was the job of education as a whole to winnow out the artificial from the
natural aristoi and create as many incentives as possible for encouraging the
learned and virtuous to assume the most important roles in a thriving republic.
In practice, the aim of separating the talented and virtuous from the wealthy
and wellborn could not work in Jefferson's system, as the system allowed too
few indigent students each year to receive education at the highest levels. So,

in effect, mostly the wealthy and wellborn would be educated at the highest levels and mostly the wealthy and wellborn would be available for public offices. It was, nonetheless, a step in the right direction.

Expound Laws and Preserve Liberties

Jefferson's vision of a happy or stable state is one in which there is fullest political participation of all citizens—each pursuant to his capacities. Full participation entails that people have the freedom to manage their own affairs as they see fit, without governmental intervention. To guarantee freedom, the domestic role of high-level government is fundamentally to preserve the rights of the citizenry. For that to happen, citizens need to have full control over their elected representatives because "governments are more or less republican as they have more or less of the element of popular election and control in their composition," as Jefferson writes to politician John Taylor (May 28, 1816).

To think that government can be found in a constitution is comparable to thinking that the essence of a person can be found in a painting of him at a given time. Jefferson was clear that government is never to be found in a constitution, which is always a rusty representative of the will of the people, but in "the spirit of the people," since the laws reflect the will of the people only at the time of their inception. Given that humans are progressive beings, a constitution is, in effect, moldy and superannuated soon after it is ratified. He writes to Samuel Kercheval (July 12, 1816):

> Laws and institutions must go hand in hand with the progress of the human mind. As that becomes more developed, more enlightened, as new discoveries are made, new truths disclosed, and manners and opinions change with the change of circumstances, institutions must advance also, and keep pace with the times. We might as well require a man to wear still the coat which fitted him when a boy, as civilized society to remain ever under the regimen of their barbarous ancestors.

Jefferson makes the same point in his "Rockfish Gap Report." It is education that has moved Americans beyond the hoary condition of Native Americans. "What chains them to their present state of barbarism and wretchedness, but a bigoted veneration for the supposed superlative wisdom of their fathers, and the preposterous idea that they are to look backward for better things, and not forward, longing, as it should seem, to return to the days of eating acorns and roots, rather than indulge in the degeneracies of civilization?" Jefferson says rhetorically. "And how much more encouraging to the achievements of science and improvement is this, than the desponding view that the condition of man cannot be ameliorated, that what has been must ever be, and that to secure ourselves where we are, we must tread with awful reverence in the footsteps of our fathers."[9]

That is why Jefferson states, in his famous usufruct letter to James Madison (September 6, 1789), no law or constitution can be perpetually binding. Every law and constitution is, in effect, illegitimate after nineteen years. To bind citizens of one generation to the laws or constitution of their parents or forebears, in effect, is to bind the living to the laws and constitution of the dead.

Harmonize and Promote Agriculture, Manufactures, and Commerce (Science)

Jefferson says that it is the business of higher education to promote the economic interests of the nation. Universities especially, in Jefferson's mature educative thinking, are supposed to be institutions where every useful branch of knowledge can be taught at its highest level. "Colleges and universities might teach many of the same subjects . . . but where the former did so to a 'competent' extent, the latter offered the most advanced instruction possible."[10] Jefferson's early vision of his fledgling nation is a state in which the people are predominantly agrarian.[11] He comes gradually to see the insufficiency of husbandry as an economic ideal because of the need for and inevitability of manufacture and commerce in the developing nation.[12] He comes to advocate husbandry, manufacture, and commerce through university-level learning that is in some sense vocational.

An 1814 letter to Peter Carr (September 7) fleshes out that vision of grammar schools as vocational schools—called "professional schools."[13] He gives a detailed outline of three departments—that of civil architecture, gardening, painting, sculpture, and music theory; that of military and naval architecture, projectiles, rural economy (agriculture, horticulture, and veterinary), technical philosophy (comprising the mariner, carpenter, shipwright, pump maker, clockmaker, machinist, optician, metallurgist, founder, cutler, druggist, brewer, vintner, distiller, dyer, painter, bleacher, soap maker, tanner, powder maker, salt maker, and glassmaker), medical practice, material medicine, pharmacy, and surgery; and that of theology and ecclesiastical history and municipal and foreign law—where "each science is to be taught in the highest degree," namely, "with more minuteness and detail than was within the scope of the general schools for the second grade [i.e., grammar schools or colleges] of instruction." Unlike his bills of 1779 and 1817, the subjects taught are to be dictated by the professions commonly practiced at the time. Professional schools concede much and are designed to promote the general practices of agriculture, manufacture, and commerce.

Develop Intelligence, Moral Sensitivity, and Habits of Reflection and Correct Action

It is clear that Jefferson, through higher education, wished to develop genius as fully as possible. Following the strict empiricism of his British triad, Bacon, Locke, and Newton, as well as the Scottish empiricists, Jefferson disavowed speculative disciplines that had uncertain bearing on observable things. Aversion to metaphysics is evident in a quote from Lord Bolingbroke in Jefferson's *Literary Commonplace Book*: "Solidity and extension are the primary qualities [of things], and in our ideas the essence of matter, of which we can frame no conception exclusively of them. what then are the primary ideas of spirit or immaterial substance?"[14] Jefferson answers Bolingbroke's question many years later, as we saw in chapter 1, in a letter to John Adams (August 25, 1820). "When once we quit the basis of sensation, all is in the wind. To talk of immaterial *existences* is to talk of *nothings*." Subjects like theology and metaphysics[15] were anathema to Jefferson and to be excluded, because of irrelevancy, from the curricula of higher education.[16]

Why, however, did Jefferson think higher education would promote moral sensitivity and habits of reflection and correct action? Reason, he often says, is unneeded for, even an obstacle to, morally correct action. Recall he disadvises Peter Carr (August 10, 1787) to pursue any course on ethics, as "it is lost time to attend lectures in this branch." He adds, "The rules of our moral conduct [are] not a matter of science." It is the role of reason to incite contagion, to encourage moral activity to keep strong the moral sense, and to prompt perfection of the moral sense through reading history—this last being the primary vehicle for moral improvement. It is not the role of reason to decide morally correct action. At the primary level of education, he writes in his *Notes on the State of Virginia*, "history by apprising them of the past will enable them to judge of the future; it will avail them of the experience of other times and other nations; it will enable them to know ambition under every disguise it may assume; and knowing it, to defeat its views." It will give the young their first and most lasting lesson in morality.[17] At the secondary level of education, the study of ancient and modern history teaches moral lessons that are politically applicable, since it is history that "informs us what bad government is."[18] The aim is political progress.

GRAMMAR SCHOOLS (COLLEGES)

"At the discharging of the pupils from the elementary schools," Jefferson writes in his 1814 letter to Peter Carr, "the two classes separate—those destined for labor will engage in the business of agriculture, or enter into apprenticeships to such handicraft art as may be their choice; their companions, destined to the pursuits of science, will proceed to the college, which will consist, 1st of general schools; and 2d, of professional schools."

In a letter to Joseph Priestley, just prior to his presidency (January 27, 1800), Jefferson writes of dividing every county into hundreds, or wards, each roughly to be five or six square miles. In the middle of each ward there is to be a ward school. The state is to be laid off into ten districts, with a college in the middle of each district.[19] To Governor Wilson C. Nicholas (April 2, 1816), Jefferson says, "I know no better rule to be assumed than to place one within a day's ride of every man's door . . . one for every eighty square miles."

In his 1779 "A Bill for the More General Diffusion of Knowledge," Jefferson states that for every ten ward schools, or roughly so, there will be one grammar school.[20] The overseers of certain counties will collect—and here Jefferson lists and groups the counties—and will designate a suitable spot for a grammar school. The spot must be central and, above all, conducive to good health. A house of brick or stone along with "necessary offices" will be built on the spot. They must accommodate a room for schooling, a dining hall, four rooms for a master and usher, and ten or twelve rooms in which students can lodge. The buildings will be funded out of the public treasury—that is, through public taxation.[21]

The subject of educating is given tersely. "In these grammar schools," Jefferson writes, "shall be taught the Latin and Greek languages, English grammar, geography, and the higher part of numerical arithmetic, to wit, vulgar and decimal fractions, and the extraction of the square and cube roots."[22]

The overseers will appoint a Visitor from each county, and the Visitors of each grammar school will meet and pick out a master and, if needed, and usher. The Visitors will be required to stop by the grammar school at least twice each year and assess the plan of instruction suggested by the Visitors of William and Mary College. A steward will be allowed to each master to procure provisions, fuel, and servants for cooking, waiting, house cleaning, washing, mending, and gardening. He will also be responsible for the buildings being in functional order. Money for the master, usher, steward, and servants will be at expense of the students—some being boarded privately, others publicly. From each ward every year, public funding is awarded one male student, "of promising genius and disposition" and whose parents have not the wherewithal for sending the boy to the grammar school.[23]

Those students who are publically funded will be on probation while being educated. The least promising of the publicly funded students who have been there one year will be discontinued. After two years, all except one of the publicly funded students will be discontinued. Yet that one of "best genius and disposition" will be educated for four more years at public expense. Of the senior scholars each year, one will be awarded publicly funded education at the College of William and Mary. That scholar will be chosen from one-half of the districts in Virginia in odd years and the other half of the districts in Virginia in even years.[24]

In Jefferson's "Bill for Establishing a System of Public Education" of 1817, the Visitors are to convene and determine the site of the college. The schoolhouse is again to be made of brick or stone, but there are to be two schoolrooms and four rooms to accommodate not one, but two professors. There are to be sixteen dormitories, each with a fireplace and each to house no more than two pupils.[25]

The subjects of study are "the Greek, Latin, French, Spanish, Italian, and German languages, English grammar, geography, ancient and modern [history], the higher branches of numerical arithmetic, the mensuration of, and the use of the globes, and the ordinary elements of navigation."[26]

The scant treatment of subjects of study in his two bills is explicable in that they are bills, designed to show the need and serviceability of Jefferson's overall educative scheme. It is not necessary at this point to proffer a detailed explication of the courses of study, and I suspect, Jefferson would think of himself as poorly qualified to do just that.

In his 1814 letter to Peter Carr, Jefferson gives a detailed explication of the courses of study in the "General [i.e., Grammar] Schools."[27] The "branches of useful science" are subsumed under the rubrics language, mathematics, and philosophy.

LANGUAGE	MATHEMATICS	PHILOSOPHY
1. Ancient and Modern Language and History	1. Pure Mathematics (Arithmetic, Algebra, Fluxions, Geometry, and Trigonometry)	1. Ideology[28]
2. Grammar	2. Physico-Mathematics (Mechanics, Statics, Hydrostatics, Hydrodynamics, Navigation, Astronomy, Geography, Optics, Pneumatics, and Acoustics)	2. Ethics
3. Belles Lettres (Poetry, General Composition, and Literary Criticism)	3. Physics	3. Law of Nature and Nations
4. Rhetoric and Oratory	4. Chemistry	4. Government
5. A School for the Deaf, Dumb, and Blind	5. Natural History (Mineralogy)	5. Political Economy
	6. Botany	
	7. Zoology	
	8. Anatomy	
	9. Theory of Medicine	

Jefferson's list certainly bespeaks his interest in useful knowledge—the unsurprising exception being the study of Ancient Greek and Latin, which he says to Carr can be studied in conjunction with reading ancient history. As he writes much earlier to son-in-law Thomas Mann Randolph (August 27, 1786): "It would be a waste of time to attend a professor of [history]. It is to be acquired from books." He adds, "The histories of Greece and Rome are worthy a good degree of attention; they should be read in the original authors."

Aegis of the study of ancient languages, a large part of the curriculum at grammar schools, seems inconsistent with his equation of worth with serviceability, so it is worth examination of his focus on them. Jefferson addresses that issue in letters to Joseph Priestley (January 27, 1800) and, especially, John Brazier years later (August 24, 1819). Greek and Latin can be studied as works of reason, he writes to Priestley, which suggests some present-day applicability, or as works of "style & fancy"—that is, imagination. He adds, "To read the Latin and Greek authors in their original, is a sublime luxury; and I deem luxury in science to be at least as justifiable as in architecture, painting, gardening or the other arts." It is "an innocent enjoyment." To Brazier, Jefferson gives several reasons for the study of ancient languages: they are "models of pure taste in writing," an invaluable luxury, and "stores of real science deposited and transmitted." He lists history, ethics, arithmetic, geometry, astronomy, and natural history as examples of ancient sciences that are still relevant today. The classical languages, he sums, are a "solid basis for most, and an ornament to all the sciences."

Jefferson's axial arguments here are three: the argument from luxury, the argument from taste, and the argument from science. I flesh out each below. The argument from luxury might be fleshed out thus:

(1) Luxury in science is at least as justifiable as luxury in the arts.
(2) Reading Greek and Latin is a scientific luxury.
(3) The arts are an aesthetic luxury.
(4) Luxury in the arts is justifiable.
(5) So, luxury in reading Greek and Latin is justifiable (1–4).

The argument from taste, thus:

(1) Greek and Latin authors are models of pure taste (i.e., "national and chaste") in writing.
(2) Familiarity with those models has made English composition national and chaste, not inflated, like the northern style or the "hyperbolic and vague," like the eastern style.
(3) So, pure taste in writing is desirable (1 & 2).
(4) So, study of Greek and Latin is justifiable (3).

The argument from science, thus:

(1) There are "stores of real science deposited and transmitted us" in Greek and Latin.
(2) So, the study of Greek and Latin is justifiable.

Jefferson likely senses that the first two arguments are not very compelling from the standpoint of utility, since he does not expatiate on them. The analogical argument from luxury is aesthetic, which might be deemed irrelevant to utility. Yet one must tread cautiously here. Kames, whose *The Elements of Criticism* Jefferson owned and recommended to friend Robert Skipwith (August 3, 1771), thought aesthetic cultivation a boon moral sensitivity. It is likely Jefferson shared that view, provided that aesthetic cultivation was not taken to excess.[29] The argument from taste is also an aesthetic argument, yet one with an economic slant. A language should be national in that it should be parochial, not cosmopolitan. It should reflect transparently parochial interests—that is, the spirit of the people using the language. A language should be chaste in that it should be unadorned, clean, measured, and precise, not aureate, vulgar, hyperbolic, and vague. That Jefferson fails to expatiate on the argument from taste—especially on premise 2—is surprising, as there is more to it than meets the eye.

Jefferson does expand on the final argument—the argument from science—in the letter to Brazier. The ancient languages are invaluable to the moralist because "they furnish ethical writings highly and justly esteemed." They are valuable to the lawyer, as Latin gives expression to "the principles of civil law most conformable with the principles of justice." They are useful to the physician, since they offer "as good a code of his art as has been given us to this day." They are availing to the statesman, for they offer him a store of history, politics, mathematics, ethics, eloquence, and love of country and the rudiments of today's sciences whose fundamental terms are derived from Greek and Latin etyma." They are needed for the merchant because ethics, mathematics, geography, political economy, and history "seem to constitute the immediate foundations of his calling." They are required of the farmer and mechanic, since he uses ethics, mathematics, chemistry, and natural philosophy.

Nonetheless, the argument from science does little to show the usefulness of Greek and Latin. It merely demonstrates the historical value of Greek and Latin. First, Jefferson acknowledges that ethics and the medicine of his time have outstripped ancient ethics and medicine. Of ethics, he says to Brazier, "In my own opinion, the moderns are far advanced beyond them in this line of science." Of medicine, he says: "Theories and systems of medicine, indeed, have been in perpetual change from the days of good Hippocrates to the days of good Rush, but which of them is the true one? the present, to be sure, as long as it is the present, but to yield its place in turn to the next novelty, which is then to become the true system, and is to mark the vast advance of medicine since the days of Hippocrates." Second, that law still relies heavily on the Latin language is not to show necessarily that Latin is "most conformable with the principles of justice." It might be merely that law is conservative. Finally, the statesman, merchant, farmer, and mechanic draw from sciences, founded in Greek and Latin science, but that is not to say that they draw from Greek and Latin sciences, but only that they draw from sciences rooted in Greek and Latin. Hence, nothing shows that Greek and Latin authors are relevant in anything but a historical sense. Even Parson James Maury, whom Jefferson lauded for his facility with Greek and Latin, questioned the relevance of studying those languages, as "he could not name a single son of parents of large fortune who had entered the learned professions."[30]

As we have seen, the world through Jefferson's eyes was inevitably progressive. He writes to son-in-law John Wayles Eppes (September 18, 1813): "We, this age, and in this country especially, are advanced beyond those [ancient] notions of natural law. We acknowledge that our children are born free; and that freedom is the gift of nature."[31] To his Greek friend Monsieur Adamantios Koraïs (October 31, 1823), he speaks of the political inferiority of ancient systems of governing:

> The government of Athens, for example, was that of the people of one city making laws for the whole country subjected to them. That of Lacedæmon was the rule of military monks over the laboring classes of people, reduced to abject poverty. These are not the doctrines of the present age. Modern times have the signal advantage, too, of having discovered the only device by which these rights can be secured, to wit: government by the people, acting not in person, but by representatives chosen by themselves, that is to say, by every man of ripe years and sane mind, who either contributes by his purse or person to the support of his country."[32]

One must conclude that the primary significance of ancient literature was its moral inspiration.

WILLIAM AND MARY

Jefferson writes of the College of William and Mary in Query XV of his *Notes on the State of Virginia*:

> The College of William and Mary is the only public seminary of learning in this State. It was founded in the time of king William and queen Mary, who granted to it 20,000 acres of land, and a penny a pound duty on certain tobaccoes exported from Virginia and Maryland. . . . The assembly also gave it, by temporary laws, a duty on liquors imported, and skins and furs exported. From these resources it received upwards of 3,000£ communibus annis. The buildings are of brick, sufficient for an indifferent accommodation of perhaps an hundred students. By its charter it was to be under the government of twenty visitors, who were to be its legislators, and to have a president and six professors, who were incorporated. It was allowed a representative in the general assembly. Under this charter, a professorship of the Greek and Latin languages, a professorship of mathematics, one of moral philosophy, and two of divinity were established. To these were annexed, for a sixth professorship, a considerable donation by Mr. Boyle, of England, for the instruction of the Indians, and their conversion to Christianity. This was called the professorship of Brafferton, from an estate of that name in England, purchased with the monies given.[33]

Jefferson matriculated at William and Mary in 1760 and was educated until 1762. There were four "schools" at the time: the Grammar School, the Divinity School, the Philosophy School, and the Brafferton. The largest and most fundamental was the Grammar School, in which boys studied catechism, Greek and Latin, and English composition. The Philosophy School, which Jefferson entered, featured Natural Philosophy—physics, metaphysics, and mathematics—and Moral Philosophy—rhetoric, logic, and ethics. The Divinity School was for those students who successfully completed the Philosophy School and were placed on "the Foundation." They studied Hebrew and Holy Scripture and were placed in Orders to function in some capacity in the Anglican Church. The Brafferton was a school for anglicizing Native Americans.

School life was indoctrination in Anglicanism, which was the religion of the government in Jefferson's Virginia at the time.[34] All public officials were sworn into the thirty-nine articles of Anglican faith. Writes scholar Mark

Wenger: "Measured in terms of its influence on people's lives, the church was a formidable institution. Any threat to it was regarded as a menace to the social order—secular and ecclesiastical affairs were inseparable."[35] School began in the chapel at 6:00 or 7:00 a.m., depending on the time of year, with prayer-book readings, dictated by the seasons and rotations of the Anglican calendar. The day ended in similar fashion.

Seating in the chapel, the hall, and especially the church enforced the various levels of social order. In the hall, where students and faculty met thrice for "Commons" or communal meals, seating reflected relative importance. The first table sat the president; the last, the Native American master and his students. In the chapel and church, the best families occupied the largest, most noticeable pews. The school, thus, reinforced the conservative tendencies of government by the artificial aristoi.

The college was essentially one building with three stories and two rear wings, each with a hall and chapel. The building enclosed a beautiful garden with graveled walkways. Lecture rooms were on the first floor, at the front of the main building. The second floor housed a Convocation Room, to accommodate the professors and visitors. Next to the Convocation Room was a Common Room, in which the professors would socialize. On the third floor, each professor had a modest living space of two rooms. Additional rooms were there for the better of the more established students, no more than four to a room. A library was added in 1773. Grammar-school students slept in dormitories over the hall and chapel of each wing.

After the tenure of William and Mary's first president, James Blair, a tough-minded politician with unquestionable political power in Virginia, the college was wracked by several scandals and numerous difficulties—riotous, drunken, and irreligious students, drunken professors, and troublesome Visitors, among other things. The college was, as one scholar says, "out of control" by the time of Jefferson's matriculation.[36]

The degenerate climate had little influence on Jefferson qua student. With matchless motivation, he took it upon himself to get what he could get from his time at the college. He found a palliative in the only non-Anglican professor at the college—William Small, professor of mathematics, an exceptional tutor, friend, and quasi father to Thomas Jefferson. Small noticed Jefferson's talent and hankering for learning. He introduced Jefferson to George Wythe, a distinguished Williamsburg lawyer who was firm in philosophy and taciturn about his religious beliefs, and Governor Francis Fauquier, humanist, Fellow of the Royal Society, and owner of a sizeable and significant library and art collection. The four frequently dined together, and such gatherings doubtless had an incalculable effect on the young scholar's maturity and philosophical thinking, including his views of education.

Examination of his views on education shows Jefferson's thoughts pertaining to reform of university-level education were shaped by observed difficulties in his educational experience at William and Mary. The college was in no sense a university or college even by the standards of Jefferson's own time but instead was structured to further the aims of Anglican Christianity. Its goals, according to a pamphlet Jefferson retained on the school, were learning and morals, readying ministers for the Church of England, and instruction of Native Americans in the ways of Anglicanism.[37] Five of the difficulties were these. First, teaching Greek and Latin "filled the college with children" and that retarded the progressive sciences, by "rendering it [the school] disagreeable and degrading to young gentlemen already prepared for entering on the sciences"—especially mathematics and moral philosophy. Second, with so many students studying the languages, the revenues of the college were exhausted on them who came only "to acquire the rudiments of science." Third, the original charter did not allow the Visitors to change the curriculum or the number and kind of professorships. That meant William and Mary was behind the times. Fourth, the Brafferton was used just to educate Native Americans in the principles of Christianity. Jefferson thought it should also be employed to gather and record their traditions, laws, customs, and languages to ascertain their relationships to other tribes and their descent from other nations. Finally, there was the college itself, which Jefferson describes as a "rude and misshapen" pile. Had it not a roof, Jefferson says, it would have been mistaken for a brick-kiln.[38]

The instability, backwardness, and orthodoxy of the college during his tenure were always in mind and prompted Jefferson to consider reforms of the college in keeping with his political philosophy. One can also see his motivation for grammar schools as conduits for education at ward schools to university-level education. While a diplomat in Europe, he made careful study of the best educational systems to which he had access, and then and thereafter he had intercourse with some of the finest minds of his day in the world on the most suitable education for citizens of a flourishing republican government.

As governor, Jefferson's "Bill for Amending the Charter of the College of William and Mary" in 1779 (Bill 80) was aimed at making it a university of the highest rank and secularizing it—in effect, making it a state university—and putting it on sound financial basis. He wished its charters to be amended to make the institution's availability to the public commensurate with its expense to the public. He wished its curriculum to be changed so that all the "useful sciences" could be taught. To do so, he advised that the number of professors be changed from six to eight. He wished to see history, medicine, modern languages, and law added, and to see divinity and the Brafferton, in which Native Americans were Anglicanized, excised. He suggested instead an appointment of a "missionary" to the Native Americans more to study their habits, laws, and languages than to Anglicanizing them.[39]

Bill 80 was countermanded. In his "Autobiography," Jefferson cited the college's Anglicanism as the chief reason for its failure. As the college was aligned with the Church of England, the Visitors were required to be Anglican, the professors had to subscribe to its thirty-nine articles, and the students needed to learn its catechism. Jefferson writes, "One of its fundamental objects was declared to be, to raise up Ministers for that church." Dissenters of Anglicanism opposed the bill, as they mistakenly saw it as giving "an ascendancy to the Anglican sect." Others objected to the college's "unhealthy autumnal climate" and "local eccentricity."[40]

Nonetheless, when he became governor of Virginia and Visitor to the college, Jefferson was able to instantiate some changes. He removed the professorships of Divinity, Oriental Languages, and Greek and Latin and put in their places professorships in Law and Government, Anatomy and Medicine, and Modern Languages. Jefferson scholar Merrill Peterson sums: "Their actual effect was small . . . and the assembly never got around to revising the charter or acting on other parts of Jefferson's bill [Bill 80]. Nothing could erase the College's reputation as a Church institution."[41]

UNIVERSITY OF VIRGINIA

Founding the University

The idea of the University of Virginia began in spring of 1814, when five leading citizens of Albemarle County, among them Peter Carr, gathered at Old Stone Tavern to discuss bringing into being a private academy, to be called Albemarle Academy, which had been chartered in 1803 by the legislature of

Virginia but hitherto not acted on. As the story goes, Jefferson chanced to be passing by the tavern on horseback and one of its citizens recognized him and invited him into the tavern. However, it is more likely that Jefferson knew beforehand of the meeting and came of his own accord. Once inside, they began discussing bringing to life the chartered academy.[42]

Months later, Jefferson wrote his lengthy 1814 letter to nephew Peter Carr in the form of a proposal for a bill that goes into great detail on his plan for wholesale educational reform and the subjects of study in secondary education—that is, Albemarle Academy. At the first level of secondary education are the "General Schools"; at the second level, the "Professional Schools." The General Schools, with a focus on languages, mathematics, and philosophy—"all the branches of useful science"—are to give the wealthy the general tools for public service or a successful private life and the "professional section" the general tools for the Professional Schools, where the particular sciences are taught with great "minuteness and detail."

With the untimely death of Carr, Jefferson enlisted the aid of Senator Joseph C. Cabell to get Albemarle Academy off the ground. Cabell proved an exceptional choice. He worked indefatigably for Jefferson.[43] By December 1815, the idea of an academy morphed into an idea for a college. A bill for a new institution, Central College, was passed by the House of Delegates and by the Senate early February 1816.[44]

As a result of great debate on educational reform—Federalist Charles F. Mercer offering a viable alternative to Jefferson's educative views—Jefferson drafted his educational bill of 1817. Remarkably similar to his Bill 79 of 1779 in terms of general structure and its call for wholesale educative reform, it too failed to be ratified in its original version. A compromise, which focused on establishing only a university, was drafted. The sum of $15,000 each year was to be appropriated for a university and a commission of twenty-four persons was to examine the subject and report to the General Assembly vis-à-vis the site, architecture, subjects of study, number and kind of professorships, and provisions for organizational and governing efficiency.[45]

The university's blueprint was drawn up in the "Rockfish Gap Report" in 1818, which proposed ten professors for ten subjects. When the university was to open, six years after the Rockfish Gap Report, only eight professorships were approved. Jefferson went ahead by weaving in the subjects of the two lost professorships to the eight approved.

Three sites were considered: Lexington, Staunton, and Central College.

Jefferson writes, "The governing considerations should be the healthiness of the site, the fertility of the neighboring country, and its centrality to the white population of the whole State."[46] Yet Jefferson's 1818 report—which was, in effect, an argument for site of Central College as the site of the University of Virginia—was so meticulous and thorough that Albemarle County was confirmed as the site in late January 1819. "We have got possession of the ground," wrote Joseph C. Cabell to Jefferson, "and it will never be taken from us."[47]

There was great opposition to the new university. Many objected that, in drawing from the state's Literary Fund, the university was taking money slated for the poor. Others criticized selection of Charlottesville, as the city was seen to be too small and the location too pastoral to draw in top-ranked professors and to be a refined setting for students.[48] Adherents of William and Mary complained of the intrusion of a new, rival institution.

Financial difficulties followed. The costs, unforeseen, were exorbitant. "It has cost two hundred and fifty thousand dollars," writes George Ticknor to politician William Prescott (December 16, 1824), "and the thorough finish of every part of it and the beautiful architecture of the whole, show, I think, that it has not cost too much." He adds, "It is . . . an experiment worth trying [and] they have . . . a mass of buildings more beautiful than anything architectural in New England, and more appropriate to an university than can be found, perhaps, in the world."

An Academic Village

"This institution will be based on the illimitable freedom of the human mind," writes Jefferson to historian William Roscoe (December 27, 1820). "For here we are not afraid to follow truth wherever it may lead, nor to tolerate any error so long as reason is left to combat it." Yet an institute of higher learning, Jefferson realized, was more than a building in which students could be spoon-fed the undissembled truths of the day, for knowledge was not just something that took place in minds suitably inquisitive and acquisitive. Like earth that needed to be cultivated prior to seeding and watered and sun-exposed thereafter, minds too needed to be readied for seeding, for anything to sprout and grow healthily. Jefferson expected the young minds at the University of Virginia to do remarkable things—to be the future leaders of the state and of the nation.

Jefferson certainly envisaged that the University of Virginia would be the model university for America.[49] He writes to Joseph C. Cabell (December 28, 1822): "The great object of our aim from the beginning, has been to make the establishment the most eminent in the United States. . . . To stop where we are, is to abandon our high hopes, and become suitors to Yale and Harvard for their secondary characters." Earlier Jefferson was even more optimistic. "I contemplate the University of Virginia as the future bulwark of the human mind in this hemisphere."[50] Writes one scholar:

> Believing the university would draw students from across the nation, Jefferson attempted to make it the incubator of a national architecture that would give shape and substance to the high aspirations of a new republic. To that end, each of the buildings correctly rendered an order from some renowned example of a modern or ancient building. . . . From the abstract domain of the printed page, Jefferson projected classical knowledge into the concrete realm of experience—empirical learning of the sort that became a touchstone of enlightenment thought.[51]

The metaphor of projection is fraught with meaning. Jefferson continually worked from thoughts that were founded in ideational space, drawn on to two-dimensional space—the page of a book or a leaflet of paper—and then given an additional dimension in the real world.[52] Thus, he was no ivory-tower progressivist. He prodigiously and generously participated in the forward movement of human affairs.

Jefferson noted that the practice of making a university one large building, as was customarily done in America, was unavailing. He recommended instead an academic village, which had its roots in the Roman villa of the sort Cato, Varro, Pliny, and Cicero used to have. One scholar writes:

> The ideal of the academic village was prompted by the same aversion to city life which animated the old Romans and led Jefferson, with them, to transfer his urban intellectual life to the country. It was enhanced by his suspicion of the moral dangers threatening young boys in urban centers. The physical form in which the ideal of the academic village expressed itself . . . was not only to be classical. Beautiful and dignified instead of medieval, baroque or nondescript; it was to be an aggregation of individual buildings on a hill, spread out in the open country and connected by porticoes.[53]

In setting up his plan for the University of Virginia, Jefferson addressed the defects of William and Mary College. His plan was twofold: architectural reform and curricular reform. Apropos of the former, the university would be nestled in a healthy geographical setting and the architecture was to be thought up and drawn up to maximize physical health, encourage moral refinement, and promote intellectual advance.[54] Apropos of the latter, Greek and Latin would be taught chiefly through the reading of Greek history, while grammar would be taught mostly at the college level; the curriculum would be flexible and the various departments would function relatively independently of each other; and the university's aims would be secular, scientific, and progressive, not religious, metaphysical, and conservative.

Architecture

Jefferson placed considerable thought into the design and location of the university. "Much observation and reflection on these institutions," Jefferson writes to Hugh G. White (May 6, 1810), "have long convinced me that the large and crowded buildings in which youths are pent up, are equally unfriendly to health, to study, to manners, morals and order." Instead of cramming everyone into one large building,

> it is infinitely better to erect a small and separate lodge for each separate professorship, with only a hall below for his class, and two chambers above for himself; joining these lodges by barracks for a certain portion of the students, opening into a covered way to give a dry communication between all the schools. The whole of these arranged around an open square of grass and trees, would make it, what it should be in fact, an academical village, instead of a large and common den of noise, of filth and of fetid air. It would afford that quiet retirement so friendly to study, and lessen the dangers of fire, infection and tumult. Every professor would be the police officer of the students adjacent to his own lodge, which should include those of his own class of preference, and might be at the head of their table, it, as I suppose, it can be reconciled with the necessary economy to dine with them in smaller and separate parties, rather than in a large and common mess. These separate buildings, too, might be erected successively and occasionally, as the number of professorships and students would be increased, or the funds become competent.

Similarities to his divide-and-divide-again political policy should be obvious. Moreover, the motivation, I suspect, is identical. Jefferson is essaying to eschew adherence to a one-size-fits-all conception of university-level education.

To instantiate the aims of an academic village, Jefferson recognized that he would have to be involved in all phases of planning and construction. He oversaw the architecture, supervised the construction, raised money for construction, selected the faculty, chose some of the books to be used, laid out the curriculum, and functioned as the first rector for the faculty. As one author notes, "The University of Virginia was truly the work of one man."[55] The Board of Visitors almost always yielded to Jefferson's views, in part, because of their "unaffected deference" for his judgment and experience, and, in part, because "the scheme was originally Mr. Jefferson's, and the chief responsibility for its success or failure would fall on him."[56]

Curricular Concerns

Jefferson was also greatly involved in all other areas of implementation, including procurement of professors. He wished to stock his fledgling institution with the best available teachers, since he envisaged the university for the most part as the country's leading institution of higher education. To philosopher Dugald Stewart (April 26, 1824), he lists both knowledge and character as qualifications: "Besides the first degree of eminence in science, a professor with us must be of sober and correct morals and habits, having a talent of communicating his knowledge with facility, and of an accommodating and peaceable temperament. The latter is all-important for the harmony of the institution." Finding insufficient talent at home, Jefferson sent abroad Francis Walker Gilmer in May 1824 to procure professors of the first rank from Oxford, Cambridge, and Edinburgh. As a result of that trip, Gilmer secured five men—Thomas Hewett Key for mathematics, Robley Dunglison for anatomy and medicine, Charles Bonnycastle for natural philosophy, George Blaetterman for modern languages, and George Long for classics. They accompanied two Americans—John Taylor Lomax for law and St. George Tucker for moral philosophy. Irishman John Patten Emmet was added shortly to teach natural history.

Following the bottom-up pattern of his ward schema, the university was a loose-knit collection of what might be called "schools." Each school, housed separately, was distinct and with its own professor. The pattern embraced flexibility. It allowed for needed periodic changes in keeping with progressive changes in society. It also allowed for additional professorships—there were eight when the school opened—and for alteration of the overall curriculum. The distinct and relatively independent schools encouraged student independence and student interaction with professors, who themselves were granted considerable independence.[57]

The new university would "expound the principles and structure of government" and "a sound spirit of legislation."[58] Pace today's colleges and universities, the institution was not top-heavy with governors and administrators to oversee and direct professors and all facets of education. The Board of Visitors, trimmed to seven, was given full control over the running of the university. Each professor would be compensated remuneratively the same as all others (or roughly so), had an equal voice in the institution's affairs, and was to teach as he saw fit—the exception being the professorship of government.[59] Of the eight, one was to be elected each year to the office of chairman, who functioned to some extent as would today a president of a university.[60]

Professors were expected to lecture six hours per week in three sessions. That suggests that he thought professors ought to be preeminent scholars— that is, they needed a large amount of time for preparation and research. They were also expected to spend considerable time with students. Jefferson says to friend William Short (October 31, 1819): "No secondary character will be received among them. Either the ablest which America or Europe can furnish, or none at all. They will give us the selected society of a great city separated from the dissipations and levities of its ephemeral insects." With an equal emphasis on character, professors were to be not only specialists but also full-rounded persons, not mere databases of information. No one knowledgeable in his own discipline but ignorant of others' would be culled. Each professor was to be knowledgeable in and conversant with all sciences. Moreover, professors were expected to be moral cynosures—exemplars of virtue and good judgment for students to emulate.

There were no entrance exams at the University of Virginia, but according to the minutes of the Visitors: "No student is to be received under sixteen years of age, rigorously proved. None to be admitted into the mathematical school, or that of natural philosophy, who is not an adept in all the branches of numerical arithmetic, and none into the school of ancient languages, unless qualified, in the judgment of the professor, to commence reading the higher Latin classics; nor to receive instruction in Greek, unless qualified in the same degree in that language."[61]

Once matriculated, students could attend as many of the schools as they wished to attend, so long as they attended at least three and paid for each. Jefferson writes to Francis Wayles Eppes (December 13, 1820): "It either is, or ought to be the rule of every collegiate institution to teach to every particular student the branches of science which those who direct him think will be useful in the pursuits proposed for him, and to waste his time on nothing which they think will not be useful to him. This will certainly be the fundamental law of our University to leave every one free to attend whatever branches of instruction he wants, and to decline what he does not want." The aim was well-rounded students, chock-full of useful knowledge so as to be of service to themselves, their country, and their fellow men.[62] "You know that our views in giving you opportunities of acquiring sciences are directed to your own good alone," he tells grandson Thomas Jefferson Randolph (March 14, 1810), "to enable you, by the possession of knolege, to be happier and more useful to yourself, to be beloved by your friends, and respected and honored by our country."

Jefferson was, thus, the father of American elective education, and it was an extreme sense of "elective," much unlike allowing for electives related to required courses.[63] Students were completely free to choose their subjects. The elective system encouraged a voluntary intellectual pairing of student with professors of like interests. It also discouraged any sort of ranking of students, which is endemic to American institutions today.

Students were judged by their performance on semiannual examinations, writing and oral, with a preference for the written examinations. The recitation system, which encouraged rote memorization and not assimilation of material, prevailed at most institutions at the time. However, Jefferson opted for the lecture system and students could come and go as they pleased. The notions of grading and of making attendance part of one's grade would have been repugnant to him. It would have discouraged the sort of enlightened autonomy he sought to encourage.

A certificate of graduation stating merely the courses that a student had completed was awarded to those who distinguished themselves orally and through writing upon demonstrated proficiency. There were no degrees— nothing like a BA or an MA—except in medicine. There was merely a diploma to be received upon graduation.

Infusion of Jefferson's liberalism into his pedagogical views was evident in his view of handling student discipline. Though he championed independence, he also championed responsibility. He writes to Professor Thomas Cooper (November 2, 1822): "The article of discipline is the most difficult in American education. Premature ideas of independence, too little repressed by parents, beget a spirit of insubordination, which is the great obstacle to science with us, and a principle cause of its decay since the revolution. I look to it with dismay at our institution, as a breaker ahead, which I am far from being confident we shall be able to weather." To George Ticknor (July 16, 1823), he says that too much governing might be the cause of insubordination. "The rock which I most dread is the discipline of [the University of Virginia], and it is that on which most of our public schools labor. The insubordination of our youth is now the greatest obstacle to their education. We may lessen the difficulty, perhaps, by avoiding too much government, by requiring no useless observances, none which shall merely multiply occasion for dissatisfaction, disobedience and revolt by referring to the more discreet of themselves the minor discipline, the grayer to the civil magistrates, as in Edinburgh." Jefferson had put in place a system of student government, run by a student-based Board of Censors, to handle deviant behavior.

Jefferson believed that punishment was a poor conduit to virtue. "Pride of character, laudable ambition, and moral dispositions are innate correctives of the indiscretions of that lively age; and when strengthened by habitual appeal and exercise, have a happier effect on future character than the degrading motive of *fear*." Fear merely hardens youth through disgrace, physical punishment, and servile humiliations. Reward of right action through ingenuous praise is the proper motivator. It strengthens the moral sense through positive reinforcement of right action. Jefferson's model here is paternal—that is, that of father and son—not paternalistic. The aim is not only to prompt intellectual advance but also to encourage moral improvement in students through allowing for numerous avenues of responsible student expression.

Jefferson's republicanism doubtless influenced governance of the University of Virginia. He disdained strong government because it tended to autocracy in the service of the autocrat's own interests, not the interests of the people. It was likewise for his university. Thus, the Board of Visitors in 1824 adopted the plan of electing one of the faculty to oversee affairs as rector each year, but there was no president of the institution to oversee affairs. That policy remained in effect until 1904,[64] though before it the presiding rector functioned much like a university president.

Finally, in keeping with Jefferson's empiricism and progressivism, there was to be no professorship of theology at the University of Virginia—a move that mobilized dissenters and religious critics and inclined them to consider the university to be a "godless" institution and its most energetic patron a "godless" man.

The Philosophy behind the Curriculum

When the university opened, Jefferson regularly visited it. Plain in appearance and unassuming in manners, he would make almost daily visits on horseback to the university, though he was eighty-three years old, and had frequent intercourse with the faculty and students. He dined with faculty and their families two or three times per week; with students, once per week. One author states:

> Mr. Jefferson had a wonderful tact in interesting his youthful visitors, and making even the most diffident feel at ease in his company. He knew from what county each student came, and being well-acquainted with the most prominent men in every part of the State, he would draw out the student by asking questions about them, or about something remarkable in his neighborhood, thus making one feel that he was giving instead of receiving information; or he would ask about the studies of the students, and make remarks about them or the Professors, for all of whom he had a high admiration. He was thus careful to pay attention to each individual student.[65]

Overall, Jefferson was proposing radical renovation of institutionalized learning at colleges and universities that was in keeping with his liberalism. His model of education at the University of Virginia was patterned after his republicanism. The powers of the government ought to be few—that is, restricted chiefly in securing citizens' rights—and government is best when all are participating as fully as possible and each is directing his own affairs. Likewise, "this institution will be based on the illimitable freedom of the human mind," Jefferson writes to historian William Roscoe (December 27, 1820). "For here we are not afraid to follow truth wherever it may lead, nor to tolerate any error so long as reason is left free to combat it." The statements contain the germ of Jefferson's philosophy of pedagogy: liberty, truth, reason, respect for personhood, and toleration of error are key guiding principles of that philosophy.

For there to be liberty, Jefferson supplanted the authoritarian or paternalistic model of pedagogy of William and Mary with a model based on equality, mutual respect, and periodic change, consistent with social and moral progress. Professors were superiors of students mostly insofar as they possessed knowledge and moral sensitivity that students lacked. Students and faculty were each to be lodged at the university. Professors were to live in separate pavilions, each set off from others by students' dormitories, sandwiched between the pavilions.

Education was in the service of liberty.[66] Liberty meant nonintervention in the affairs of students, and that allowed for self-disclosure and self-determination. Absent were the numerous rules and regulations that characterized other institutions like William and Mary College, Harvard, and Yale. Punishment for miscreants, except in extreme cases, was handed down by the board of six students, appointed by the Visitors, not by faculty or the Visitors. "When testimony is required of a student, it shall be voluntary, and not on oath. And the obligation to give it shall be left to this own sense of right."[67] A gentleman's word was to be binding and no one was compelled to "rat" on another. Jefferson hoped, by empowering students, to avoid the skirmishes and riots that often occurred at William and Mary College and other institutions.[68] He hoped to show that other institutions of learning underappreciated the motives, morals, and talents of scholars.

Jefferson also recognized that reason and truth could not flourish in a religion-sanctioned institution. Religious ritual and dogmata, paying obeisance to conservatism, choked off individuality and initiative. Therefore, there was need of a wholly secular, scientific institution. In a letter to Thomas Cooper (November 2, 1822), Jefferson writes of the Aesopian criticisms of that move. "In our university . . . there is no Professorship of Divinity. A handle has been made of this, to disseminate an idea that this is an institution, not merely of no religion, but against all religion." That certainly was not the case.

In one of the university's annual reports, there was the suggestion of making an offering to all religious sects to establish a professorship of their own tenets on the confines of the university so that students could avail themselves of their lectures and of the university's library, while they remained independent of the university and each other. The invitation was indeed a concession to religious critics apropos of the secularism of the institution.[69] Jefferson writes in the 1822 letter to Cooper, "By bringing the sects together, and mixing them with the mass of other students, we shall soften their asperities, liberalize and neutralize their prejudices, and make the general religion a religion of peace, reason, and morality." No religious sect availed themselves of the offer.

Some have argued that Jefferson, in disallowing a professor of divinity at the University of Virginia, was guilty of beginning his own secular sect. For instance, two authors write:

> Jefferson intended the university to reflect the rational ideal image of himself its maker. The University of Virginia was, we believe, created according to Jefferson's rational blueprint for the ideal civil society on a small scale meant to inspire its students to reproduce the structure on the state and national level. Certainly it was meant to supply a non-sectarian alternative to the Anglican College of William and Mary. We suspect that Jefferson envisioned a place where he would no longer be a sect unto himself, or at least a place where all others would be a sect among themselves as independent followers of the same or similar natural religion.[70]

Thus, Jefferson, in plotting to establish an institution that was free of religious intolerance, was himself guilty of religious intolerance of a naturalistic sort. Jefferson, it seems, was schooling his students in the sort of natural religion that he embraced.

The argument—Jefferson beefs about the stifling dogmata of religion-based education, yet he propounds a sort of naturalistic religion-based education, exempt from metaphysics and based on experience—fails. Jefferson's point is that the University of Virginia is to be a science-based, progressive institution, and science can only flourish in a free milieu. Sectarian religion, based on metaphysical asperities and prejudices, suffocates freedom. As the letter to Cooper suggests, if all religions are brought together on the university's grounds and allowed to mix with each other and the mass of students, they will find their common ground or cancel out each other through stultifying metaphysical debate. If the first obtains, there will be fertile ground for progressive moral discussion. If the second obtains, the various sects will prove themselves scrap and in the end little harm will be done.

Without the metaphysical taint of religiosity, the University of Virginia would not be in service of Anglican aims and would be free to pursue all the most useful sciences at their highest level.[71] While president of the country, Jefferson writes to politician Littleton Waller Tazewell (January 5, 1805) apropos of his notions about an appropriate curriculum for William and Mary:

"It's object should be defined only generally for teaching the useful branches of science, leaving the particulars to the direction of the day. Science is progressive. What was useful two centuries ago is not become useless, e.g. one half of the professorships of wm & Mary. What is now deemed useful will in some of it's parts become useless in another century." The sentiment is that "useful" is the soul mate of "progressive."

Another author objects that Jefferson's pedagogical aims were elitist and provincial, not cosmopolitan. "First, Jefferson shifted priorities from educating the masses through primary education to training statesmen at the university level. Second, the education of these statesmen no longer consisted in the broad exposure to modern learning but instead took on the forms of a narrow political indoctrination, one meant to inculcate a southern version of what some might now call political correctness."[72] The depiction of Jefferson is not unlike numerous scholars' take on Plato, whose educative views in *The Republic* were in service of a questionable vision of human nature and the good life.

A third writer makes a similar point about Jefferson's elitism. He believes that Jefferson was focused on university-level education at the expense of elementary education. "Jefferson was far more concerned with what books were read by the intellectual elite than with the reading matter which found its way into the hands of the common people—by the educated, the talented, the born leaders whom Nature had clearly designated as superiors. It was with the best interests of this 'natural aristocracy' in mind that he compiled a list of good and bad books designed to serve as a guide to students at the University of Virginia."[73]

The objections are unsustainable.

First, Jefferson shifted priorities to higher education only because options for implementing wards and wards schools were blocked. As we have seen, Jefferson consistently claimed that educational reform ought to be wholesale and that he would prefer instantiation of ward schools to a new university if only one of the two could be had, because representative government could not occur without education of the common people. Despite his preference for instantiating wards and ward schools,[74] it became a matter of moving forward with higher education or of doing nothing. The whole pie being unavailable, he could have a piece or none at all. He chose a piece.

Second, that Jefferson's educational views were shaped by his political thinking is not debatable. The issue concerns the narrowness of his political views. Jefferson's political thinking championed open-mindedness, trust in the judgment of the people to run their own lives and to elect honest governors, disinterestedness, rationality, and pursuit of truth. Most significant, his polit-ical thinking was ultimately grounded in his moral thinking—namely, human well-being or flourishing. To bring about that end, he sought to avoid the suffo-cating strictures of the Christian "piety" of organized religion and instill morally responsible behavior through a milieu of freedom and intellectual engagement through hard and challenging work.[75] It is incredible to think that such views could be construed as "narrow political indoctrination" and southern "political correctness." Jefferson allowed even bigotry its say. He merely did not think it should be part of the curriculum of the University of Virginia. Apropos of reli-gion, he grasped that any institution whose chief aim was religious indoctrina-tion in any particular religious sect could not be progressive because each was fouled by dogmata. Thus, the second objection is nullified.

Finally, the University of Virginia was to distinguish itself from religious institutions in toleration of error. Jefferson, like Socrates, grasped that error exposed is the best goad to pursuit of truth. Thus, while religious institutions suffered from metaphysical mulishness—dissent from the thirty-nine articles of Anglican faith was anathema and disavowed at William and Mary Col-lege—a secular institution was necessary if the university was to be scientific and progressive, that is, open to admission of error. Following the strictures of Baconian induction, science—even in the broad sense in which Jefferson grasped it—was essentially a fallible discipline.[76] The truths of one day might not be the truths of another day. Yet through patient use of enumerative and eliminative induction, falsity would gradually be stripped away, thereby leaving truth exposed and paving the path to human progress.

UPSHOT

It is commonly objected that Jefferson's hands-off vision of the University of Virginia, once instantiated, was a nonstarter. The liberties afforded the stu-dents—their relative equality with respect to each other, the dearth of differ-ence of status between professors and students, accountability only in front of a student board, and an elective system of class selection, among other things—led to insubordination, drunkenness, riots, and even the death of one professor by students.

The difficulty, scholar Joseph Kett says, is that "Jefferson attributed to all students the same intellectual curiosity and maturity that he had carried with him to William and Mary."[77] The statement is, I think, misleading. Jefferson was too savvy to ascribe his own intellectual curiosity and maturity to each matriculating student. If that were the case, then I suspect that it would not have mattered so substantially whether the university was an academic village or a dungy prison, filled with books. What other thinkers construed to be ancillary features or superfluities of university—that is, location, architecture, cleanliness, and freedom of students, etc.—Jefferson construed to be essentialities. Because of that, it is likely Jefferson thought all matriculating students had the same intellectual curiosity and maturity in potentiality, not the same intellectual curiosity and maturity in actuality. It was his role, as father and founder of the University of Virginia, to create something new—an academic village—in which to nurture students' capacities to mold natural aristoi to serve the general citizenry, the state, and even the nation.

If anything, Jefferson is to be chided for espousing a view of human nature and human capacities that is too pie-in-the-sky, too roseate. What is perhaps especially problematic is that he thinks too highly of moral integrity and not enough about enormity. Thus, his educative views might be said to be unrealizable because they are founded on a view of human nature that is ethically unrealistic.

That might well be and probably is the case. Yet the problems of a faulty plan that is excessively optimistic of human capacities are much less pernicious than the problems of a faulty plan that is insufficiently optimistic. The former are remediable by, perhaps, tighter controls on human liberties in the educative setting. The latter are difficult to remedy because they are unrecognizable. An educational plan that sets the standards much too low will not have students rising above those standards because the standards fail to reward, much less recognize, human achievement beyond a certain basal level. Undervaluation of human capacities burkes human achievement through underestimating human capacities. Consequently, for Jefferson to be chided for being overly sanguine is to be chided for believing in the intellectual and moral capacities of his fellow human beings both at the level of the general citizenry and at the level of the natural aristoi. Genuine belief in his fellow human beings sets apart Jefferson from other reformers of his day—Federalists like Alexander Hamilton and John Adams, fellow Republicans like James Madison, and even transoceanic friends like the Marquis de Lafayette—and places him on the shoulders of Francis Bacon, John Locke, and Isaac Newton.

NOTES

PREFACE

1. Exceptions are Koch and perhaps Sheldon. Adrienne Koch, *The Philosophy of Thomas Jefferson* (New York: Columbia University Press, 1943), and Garrett Ward Sheldon, *The Political Philosophy of Thomas Jefferson* (Baltimore: Johns Hopkins University Press, 1993).

2. For example, Merrill D. Peterson, *The Jefferson Image in the American Mind* (Cambridge: Oxford University Press, 1960); Peter Onuf, *The Mind of Thomas Jefferson* (Charlottesville: University of Virginia Press, 2007); and Andrew Burstein, *Jefferson's Secrets* (New York: Basic Books, 2005).

3. Thomas Jefferson, "Sixth Annual Message," December 2, 1806.

4. Barbara McEwan, *Thomas Jefferson: Farmer* (Jefferson, NC: McFarland, 1991), 173.

5. Onuf, *Mind of Thomas Jefferson*, 99–108.

6. This is the subject of a forthcoming book on Jefferson's political vision, provisionally titled *Pathological Moralist & Moral Pathologist: The Political Philosophy and Moral Vision of Thomas Jefferson*.

7. Dumas Malone, *Jefferson and His Time*, vol. 6, *The Sage of Monticello* (Charlottesville: University of Virginia Press, [1981] 2005), 169–70.

8. See M. Andrew Holowchak, *Dutiful Correspondent: Philosophical Essays on Thomas Jefferson* (Lanham, MD: Rowman & Littlefield, 2012).

9. See Alan Pell Crawford, *Twilight at Monticello: The Final Years of Thomas Jefferson* (New York: Random House, 2008), xvi.

10. See Douglas Wilson, *Jefferson's Books* (Charlottesville, VA: Thomas Jefferson Memorial Foundation, 1996), 42–44.

11. James Golden and Alan L. Golden, *Thomas Jefferson and the Rhetoric of Virtue* (Rowman & Littlefield, 2002), 140.

12. William G. Merkel, "A Founding Father on Trial: Jefferson's Rights Talk and the Problem of Slavery during the Revolutionary Period," *64 Rutgers Law Review* 595 (2011–2012): 617.

13. TJ to Samuel Adams, March 29, 1801; TJ to John Dickinson, July 23, 1801; and TJ to John Randolph, December 1, 1803.

14. Lester P. Coonen et al., "Thomas Jefferson and American Biology," 746.

15. Alf J. Mapp Jr., *Thomas Jefferson: America's Paradoxical Patriot* (Lanham, MD: Rowman & Littlefield, 1987), 416.

16. Karl Lehmann, *Thomas Jefferson: American Humanist* (Charlottesville: University of Virginia Press, [1965] 1994), 5.

17. Merrill D. Peterson, *The Jefferson Image in the American Mind* (Charlottesville: University of Virginia Press, 1998), 444.

18. Pace Pole, who maintains "philosophy" apropos of Jefferson should be taken "not so much as a self-consistent system of thought as an outlook on life, a composition of imperfectly reconciled sentiments and opinions, and sometimes impulses." J. R. Pole, "Jefferson and the Pursuit of Equality," in *Reason and Republicanism: Thomas Jefferson's Legacy of Liberty*, ed. Gary L. McDowell and Sharon L. Noble (Lanham, MD: Rowman & Littlefield, 1997), 219. See also Helo, who argues Jefferson never aimed at consistent theory on philosophical issues but rather on "keeping ethical discourse alive." Ari Helo, *Thomas Jefferson's Ethics and the Politics of Human Progress: The Morality of a Slaveholder* (Cambridge: Cambridge University Press, 2014), 6.

19. In that regard, I eschew the sort of analysis given by Koch in her estimable booklet *The Philosophy of Thomas Jefferson*. She takes Jefferson's categorization of "philosophy"—comprising ideology, ethics, the law of nature and nations, government, and political economy—and proceeds investigation on Jefferson's own terms, as it were. Adrienne Koch, *The Philosophy of Thomas Jefferson* (Gloucester, MS: Peter Smith, 1957), xiii.

20. For example, Robert D. Heslep, "Thomas Jefferson's Major Philosophical Principles," *Educational Theory* 16 (1966): 151–62; and Robert D. Heslep, *Thomas Jefferson and Education* (New York: Random House, 1969); and Stuart Gerry Brown, "The Mind of Thomas Jefferson," *Ethics* 73, no. 2 (1963): 79–99.

INTRODUCTION

1. That Hamilton did not recognize any of the figures on sight of their portraits is remarkable. It shows profound ignorance of the philosophy and science of his day.

2. See TJ to George F. Hopkins, September 5, 1822.

3. For Jefferson's abhorrence of metaphysics, see Chinard, who notes that Comte himself called Jefferson the prophet of a new social philosophy—that is, Positivism. Gilbert Chinard, "Jefferson and the Philosophers," *Ethics* 53, no. 4 (1943): 266–68. Elsewhere Chinard explains Jefferson's aversion to metaphysics by his early training in law. "His was eminently the mind of a lawyer, and it is not for a lawyer to arrive at a definition of justice but to determine what the law says on a particular

point." Gilbert Chinard, *Thomas Jefferson: The Apostle of Americanism* (Ann Arbor: University of Michigan Press, [1929] 1962), 31.

4. It was an age of experiments with constitutional governments in, for instance, Switzerland, Holland, France, Spain, and South America. See John Adams to TJ, July 16, 1814.

5. Thomas Jefferson, *Thomas Jefferson: Writings*, ed. Merrill D. Peterson (New York: Library of America, 1984), 484–85. See also Thomas Jefferson, *Notes on the State of Virginia* (book 18; Thomas Jefferson, Opinion on Communications to Congress, April 1790; TJ to George Mason, February 4, 1791; TJ to Archibald Stuart, December 23, 1791; TJ to M. D'Ivernois, February 6, 1795; TJ to John Adams, February 28, 1796; TJ to Harry Innes, January 23, 1800; TJ to Joseph Priestley, June 19, 1802; TJ to Gov. Hall, July 6, 1802; TJ to Abigail Adams, September 11, 1804; Thomas Jefferson, Second Inaugural Address, 1805; TJ to Thomas Seymour, February 11, 1807; TJ to Benjamin Rush, September 22, 1809; TJ to William Duane, November 13, 1810; TJ to A. C. V. C. Destutt de Tracy, January 26, 1811; TJ to Francis Van der Kemp, March 22, 1812; TJ to Dr. Walter Jones, January 2, 1814; and TJ to James Madison, December 24, 1824.

6. See for example, William L. Chew, "Thomas Jefferson in France: An Imagological and 'Comparative Cohort' Approach," in *Consortium on the Revolutionary Era: Selected Papers* (Tallahassee, FL: Consortium on the Revolutionary Era, 2006), 41; and Colin Bonwick, "Jefferson as Nationalist," in *Reason and Republicanism: Thomas Jefferson's Legacy of Liberty*, ed. Gary L. McDowell and Sharon L. Noble (Lanham, MD: Rowman & Littlefield, 1997), 151–54.

7. Robert K. Faulkner, "Jefferson and the Enlightened Science of Liberty," in McDowell and Noble, *Reason and Republicanism*, 42.

8. Dumas Malone, *Jefferson the President: First Term* (Boston: Little, Brown, 1970), xvii.

9. TJ to Count de Moustier, May 17, 1788.

10. Adrienne Koch, *The Philosophy of Thomas Jefferson* (Gloucester, MA: Peter Smith, 1957), 186.

11. M. Andrew Holowchak, *Dutiful Correspondent: Philosophical Essays on Thomas Jefferson* (Lanham, MD: Rowman & Littlefield, 2012), chap. 3.

12. Not to deny the possibility of a naturalistic or rationalistic strain in Jefferson's thought—for example, his appeal to natural rights—which some think were not for Jefferson outside the realm of experiential confirmation or disconfirmation. See J. R. Pole, "Jefferson and the Pursuit of Equality," in McDowell and Noble, *Reason and Republicanism*, 220–21.

13. Gilbert Chinard, "Jefferson among the Philosophers," *Ethics* 53, no. 4 (1943): 268.

14. Grasping "scientific" here more flexibly and broadly, as did Jefferson, to include, for example, morality, architecture, invention, and military technology.

15. Sedgwick even speaks of Jefferson's eclectic approach to collecting things as scientific. "Jefferson treated acquisitions as he treated natural history: an aggregation of discrete and apparently unrelated items from which he was free to derive universal principles." Jeffrey Leigh Sedgwick, "Jeffersonianism in the Progressive Era," in McDowell and Noble, *Reason and Republicanism*, 191. See also Caleb Perry Patterson, *The Constitutional Principles of Thomas Jefferson* (Austin: University of Texas Press, 1953), 63.

16. Densford mistakenly claims that Jefferson was epistemically eclectic—namely, that he was at times empiricist and at other times rationalist. He cites Jefferson's self-evident truths in the Declaration of Independence as well as Jefferson's moral sense as evidence of a purchase of rationalism. Such eclecticism on fundamental issues ascribes a profound epistemic confusion to a thinker of considerable depth and breadth. John P. Densford, "The Educational Philosophy of Thomas Jefferson," *Peabody Journal of Education* 38, no. 5 (1961): 265–75.

17. Charles A. Miller, in a study of Jefferson's conception of nature, writes that Jefferson's "book of nature was primarily the book of experience." Charles A. Miller, *Jefferson and Nature: An Interpretation* (Collingdale, PA: Diane, 1988).

18. I address fully Jefferson's empiricism in my essay, "'To Do a Little with Certainty': Thomas Jefferson's Debt to Isaac Newton in *Notes on Virginia*" (forthcoming).

19. Aristotle, *Nicomachean Ethics*, trans. Terence Irwin (Indianapolis: Hackett, 1999), 1103a14–17.

20. Ibid., 1098b13–18 and 1098b13–18. For a fuller discussion, see M. Andrew Holowchak, *Greek Ethics and Happiness* (New York: Continuum International, 2008), chap. 2.

21. Seneca, "Benefits," in *Moral Essays*, vol. 3, trans. John W. Basore (Cambridge: Harvard University Press, 2001), V.xiii.2.

22. See M. Andrew Holowchak, *The Stoics: A Guide for the Perplexed* (New York: Continuum International, 2008), chap. 1, esp. 29–35.

23. For example, TJ to John Adams, February 28, 1796; and TJ to Pierre Samuel Dupont de Nemours, April 24, 1816.

24. Holowchak, *Dutiful Correspondent*, chap. 4; and M. Andrew Holowchak, "The Paradox of Public Service: Jefferson, Education, and the Problem of Plato's Cave," *Studies in Philosophy and Education* 32, no. 1 (2013): 73–86.

25. From the Greek aristoi, meaning "best men," and *kratein*, meaning "to rule" or "to be strong."

26. Richard Matthews states: "*Bonheur*, happiness, is [for Jefferson] man's *telos*. Rights—property and other—are mere instruments to aid men in their pursuit of hap-

piness. And governments must either be structured or dissolved and restructured so that all men will have access to this pursuit." Richard K. Matthews, *The Radical Politics of Thomas Jefferson: A Revisionist View* (Lawrence: University Press of Kansas, 1984), 122.

27. TJ to Joseph Priestley, January 27, 1800. See also TJ to Count de Moustier, May 17, 1788; TJ to Elbridge Gerry, January 26, 1799; and TJ to William Green Munford, June 18, 1799.

28. The subject of another work that is forthcoming: *Pathological Moralist & Moral Pathologist: The Political Philosophy and Moral Vision of Thomas Jefferson.*

PART 1: JEFFERSON ON NATURE

Chapter 1. "I Cannot Reason Otherwise": Jefferson's Cosmos

1. See Brooke Allen, "Jefferson the Skeptic," *Hudson Review* 59, no. 2 (2006): 193.

2. John Adams to TJ, May 12, 1820; and TJ to John Adams, August 15, 1820.

3. Jefferson is without doubt following Destutt de Tracy here in the latter's *Élémens d'Ideologie*, 5 vols. (Brussels: Courcier, 1827), 3:164.

4. Again following Tracy in the latter's *Élémens d'Ideologie*, 3:164.

5. Isaac Newton, *Principia*, vol. 1, *The Motion of Bodies*, trans. Florian Cajori (Berkeley: University of California Press, 1962), 1–13.

6. Epicurus, *Letter to Herodotus*, trans. Brad Inwood and L. P. Gerson (Indianapolis: Hackett, 1994), §§39–40.

7. Ibid., §§62–68.

8. TJ to William Short, October 31, 1819.

9. The ad hoc collisions, he realized, were needed to bring atoms together. Epicurus, *Letter to Herodotus*, §§42 and 54–62.

10. John Locke, *An Essay concerning Human Understanding*, ed. A. D. Woozley (New York: New American Library, 1964), III.iii.1.11.

11. See *Posterior Analytics* (71b33–72a5), *Topics* (141b3–14), *Physics* (184a16–23), *Metaphysics* (1029b3–12), and *Nicomachean Ethics* (1095b2–4). Aristotle, *Selections*, ed. Terence Irwin and Gail Fine (Indianapolis: Hackett, 1995).

12. Lord Kames, *Essays on the Principles of Morality and Natural Religion*, 2nd ed. (London, 1758), 113–14.

13. Epicurus, *Letter to Herodotus*, IV.123. His Roman disciple Lucretius gives the evidence of large and perfect humanlike simulacra in sleep. Lucretius, *On the Nature of Things*, trans. Martin Ferguson Smith (Indianapolis: Hackett, 2001), V.1170–82.

14. Epicurus, *Letter to Menoeceus*, in *The Epicurus Reader*, trans. Brad Inwood and

L. P. Gerson (Indianapolis: Hackett, 1994), §§ 123–24; and Cicero, *On the Nature of the Gods*, trans. H. Rackham (Cambridge: Harvard University Press, 2000), §§46–53 and 71.

15. See Roger Heslep, *Thomas Jefferson and Education* (New York: Random House, 1969), 74–75.

16. Thomas Jefferson, "Autobiography," in *Thomas Jefferson: Writings*, ed. Merrill D. Peterson (New York: Library of America, 1984), 97.

17. One speculates that Jefferson would nowise marvel at current global trends toward democratization—for example, the "fall" of the Soviet Union, the unification of East Germany and West Germany, and the upheavals in Egypt and Syria.

18. Destutt de Tracy, *Élémens d'Ideologie*, 3:164.

19. Tucker asserts that Jefferson's god is subject to and not creator of the laws of nature, as "the laws of nature were an authority even for God." David Tucker, *Enlightened Republicanism: A Study on Jefferson's* Notes on the State of Virginia (Lanham, MD: Lexington Books, 2008), 26.

20. For example, TJ to Joseph Priestley, April 9, 1803; and TJ to Benjamin Rush, April 21,1803.

21. Jefferson might have had another source in mind, when writing about deity— John Locke. Writes Locke in *Questions concerning the Law of Nature*: "Thus, for anyone to know that he is bound by law, he must first know that there is a legislator, a superior; that is, some power to which he is rightfully suspect." Locke, too, in appealing to the senses, uses the argument from design to show that the senses, with the aid of reason, can know of the existence of a creator, "more powerful and wiser" than humans, and who has the power to generate, preserve, and destroy humans. Not making the cosmos at random, but for the sake of some end, the creator has made humans so that they have a duty to themselves, their fellow humans, and to deity. John Locke, *Questions concerning the Law of Nature*, ed. Robert Horwitz, Jenny Strauss Clay, and Diskin Clay (Ithaca, NY: Cornell University Press, 1990), 159–69.

22. Jefferson, "Autobiography," 96; and Thomas Jefferson, "Query VI," in *Notes on the State of Virginia*, in *Thomas Jefferson: Writings*, ed. Peterson, 188.

23. For example, TJ to John Adams, July 5, 1814 and December 10, 1819.

24. TJ to Benjamin Rush, April 21, 1803.

25. Cicero, *On the Nature of the Gods*, II.i.3.

26. Locke in states that we know that deity is "most powerful" and "most knowing." John Locke, *Essay concerning Human Understanding*, 379–80.

27. See, for comparison, Kames: "When we at last take in at one view the material and moral worlds, full of harmony, order, and beauty, happily adjusted to answer great and glorious purposes; there is in this grand production necessarily involved the conviction of a cause, unbounded in power, intelligence, and goodness." Kames, *Essays on the Principles of Morality and Natural Religion*, 258.

28. Cicero, *On the Nature of the Gods*, II.87.

29. For more, see M. Andrew Holowchak, "The Fear, Honor, and Love of God: Thomas Jefferson on Jews, Philosophers, and Jesus," *Forum Philosophicum* 18, no. 1 (2013): 49–71.

30. Cicero, *On the Nature of the Gods*, II.73–75.

31. M. Andrew Holowchak, *The Stoics: A Guide for the Perplexed* (London: Continuum Books, 2008), 20–21.

32. Cicero, *On the Nature of the Gods*, II.12.

33. Ibid., II.ii.5.

34. See, for example, Thomas Jefferson, "Notes on Religion," 1776, in *The Papers of Thomas Jefferson*, vol. 1, *1760–1776*, ed. Julian P. Boyd (Princeton: Princeton University Press, 1950) 555–58; Thomas Jefferson, "Bill for Religious Freedom," 1779, in *The Works of Thomas Jefferson*, vol. 2, ed. Paul Leicester Ford (New York: G. P. Putnam's Sons, 1904), 438–41; TJ to Peter Carr, August 19, 1785; and TJ to Judge John Tyler, June 28, 1804.

35. To Styles, Jefferson says of deity, "I am, therefore of His theology, believing that we have neither words nor ideas adequate to that definition." TJ to Ezra Styles, June 25, 1819.

36. It is possible, though not probable, that Jefferson is not so much arguing for the existence of deity in his letter to Adams as he is illustrating à la Kames humans' intuitive "knowledge" of deity through internal senses: "To found our knowledge of the Deity upon reasoning solely, is not agreeable to the analogy of nature. We depend not on abstract reasoning, nor indeed on any reasoning, for unfolding our duty to our fellow creatures: it is engraved upon the table of our hearts. We adapt our actions to the course of nature, by mere instinct, without reasoning, or even experience. Therefore, if analogy can be relied on, it ought to be thought that God will discover himself to us, in some such manner as may take in all mankind, the vulgar and illiterate as well as the deep-thinking philosopher." Kames, *Essays on the Principles of Morality and Natural Religion*, 250. See also 259–60.

37. Cicero, *On the Nature of the Gods*, II.13–31.

38. Ibid., II.33 and 44, respectively.

39. TJ to John Adams, April 11, 1823. Thomson strangely uses this same letter as evidence that Jefferson never bought into extinction, though he admits to some puzzlement vis-à-vis Jefferson's use of "restoring power." One prominent reason for disbelief in extinction, Thomson says, is Jefferson's belief that creation of the world occurred consonant with the account in Genesis ("Jefferson believed that the earth had been created by God as described in the Book of Genesis"). Thomson unsurprisingly cites none of Jefferson's writings as evidence for that claim. Keith Thomson, *Jefferson's Shadow: The Story of His Science* (New Haven: Yale University Press, 2012), 90–96 and 73–76, respectively.

40. This can be translated thus: "Injuries of the gods are the concerns of the gods."

41. For example, TJ to Thomas Lomax, March 12, 1799; and TJ to Elbridge Gerry, January 26, 1799.

42. Holowchak, *Stoics*, 21.

43. There was a political motivation as well. To acknowledge the extinction of the mammoth would be to play into Buffon's hand, for that would give evidence of the inhospitableness of the Americas to biota.

44. Jefferson, "Query VI," 176.

45. For example, TJ to Francis Adrian Van der Kemp, April 25, 1816; and TJ to Daniel Salmon, February 15, 1808.

46. Plato's *Timaeus* and Aristotle's *Physics* (VIII.6; 258b10–33). The Greek *kosmos* means principally "order" or "arrangement," which itself bespeaks an artificer.

47. See, by way of comparison, Hume, for whom "deity . . . govern every thing by those general and immutable laws, which have been established from the beginning of time." David Hume, "Of Suicide," in *Essays: Moral, Political, and Literary*, ed. Eugene F. Miller (New York: Liberty Fund, 1987), 581.

48. Writes Charles Sanford: "Jefferson went beyond his deistic teachers in attributing love, care, concern, guidance, providence, protection, and wisdom to God, the Creator of the universe, but he agreed with them in stressing the might and power of God. . . . This belief in God's guidance gave Jefferson a confidence which lesser leaders lacked." Charles B. Sanford, *The Religious Life of Thomas Jefferson* (Charlottesville: University Press of Virginia, 1984), 96.

49. TJ to William Short, October 31, 1819. Mario Valsania mistakenly writes, "A sound Epicurean, Jefferson did not renounce his opinion that humans . . . are left alone in this world, God dwelling in an untouched physical space, 'not meddling with the concerns of the scale of beings below them,' God is a relatively distant figure for him." Maurizio Valsania, "'Our Original Barbarism,'" 638–41.

50. For example,, TJ to Dr. Benjamin Waterhouse, June 26, 1822; TJ to Rev. James Madison, January 31, 1800; TJ to Thomas Jefferson Grotian, January 10, 1804; TJ to George Logan, November 12, 1816; and TJ to George Tinckner (November 25, 1817.

51. Thomas Jefferson, *Jefferson's Literary Commonplace Book: The Papers of Thomas Jefferson, Second Series*, ed. Douglas L. Wilson (Princeton: Princeton University Press, 1989), §46.

52. Andrew Burstein, *Lincoln Dreamed He Died* (New York: Palgrave MacMillan, 2013), 89–90.

53. See note 34 above.

54. Or at least is equivalent to the cosmos, in which case the creation is a matter of a sort of divine unfolding.

55. See also TJ to Adams, April 8, 1816.

56. A letter to Abigail Adams displays cynicism: "Nothing proves more than this that the being who presides over the world is essentially benevolent, stealing from us, one by one, the faculties of enjoyment, searing our sensibilities, leading us, like the horse in his mill, round and round the same beaten circle." He then speaks of an aging friend, neither a poet nor a philosopher, who complained of being tired of pulling off his shoes and stockings at night, only to pull them back on in the morning. TJ to Abigail Adams, January 11, 1817.

57. For more on Jefferson's notions of the sublime and the beautiful, see M. Andrew Holowchak, *Dutiful Correspondent* (Lanham, MD: Rowman & Littlefield, 2012), 135–38.

58. Adrienne Koch, *Power, Morals, and the Founding Fathers* (Ithaca, NY: Cornell University Press, 1961), 44–45.

59. Michelle L. Browers, "Jefferson's Land Ethic: Environmentalist Ideas in *Notes on the State of Virginia*," *Environmental Ethics* 21 (1999): 46–47.

60. Maurizio Valsania, "'Our Original Barbarism': Man vs. Nature in Thomas Jefferson's Moral Experience," *Journal of the History of Ideas* (2005): 643. Valsania's syllogism is, I believe, somewhat puzzleheaded and wrongly framed. First, it is implausible to assert, as a blanket statement, that self-government is the result of moral rectitude. It might be the case that morally advanced persons are themselves self-governed in that they are self-possessed, but it nowise follows that self-government of the Jeffersonian sort results from moral rectitude. It is also implausible to think that Jefferson thought self-governing was the result of moral rectitude. Were that the case, Jefferson would have been more brazen and have asserted that his republican vision was more than a mere experiment, but rather comprised ontological truths. Nowhere does Jefferson say that. Second, for Valsania, self-government is Jefferson's aim and moral rectitude is the means. As I have argued in *Dutiful Correspondent*, Jefferson views autonomy and morally correct activity as each crucial for human thriving, but morality (i.e., happiness) is the end, not the means. Jefferson's liberalism has its tether: Liberty serves the end of human happiness; happiness is not for the sake of liberty. Failure to recognize that is to paint Jefferson a liberal anarchist, as does Conor Cruise O'Brien (see chapter 4 of this book), and there is no warrant for that. The syllogism should read: Human happiness is the result of self-governing (*inter alia*), Americans wish to be happy, so Americans wish to be self-governed.

61. Charles A. Miller, *Jefferson and Nature: An Interpretation* (Baltimore: Johns Hopkins University Press, 1988), 7.

62. Ibid., 17.

63. Ibid., 23.

64. Thomas Hobbes, *Leviathan*, ed. Edwin Curley (Indianapolis: Hackett, 1994), §§XIII–XIV.

65. Jean-Jacques Rousseau, "Discourse on the Origin of Inequality," in *Jean Jacques Rousseau: The Basic Political Writings*, trans. Donald A. Cress (Indianapolis: Hackett, 1987), 49–54, 60–63, and 80.

66. Leo Marx, *The Machine in the Garden: Technology and the Pastoral Ideal in America* (New York: Oxford University Press, 1964), 104–105.

67. Thomas Jefferson, "Opinion on the Question Whether the United States Has a Right to Intervene to Renounce Their Treaties with France," in *The Works of Thomas Jefferson, vol. 3, ed. Paul Leicester Ford, 12 vols. (New York: Putnam,*1903), 227.

68. I follow Smith here. John E. Smith, "Philosophical Ideas behind the 'Declaration of Independence,'" *Revue Internationale de Philosophia* 31 (1977): 366.

69. Smith, "Philosophical Ideas behind the 'Declaration of Independence,'" 367–68.

70. One must be cautious here, for Jefferson's conception of liberty, the subject of chapter 3, implies as with the Stoics social engagement.

71. Smith, "Philosophical Ideas behind the 'Declaration of Independence,'" 366.

72. TJ to Isaac McPherson, August 13, 1813.

73. For example, see TJ to Jonathan Williams, July 3, 1796; and TJ to Robert Livingston, April 30, 1800.

74. Silvio A. Bedini, *Jefferson and Science* (Charlottesville, VA: Thomas Jefferson Foundation, 2002), 61–62.

75. Thomas Hobbes, *Leviathan, with Selected Variants from the Latin Edition of 1668*, ed. E. Curley (Indianapolis: Hackett, 1994), chap. 4.

76. Kerry H. Whiteside, "Nominalism and Conceptualism in Hobbes' Political Theory," *Commonwealth: A Journal of Political Science* 1, no. 1 (1987): 1–3.

77. For example, Jefferson's depiction of the Natural Bridge, at the end of Query V. Jefferson, *Thomas Jefferson: Writings*, ed. Peterson, 148.

78. See M. Andrew Holowchak, "'To Do a Little with Certainty': Thomas Jefferson's Debt to Isaac Newton in *Notes on Virginia*" (forthcoming).

79. Jefferson, "Query VI," 169–70.

80. Ibid., 170. Jefferson was, of course, one of the foremost meteorologists of the New World. See M. Andrew Holowchak, *A Utopian Dream: Thomas Jefferson's Philosophy of Education* (London: Taylor & Francis, 2014), chap. 5.

81. Jefferson, "Query VI," 170.

82. Jefferson was indebted to Archibald Cary and Thomas Walker for his data on animal sizes in America for these comparative tables and Walker for information on Native Americans. Archibald Cary to TJ, October 12, 1783; and TJ to Thomas Walker, September 25, 1783.

83. Roughly, "I appreciate a person who relieves me of an error as much as

another who teaches me a truth, since in effect an error corrected is a truth." Jefferson, "Query VI," 172–77.

84. Ibid., 165–69. See also TJ to Jean Baptiste Le Roy, November 17, 1786; and TJ to Thomas Cooper, August 10, 1810.

85. Jefferson, "Query VI," 191.

PART 2: JEFFERSON ON POLITICS

Chapter 2. "Prophecy Is One Thing, History Another": Jefferson's Mother Principle

1. Merrill Peterson, *The Jefferson Image in the American Mind* (Charlottesville: University of Virginia Press, 1998), 33–35.

2. Dumas Malone, *Jefferson and His Time*, vol. 1, *Jefferson the Virginian* (Boston: Little, Brown, 1948), 173.

3. Peter S. Onuf, "The Scholar's Jefferson," *William and Mary Quarterly* 50, no. 4 (1993): 697.

4. For example, TJ to William Carmichael, December 26, 1786; TJ to Edward Carrington, January 16, 1787; TJ to James Madison, December 20, 1787, and May 15, 1794; TJ to David Humphreys, March 18, 1789; TJ to Gouverneur Morris, November 7, 1792; TJ to John Taylor, June 1, 1798; TJ to Edmund Randolph, August 18, 1799; TJ to John Breckinridge, January 29, 1800; TJ to Elbridge Gerry, March 29, 1801; Thomas Jefferson, First Inaugural Address, April 30, 1801; TJ to Dr. William Eustis, January 14, 1809; TJ to Caesar A. Rodney, February 10, 1810; TJ to P. S. Dupont de Nemours, April 14, 1816; TJ to Francis Gilmer, June 7, 1816; TJ to Marquis de Lafayette, May 14, 1817; and TJ to Alexander von Humboldt, June 13, 1817.

5. Thomas Jefferson, "First Inaugural Address," in *Thomas Jefferson: Writings*, ed. Merrill D. Peterson (New York: Library of America, 1984), 493.

6. In his book *L'An 2440*, or *The Year 2440*.

7. TJ to John Adams, April 8, 1816.

8. Many of Jefferson's own thoughts were "validated" by Destutt de Tracy in his 1809 *Commentary and Review of Montesquieu's* Spirit of Laws. Tracy argued that much of what Montesquieu had written in 1767 has not passed the test of time. Tracy opted for communication and education instead of coercion for establishing a republic, individual liberty and freedom of the press, dissemination of knowledge and correction of error, and morality taught by the most enlightened, not by putative religious authorities.

9. TJ to John Taylor, May 28, 1816.

10. Conor Cruise O'Brien, *The Long Affair: Thomas Jefferson and the French Revolution, 1785–1800* (Chicago: University of Chicago Press, 1996), 115.

11. "Democracy" was not in vogue, as it connoted for many a sort of anarchic rule of the many. Dumas Malone notes that Jefferson, habitually employing lower-case letters, avoided the terms *federalist* and *antifederalist* in favor of *republican* and *antirepublican*. Thus, by *republicanism*, Jefferson was likely most often referring not to political parties but to a general democratic movement away from the British aristocratic system of governing. Dumas Malone, *Jefferson and His Time*, vol. 3, *Jefferson and the Ordeal of Liberty* (Boston: Little, Brown, 1962), 265.

12. TJ Joseph Priestley, March 21, 1801. Renowned Federalist John Quincy Adams recognized that fully in a letter to Rufus King. See Dumas Malone, *Jefferson and His Time*, vol. 4, *Jefferson as President: First Term, 1801–1805* (Boston: Little, Brown, 1970), 139.

13. This sentiment he reiterates almost verbatim in a letter to Thomas Pinckney on the same day.

14. The Federalist Noah Webster objected to terms such as *the people*, *democracy*, and even *equality*, for such categories were meaningless "metaphysical abstractions." Joseph J. Ellis, *After the Revolution: Profiles of Early American Culture* (New York: W. W. Norton, 1979), 199 and 206.

15. Gilbert Chinard, *Thomas Jefferson: The Apostle of Americanism* (Ann Arbor: University of Michigan Press, [1929] 1962), 204.

16. "Madison's Report of 1800" in Dumas Malone, *Jefferson and His Time*, 3:402.

17. Thomas Jefferson, "Travelling Notes for Mr. Rutledge and Mr. Shippen," in *Thomas Jefferson: Writings*, ed. Peterson, 660. See also TJ to Marquis de Lafayette, April 11, 1787.

18. "All in all, there is not much truth in the conventional image of Jefferson as an advocate of little government with minimum spending and minimum taxation," says Helo. His point is well taken, but one must concede that advocacy of government spending of the sort Helo mentions—internal improvements, the Louisiana Purchase, and district taxes for local education—were for the sake of advancing human flourishing. Ari Helo, *Thomas Jefferson's Ethics and the Politics of Human Progress: The Morality of a Slaveholder* (Cambridge: Cambridge University Press, 2014), 166. Kaplan's assessment, in contrast, is sound. Jefferson's domestic program "centered on executive restraint," while his foreign policy required the president to be "the prime mover." Lawrence S. Kaplan, *Thomas Jefferson: Westward the Course of Empire* (Wilmington, DE: SR Books, 1999), 128.

19. That is, England wishes to control the seas; France, the continents. See Jefferson's letter to Madame de Staël, May 24, 1813.

20. Merrill D. Peterson, *Thomas Jefferson and the New Nation: A Biography* (New York: Oxford University Press, 1970), 936–37.

21. TJ to Alexander von Humboldt, December 6, 1813.

22. Stanley Mellon, "Jefferson and the French Revolution," *Consortium on Revolutionary Europe: 1750–1850* 22 (1993): 277–89.

23. Gilbert Chinard, "Jefferson among the Philosophers," *Ethics* 53, no. 4 (1943): 261.

24. Chinard, *Thomas Jefferson*, 215–16.

25. For instance, French unwillingness to open their ports to American commerce for exchange of goods as equals, their expansionist aims pertaining to North America, and of course the rise of Bonaparte. See Kaplan, *Thomas Jefferson: Westward the Course of Empire*, 91–93 and 99.

26. For more, see M. Andrew Holowchak, "An Education Directed to Freedom and Happiness: The Usefulness of 'American' Education," in *Thomas Jefferson's Philosophy of Education: A Utopian Dream* (London: Taylor & Francis, 2014), 141–79.

27. "Never was there a country where the practice of governing too much had taken deeper root and done more mischief." TJ to James Madison, August 28, 1789.

28. "The liberty of the whole earth was depending on the issue of the contest," Jefferson writes to William Short (January 3, 1793), "and was ever such a prize won with so little innocent blood?"

29. Politically, Jefferson favored neither France nor Britain but recognized that American growth and prosperity depended on a balance of power between what could then be called the two European superpowers.

30. See also TJ to James Madison, April 23, 1804 and May 4, 1806; TJ to John Melish, December 10, 1814; and TJ to James Monroe, October 16, 1816.

31. Garrett Ward Sheldon, *The Political Philosophy of Thomas Jefferson* (Baltimore: Johns Hopkins University Press, 1991), 23.

32. TJ to John Banister, October 15, 1785.

33. Jefferson was, however, taken aback by British "cuisine." See, for instance, Kaplan, *Thomas Jefferson*, 38.

34. TJ to John Page, May 4, 1786.

35. Thomas Jefferson, *Thomas Jefferson: Writings*, ed. Peterson, 105–106. For more on Whig and Tory history, see H. Trevor Colbourn, "Thomas Jefferson's Use of the Past," *William and Mary Quarterly* 15, 3rd ser. (1958): 59 and 64.

36. Colbourn elaborates, "The seeming failure of England to reinstitute the happy system of her ancestors played an important part in Jefferson's decision to institutionalize such a system in the Saxon settlements in the New World." He adds, "Jefferson's acceptance and exposition of the Anglo-Saxon myth in his *Summary View* is . . . an acceptance, both proper and predictable for the eighteenth century, of an historical realization of Locke's first compact-founded society." Jefferson was, there-

fore, determined that George III would not be the second William the Conqueror. H. Trevor Colbourn, "Thomas Jefferson's Use of the Past," *William and Mary Quarterly* 15, 3rd ser. (1958): 67–8. For the relationship of Jefferson's Saxon myth and his take on common law, see James R. Stoner, "Sound Whigs or Honeyed Tories? Jefferson and the Common Law Tradition," in *Reason and Republicanism: Thomas Jefferson's Legacy of Liberty*, ed. Gary L. McDowell and Sharon L. Noble (Lanham, MD: Rowman & Littlefield, 1997), 103–17.

37. Merrill D. Peterson, *The Jefferson Image in the American Mind* (Charlottesville: University Press of Virginia, 1998), 375.

38. Writes Fleming: "American or Jeffersonian democracy is not so much a political ideology as it is the general American habits of self-reliance and local self-governance, both formal and informal. This is exemplified in the two great institutions . . . : New England town meetings and Southern Lynch law, understood in the broadest sense to include the entire panoply of rough justice, from the shivarees staged to protest an unsuitable marriage to the great vigilante movements of Montana and San Francisco. Early American democracy was the determination to mind one's own business." Thomas Fleming, "Three Faces of Democracy: Cleisthenes, Jefferson, and Robespierre," *Telos* (1995): 53.

39. Dumas Malone, *Jefferson and His Time*, vol. 6, *The Sage of Monticello* (Charlottesville: University of Virginia Press, 1981), 36.

40. Colin Bonwick, "Jefferson as Nationalist," in *Reason and Republicanism*, 151–57.

41. The constitution, in effect, allowed for a dictatorship, which almost came to pass. Virginia, at the time of Jefferson's writing of his *Notes on the State of Virginia*, was in political turmoil and the possibility of a democratic republic for the state was mere possibility. See Michelle L. Browers, "Jefferson's Land Ethic: Environmentalist Ideas in *Notes on the State of Virginia*," *Environmental Ethics* 21 (1999): 45.

42. Rahe argues correctly that Jefferson was not so much motivated by trust of the people as he was by distrust of those in power. "Although he was convinced that human beings are endowed with an innate moral sense that renders them fit for society, able to manage their own affairs, and capable of cooperative self-government, he nonetheless doubted whether any individual can really be trusted to rule on another's behalf." His stay in France disabused him of the European politics of "implicit confidence and trust," where nations were divided into wolves and sheep. His method was not to convince those ruling not be wolves, but them being ruled not to be sheep. Paul A. Rahe, "Jefferson's Machiavellian Moment," in *Reason and Republicanism*, 57–58 and 76.

43. Happiness might include the right to property. He maintained that the right to property could be violated in cases of national security or in cases of poverty—that is,

when large landholders with unproductive land prohibit persons without property from holding property. TJ to James Madison, October 28, 1785.

44. See M. Andrew Holowchak, "Individual Liberty and Political Unity in an Expanding Nation: The Axiological Primacy of Wards in Jefferson's Republican Schema," in *Thomas Jefferson and Philosophy: Essays on the Philosophical Cast of Jefferson's Writings* (Lanham, MD: Lexington Books, 2013), chap. 3.

45. See, by way of comparison, James Harrington's account of the commonwealth of Israel, whose first grouping was "parish," and some one hundred of them being grouped into a "hundred." James Harrington, *The Oceana and Other Works of James Harrington Esq; Collected, Methodiz'd, and Review'd with an Exact Account of His Life*, ed. John Toland (London, 1747), 89.

46. In Richard E. Ellis, "Comment on Executive Privilege in Light of the United States v. Nixon," 9 *Loy. L.A. L. Rev.* 33 (1975): 38–39.

Chapter 3. "Turbulent Liberty [or] Quiet Servitude": Jefferson and Liberty

1. T. V. Smith, "Thomas Jefferson and the Perfectibility of Mankind," *Ethics* 53, no. 4 (1943): 304.

2. Carl Becker, *The Declaration of Independence: A Study in the History of Political Ideas* (New York: Random House, 1958), 27 and 79. See also Daniel Boorstin, *The Lost World of Thomas Jefferson* (New York: Henry Holt, 1948); Dumas Malone, *Jefferson in His Time*, vols. 1–6 (Boston: Little, Brown, 1948–1981); Gordon Wood, *The Creation of the American Republic, 1776–1787* (Chapel Hill: University of North Carolina Press, 1969); and Merrill D. Peterson, *Thomas Jefferson and the New Nation* (New York: Oxford University Press, 1970).

3. A point readily recognized in Jefferson's day. For example, see David Hume, "Idea of a Perfect Commonwealth," in *Essays: Moral, Political, and Literary*, ed. Eugene F. Miller (Indianapolis: Liberty Fund, 1987), 528.

4. "Turbulent liberty is preferable to quiet servitude."

5. Beitzinger notes indecisiveness in Jefferson's commitment to the second form of government. "Convinced that man is a social animal, Jefferson seems to have entertained a strong doubt that nature intended man to be a political animal. His ideal appears to have been a healthy natural society without coercive government." And so, he was "'not clear' in his mind that the first condition 'is not the best.'" A. J. Beitzinger, "Political Theorist," in *Thomas Jefferson: A Reference Biography*, ed. Merrill D. Peterson (New York: Charles Scribner's Sons, 1986), 87–88.

6. Thomas Jefferson, "Query XI," in *Notes on the State of Virginia*, in *Thomas Jefferson: Writings*, ed. Merrill D. Peterson (New York: Library of America, 1984), 220.

7. See Michael Hardt, "Jefferson and Democracy," *American Quarterly* 59, no. 1 (2007): 69.

8. In that, he differs from Plato and Aristotle, for whom the good of the state was paramount, if only because of the axiological priority of the state.

9. For example, Adrienne Koch, *The Philosophy of Thomas Jefferson* (Gloucester, MA: Peter Smith, 1957), 137.

10. Hutcheson writes of "perfect rights," the universal violation of "would make human Life intolerable"; "imperfect rights," the universal violation of which "would not make Men miserable"; and "external rights," which allow for actions contrary to the public good, because suppression of such actions would be a greater public ill. Francis Hutcheson, *Inquiry into the Original of Our Ideas of Beauty and Virtue*, ed. Wolfgang Leidhold (Indianapolis: Liberty Fund, [1725] 2004), 182–84.

11. Thomas Jefferson, "Commissioners' Report on University of Virginia," in *Thomas Jefferson: Writings*, ed. Peterson, 461–62.

12. Merrill Peterson says that early conservative critics took Jefferson's conception of liberty to mean the power of the people to rule. Less generally and with a political sense, liberty was a code of restraint on sovereignty, exercised by a few or many. Thus, liberty involved minifying and decentralizing government. "He was the first to see that strength, the progress, even the splendor, of the nation might come, not from the consolidation of loyalties, not from the vastness of governing power, but from the release of its myriad individual talents and energies. Merrill D. Peterson, "Thomas Jefferson and the National Purpose," in *Proceedings of the American Philosophical Society* 105, no. 6 (1965): 518. J. W. Cooke notes that Jefferson had available to him three different conceptions of "freedom." First, there was the liberty afforded citizens by external circumstances being such that persons could act "as they wished in pursuing their chosen interests." Second, there was the liberty afforded them by self-induced change in thinking, character, or personality—that is, a life in accordance with a moral ideal of their own choosing. Last, there was the liberty afforded all persons by virtue of being God-loved creatures, though this capacity to exercise such liberty might be impeded through external circumstances or underdeveloped faculties. Overall, "Jefferson . . . sought to create an atmosphere congenial to liberty by stressing the need to consider all relevant circumstances—population density, geography, the level of literacy, experience in self-government, virtue, and the like—in determining the type of government best suited for Americans." He concludes that Jefferson's conception of liberty is closest to Berlin's notion of "negative liberty"—that is, freedom from the coercion of other person and institutions in some significant areas of endeavor. J. W. Cooke, "Jefferson on Liberty," *Journal of the History of Ideas* 34 (1973): 571–75. Robert Faulkner says that liberty, for Jefferson, is rational and accords with what is useful. It is not spontaneous but planned, and it serves to engender useful

power—that is, the rights to life, liberty, and happiness. It turns loose the passions and uncages ingenuity. It disencumbers persons from fear of death and useless desires. It devises useful arts and inventions. Robert K. Faulkner, "Jefferson and the Enlightened Science of Liberty," in *Reason and Republicanism: Thomas Jefferson's Legacy of Liberty*, ed. Gary L. McDowell and Sharon L. Noble (Lanham, MD: Rowman & Littlefield, 1997), 43.

13. What Jefferson calls "personal liberty" in "Argument in the Case of Howell vs. Netherland" (April 1770). See Thomas Jefferson, *The Writings of Thomas Jefferson*, vol. 1, ed. Andrew A. Lipscomb and Albert E. Bergh (Washington, DC: Thomas Jefferson Memorial Association, 1903–1904), 376.

14. T. V. Smith, "Thomas Jefferson and the Perfectibility of Mankind," *Ethics* 53, no. 4 (1943): 304.

15. Horace Kallen, "The Arts and Thomas Jefferson," *Ethics* 53 (1943): 278. See also Becker, *Declaration of Independence*; Boorstin, *Lost World of Thomas Jefferson*; Malone, *Jefferson in His Time*, vols. 1–6; Wood, *Creation of the American Republic, 1776–1787*; and Peterson, *Thomas Jefferson and the New Nation*.

16. Joyce Appleby, "What Is Still American in the Political Philosophy of Thomas Jefferson?" *William and Mary Quarterly* 39 (1982): 291–93 and 295–96.

17. Jeffrey Leigh Sedgwick, "Jeffersonianism in the Progressive Era," in *Reason and Republicanism*, ed. McDowell and Noble, 194–95.

18. Conor Cruise O'Brien, "Thomas Jefferson: Radical and Racist," *Atlantic Monthly*, October 1996, 53–74.

19. Jefferson's correspondence is replete with expressions of his execration of public service to the neglect of his own affairs as well as his desire to return to Monticello and pursue a life of domestic tranquility. For example, TJ to John Randolph, August 25, 1775; TJ to Richard Henry Lee, June 17, 1779; TJ to Marquis de Lafayette, August 4, 1781; TJ to Colonel James Monroe, May 20, 1782; TJ to James Steptoe, November 26, 1782; TJ to James Madison, November 11, 1784; TJ to Francis Hopkinson, March 13, 1789; TJ to William Short, December 14, 1789; TJ to George Washington, December 15, 1789; TJ to William Short, March 12, 1790; TJ to Madame la Duchesse D'Auville, April 2, 1790; TJ to President George Washington, February 19, 1791; TJ to Thomas Mann Randolph, January 1, 1792; TJ to Thomas Pinckney, November 8, 1792; TJ to Martha Jefferson Randolph, January 26, 1793; TJ to James Madison, April 3, 1794; TJ to John Adams, April 25, 1794; TJ to John Taylor, May 1, 1794; TJ to James Madison, April 27, 1795; TJ to Edward Rutledge, November 30, 1795; TJ to Edward Rutledge, December 27, 1796; TJ to John Adams, December 28, 1796; TJ to James Madison, January 1, 1797; TJ to Count Volney, January 8, 1797; TJ to James Sullivan, February 9, 1797; TJ to Mary Jefferson Eppes, October 26, 1801; TJ to James Monroe, January 13, 1803; TJ to John Taylor, January 6, 1805; TJ to Martha Jefferson Randolph, July

6, 1806; TJ to John Dickinson, January 13, 1807; TJ to Charles Thomson, January 11, 1808; and to Pierre Samuel Dupont de Nemours, March 2, 1809.

20. An exception being J. W. Cooke. "Jefferson on Liberty," *Journal of the History of Ideas* 34 (1973): 565–71. Cooke, however, makes Jefferson a Benthamite. He was not. Political harmony, not social control, was Jefferson's aim. The latter is a Hamiltonian notion.

21. For example, Garry Wills, *Inventing America: Jefferson's Declaration of Independence* (Garden City, NY: Doubleday, 1977); Richard Matthews, *The Radical Politics of Thomas Jefferson: A Revisionist View* (Lawrence: University Press of Kansas, 1984), 17–18; and Beitzinger, "Political Theorist," in *Thomas Jefferson: A Reference Biography*, ed. Peterson, 93.

22. Sheldon assumes the priority of liberalism in Jefferson's political thinking prior to the revolution and the emergence or predominance of classical communitarianism after the revolution. The communitarian strain was in Jefferson's thinking all along. Garrett Ward Sheldon, "Eclectic Synthesis: Jesus, Aristotle, and Locke," in *Thomas Jefferson and the Politics of Nature*, ed. Thomas S. Engeman (Notre Dame: University of Notre Dame Press, 2000), 87–88.

23. Never was he so preoccupied with the issue of a free press as he was at the time of what we would today call his presidential campaigns. Prior to his first term, the constitutionality of the Alien and Sedition Acts were vigorously debated. Numerous Republicans were charged with sedition and imprisoned for writings that presumably undermined the federal government—namely, attacks on Federalists or Federalism. That no Federalists were similarly charged is sufficient evidence of the partisan nature of the legislation. Prior to both terms, the brickbats hurled at Jefferson were ponderous and numerous. In 1803, he writes to Gov. Thomas Seymour (February 11) of the calumny: "I have lent myself willingly as the subject of a great experiment, which was to prove that an administration, conducting itself with integrity and common understanding, cannot be battered down, even by the falsehoods of a licentious press, and consequently still less by the press, as restrained within legal & wholesome limits of truth. This experiment was wanting for the world to demonstrate the falsehood of the pretext that freedom of the press is incompatible with orderly government."

The tension climaxes in his Second Inaugural Address. Jefferson writes that a free press is needed for freedom and scientific advance. Here he calls "freedom of discussion," of which a free press is a critical part, an "experiment." Jefferson writes: "Nor was it uninteresting to the world that an experiment should be fairly and fully made, whether freedom of discussion, unaided by power, is not sufficient for the propagation and protection of truth—whether a government conducting itself in the true spirit of its constitution, with zeal and purity, and doing no act which it would be unwilling the whole world should witness, can be written down by falsehood and defamation." The experiment, he adds, has been tried and has met with success. The brickbats hurled at Jefferson have not deterred the public, seeing truth behind the façade of prevarication, from electing him for a second term. "[The citizens] gathered around their public functionaries, and when the Constitution called them to the decision by suffrage, they pronounced their verdict, honorable to those who had served them and consolatory to the friend of man who believes that he may be trusted with the control of his own affairs." He sums: "But the experiment is noted to prove that, since truth and reason have maintained their ground against false opinions in league with false facts, the press, confined to truth, needs no other legal restraint; the public judgment will correct false reasoning and opinions on a full hearing of all parties; and no other definite line can be drawn between the inestimable liberty of the press and its demoralizing licentiousness."

24. Taken from Karl Lehmann, *Thomas Jefferson: American Humanist* (Charlottesville: University of Virginia Press, [1965] 1994), 112.

25. See also TJ to James Maury, April 25, 1812.

26. Malone contends that Jefferson's concern was large extensions of power for minor convenience. Dumas Malone, *Jefferson and the Rights of Man* (Boston: Little, Brown, 1951), 344. And elsewhere, "Few who have exercised great authority ever valued it less for its own sake or have been less tyrannical in person." Dumas Malone, *Jefferson the President: Second Term, 1805–1809* (Charlottesville: University of Virginia Press, 1974), 589.

27. See also his speech to the Senate, February 28, 1801; TJ to James Monroe, March 7, 1801; TJ to Horatio Gates, March 8, 1801; TJ to Samuel Adams, March 29, 1801; and TJ to John Randolph, December 1, 1803.

28. Malone, *Jefferson and the Rights of Man*, 341–42 and 350.

29. Thomas Jefferson, "Draft Constitution for Virginia," in *Thomas Jefferson: Writings*, ed. Peterson, 343.

30. Thomas Jefferson, "Sixth Annual Message," in *Thomas Jefferson: Writings*, ed. Peterson, 529.

31. Plato, *The Republic*, trans. G. M. A. Grube (Indianapolis: Hackett, 1992), 419a–420b.

32. Thomas Jefferson, "Howell v. Netherland," in *The Works of Thomas Jefferson*, vol. 1, ed. Paul Leicester Ford (New York: G. P. Putnam's Sons, 1904), 471–81, http://oll.libertyfund.org/?option=com_staticxt&staticfile=show.php%3Ftitle=800&chapter=85803&layout=html&Itemid=27 (accessed June 27, 2013).

33. Compare to Kames, who distinguishes between actions from will and actions from consciousness of duty. "With respect to the latter, we have no liberty, but ought to proceed to action; with respect to the former, we may freely indulge every natural impulse, where the action is not disapproved by the moral sense." Both nonetheless

are subject to natural necessity. Lord Kames, *Essays on the Principles of Morality and Natural Religion*, 2nd ed. (London, 1756), 93.

34. Disrelish of reason apropos of moral judgments and knowledge of certain "metaphysical" truths—for example, the nature of deity, the uniformity of nature, and the existence of causality in the cosmos—Kames expresses often. It is too slippery a guide and too inaccessible by the majority of humans, ill-suited for reasoning. For instance, Kames, *Essays on the Principles of Morality and Natural Religion*, 259, 265, 267, and 284.

35. I add "convenience," because, while some intuitive perceptions are truths—for example, the self-existence of deity—others are untruths that are of utmost usefulness for humans—for instance, the existence of good, bad, beauty, and ugliness. In that regard, human faculties are given to them by deity to be of utmost use to them in flourishing, and truth is not always suited to human flourishing.

36. Lord Kames, *Essays on the Principles of Morality and Natural Religion*, 265–75 and 298–309.

37. See M. Andrew Holowchak, *Dutiful Correspondent: Philosophical Essays on Thomas Jefferson* (Lanham: Rowman & Littlefield, 2012), 159–76.

38. Kames, *Essays on the Principles of Morality and Natural Religion*, 34–36, 44–52, 55–58, 73, and 89.

39. TJ to John Adams, July 5, 1814.

40. As Kames in his essay "Liberty and Necessity" shows, choosing to disregard moral law is liberty to follow one's strongest passion, which is not under one's power. That, of course, is not liberty. Kames, *Essays on the Principles of Morality and Natural Religion*, 130–31.

41. Both scenarios are in accord with the ancient Stoics, for whom self-regard and other regard are both natural impulses and for whom a vicious action is a mistake of reasoning. The difference is that for the Stoics virtue is a matter of sound reasoning, while for Jefferson virtue is a matter of moral sensibility, which is irrational.

42. R. R. Palmer argues that the differences between Adams and Jefferson were not so great. Adams wished for executive independence and feared the impact of privileged oligarchies. Jefferson feared the abuses of monarchy. R. R. Palmer, "The Dubious Democrat," *Political Science Quarterly* 72, no. 3 (1957): 390–95.

43. Govan is correct to note that Hamilton's writings offer no confirmatory evidence of great esteem for Julius Caesar. Thomas P. Govan, "Alexander Hamilton and Julius Caesar: A Note on the Use of Historical Evidence," *William and Mary Quarterly* 32, no. 3 (1975): 475–80.

44. To Madison, Jefferson writes of Ben Franklin's assessment of Adams: "Always an honest man, often a great one, but sometimes absolutely mad" (July 29, 1789).

45. TJ to Benjamin Rush, January 16, 1811.

46. Paul Thompson, "Agrarianism and the American Philosophical Tradition," *Agriculture and Human Values* 7, no. 1, 4–5.

47. Joyce Appleby, *Capitalism and the New Social Order* (New York: New York University Press, 1984), 50–53 and 86–97. See also Max Lerner, *Thomas Jefferson: America's Philosopher-King* (New Brunswick: Transaction, 1996), 129.

48. Jeffrey Leigh Sedgwick, "Jeffersonianism in the Progressive Era," in *Reason and Republicanism*, ed. McDowell and Noble, 194.

49. Shannon Kincaid, "Democratic Ideals and the Urban Experience," *Philosophy and Geography* 6, no. 2 (2003): 146.

50. See also Matthews and Malone. Writes Matthews: "[Jefferson] freely acknowledges that the Native Americans have no government, but he disagrees that they lack society. . . . To Jefferson as to Karl Marx, the Native Americans constituted empirical evidence of moral agents who did not need the presence of a Leviathan to hold them in check; chiefs held "power" through their ability to earn the respect of their fellow tribesmen who exercised their "moral sense of right and wrong" and were receptive to community pressures of loss of esteem, expulsion, and in extreme case, execution carried out by the person who was harmed." Richard K. Matthews, "The Radical Political Philosophy of Thomas Jefferson: An Essay in Retrieval," *Midwest Studies in Philosophy* 28 (2004): 48. Writes Malone: "The extreme against which Jefferson had recoiled was despotism such as he had observed in pre-revolutionary Europe, and which his countrymen had revolted against in a much milder form in their own Revolution." Dumas Malone, *Jefferson in His Time*, vol. 4, *Jefferson the President: First Term, 1801–1805* (Boston: Little, Brown, 1970), 25.

51. Peter Onuf, *The Mind of Thomas Jefferson* (Charlottesville: University of Virginia Press, 2007), 87. See also 69, 71, and 95.

52. Henry Adams, *History of the United States during the Administrations of Thomas Jefferson* (New York: Library of America, 1986).

53. He was not averse to an executive acting with a heavy hand, at least in extreme circumstances—for example, when the unity of a state was at issue. See Thomas Jefferson, "Opinion on the French Treaties," April 28, 1873; TJ to W. C. C. Claiborne, February 3, 1807; TJ to Dr. James Brown, October 27, 1808; TJ to John Colvin, September 20, 1810; and TJ to James Barbour, January 22, 1812.

54. For example, TJ to John F. Mercer, October 9, 1804.

55. Mark Roelofs argues that the differences are slight—"one of shading and emphasis." Both are commercial liberals, schooled in the economic thought of Adam Smith and likeminded thinkers, and both are committed to nascent capitalism. H. Mark Roelofs, *Ideology and Myth in American Politics* (Boston: Little, Brown, 1976), 247. This view is untenable.

56. Plato, *Republic*, 457c.

57. For more, see Lawrence S. Kaplan, *Thomas Jefferson: Westward the Course of Empire* (Wilmington, DE: SR Books, 1999), 87–88.

58. Alexander Hamilton, "Opinion on the Constitutionality of the Bank" (March 23, 1791).

59. Noble E. Cunningham Jr., "Political Parties," in *Thomas Jefferson: A Reference Biography*, ed. Peterson, 299–300.

60. Patterson suggests the difference is one of adaptation versus molding. "Jefferson insisted that government should be adapted to society rather than that society should be reconstructed to fit the doctrinaire type of government." Hamilton, in contrast, wished to mold persons to a particular one-size-fits-all constitution. Caleb Perry Patterson, *The Constitutional Principles of Thomas Jefferson* (Austin: University of Texas Press, 1953), 27–28.

61. Thomas Jefferson, "The Anas," in *Thomas Jefferson: Writings*, ed. Peterson, 665–66. To John Melish (January 13, 1813), Jefferson writes of the differences between three types of "federalism": Essex federalism, Hamiltonian federalism, and federalism. "Anglomany, monarchy, and separation . . . are the principles of the Essex federalists. Anglomany and monarchy, those of the Hamiltonians, and Anglomany alone, that of the portion among the *people* who call themselves federalists."

62. See Patterson, *Constitutional Principles of Thomas Jefferson*, 37.

63. Each having an elementary school, a company of militia, a justice of peace and constable, a police force, and jurors, and each caring for their own poor, roads, and police. TJ to John Cartwright, June 5, 1824.

64. TJ to Thomas Kercheval, June 12, 1816.

65. The XYZ Affair (1797–1798) was a diplomatic rift between America and France, begun by French attacks on US merchant ships because of US refusal to aid the French in their war with England. It involved three French officials, named X, Y, and Z, by John Adams in the altered correspondence between his administration and the French that was given over to Republicans, upon demand, for inspection. The rift resulted in what is now known as the Quasi-War. The Alien and Sedition Acts (1798) were four laws, avowedly aimed at French revolutionists but almost certainly aimed at nullifying Jeffersonian republicanism. The Naturalization Act postponed citizenship of aliens to fourteen years of residence (not five) in the United States, thereby disallowing voting privileges for prospective Republicans. The Alien Act and Alien Enemies Act gave Adams the power to deport or imprison any alien suspected of actions aimed at usurpation. The Sedition Act was specifically aimed at "subversive" republicans, and a clear violation of the First Amendment. It disallowed any criticism of the US government, which was Federalist in essence, or its officials. Many republicans—journalists especially—were tried and imprisoned.

66. Thomas Jefferson, "Draft Constitution for Virginia," 338.

67. As John Howe notes, "Laws clear in their meaning, just in their purposes, and equitably administered were the ligaments that held a republican order together." John Howe, "Republicanism," in *Thomas Jefferson: A Reference Biography*, ed. Peterson, 66.

68. Writes Garrett Ward Sheldon: "Hamilton's corrupting fiscal policy derived from a corrupt [Hobbesian] political theory, which strove to govern men by appealing solely to their private interests, and expected to somehow create a just and orderly society out of the aggregate of those interests, rather than acknowledging and cultivating the highest faculty in man: his social, ethical nature." Garrett Ward Sheldon, *The Political Philosophy of Thomas Jefferson* (Baltimore: Johns Hopkins University Press, 1993), 92. Malone adds: "By catering to a relatively small but highly articulate and influential group, [Hamilton] had bound these men to himself by ties of interest and become their champion. In effect he had created a 'machine,' which would continue to be used in the interest of the favored few." Malone, *Jefferson and the Rights of Man*, 340.

69. McDonald states that though Hamilton refers to Hobbes in "The Farmer Refuted" and perhaps even considers himself a Hobbesian, there is no evidence that he ever read Hobbes and good reason to believe he did not. Forrest McDonald, *Alexander Hamilton: A Biography* (New York: W. W. Norton, 1979), 374 n. 18.

70. Hamilton acknowledges similitude of political principles, but not axial similitude, for he believes in a deity that made man and established the laws of nature prior to "any human institution whatsoever" and protective of each man's life, limb, property, and liberty. The laws of nature prohibit any form of governing other than one of mutual consent of the governing and the governed. Alexander Hamilton, *The Farmer Refuted*, The Online Library of Liberty, http://oll.libertyfund.org/?option=com _staticxt&staticfile=show.php%3Ftitle=2121&chapter=164944&layout=html&Itemid =27 (accessed October 12, 2012).

71. TJ to Destutt de Tracy, January 26, 1811.

72. For the influence of Scottish culture, see Gilman M Ostrander, "Jefferson and Scottish Culture," *Réflexions Historiques* 5, no. 2 (1978): 246. See also Garry Wills, *Inventing America: Jefferson's Declaration of Independence* (New York: 1978), 174 and 239.

73. Pace Fowler, who argues, "It is not really clear that Jefferson cared much about natural rights, except as a lever to promote his understanding of the good society." Robert Booth Fowler, "Mythologies of a Founder," in *Thomas Jefferson and the Politics of Nature*, ed. Engeman, 134.

74. Concerning the last point, Donovan says: "Thus, the political process that Locke endorses can be described as a constant check between separate and conflicting powers. The government determines the laws that rule the people and the people choose the officials who determine those laws. Both lack a power the other possesses.

Both possesses a power that limits the other. The process is mutually restricted conflict. Locke's writings become an attempt to empower a people who, nonetheless, do not and should not govern themselves." Michael Donovan, "Pursuing Democracy as Moral Task: A Deweyan Response to Jeffersonian Revolution," *International Studies in Philosophy* 26, no. 1 (1994): 2.

75. For Jefferson, Browers contends, his three unalienable rights entailed a right to property. That proved good politics because it was a moral stance. Claude Browers, "Jefferson's Land Ethic," *Ethics* 53, no. 4 (1943): 53. Katz argues otherwise. Citing Jefferson's letter to McPherson (August 13, 1813), he shows that Jefferson did not believe in a right to property but merely a right to occupancy—that is, a right to appropriate. Following Locke, a right to occupancy is conditioned on no harm done through surfeit or neglect. He deviates from Locke in maintaining that only settled husbandry confers authentic occupancy. Selling off one's labor to another for manufacture was illegitimate. "Jefferson draws the boundary between freedom and bondage quite differently [than Locke]. He contends that laborers are meaningfully free only if they employ their own property and work for themselves, and not for an employer who puts them to work. To be constrained by necessity to subject oneself to another's will is equivalent to wage-slavery." Claudio J. Katz, "Thomas Jefferson's Liberal Anticapitalism," *American Journal of Political Science* 47, no. 1 (2003): 10–13.

76. John Locke, *Second Treatise of Government*, ed. C. B. Macpherson (Indianapolis: Hackett, 1980), §4.

77. Sandler argues that Jefferson's "Bill for Establishing Religious Freedom" is, through a folio containing Jefferson's notes on Locke's *A Letter concerning Toleration*, linked to the latter. He establishes five key points: the notion of belief being inspired by reason, not force; the fallibility, justified by history, of civil magistrates in religious affairs; the separation of religious opinions from their capacities to perform civil roles; the right of government to interfere with religious activities that are designed to interfere with peace and social order; and the notion of truth, unaided, being sufficiently powerful to prevail over untruth. S. Gerald Sandler, "Lockean Ideas in Thomas Jefferson's Bill for Establishing Religious Freedom," *Journal of the History of Ideas,* 21, no. 1 (1960): 110–16.

78. John Locke, *The Reasonableness of Christianity as Delivered in the Scriptures* (Oxford: Oxford University Press, 1999).

79. Thomas Jefferson, *Notes on the State of Virginia*, in *Writings*, 285. Brown sums, "The identity of church and state is tyranny; toleration is offensive to reason; only full freedom of conscience is compatible with free government." Stuart Gerry Brown, "The Mind of Thomas Jefferson," *Ethics* 73, no. 2 (1963): 87.

80. Locke, *Second Treatise of Government*, §125. See note 74 above for Donovan's opinion.

81. Taken from Thomas Jefferson and James Madison, *The Republic of Letters: The Correspondence of Thomas Jefferson and James Madison, 1776–1826*, vol. 1, ed. James Morton Smith (New York: W. W. Norton, 1995), 1–2.

82. Merrill D. Peterson, *Thomas Jefferson and the New Nation: A Biography* (Cambridge: Oxford University Press, 1970), 266.

83. Given the bond of the friendship, the correspondence is surprisingly serious and dry.

84. James Morton Smith, "Introduction: An Intimate Friendship," in *The Republic of Letters: The Correspondence between Thomas Jefferson and James Madison, 1776–1826*, vol. 1 (New York: W. W. Norton, 1995), 12.

85. See Adrienne Koch, *Jefferson and Madison: The Great Collaboration* (New York: Alfred A. Knopf, 1950).

86. For Hutcheson, "alienable Rights" are transferable for the possibility of promoting some good; "inalienable Rights," for instance, a right over our own lives, are nontransferable. Francis Hutcheson, *Inquiry into the Original of Our Ideas of Beauty and Virtue*, ed. Wolfgang Leidhold (Indianapolis: Liberty Fund, [1725] 2004), 185.

87. Gilbert Chinard, "Jefferson among the Philosophers," *Ethics* 43, no. 4 (1943): 260.

88. Peter Onuf, *The Mind of Thomas Jefferson* (Charlottesville: University of Virginia Press, 2007), 74.

89. Madison disclaimed any right to be called "father of the Constitution," though modern scholarship suggests he was more modest than accurate. Smith, "Constitution and the Movement for a Bill of Rights," in *Republic of Letters*, 518.

90. After reading a copy of the Constitution from Madison, Jefferson wrote: "My first wish was the 9. first conventions might accept the constitution, as the means of securing to us the great mass of good it contained, that the 4. last might reject it, as the means of obtaining amendments." Letter to Hopkinson, March 13, 1789. His ambivalence was due to its not having a bill of rights affixed.

91. See also TJ to James Madison, March 15, 1789. Wood makes the absurd assertion that Jefferson supported a bill of rights "not because he had thought through the issue the way Madison had, but largely because a bill of rights was what good governments were supposed to have." Gordon S. Wood, "The Trials and Tribulations of Thomas Jefferson," *Jeffersonian Legacies*, ed. Peter S. Onuf (Charlottesville: University Press of Virginia, 1993), 396.

92. Jefferson consistently objected to any political service without term. The issue was a growing sense of infallibility through unaccountability.

93. Richard K. Matthews, *The Radical Politics of Thomas Jefferson: A Revisionist View* (Lawrence: University Press of Kansas, 1986), 17 and 98–118.

94. James Madison to TJ, October 17, 1788.

95. One must be cautious. As Banning has shown more recently, Madison was

not the sort of nationalist that many have made him out to be. Lance Banning, *The Sacred Fire of Liberty: James Madison and the Founding of the Federal Republic* (Ithaca, NY: Cornell University Press, 1995).

96. See Cunningham, "Political Parties," 295–310.

97. That is not to say that Jefferson did not think there were times that the executive had to act quickly and firmly, and even without constitutional sanction. Enforcement of the embargo was one such instance. See, for example, TJ to Albert Gallatin, August 11, 1808.

98. See also TJ to Thomas Pinckney, May 29, 1797; TJ to Henry Lee, August 10, 1824; and TJ to William Short, January 8, 1825.

Chapter 4. "The Earth Belongs . . . to the Living": Jefferson on Revolution and Political Renewal

1. The rebellion of a group of Massachusetts' farmers, some 1,500 in all, in protest to increasing debts. The farmers, led by Daniel Shays, demanded that the government relieve their debts by printing up more paper money. The state legislature did not reply. Consequently, the farmers rose up in arms against their government.

2. James Madison to TJ, October 17, 1788.

3. Conor Cruise O'Brien, "Thomas Jefferson: Radical and Racist," *Atlantic Monthly*, October 1996, 53–74.

4. Ibid., 60–61.

5. Compare to Hutcheson: "It follows 'That all human Power, or Authority, must consist in a Right transferr'd to any Person or Council, to dispose of the alienable Rights of others; and that consequently, there can be on Government so absolute, as to have even an external Right to do or command every thing.' For wherever any Invasion is made upon unalienable Rights, there must arise either a perfect, or external Right to Resistance." Francis Hutcheson, *An Inquiry into the Original of Our Ideas of Beauty and Virtue in Two Theses*, ed. Wolfgang Leidhold (Indianapolis: Liberty Fund, 2004), 191.

6. Dumas Malone, *Jefferson and the Rights of Man* (Boston: Little, Brown, 1951), 166–67.

7. For more, see M. Andrew Holowchak, *Dutiful Correspondent: Philosophical Essays on Thomas Jefferson* (Lanham, MD: Rowman & Littlefield, 2012), 51–68.

8. M. Andrew Holowchak, *Framing a Legend: Exposing the Distorted History of Thomas Jefferson and Sally Hemings* (New York: Prometheus Books, 2013), 98–99.

9. O'Brien, "Thomas Jefferson: Radical and Racist," 54.

10. Dumas Malone, *Jefferson the Virginian* (Boston: Little, Brown, 1948), xiii.

11. For example, TJ to Thomas Jefferson Randolph, December 30, 1809.

12. See Kevin R. C. Gutzman, "Thomas Jefferson's Federalism, 1774–1825," *Modern Age* (September 2011): 78.

13. For example, TJ to James Monroe, March 7, 1801; and TJ to John Randolph, December 1, 1803.

14. O'Brien, "Thomas Jefferson: Radical and Racist," 64–66.

15. Ibid., 71.

16. Ibid.

17. Not to be taken in its political sense, linked to the movement that took root early in the twentieth century.

18. Malone, *Jefferson and the Rights of Man*, 158.

19. Writes McDonald: "Jefferson really did not believe in law—or not, at any rate, in the historical English concept of law as something fixed, immutable, handed down through the ages. Rather, they believed in government by the good and wise, acting in the interest of the whole and restrained only by the virtue of an enlightened and informed people." Forrest McDonald, *The Presidency of Thomas Jefferson* (Lawrence: University Press of Kansas, 1976), 49.

20. Michael Hardt, "Jefferson and Democracy," *American Quarterly* 59, no. 1 (2007): 58–65.

21. Ibid., 62.

22. Holowchak, *Framing a Legend*, 232–40.

23. See M. Andrew Holowchak, "Jefferson's Moral Agrarianism: Poetic Fiction or Normative Vision?" *Agriculture and Human Values* 28, no. 4 (2011): 497–506.

24. Hardt, "Jefferson and Democracy," 62.

25. TJ to James Madison, December 20, 1787.

26. Hardt, "Jefferson and Democracy," 62–63.

27. Ibid., 65.

28. Thomas Jefferson, First Inaugural Address, April 30, 1801.

29. For example, see TJ to L'Abbé Arnoux, July 19, 1789.

30. Hardt, "Jefferson and Democracy," 70–71.

31. For example, TJ to William Carmichael, December 26, 1786; TJ to Edward Carrington, January 16, 1787; TJ to James Madison, December 20, 1787, and May 15, 1794; TJ to David Humphreys, March 18, 1789; TJ to Gouverneur Morris, November 7, 1792; TJ to John Taylor, June 1, 1798; TJ to Edmund Randolph, August 18, 1799; TJ to John Breckinridge, January 29, 1800; TJ to Elbridge Gerry, March 29, 1801; Jefferson, First Inaugural Address; TJ to Dr. William Eustis, January 14, 1809; TJ to Caesar A. Rodney, February 10, 1810; TJ to P. S. Dupont de Nemours, April 14, 1816; TJ to Francis Gilmer, June 7, 1816; TJ to Marquis de Lafayette, May 14, 1817; and TJ to Alexander von Humboldt, June 13, 1817.

32. TJ to James Madison, September 6, 1789.

33. TJ to Thomas Nelson, May 16, 1776.

34. See TJ to Noah Webster, December 4, 1790; TJ to Thomas Pinckney, May 29, 1797; TJ to James Monroe, March 7, 1801; TJ to Horatio Gates, March 8, 1801; and TJ to Samuel Adams, March 29, 1801.

35. Palmer notes that the Declaration of Independence is "an essentially conservative document, explaining why the Americans are not really revolutionary, a kind of lawyerlike announcement of breach of contract. Its aim is not to transform the world but to announce the arrival of the United States in the circle of existing and established powers." R. R. Palmer, "A Neglected Work: Otto Vossler on Jefferson and the Revolutionary Era," *William and Mary Quarterly* 12, 3rd ser., no. 3 (1955): 464.

36. John Locke, "Of Tyranny," in *Second Treatise of Government*, ed. C. B. Macpherson (Indianapolis: Hackett, 1980), §199.

37. Roughly, "justice concerning the beginning of a war." On Jefferson's views of war as compared with just-war theory, see Holowchak, *Dutiful Correspondent*, 177–200.

38. Ari Helo, "Jefferson's Conception of Republican Government," in *The Cambridge Companion to Thomas Jefferson*, ed. Frank Shuffleton (New York: University of Cambridge Press, 2009), 36.

39. Difficulties with this argument are the topic of my paper, "Eudaemonism or Survivalism: Jefferson and the Unwritten Laws of Self-Preservation" (forthcoming).

40. For a fine analysis of the context of the letter and its implications, see Herbert Sloan, "'The Earth belongs in Usufruct to the Living,'" in *Jeffersonian Legacies*, ed. Peter S. Onuf (Charlottesville: University Press of Virginia, 1993), 281–315.

41. See Adrienne Koch, *The Philosophy of Thomas Jefferson* (Gloucester, MA: Peter Smith, 1957), 141.

42. TJ to C. F. W. Malone, September 10, 1787.

43. See also Laurence Sterne, *The Life and Opinions of Tristram Shandy, Gentleman* (New York: Penguin Books, [1759–1767] 2003), 416. It was also designed to promote general prosperity, as there would be no lengthy debts and the wars of one generation would not be the wars of the next.

44. For example, Lerner states, "His theory of revolution was therefore not utopian but purgative: revolutions were not intended to create an ideal state or society but to get rid of the obstructions of the past and prevent what had served an earlier generation from hardening into a tyrannical habit which could no longer serve the present one." Max Lerner, *Thomas Jefferson: America's Philosopher-King* (New Brunswick: Transaction, 1996), 112.

45. "Virginia's republican order would be new, but it would emerge organically from what had existed before," Howe says. "At no time did he reject Virginia's established social and political orders." John Howe, "Republicanism," in *Thomas Jef-*

ferson: A Reference Biography, ed. Merrill D. Peterson (New York: Charles Scribner's Sons, 1986), 63.

46. Thomas Jefferson, "First Inaugural Address," in *Thomas Jefferson: Writings*, ed. Merrill D. Peterson (New York: Library of America, 1984), 493.

47. See also TJ to Count de Moustier, May 17, 1788; TJ to Elbridge Gerry, January 26, 1799; and TJ to William Green Munford, June 18, 1799.

48. February 1826. Thomas Jefferson, *The Works of Thomas Jefferson*, vol. 12, ed. Paul Leicester Ford (New York: G. P. Putnam's Sons, 1904–1905), 273.

49. For example, according to May, for instance, who paints Jefferson a "historical relativist"—rights endure but everything else must change. Henry F. May, "The Enlightenment," in *Thomas Jefferson: A Reference Biography*, ed. Peterson, 52; Dumas Malone, *Jefferson and His Time*, vol. 6, *The Sage of Monticello* (Charlottesville: University of Virginia Press, 1981), 138; and Gilbert Chinard, *Thomas Jefferson: The Apostle of Americanism* (Ann Arbor: University of Michigan Press, [1929] 1962), 132–35; Julian Boyd, *The Papers of Thomas Jefferson*, vol. 30 (Princeton: Princeton University Press, 2003), 384.

50. Jefferson calls it a "book of paradoxes; having, indeed, much truth and sound principle, but abounding also with inconsistencies, apochryphal facts and false inferences." TJ to William Duane, August 12, 1810.

51. TJ to M. D'Ivernois, February 6, 1795; TJ to A. C. V. C. Destutt de Tracy, January 26, 1811; and TJ to François Barbé-Marbois, June 14, 1817. See Holowchak, *Dutiful Correspondent*, 29–50.

52. Adrienne Koch, *The Philosophy of Thomas Jefferson* (Gloucester, MA: Peter Smith, 1957), 132.

53. See Holowchak, *Dutiful Correspondent*, 93–110.

54. For example, TJ to John Adams, July 5, 1814; TJ to I. H. Tiffany, August 6, 1816; TJ to John Adams, December 10, 1819; and TJ to A. Koraïs, October 31, 1823.

55. For more, see M. Andrew Holowchak, *Pathological Moralist & Moral Pathologist: The Political Philosophy and Moral Vision of Thomas Jefferson* (forthcoming).

56. Peterson goes on to say that Jefferson recognized, at least in the short term, that he needed to exercise power to curb power. Merrill D. Peterson, *Thomas Jefferson and the New Nation: A Biography* (Oxford: Oxford University Press, 1970), 689.

57. See also TJ to John Waldo, August 16, 1813.

58. Condorcet maintained that political authorities always lag behind the science of politics and morals and even the masses, when educated. Jean-Antoine Nicolas de Caritat, *Outlines of an Historical View of the Progress of the Human Mind: Being a Posthumous Work of the Late M. de Condorcet* (London: J. Johnson, 1795), 230.

59. For an excellent account of a paternalistic strand in Jefferson's use of "neology," see Peter Thompson, "'Judicious Neology': The Imperative of Paternalism in Thomas

Jefferson's Linguistic Studies," *Early American Studies* (fall 2003): 187–224.

60. Jefferson, "First Inaugural Address," in *Thomas Jefferson: Writings*, ed. Merrill D. Peterson (New York: Library of America, 1984), 492–93.

61. TJ to Pierre Samuel Dupont de Nemours, April 24, 1816.

62. See also TJ to Tench Coxe, June 1, 1795.

63. As Condorcet noted, "establishing by law a regular and peaceable mode of reforming the constitution" was critical in republican government. Caritat, *Outlines of an Historical View of the Progress of the Human Mind*, 264.

64. TJ to George Wythe, August 13, 1786.

65. Garret Ward Sheldon, *The Political Philosophy of Thomas Jefferson* (Baltimore: Johns Hopkins University Press, 1993), 27.

66. Thomas Jefferson, "Summary View of the Rights of British America," in *Thomas Jefferson: Writings*, ed. Peterson, 105–106.

67. See also TJ to Phillip Mazzei, ca. November 1785; Jefferson, "Autobiography" (1821), in *Thomas Jefferson: Writings*, ed. Peterson; and TJ to John Cartwright, June 5, 1824.

68. Jefferson, "Autobiography," in *Writings*, 63.

69. James R. Stoner, "Jefferson and the Common Law Tradition," in *Reason and Republicanism: Thomas Jefferson's Legacy of Liberty*, eds. Gary L. McDowell and Sharon L. Noble (Lanham, MD: Rowman & Littlefield, 1997), 110.

70. Meaning "the written law."

71. Jefferson, "Summary View of the Rights of British America," 119.

PART 3: JEFFERSON ON MORALITY

Chapter 5. "Not to Lean on Others": Jefferson on Man and Morality

1. Lehmann says Jefferson "read more of ancient literature . . . than any other man of his time," except the best professional classicists. Karl Lehmann, *Thomas Jefferson: American Humanist* (Charlottesville: University Press of Virginia, [1965] 1994), 15. Chinard writes, "Through constant and systematic study he really lived in the commerce of the Greeks." Gilbert Chinard, *The Literary Bible of Thomas Jefferson: His Commonplace Book of Philosophers and Poets* (New York: Greenwood Press, [1928] 1969), 11.

2. Book II.4 (1105a30–5). Aristotle, *Nicomachean Ethics*, trans. Terrence Irwin (Indianapolis: Hackett, 1999). See M. Andrew Holowchak, "Virtue, Craft, & Contest: An Aristotelian Approach to Competitive Sport," *Sport in Society* 8, no. 1 (2005): 65–75.

3. Cicero, *On Duties*, trans. Walter Miller (Cambridge: Harvard University Press, 2001), I.xxx.107–117.

4. M. Andrew Holowchak, *Ancient Science and Dreams: Oneirology in Greco-Roman Antiquity* (Lanham, MD: University Press of America, 2002), 13.

5. Richard K. Matthews, "The Radical Political Philosophy of Thomas Jefferson: An Essay in Retrieval," *Midwest Studies of Philosophy* 28 (2004): 39.

6. Caleb Perry Patterson, *The Constitutional Principles of Thomas Jefferson* (Austin: University of Texas Press, 1953), 50. Patterson's view is essentially correct, only if we grasp the "theory of government," as I have urged we do, as a political schema for good government and not as any particular form of instantiated constitution. Constitutions must change with the progress of a people; a schema—laid out to offer direction for progressive, liberal constitutions—need not change.

7. Diogenes Laertius, *Lives of the Eminent Philosophers*, vol. 2, trans. R. D. Hicks (Cambridge, MA: Harvard University Press, 1991), Book VII.87.

8. Ibid., Book VII.88.

9. A distinction noted by the Scottish empiricists that Jefferson so admired. See, for example, Lord Kames, *Essays on the Principles of Morality and Natural Religion*, 2nd ed. (London, 1758), 62–63.

10. Seneca, *Epistles*, vols. 1–3, trans. Richard M. Gummere (Cambridge, MA: Harvard University Press, 2000–2002), CXXI.21.

11. Cicero, *On Ends*, trans. H. Rackham (Cambridge, MA: Harvard University Press, 1994), III.xix–xx.62–66.

12. Seneca, *Epistles*, XCV.52–53.

13. This shows Latin was ill-equipped to accommodate Greek Stoicism.

14. Because other animals are capable of a *kathekon* or *officium*, "duty" and "appropriate act" (which are often used as a suitable translations) are not ideal when it comes to humans.

15. Cicero, *On Ends*, III.vi.22.

16. Ibid., III.vi.20.

17. Carolus Müllerus, ed., *Fragmenta Historicum Graeco*, vol. 4, *Hierocles* (Paris, 1868), §671.7–673.11.

18. A similar privileging occurs in Hutcheson's *Inquiry*. He notes that humans are by nature more inclined to parochial ties—for instance, family and friends—and that action from pure disinterest, without consideration of local ties, would be practically impossible. He illustrates this privileging by a comparison with universal gravitation, a force which acts strongest on those bodies nearest it and diminishes rapidly with distance. His point here is that even the remotest objects in the universe are gravitationally bound, if only to the slightest extent. Francis Hutcheson, *Inquiry into the Original of Our Ideas of Beauty and Virtue*, ed. Wolfgang Leidhold (Indianapolis: Liberty Fund, [1725] 2004), 149; and Francis

Hutcheson, *A Short Introduction to Moral Philosophy in Three Books; Containing the Elements of Ethicks and the Law of Nature*, 2nd ed. (Glasgow: Robert and Andrew Foulis, 1753), 79. See also Charron, for whom justice entails duties to self, others, and deity. Pierre Charron, *On Wisdom*, vol. 3, trans. George Stanhope (London, 1729), 1017ff.

19. Seneca, *Benefits, Essays*, vols. 1–3, trans. John W. Basadore (Cambridge, MA: Harvard University Press, 1998–2001), III.xxviii.1.

20. Seneca, *Benefits*, III.xviii.2.

21. M. Andrew Holowchak, "Liberal Individualism, Autonomy, and the Great Divide," *Philosophy in the Contemporary World* 13, no. 1 (2006): 20–21.

22. See TJ to Benjamin Rush, April 21, 1803.

23. Taken from Stanley R. Hauer, "Thomas Jefferson and the Anglo-Saxon Language," *PMLA* 98, no. 5 (1983): 880.

24. See M. Andrew Holowchak, *The Stoics: A Guide for the Perplexed* (New York: Continuum, 2008), 99–103. Yarbrough mistakenly takes this as an appeal to publicity—"the appeal to majority sentiment." That view makes the correctness or incorrectness of moral decision making merely a democratic and arbitrary process. Jean Yarbrough, "The Moral Sense, Character Formation, and Virtue," in *Reason and Republicanism: Thomas Jefferson's Legacy of Liberty*, ed. Gary L. McDowell and Sharon L. Noble (Lanham, MD: Rowman & Littlefield, 1997), 284.

25. For example, Adam Smith, *Theory of Moral Sentiments* (Indianapolis: Liberty Classics, 1969).

26. Thomas Jefferson, *Thomas Jefferson: Writings*, ed. Merrill D. Peterson (New York: Library of America, 1984), 423.

27. See M. Andrew Holowchak, *Dutiful Correspondent: Philosophical Essays on Thomas Jefferson* (Lanham, MD: Rowman & Littlefield, 2012), 189.

28. For more on Jefferson and war, see ibid., 177–200.

29. Francis Hutcheson, *Illustrations on the Moral Sense*, ed. Bernard Peach (Cambridge: Belknap, 1971), 188–89.

30. While Yarbrough asserts that Jefferson generally disacknowledges that virtue is often difficult and painful, these passages show otherwise. Yarbrough, "Moral Sense, Character Formation, and Virtue," 273.

31. Various manifestations of cognitivist (i.e., descriptivism and naturalism) and noncognitivist (i.e., prescriptivism, emotivism, and postmodernism) accounts of morality today—in reducing morality to wanting or desiring—have by fiat reduced morality to one form or another of hedonism.

32. David Hume, *An Enquiry concerning the Principles of Morals*, ed. J. B. Schneewind (Indianapolis: Hackett, 1983), 16.

33. Kames rejects reason as the faculty for morality, because it is too weak in the general public, who have "little capacity to enter into abstract reasoning" and who

show every capacity to form correct moral judgments and act accordingly. Kames, *Essays on the Principles of Morality and Natural Religion*, 73.

34. Justice was an exception. Hume believed that its "sole" ground was public utility. Hume, *Enquiry concerning the Principles of Morals*, 34.

35. The problem, of course, was redoubled in that Hume lacked a unitary conception of personhood in which to ground social sentiment. Ibid., 50 and 77.

36. David Hume, *A Treatise on Human Nature* (Harmondsworth, Middlesex: Penguin, 1969), 462.

37. Ibid., 510.

38. Simon Blackburn, *Ruling Passions: A Theory of Practical Reasoning* (Oxford: Clarendon, 1998), 239.

39. Ibid., 240.

40. Ibid., 241.

41. Ibid., 250–51.

42. Ibid., 254–56.

43. Ibid., 257–59.

44. David Hume, "Of the Standard of Taste," in *Essays: Moral, Political, and Literary*, ed. Eugene F. Miller (Indianapolis: Liberty Fund, 1987), 246.

45. David Hume, "The Sceptic," in *Essays*, ed. Miller, 180.

46. TJ to Peter Carr, August 19, 1785; TJ to John Randolph, December 1, 1803; TJ to James Fishback, September 27, 1809; TJ to Thomas Law, June 13, 1814; TJ to Thomas Cooper, December 11, 1823; and TJ to Edward Livingston, April 4, 1824.

47. Lehmann notes that Jefferson subsumes moral philosophy under reason in his library catalog, though "it would have been more logical to replace that Baconian category by his moral sense, which seemed to be the root rather than the offspring of organized reason." Karl Lehmann, *Thomas Jefferson: American Humanist* (Charlottesville: University of Virginia Press, [1965] 1994), 132.

48. Aristotle, *On the Soul*, trans. W. S. Hett (Cambridge, MA: Harvard University Press, 1957), III.9–10.

49. Dred Scott speech, 1857.

50. Eric Slauter, "The Declaration of Independence and the New Nation," in *The Cambridge Companion to Thomas Jefferson*, ed. Frank Shuffleton (New York: Cambridge University Press, 2009), 12–34.

51. See R. R. Palmer, "A Neglected Work: Otto Vossler on Jefferson and the Revolutionary Era," *William and Mary Quarterly* 12, 3rd ser., no. 3 (1955): 464.

52. See Michael Zuckert, "Founder of the Natural Rights Republic," in *Thomas Jefferson and the Politics of Nature*, ed. Thomas S. Engeman (Notre Dame: University of Notre Dame Press, 2000), 17–18.

53. Roughly following Smith. John E. Smith, "Philosophical Ideas behind the

'Declaration of Independence,'" *Revue Internationale de Philosophia* 31 (1977): 374–75.

54. For equality of status and property, see Adam Ferguson, *An Essay on the History of Civil Society*, 2nd ed. (London, 1768), 239.

55. Thomas Jefferson, "Rules of Etiquette," in *Thomas Jefferson: Writings*, ed. Peterson, 705. It is a common criticism that Jefferson's actions were inconsistent with his words. "But Jefferson, although he may have affected simplicity of dress even in the White House, ate and drank like a lord." If democracy is to mean anything, it must be about "equal or proportionate access to justice and the political process." Thomas Fleming, "Three Faces of Democracy: Cleisthenes, Jefferson, and Robespierre," *Telos* (1995): 53–54.

56. "First among equals."

57. For more, see M. Andrew Holowchak, "The Fear, Honor, and Love of God: Thomas Jefferson on Jews, Philosophers, and Jesus," *Forum Philosophicum* 18, no. 1 (2013): 49–71.

58. See Jennings L. Wagoner, "Honor and Dishonor at Mr. Jefferson's University: The Antebellum Years," *History of Education Quarterly* 26, no. 2 (1986): 162.

59. TJ to Martha Jefferson, May 21, 1787.

60. TJ to Martha Jefferson, April 7, 1787. See also April 25, 1790; April 26, 1790; and May 30, 1791.

61. TJ to Martha Jefferson Randolph, February 5, 1801.

62. On Jefferson as mentor, see Harold Hellenbrand, *The Unfinished Revolution: Education and Politics in the Thought of Thomas Jefferson* (Newark: University of Delaware Press, 1990), 65–67.

63. There is another discernable Stoic strain in his thinking. Jefferson says to Mary (June 14, 1787), vis-à-vis her wishes to marry, that her future husband is a person for whom he has high esteem. The coupling, "in compleating the circle of our family," promises "long years of domestic concord and love, the best ingredient in human happiness." It will allow for good sense, good humor, liberality, and prudent care of domestic affairs. The sentiment, following the Stoic Hierocles, is that happiness begins with oneself and one's family circle. It is repeated in another letter to Mary a year and a half later and in a 1782 letter to James Monroe. TJ to Mary Jefferson Eppes, January 1, 1799; and TJ to James Monroe, May 20, 1782. See also, TJ to Mary Jefferson Eppes, October 26, 1801.

64. M. Andrew Holowchak, "Jefferson's Moral Agrarianism: Poetic Fiction or Normative Vision?" *Agriculture and Human Values* 28, no. 4 (2001): 497–506; and M. Andrew Holowchak, "Jefferson's Moral Agrarianism," in *Encyclopedia of Food and Agricultural Ethics*, ed. Paul B. Thompson and David M. Kaplan (Netherlands: Springer, 2013).

65. Thomas Jefferson, "Memorandum," in *Thomas Jefferson: Writings*, ed. Peterson, 702–704.

66. Thomas Jefferson, "Travelling Notes for Mr. Rutledge and Mr. Shippen," in *Thomas Jefferson: Writings*, ed. Peterson, 659–60.

67. John Locke, "Of Property," in *Second Treatise of Government*, ed. C. B. Macpherson (Indianapolis: Hackett, 1980), §25.

68. Ibid., §42.

69. Jefferson bracketed Lafayette's "droit à la propriété" when the latter had sent to him his manuscript "Déclaration des droits de l'homme," which suggests that property was not an unqualified natural right. Gilbert Chinard, *Thomas Jefferson: The Apostle of Americanism* (Ann Arbor: University of Michigan Press, [1929] 1962), 84.

70. John Locke, "Of the State of Nature," in *Second Treatise of Government*, ed. Macpherson, §6.

71. Locke, "Of Property," §§32, 34, and 42–43. As Claudio Katz notes, Locke's purpose "to redefine property relations in the interest of an emerging agrarian capitalism," as "only settled husbandry merits this description." He sums, "capitalist agriculture best serves the preservation of life and liberty." Because Locke believed that a person owned his own labor, working for another was not "wage slavery" and a violation of one's independence. Claudio J. Katz, "Thomas Jefferson's Anticapitalism," *American Journal of Political Science* 47, no. 1 (2003): 3–5.

72. Thomas Jefferson, *The Commonplace Book of Thomas Jefferson: A Repertory of His Ideas on Government* (Baltimore: Johns Hopkins University Press, 1926). Chinard writes, "By the mere fact of expatriating themselves [the colonists] had severed all ties with the mother country, they had recovered full possession of all their natural rights and were at liberty to agree on a new social compact; they derived their rights of property not from the king but from their occupancy of a new and unsettled territory." Chinard, *Thomas Jefferson: The Apostle of Americanism*, 50.

73. See Michelle L. Browers, "Jefferson's Land Ethic: Environmental Ideas in *Notes on the State of Virginia*," *Environmental Ethics* 21, no. 1 (1999): 54–55.

74. For example, TJ to Richard Henry Lee, June 17, 1779; TJ to Edmund Randolph, September 16, 1781; TJ to James Monroe, May 20, 1782; and TJ to Martha Jefferson Randolph, February 27, 1809.

75. Thomas Jefferson, "The Anas," in *The Writings of Thomas Jefferson*, vol. 1, *1760–1775*, ed. Paul Leicester Ford (New York: G. P. Putnam's Sons, 1892), 337.

76. Anonymous Hippocratic Author, *The Nature of Man*, in *Hippocratic Writings*, ed. G. E. R. Lloyd (New York: Penguin Books, 1983), 261.

77. Anonymous Hippocratic Author, *Airs, Waters, Places*, in *Hippocratic Writings*, ed. Lloyd 148.

78. My translation (following Rackham). Aristotle, *Politics*, trans. H. Rackham (Cambridge: Harvard University Press, [1932] 1990), 1327b29–38.

79. Hume who, distinguishing between moral and physical causes—the former

work on the mind as motives or reasons, while the latter work on the temper—conceded that physical causes greatly influence all other animals but man. With man, the moral causes predominate in shaping character, not such things as climate and air. His argument draws plentifully from experience—he shows that generalizations of others concerning how physical causes determine national characters are unsustainable—and one wonders why it did not have more of an influence on Jefferson and others than it did. David Hume, "Of National Characters," in *Essays*, ed. Miller, 197–215. "The character of nations," writes author John Bristed in *Resources of the United States of America*, "is formed not by *physical*, but by *moral* causes and influences, as government, religion, and education." Edward T. Martin, *Thomas Jefferson: Scientist* (New York: Henry Schuman, 1952), 210.

80. Ibid., 193–94.

81. Ibid., 199.

82. Ibid., 198–99.

83. Though the amount of precipitation is greater in America, it falls in "half the time."

84. Martin, *Thomas Jefferson: Scientist*, 208.

85. Compare to Millar, who writes of climate on behavior: "To labour under the extreme heat of the sun is, at the same time, exceedingly troublesome and oppressive. The inhabitants, therefore, of such countries, while they enjoy a degree of affluence, and, while by the mildness of the climate they are exempted from many inconveniencies and wants, are seldom disposed to any laborious exertion, and thus, acquiring habits of indolence, become addicted to sensual pleasure, and liable to all those infirmities which are nourished by idleness and sloth. The people who live in a cold country find, on the contrary, that little or nothing is to be obtained without labour; and being subjected to numberless hardships, while they are forced to contend with the ruggedness of the soil, and the severity of the seasons, in earning their scanty provision, they become active and industrious, and acquire those dispositions and talents which proceed from the constant and vigorous exercise both of the mind and body." John Millar, *The Origin of the Distinction of Ranks: Or, An Inquiry into the Circumstances Which Give Rise to Influence and Authority, in the Different Members of Society*, 4th ed. (Edinburgh, 1806), 8–9.

86. It is unclear why Jefferson would label virtue an "extreme." For Aristotle, only vice was an extreme. Each virtue was situated in a mean state between extremes of vice—an excess of that virtue and a defect of it.

87. Charles A. Miller, *Jefferson and Nature: An Interpretation* (Baltimore: Johns Hopkins University Press, 1988), 59–60.

88. Ibid.

89. TJ to Gov. Patrick Henry, March 27, 1779; TJ to Peter Carr, August 19, 1785;

TJ to Maria Cosway, October 12, 1786; TJ to Peter Carr, August 10, 1787; TJ to John Randolph, December 1, 1803; TJ to James Fishback, September 27, 1809; and TJ to Thomas Law, June 13, 1814.

90. Hume, "Of National Characters," 198.

91. Ibid., 212.

92. For example, see TJ to von Humboldt, April 14, 1811; and TJ to John Adams, September 4, 1823.

93. TJ to von Humboldt, April 14, 1811. Jefferson was not deluded into thinking that the result of every revolution would be independence of citizenry. The Latin nations he thought would likely end in military despotisms. "The different casts of their inhabitants, their mutual hatreds and jealousies, their profound ignorance and bigotry, will be played off by cunning leaders, and each be made the instrument of enslaving others." Letter to von Humboldt, December 6, 1813.

94. See also TJ to Thomas Pinckney, May 29, 1797; TJ to Joel Barlow, May 3, 1802; TJ to Henry Lee, August 10, 1824; and TJ to William Short, January 8, 1825.

95. Pace Aristotle, who maintained that farming did not provide leisure enough for one to cultivate virtue, a public ideal (*Politics*, VII.9, 1328b40). Jefferson, of course, advocated scientific farming, which would allow for crop abundance and a certain amount of leisure for public participation. It was also commonly believed that the clearing of trees and brush, inclining the land to greater exposure to sunlight and entrance of easterly winds, would make the land, climate, and people more moderate. Martin, *Thomas Jefferson: Scientist*, 203–209.

96. James Morton Smith, *The Republic of Letters: The Correspondence between Thomas Jefferson and James Madison 1776–1826*, vol. 1 (New York: W. W. Norton, 1995), 12–13.

97. See also TJ to James Monroe, May 20, 1782.

98. Thomas Jefferson, "Commissioners' Report on University of Virginia," in *Thomas Jefferson: Writings*, ed. Peterson, 461–62. See Holowchak, *Dutiful Correspondent*, 286.

99. Thomas Jefferson, *Notes on the State of Virginia*, in *Thomas Jefferson: Writings*, ed. Peterson, 267–70.

100. Jefferson's fullest discussion occurs in his *Notes on the State of Virginia*. Thomas Jefferson, *Thomas Jefferson: Writings*, ed. Peterson, 264–70.

101. For more on blacks and Native Americans, see Holowchak, *Dutiful Correspondent*, 203–49; and M. Andrew Holowchak, "Empiricist and Mindful, not Racist and Pococurante: Jefferson's 'Denigration' of Blacks in Query XIV" (forthcoming).

Chapter 6. "This Faithful, Internal Monitor": Jefferson on the Moral Sense

1. See M. Andrew Holowchak, "The Fear, Honor, and Love of God: Thomas Jefferson on Jews, Philosophers, and Jesus," *Forum Philosophicum* 18, no. 1 (2013): 49–71.

2. For example, Adrienne Koch, *The Philosophy of Thomas Jefferson* (New York: Columbia University Press, 1943); Jean M. Yarbrough, "The Moral Sense, Character Formation, and Virtue," in *Reason and Republicanism: Thomas Jefferson's Legacy of Liberty*, ed. Gary L. McDowell and Sharon L. Noble (Lanham, MD: Rowman & Littlefield, 1997), 271–303; and M. Andrew Holowchak, "The Reluctant Politician: Thomas Jefferson's Debt to Epicurus," *Eighteenth-Century Studies* 45, no. 2 (2012): 277–97.

3. See also M. Andrew Holowchak, "The March of Morality: Making Sense of Jefferson's Moral Sense," in *Thomas Jefferson and Philosophy: Essays on the Philosophical Cast of Jefferson's Writings* (Lanham, MD: Lexington Books, 2013), 147–64; M. Andrew Holowchak, "Reasoning and the Moral Sense," in *Dutiful Correspondent: Philosophical Essays on Thomas Jefferson* (Lanham, MD: Rowman & Littlefield, 2012), 159–75; as well as M. Andrew Holowchak, *Taking Things by Their Smooth Handle: Jefferson on Morality, the Moral Sense, and Good Living* (forthcoming).

4. Compare to Seneca: "There are more things likely to frighten us than there are to crush us. We suffer more often from imagination than from reality." Seneca, *Letters*, vol. 1, trans. Richard M. Gummere, Loeb Classical Library (Cambridge: Harvard University Press, 2000), XIII.4.

5. Exceptions being the middle-Platonist Stoics, Panaetius and Posidonius.

6. Seneca, *Epistles*, CXVI.1. M. Andrew Holowchak, *The Stoics: A Guide for the Perplexed* (London, Continuum Books, 2008), 49.

7. For Aristotle, the soul is characterized functionally. The soul had nutritive, perceptive, desiderative, locomotive, and intellective functions. Aristotle, *On the Soul*, trans. W. S. Hett, Loeb Classical Library (Cambridge: Harvard University Press, 1986), II.3.

8. Aristotle, *Politics*, trans. H. Rackham, Loeb Classical Library (Cambridge: Harvard University Press, 1990), VIII.V (1339a25 ff.) and (1341b32–1342a16 and 1342b17–18).

9. Aristotle, *Nicomachean Ethics*, trans. H. Rackham (Cambridge, MA: Harvard University Press, 1900), III.6–9 and IV.5.

10. Chinard notes that this list is taken almost verbatim from Kames's *Essays on the Principles of Morality and Natural Religion*. Gilbert Chinard, "Jefferson among the Philosophers," *Ethics* 53, no. 4 (July 1943): 258.

11. Henry St. John Bolingbroke, *Reflections concerning Innate Moral Principles* (London: S. Blandon, 1752).

12. TJ to Benjamin Rush, April 21, 1803. For more, see Holowchak, "Fear, Honor, and Love of God," 49–71.

13. He notes its lack in Bonaparte in a letter to Adams. TJ to John Adams, February 25, 1823.

14. TJ to Thomas Law, June 13, 1814.

15. For example, TJ to Robert Skipwith, August 3, 1771; TJ to Peter Carr, August 19, 1785; TJ to Maria Cosway, October 12, 1786; and TJ to Joseph Priestley, January 29, 1804. Hume and Smith steered clear of the difficulties of treating the moral sense as a faculty and instead focused on it as comprising the appropriate moral sentiments that led to virtuous actions. David Hume, *An Enquiry concerning the Principles of Morals*, ed. J. B. Schneewind (Indianapolis: Hackett, 1983), sec. 3; and Adam Smith, *The Theory of Moral Sentiments* (Indianapolis: Liberty Classics, 1969), 47–53.

16. Lord Kames, *Essays on the Principles of Morality and Natural Religion*, 2nd ed. (London, 1758), 19.

17. Ibid., 111. For Jefferson's comments at the bottom of the page of his copy of Kames's work, see Douglas L. Wilson, "Thomas Jefferson's Library and the French Connection," *Eighteenth-Century Studies* 26, no. 4 (1993): 672.

18. Thomas Jefferson, "Declaration concerning Ethan Allen," December 2, 1775, in *The Works of Thomas Jefferson*, vol. 2, ed. Paul Leicester Ford (New York: G. P. Putnam's Sons, 1904), 145–47; TJ to James Madison, August 28, 1789; TJ to Gov. Patrick Henry, March 27, 1779; TJ to David Williams, November 14, 1803; TJ to Caesar A. Rodney, February 10, 1810; TJ to Correia da Serra, June 28, 1815; TJ to John Adams, January 11, 1816; TJ to John Adams, September 12, 1821; and TJ to Cornelius Blatchly, October 21, 1822.

19. See Merrill D. Peterson, *Thomas Jefferson & the New Nation: A Biography* (Oxford: Oxford University Press, 1970), 885.

20. TJ to Joseph Priestley, April 9, 1803.

21. TJ to Martha Jefferson, December 11, 1783.

22. Francis Hutcheson, *Inquiry into the Original of Our Ideas of Beauty and Virtue*, ed. Wolfgang Leidhold (Indianapolis: Liberty Fund, [1725] 2004), 178–79.

23. Zuckert takes this statement as elliptical for a *modus tollens* argument for the existence of a moral sense. "From the premise that we are made by a wise artisan and not a 'pitiful bungler,' Jefferson concludes that we have been endowed directly with the moral sense." Schematically: 1. The Creator would have been a pitiful bungler, if he had made moral rules a matter of science. 2. We are not made from a pitiful bungler. 3. So, we are endowed with a moral sense. He fails to note the conditional sentence is expressed counterfactually—that is, the antecedent is assumed false and the conse-

quent is merely given as an implication of what would obtain, were the consequent true. Thus, we are given a statement that affirms humans have a moral sense, not an argument for the moral sense. Michael P. Zuckert, "Thomas Jefferson and Natural Morality: Classical Moral Theory, Moral Sense, and Rights," in *Thomas Jefferson, the Classical World, and Early America*, eds. Peter S. Onuf and Nicholas P. Cole (Charlottesville: University of Virginia Press, 2011), 66.

24. Aristotle contrasts ethical excellence in general (virtue) with its particular instantiations (virtues)—that is, friendliness, generosity, magnanimity, sense of humor, and others.

25. Aristotle, *Nicomachean Ethics*, 1103a14–26, with modifications.

26. For a thorough refutation of that thesis, see M. Andrew Holowchak, "The Reluctant Politician," in *Dutiful Correspondent*, 277–97.

27. This is, however, not an Epicurean claim, as friendship had a special status in Epicurean communities.

28. Engels maintains that the dialogue is a triumph of Head over Heart—that is, that "for [Jefferson] the moral sense was subordinate to his head's rational calculation." Engels argues that Jefferson's letter is a "dramatization of Smith's psychological theories" of a divided self in which disputes are ultimately solved by "the man within the breast"—that is, the ideal spectator of sentiments and moral conduct—in the latter's *The Theory of Moral Sentiments*. For Jefferson, it is Head, not Heart, that assumes the position of ideal spectator and trumps the sentiments of Heart at letter's end. His main argument is stylistic. Heart adopts the language and reasoning of Head to win its victory and, thus, the ostensible victory of Heart is apparent, not real. Heart is a tin god. The overall argument presupposes a relationship between reason and the moral sense that, as we shall see, did not exist for Jefferson. Thus, the view is tenuous. Jeremy Engels, "Disciplining Jefferson: The Man within the Breast and the Rhetorical Norms of Producing Order," *Rhetoric and Public Affairs* 9, no. 3 (2006): 411–36, but especially 419–23. The overall correspondence between Jefferson and Carr suggests strongly that Head does triumph over Heart (e.g., TJ to Maria Cosway November 19, 1786, and November 29, 1786). Some letters intimate that Cosway had a small coterie of male admirers, among whom Jefferson was one, and that Jefferson was in over his head, so to speak. For example, Maria Cosway to TJ, April 29, 1788; and TJ to Maria Cosway, July 30, 1788. Thomas Jefferson and Maria Cosway, *Jefferson in Love: The Love Letters between Thomas Jefferson & Maria Cosway*, ed. John P. Kaminski (Lanham, MD: Rowman & Littlefield, 1999), 105 and 111.

29. For example, Max Lerner, *Thomas Jefferson: America's Philosopher-King* (New Brunswick: Transaction, 1996), 106 and 111.

30. Zuckert, "Thomas Jefferson and Natural Morality," 58–67.

31. Ari Helo, "Jefferson's Conception of Republican Government," in *The Cam-*

bridge Companion to Thomas Jefferson, ed. Frank Shuffleton (New York: University of Cambridge Press, 2009), 36.

32. Hume, *Enquiry concerning the Principles of Morals*, 20–34.

33. Zuckert argues that Jefferson, for whom "right is derived independently of good," was Lockean and even a bit of a Hobbesian. The moral instinct is "neither a necessary nor sufficient condition for moral conduct," for the social and selfish passions, guiding behavior, interact in complex ways. "Without the system of rights, the moral sense appears to be a dismal failure in procuring the good of all," he adds. The view is untenable. Zuckert, "Thomas Jefferson and Natural Morality," 61 and 73–75.

34. Son of George Gilmer, a close friend of Jefferson.

35. Tadashige Shimizu, "The Meaning of Moral Sense in Thomas Jefferson's Political Thought," *Japanese Journal of American Studies* 6 (1995): 72.

36. The law of the land.

37. Shimizu, "Meaning of Moral Sense in Thomas Jefferson's Political Thought," 72.

38. Ibid., 71–72.

39. TJ to James Madison, August 28, 1789; and TJ to William Findley, March 24, 1801.

40. Thomas Jefferson, *Jefferson: Writings*, ed. Merrill D. Peterson (New York: Library of America, 1984), 423.

41. Valsania argues that Jefferson's moral thinking is, at least in part, propaganda for his political views—a view I find implausible. Maurizio Valsania, "'Our Original Barbarism': Man vs. Nature in Thomas Jefferson's Moral Experience," *Journal of the History of Ideas* (2005): 643.

42. Shimizu, "Meaning of Moral Sense in Thomas Jefferson's Political Thought," 70.

43. See Koch, *Philosophy of Thomas Jefferson*, 138.

44. For more on Jefferson's take of *salus populi*, see M. Andrew Holowchak, "Eudaemonism or Survivalism: Jefferson and the Unwritten Laws of Self-Preservation" (forthcoming).

45. This is a mistake made by Stephanie Newbold, who, following Walzer, asserts that the purchase was a contravention of moral principle by Jefferson for beneficial consequences. Jefferson neither embraced moral absolutes nor was a consequentialist. Stephanie P. Newbold, "Statesmanship and Ethics: The Case of Thomas Jefferson's Dirty Hands," *Public Administration Review* 65, no. 6 (2005): 672.

46. Kames, *Essays on the Principles of Morality and Natural Religion*, 2nd ed., 72–73.

47. He then cites the writings of clergyman and novelist Laurence Sterne "as the best course of morality that ever was written." TJ to Peter Carr, August 10, 1787.

48. Thomas Jefferson, *Thomas Jefferson: Writings*, ed. Peterson, 273.

49. Thomas Jefferson, "Declaration concerning Ethan Allen," in Dumas Malone, *Jefferson and His Time*, vol. 1, *Jefferson the Virginian* (Boston: Little, Brown, 1948), 291.

50. Kames, *Essays on the Principles of Morality and Natural Religion*, 2nd ed., 110.

51. Hutcheson, *Inquiry into the Original of Our Ideas of Beauty and Virtue*, 186–88.

52. Gilbert Chinard, *The Literary Bible of Thomas Jefferson: His Commonplace Book of Philosophers and Poets* (New York: Greenwood Press, [1928] 1969), 6 and 16.

53. Robert Booth Fowler, "Mythologies of a Founder," in *Thomas Jefferson and the Politics of Nature*, ed. Thomas S. Engeman (Notre Dame: University of Notre Dame Press, 2000), 134–37.

54. Koch, *Philosophy of Thomas Jefferson*, 40.

55. Ibid., 8.

56. M. Andrew Holowchak, "The Reluctant Politician: Thomas Jefferson's Debt to Epicurus," *Eighteenth-Century Studies* 45, no. 2 (2012): 277–97.

57. See Holowchak, *Dutiful Correspondent*, 93–110.

58. Yarbrough, "Moral Sense, Character Formation, and Virtue," 281–82.

59. Ibid., 282–83.

60. For example, TJ to John Adams, January 11, 1816; and TJ to P. S. Dupont de Nemours, April 24, 1816.

61. TJ to Benjamin Waterhouse, 1818.

62. Mercier, a contemporary of Jefferson, writes no less at discovery of "those simple and efficacious laws by which mankind should be governed." Louis-Sébastien Mercier, *Memoirs of the Year Two Thousand Five Hundred* (Philadelphia: Thomas Dobson, 1795), 258.

63. Holowchak, *Dutiful Correspondent*, 159–76.

64. Lord Kames, *Essays on the Principles of Morality and Natural Religion*, 3rd ed. (London, 1779), 76 and 92.

Chapter 7. "The Most Precious Gift of Nature": Jefferson on the "Natural Aristoi"

1. TJ to Peter Carr, August 19, 1787.

2. For those who note this distinction but make little of it, see William E. Phipps, "Jefferson on Political Obligation," *Journal of the West Virginia Philosophical Society* 12 (1977): 3.

3. Greek for "best" (masc. and pl.).

4. It must be acknowledged that Jefferson's presidency was itself in some respects inconsistent with his republicanism and limited executive privileges. In his first term, Jefferson knew that the Constitution did not grant him the authority to authorize his purchase of the Louisiana territories. He did so anyways and justified his strong-armed action "on the grounds of expediency" and drafted an amendment to the

Constitution. He maintained, "The executive in seizing the fugitive occurrence which so much advances the good of this country have done an act beyond the Constitution." In his second term, he authorized the Embargo Act of 1807—a temporary freeze on importation and exportation of goods in response to the French and British maritime wars, which harmed American ships. Garrett Ward Sheldon, *The Political Philosophy of Thomas Jefferson* (Baltimore: Johns Hopkins University Press, 1993), 95–102. In his letter to John Colvin (September 20, 1810), he is anything but remorseful. "A strict observance to the written laws is doubtless one of the *high* duties of a good citizen, but it is not *the highest*. The laws of necessity, of self-preservation, of saving our country by a scrupulous adherence to written law, would be to lose the law itself, with life, liberty, property and all those who are enjoying them with us; thus absurdly sacrificing the end to the means."

5. Adams is referring to reaction to his unpopular works *Defence of the Constitutions of the United States* and "Discourses on Davila" (a series of newspaper articles), which were pro-British in sentiment and, he thought, greatly misapprehended. For example, John Adams to TJ, September 15, 1813, and July 15, 1813. Appleby writes, "Adams' underlying theme [in his *Defence*] was that democracy would not work, that elites were inevitable, and that stability demanded that a constitutional place be given them." Joyce Appleby, "The Jefferson-Adams Rupture and the First French Translation of John Adams' *Defence*," *American Historical Review* 73, no. 4 (1968): 1088.

6. Greek poet from Megara, sixth century BCE.

7. Compare to Harrington, whom Jefferson certainly read. Harrington considers in his "Oceana" a commonwealth of twenty persons. A third of them over time will be found to be wiser, or at least less foolish, than the others. Consequently, in matters of common concernment, difficulty, or danger the other fourteen will appeal to the six as do children to their fathers. "Wherefore this can be no other than a natural Aristocracy diffus'd by God throout the whole Body of Mankind to this end and purpose; and therefore such as the People have not only a natural, but a positive Obligation to make use of as their Guides. . . . The fix then approv'd of . . . not by hereditary Right, or in regard of the greatness of their Estates only . . . but by election for their excellent Parts, which tends to the advancement of the influence of their Virtue or Authority that leads the People." Senators, he concludes, are not to be commanders, but people's counselors, whose jobs are to debate legislation and advise the people, whose job is to choose. James Harrington, *The Oceana and Other Works of James Harrington Esq; Collected, Methodiz'd, and Review'd with an Exact Account of His Life*, ed. John Toland (London, 1747), 47–49.

8. Jefferson, however, notes a difficulty Plato in *The Republic* noted. The true best, the natural aristoi, will be disinclined to govern and inclined to participate more directly in matters related to virtuous activity. In a letter to Jefferson, Rush mentions

the naming of towns after virtuous persons an incentive to virtuous activity. Benjamin Rush to TJ, August 22, 1800. See M. Andrew Holowchak, "The Paradox of Public Service: Jefferson, Education, and the Problem of Plato's Cave," *Studies in Philosophy and Education* 32, no. 1 (2013): 73–86.

9. Charles A. Miller, *Jefferson and Nature: An Interpretation* (Baltimore: Johns Hopkins University Press, 1988), 84.

10. John Zvesper, "Jefferson on Liberal Natural Rights," in *Reason and Republicanism: Thomas Jefferson's Legacy of Liberty*, ed. Gary L. McDowell and Sharon L. Noble (Lanham, MD: Rowman & Littlefield, 1997), 23; and Sheldon, *Political Philosophy of Thomas Jefferson*, 90.

11. Thomas Jefferson, "Autobiography," in *Thomas Jefferson: Writings*, ed. Merrill D. Peterson (New York: Library of America, 1984), 38–39 and 44.

12. Dumas Malone, *Jefferson and His Time*, vol. 1, *Jefferson the Virginian* (Boston: Little, Brown, 1948), 257.

13. Writes Helo: "Jefferson's democratic idealism could well include those lucky few who were genuinely 'good and wise' as well as rich and well-born. They could qualify to any government office, provided that the public deemed them worth their trust. Moreover, given that the simple majority of the people occasionally err in such judgment, the constant rotation of offices would keep every representative aware of being bound to 'return to the mass of the people' and become one of the governed in turn." Ari Helo, "Jefferson's Conception of Republican Government," in *The Cambridge Companion to Thomas Jefferson*, ed. Frank Shuffleton (New York: University of Cambridge Press, 2009), 42.

14. For example, TJ to George Washington, May 10, 1789; TJ to Edmund Randolph, May 8, 1793; TJ to Dr. Benjamin Smith, February 14, 1801; TJ to Levi Lincoln, July 11, 1801; TJ to A. L. C. Destutt de Tracy, January 26, 1811; and TJ to Joel Barlow, April 16, 1811.

15. Writes Peter Paret: "Jefferson . . . never allowed his belief in a natural aristocracy of talent and his concern over the political immaturity of the poor to lessen his faith in the supreme value of individual freedom and in the rightness and, indeed, necessity of truly representative government. He was very conscious of the difficulties the American experiment in freedom continued to face, but as he wrote in 1791, 'I would rather be exposed to the inconveniences attending too much liberty than those attending too small a degree of it.'" Peter Paret, "Jefferson and Birth of European Liberalism," *Proceedings of the American Philosophical Society* 137, no. 4 (1993): 492.

16. TJ to Martha Jefferson, April 7, 1787. See also April 25, 1790, and April 26, 1790.

17. For a fuller articulation of Jefferson's views on Jesus and his teachings, see M. Andrew Holowchak, *Dutiful Correspondent: Philosophical Essays on Thomas Jefferson* (Lanham, MD: Rowman & Littlefield, 2012), 93–110.

18. In a later letter to Carr, only the ancient authors are listed and Plato is added. TJ to Peter Carr, August 1785.

19. TJ to William Short, October 31, 1819.

20. Thomas Jefferson, *Jefferson's Literary Commonplace Book*, ed. Douglas L. Wilson (Princeton: Princeton University Press, 1989), §§22–58.

21. See Dickinson W. Adams, "Introduction," in Thomas Jefferson, *Jefferson's Extracts from the Gospels*, ed. Dickinson W. Adams (Princeton: Princeton University Press, 1983), 5–7.

22. For this "Syllabus," Jefferson was greatly indebted to Joseph Priestly in whose published works he found, to some extent, support and a religious ally. Priestly published, at the request of Jefferson, a comparative analysis of classical and Christian morality, *The Doctrines of Heathen Philosophy, Compared with Those of Revelation*, which Jefferson received on February 6, 1805, the day of Priestley's death. The work greatly disappointed Jefferson (TJ to Benjamin Smith Barton, February 14, 1805), as it was supposed to be a fleshing out of Jefferson's "Syllabus." Instead, it gave strong evidence of Priestley's failing health.

23. Rush admonished Jefferson for not accepting the divinity of Christ, as without his divinity, Jesus life and death were without meaning (August 29, 1804). Jefferson never sent his "The Life of Jesus" to Rush. The tension between Rush and Jefferson over the divinity of Christ remained unresolved when Rush died.

24. The compilation is never mentioned in his correspondence, and it became evident to family members only after Jefferson's death. See Dickinson W. Adams, "Introduction," in Jefferson, *Jefferson's Extracts from the Gospels*, ed. Adams, 38.

25. Richard Samuelson, "Jefferson and Religion: Private Belief, Public Policy," in *Cambridge Companion to Thomas Jefferson*, ed. Shuffleton, 146.

26. TJ to Benjamin Rush, April 21, 1803.

27. Jefferson here was influenced by Priestley. Joseph Priestley, *An History of Early Opinions concerning Jesus Christ, Compiled from Original Writers; Proving that the Christian Church was at First Unitarian* (Birmingham: Pearson and Rollason, 1786), 383–84.

28. See also TJ to Francis Adrian Van der Kemp, April 25, 1816; and TJ to Daniel Salmon, February 15, 1808.

29. He had in mind especially *A Free Inquiry into the Miraculous Powers in the Christian Church* (1750). Jefferson had in his library Middleton's four-volume *Miscellaneous Works*, published posthumously in 1752.

30. David Hume, "On Miracles," in *Dialogues concerning Natural Religion*, ed. Richard H. Popkin (Indianapolis: Hackett, 1998), 111.

31. Compare to Mercier's reference to Paris as a diamond in the dunghill of France. Louis-Sébastien Mercier, *Memoirs of the Year Two Thousand Five Hundred* (Philadelphia: Thomas Dobson, 1795), 4.

32. See George Harmon Knoles, "The Religious Ideas of Thomas Jefferson," *Mississippi Valley Historical Review* 30, no. 2 (1943): 96.

33. TJ to Joseph Priestley, April 9, 1803; and TJ to Benjamin Rush, April 22, 1803.

34. For a more detailed examination, see M. Andrew Holowchak, "The Fear, Honor, and Love of God: Thomas Jefferson on Jews, Philosophers, and Jesus," *Forum Philosophicum* 18, no. 1 (2013): 49–71.

35. He was cousin of republican James Madison, fourth president of the United States.

36. Aristotle, *Nicomachean Ethics*, trans. Terrence Irwin (Indianapolis: Hackett, 1999), 1098b30–35.

37. See also Pierre Volney, *On Wisdom*, vol. 3, trans. George Stanhope (London, 1729), 1089.

38. Francis Hutcheson, *Inquiry into the Original of Our Ideas of Beauty and Virtue*, ed. Wolfgang Leidhold (Indianapolis: Liberty Fund, [1725] 2004), 116 and 137–46.

39. David Hume, *An Enquiry concerning the Principles of Morals*, ed. J. B. Schneewind (Indianapolis: Hackett, 1983), sec. 2.

40. Later he goes on to say that benevolence in the abstract—that is, aiming at abstract groups of persons and not as a principle of equal benevolence to all individuals—is by nature a moral duty. Lord Kames, *Essays on the Principles of Morality and Natural Religion*, 2nd ed. (London, 1758), 43 and 58–63.

41. Compare to Mercier who says: "It is with religion as with laws; the most simple are the best. Adore God, love thy neighbor; hearken to that conscience, that judge which continually attends thee; never stifle that secret and celestial voice; all the rest is imposture, fraud, falshood." Mercier, *Memoirs of the Year Two Thousand Five Hundred*, 104.

42. TJ to James Smith, December 8, 1822.

43. Jefferson is not, I suspect, referring to Unitarianism as the particular religious movement of his day, but using the term generically—namely, to note belief in one deity. Unitarianism had its own problems apropos of the status of Jesus.

44. See also Thomas Jefferson, "Notes on Religion," 1776, in *The Papers of Thomas Jefferson*, vol. 1, *1760–1776*, ed. Julian P. Boyd (Princeton: Princeton University Press, 1950), 555–58; TJ to Thomas Parker, May 15, 1819; TJ to Dr. Benjamin Waterhouse, June 26, 1822; TJ to John Adams, April 11, 1823; TJ to George Thatcher, January 26, 1824; and TJ to John Davis, January 18, 1824.

45. Repentance being sufficient for undoing a wrong was anathema to Greek ethicians.

46. TJ to William Short, October 31, 1819.

47. TJ to Joseph Priestley, April 9, 1803.

48. TJ to John Adams, April 8, 1816.

49. Robert Dawidoff, "The Jeffersonian Option," *Political Theory* 21, no. 3 (1993): 438.

50. Howard Temperly, "Jefferson and Slavery: A Study in Moral Philosophy," in *Reason and Republicanism*, ed. McDowell and Noble, 86 and 89–90. See also, for instance, Robert McColley, *Slavery and Jeffersonian Virginia* (Urbana: University of Illinois Press, 1964), 124; Winthrop D. Jordan, *White over Black: American Attitudes toward the Negro, 1550–1812* (Baltimore: Penguin Books, 1969), 429–31; Nicholas E. Magnis, "Thomas Jefferson and Slavery: An Analysis of His Racist Thinking as Revealed by His Writings and Political Behavior," *Journal of Black Studies* 29, no. 4 (1999): 491–509; and Paul Finkelman, "Thomas Jefferson and Antislavery: The Myth Goes On," *Virginia Magazine of History and Biography* 102, no. 2 (1994): 203–208.

51. Peter Onuf, *The Mind of Thomas Jefferson* (Charlottesville: University of Virginia Press, 2007), 38. For a critique of Onuf, see M. Andrew Holowchak, "Review of Peter Onuf's *The Mind of Thomas Jefferson*," *History News Network*, http://hnn.us/article/156482 (accessed August 18, 2014).

52. For example, see John M. Mason, *The Voice of Warning, to Christians, on the Ensuing Election of a President of the United States* (New York, 1800), 9–14; and Clement C. Moore, *Observations upon Certain Passages in Mr. Jefferson's* Notes on Virginia, *Which Appear to Have a Tendency to Subvert Religion, and Establish a False Philosophy* (New York, 1804).

53. *The Life and Morals of Jesus*, constructed years later, was "strictly a product of his private search for religious truth." Adams, "Introduction," 12–13, 19, and 30.

54. TJ to John Adams, October 12, 1813.

55. That too explains his preference for Epicurean ethics over other ancient views. Francis Adrian Van der Kemp writes to Jefferson that any divinely inspired doctrine must be so plain that "any man, of the meanest capacities, but with a sound head and honest heart, could discover it with ease." TJ to Jefferson, June 4, 1816. Jefferson, *Jefferson's Extracts from the Gospels*, ed. Adams.

56. TJ to Peter Carr, August 10, 1787.

57. Cicero, *On Duties*, trans. Walter Miller, Loeb Classical Library (Cambridge: Harvard University Press, 2001), I.xxx.107–17.

58. Ibid., III.x.42.

59. Hutcheson, *Inquiry into the Original of Our Ideas of Beauty and Virtue*, 166 and 184–87.

60. Laurence Sterne, *The Sermons of Mr. Yorick*, vol. 4 (London, 1776), 1–3.

61. When Thomson informed Jefferson that there were families in Virginia without a Bible and asked for a contribution to the Bible Society, Jefferson uttered his astonishment and enclosed fifty dollars—a considerable sum for the day. TJ to Charles Thomson, January 21, 1814.

62. John W. Oliver, "Thomas Jefferson—Scientist," *Scientific Monthly* 56, no. 5 (1943): 461–65.

63. In general, he thought inventors should benefit from their inventions, but not for all time, as that would prove injurious to humankind. TJ to Oliver Evans, May 2, 1807.

64. See Holowchak, *Dutiful Correspondent*, 3–26 and 131–56.

65. Heracles faced the choice between two goddesses—Hēdonē, a life of ease and pleasure, and Aretē, a life of hardship and toil, but one dear to the gods. He chose the latter. Xenophon, *Memorabilia*, ed. E. G. Marchant and O. J. Todd (Cambridge, MA: Harvard University Press, 1923), §§21–34.

66. TJ to Thomas Jefferson Randolph, November 24, 1808.

67. See M. Andrew Holowchak, *The Stoics: A Guide for the Perplexed* (London: Continuum Books, 2008), 221.

PART 4: JEFFERSON ON EDUCATION

Chapter 8. "Uniting Merit with . . . Learning": Jefferson's Philosophy of Education

1. A version of this chapter was published in the journal *Democracy and Education* (vol. 21, no. 2, 2013) and is reprinted here with permission.

2. Thomas Jefferson, *Notes on the State of Virginia*, in *Thomas Jefferson: Writings*, ed. Merrill D. Peterson (New York: Library of America, 1984), 274.

3. For a complete examination of Jefferson's views on education, see M. Andrew Holowchak, *Thomas Jefferson's Philosophy of Education: A Utopian Dream* (London: Taylor & Francis, 2014).

4. Thomas Jefferson, "Autobiography," in *Thomas Jefferson: Writings*, ed. Peterson, 31–44.

5. Ibid., 43–44.

6. TJ to George Wythe, August 13, 1786.

7. It was Jefferson's favorite bill (see ibid.) and did not pass, because the burden of expense for the schools would have been mostly on the well-to-do and "the justices, being generally of the more wealthy class, were unwilling to incur that burden." In 1796, a version passed, so greatly amended that it defeated its original purpose (Jefferson, "Autobiography," 274). In a memorandum (ca. 1800), he writes: "It was received by the legislature with great enthusiasm at first; and a small effort was made in 1796, by the act to establish public schools, to carry a part of it into effect, viz., that for the establishment of free English schools; but the option given to the courts has defeated the intention of the act" (Jefferson, *Thomas Jefferson: Writings*, ed. Peterson, 703–704).

8. Gilbert Chinard, *Thomas Jefferson: The Apostle of Americanism* (Ann Arbor: University of Michigan Press, [1929] 1962), 99.

9. Charles Flynn Arrowood, *Thomas Jefferson and Education in a Republic* (New York: McGraw-Hill, 1970 [1930]), 70.

10. For example, TJ to James Madison, December 20, 1787; TJ to Gouverneur Morris, December 30, 1792; TJ to John Breckenridge, January 29, 1800; and TJ to Caesar A. Rodney, February 10, 1810.

11. Thomas Jefferson, "Query XIV," in *Notes on the State of Virginia*, in *Thomas Jefferson: Writings*, ed. Peterson, 274.

12. Thomas Jefferson, "Bill for General Diffusion of Knowledge," in *Thomas Jefferson: Writings*, ed. Peterson, 365.

13. M. Andrew Holowchak, *Dutiful Correspondent: Philosophical Essays on Thomas Jefferson* (Lanham, MD: Rowman & Littlefield, 2012), 29–50.

14. TJ to John Taylor, May 28, 1816. Elsewhere, governments are republican only in proportion as "they embody the will of their people, and execute it." TJ to Sam Kercheval, July 12, 1816.

15. Thomas O. Jewett, "Thomas Jefferson and the Purposes of Education, *Educational Forum* 61 (winter 1997): 110.

16. James J. Carpenter, "Jefferson's Views on Education: Implications for Today's Social Studies," *Social Studies* (July/August 2004): 143.

17. Thomas Jefferson, "Rockfish Gap Report," in *Thomas Jefferson: Writings*, ed. Peterson, 459–60.

18. Robert D. Heslep, *Thomas Jefferson and Education* (New York: Random House, 1969), 98.

19. TJ to William Green Munford, June 17, 1799.

20. Thomas Jefferson, "Report of the Commissioners of the University of Virginia," in *Thomas Jefferson: Writings*, ed. Peterson, 461.

21. Joseph Kett, "Education," in *Thomas Jefferson: A Reference Biography*, ed. Merrill D. Peterson (New York: Charles Scribner's Sons, 1986), 238.

22. Thomas Jefferson, "Query XIV," in *Notes on the State of Virginia*, in *Thomas Jefferson: Writings*, ed. Peterson, 273.

23. Excepting, I suspect, extremes in that condition.

24. Aristotle, *Nicomachean Ethics*, trans. H. Rackham (Cambridge, MA: Harvard University Press, 1926), 1179b1–4, 1103b26–32, and 1105b13–18.

25. Jefferson, *Thomas Jefferson: Writings*, ed. Peterson, 461.

26. Ibid., 469.

27. For more, see Claude Bowers, "Jefferson and the Freedom of the Human Spirit," 53, no. 4 (1943): 243; and Craig Walton, "Hume and Jefferson on the Uses of History," in *Philosophy and the Civilizing Arts*, eds. C. Walton and J. Anton (Athens: Ohio University Press, 1976), 119.

28. Robert K. Faulkner, "Jefferson and the Enlightened Science of Liberty,"

in *Reason and Republicanism: Thomas Jefferson's Legacy of Liberty*, ed. Gary L. McDowell and Sharon L. Noble (Lanham, MD: Rowman & Littlefield, 1997), 35.

29. Aristotle, *Nicomachean Ethics*, II.4.

30. Marc Hauser, *Moral Minds: How Nature Designed Our Universal Sense of Right and Wrong* (New York: HarperCollins, 2006), xvii.

31. Ibid., xvii–xviii.

32. Ibid., xviii–xix.

33. D. C. Dalton and Thomas C. Hunt, "Thomas Jefferson's Theories on Education as Revealed through a Textual Reading of Several of His Letters," *Journal of Thought* 14 (1979): 270.

34. Charles Flynn Arrowood, *Thomas Jefferson and Education in a Republic* (New York: McGraw-Hill, 1970 [1930]), 49–50.

35. Ibid., 49–50.

36. For example, TJ to John Adams, September 28, 1787; TJ to William Short, July 28, 1791; TJ to Archibald Stuart, December 23, 1791; TJ to Edmund Randolph, May 8, 1793; TJ to James Madison, April 3, 1794; TJ to Peregrine Fitzhugh, February 23, 1798; TJ to Edmund Pendleton, February 14, 1799; TJ to John Dickinson, July 23, 1801; TJ to Caesar A. Rodney, June 8, 1810; and TJ to Colonel William Duane, March 28, 1811.

37. Arrowood, *Thomas Jefferson and Education in a Republic*, 58–59.

38. Ibid., 60.

39. For example, Conor Cruise O'Brien, *The Long Affair: Thomas Jefferson and the French Revolution, 1785–1800* (Chicago: University of Chicago Press, 1995).

40. For instance, they were allowed to choose their own texts.

41. Jennings L. Wagoner, *Jefferson and Education* (Chapel Hill: University of North Carolina Press, 2004), 131–32.

42. Jefferson refused to have a president at the University of Virginia and even tried unsuccessfully to abolish the presidency at William and Mary.

43. Lucia Stanton, "Jefferson's People: Slavery at Monticello," in *The Cambridge Companion to Thomas Jefferson*, ed. Frank Shuffleton (New York: Cambridge University Press, 2009), 87.

44. "Tree of knowledge." TJ to Thomas Cooper, August 25, 1814.

45. A copy of the letter, with modifications, is contained in a much later letter to General John Minor (August 30, 1814). For dating the letter, see Morris L. Cohen, "Thomas Jefferson Recommends a Course of Law Study," *119 University of Pennsylvania Law Review* 823 (1971).

46. Edward T. Martin, *Thomas Jefferson: Scientist* (New York: Henry Schuman, 1952), 37.

47. For example, Garrett Ward Sheldon, *The Political Philosophy of Thomas Jefferson* (Baltimore: Johns Hopkins University Press, 1991), 139; Robert Dawidoff,

"The Jeffersonian Option," *Political Theory* 21, no. 3 (1993): 438; and Howard Temperly, "Jefferson and Slavery: A Study in Moral Philosophy," in *Reason and Republicanism*, ed. McDowell and Noble, 86 and 89–90.

48. Jefferson had a great detestation of metaphysics, because it was not grounded in sensory experience. In that regard, he can be regarded as a philosopher of the practicable.

49. TJ to William Green Munford, June 18, 1799.

50. Karl Lehmann, *Thomas Jefferson: American Humanist* (Charlottesville: University Press of Virginia, 1994), 201–202.

51. Ibid., 201–202 and 206–207.

52. Plato, *The Republic*, trans. G. M. A. Grube (Indianapolis: Hackett, 1994), bk. 4.

53. See M. Andrew Holowchak, "Jefferson's Moral Agrarianism: Poetic Fiction or Moral Vision?" *Agriculture and Human Values* 28, no. 4 (2011): 497–506.

54. For more on Martha's formal education while at the Abbay de Panthemont in Paris and its influence on Jefferson's views on female education, see Catherine Kerrison, "The French Education of Martha Jefferson Randolph," *Early American Studies* (spring 2013): 378.

55. Aristotle, *Politics*, trans. C. D. C. Reeve (Indianapolis: Hackett, 1998), I.3–13.

56. Thomas Jefferson, "Second Inaugural Address," in *Thomas Jefferson: Writings*, ed. Peterson, 520.

57. See Holowchak, *Dutiful Correspondent*, 229–49.

58. See ibid., 203–27.

Chapter 9. "An Utopian Dream": Jefferson on Primary Education for Enlightened Democracy

1. See also TJ to Gov. Wilson C. Nicholas, April 2, 1816.

2. See TJ to Joseph C. Cabell, February 2, 1816.

3. Jennings L. Wagoner, *Jefferson and Education* (Chapel Hill: University of North Carolina Press, 2004), 145.

4. In that regard, one sees Jefferson advising young adults like John Banister Jr. (October 15, 1785), Peter Carr (August 19, 1785; August 10, 1787; and May 28, 1788), Thomas Mann Randolph (July 6, 1787), John W. Eppes (July 28, 1787), William Green Munford (June 18, 1799), and John Minor (August 30, 1814) on their course of education.

5. Montesquieu, *The Spirit of Laws*, trans. Thomas Nugent (London: J. Nourse, 1777), bk. 4.1 and 4.5.

6. Antoine Destutt de Tracy, *A Commentary and Review of Montesquieu's* Spirit of Laws (Philadelphia: William Duane, 1811), 19.

7. Wagoner, *Jefferson and Education*, 51–52.

8. "My partiality for that division is not founded in views of education solely, but infinitely more as the means of a better administration of our government, and the eternal preservation of its republican principles." TJ to Joseph C. Cabell, February 2, 1816.

9. See M. Andrew Holowchak, "Individual Liberty and Political Unity in an Expanding Nation: The Axiological Primacy of Wards in Jefferson's Republican Schema," in *Thomas Jefferson and Philosophy: Essays on the Philosophical Cast of Jefferson's Writings* (Lanham, MD: Lexington Books, 2013), chap. 3.

10. P. S. Dupont de Nemours to TJ, April 21, 1800.

11. Thomas Jefferson, "Rockfish Gap Report," in *Thomas Jefferson: Writings*, ed. Merrill D. Peterson (New York: Library of America, 1984), 459.

12. TJ to Peter Carr, September 7, 1814.

13. That is, there is nothing contradictory about its conception. David Hume, *A Treatise of Human Nature* (Oxford: Clarendon, [1739] 1978), 416.

14. To Thomas Law (June 13, 1814), Jefferson asserts that strictly speaking there can be no duty to oneself. That however is not to say that humans do not have self-preservative impulses and that obedience to such impulses is not an indispensable component to human happiness. Thus, for Jefferson, one might distinguish between morality, related to benevolence to others, and ethics, the right way to live (happiness).

15. Thomas Jefferson, "Query XIV," in *Thomas Jefferson: Writings*, ed. Peterson, 274.

16. See also TJ to George Washington, December 4, 1788; and TJ to Richard Price, January 8, 1789.

17. TJ to James Madison, March 15, 1789.

18. Alexander Hamilton, "Federalist 84" in *The Federalist*.

19. Dumas Malone, *Jefferson the Virginian* (Boston: Little, Brown, 1948), 281.

20. TJ to Mann Page, August 30, 1795.

21. Destutt de Tracy, *A Treatise on Political Economy* (Georgetown, DC: Joseph Milligan, 1817), 113.

22. For a fuller discussion, see M. Andrew Holowchak, "The Paradox of Public Service: Jefferson, Education, and the Problem of Plato's Cave," *Studies in Philosophy and Education* 32, no. 1 (2013): 73–86.

23. Plato, *The Republic*, trans. G. M. A. Grube (Indianapolis: Hackett, 1992), 484a–502d and 516e–520d–e. The "solution" is not without difficulties. For example, see John Cooper, "The Psychology of Justice in Plato," *American Philosophical Quarterly* 14 (1977): 151–57; Julia Annas, *An Introduction to Plato's* Republic (Oxford: Clarendon, 1981); Richard Kraut, "Return to the Cave: Republic 519–521," in *Oxford*

Readings in Philosophy: Plato: Ethics, Politics, Religion, and the Soul (Cambridge: Oxford University Press, 1999); and Donald Morrison, "The Utopian Character of Plato's Ideal City," in *Cambridge Companion to Plato's* Republic (Cambridge: Cambridge University Press, 2007), 232–55.

24. Aristotle, *Nicomachean Ethics*, trans. Terence Irwin (Indianapolis: Hackett, 1999), 1119b23–1122a19.

25. For a fuller discussion, see Holowchak, "Paradox of Public Service."

26. TJ to George Washington, January 4, 1786.

27. For example, TJ to James Madison, December 20, 1787. See also TJ to John Adams, November 13, 1787.

28. Constantin François de Volney, *The Ruins, or Meditation on the Revolutions of Empires* (Fairford, England: Echo Library, 2010), 73.

29. Adrienne Koch, *The Philosophy of Thomas Jefferson* (Gloucester, MA: Peter Smith, 1957), 162.

30. "Since the character of agriculture in Virginia seemed to discourage communities," writes Kett, "Jefferson thought that the legislature would have to create them." Joseph Kett, "Education," in *Thomas Jefferson: A Reference Biography*, ed. Merrill D. Peterson (New York: Charles Scribner's Sons, 1986), 237.

31. Thomas Jefferson, "Bill for the General Diffusion of Knowledge," in *Thomas Jefferson: Writings*, ed. Peterson, 366.

32. TJ to Major John Cartwright, June 5, 1824.

33. See M. Andrew Holowchak, "Individual Liberty and Political Unity in an Expanding Nation: The Axiological Primacy of Wards in Jefferson's Republican Schema," in *Thomas Jefferson and Philosophy: Essays on the Philosophical Cast of Jefferson's Writings* (Lanham, MD: Lexington Books, 2013), chap. 3.

34. For more on the relationship between progress and education, see J. M. Beach, "The Ideology of the American Dream: Two Competing Philosophies of Education," *Educational Studies* 41 (April 2007): 151.

35. Ari Helo, "Jefferson's Conception of Republican Government," in *The Cambridge Companion to Thomas Jefferson*, ed. Frank Shuffleton (New York: University of Cambridge Press, 2009), 43.

36. Dumas Malone, *Jefferson and His Time*, vol. 6, *The Sage of Monticello* (Charlottesville: University of Virginia Press, 1981), 233.

37. See Holowchak, "Individual Liberty and Public Unity in an Expanding Nation."

38. My translation. Aristotle, *Politics*, trans. H. Rackham (Cambridge: Harvard University Press, [1932] 1990), 1326a25–b6.

39. Montesquieu, *Spirit of Laws*, bk. 8.16.

40. Thomas Jefferson, "Second Inaugural Address," in *Thomas Jefferson: Writ-*

ings, ed. Peterson, 519. See also TJ to Nathaniel Niles, March 22, 1801; and TJ to François Barbé-Marbois, June 14, 1817.

41. Compare to Millar, who argues via analogy with dice. "In a multitude of dice thrown together at random, the result, at different times, will be nearly equal; but in one or two throws of a single die, very different numbers may often be produced. It is to be expected, therefore, that, though the greater part of the political system of any country be derived from the combined influence of the whole people, a variety of peculiar institutions will sometimes take their origin from the casual interposition of particular persons, who happen to be placed at the head of a community, and to be possessed of singular abilities, and views of policy. This has been regarded, by many writers, as the great source of those differences which are to be found in the laws, and government of different nations." John Millar, *The Origins of the Distinction of Ranks: Or, An Inquiry into the Circumstances Which Give Rise to Influence and Authority, in the Different Members of Society*, 4th ed. (Edinburgh, 1806), 5–6.

42. See James E. Lewis Jr., *The American Union and the Problem of Neighborhood: The United States and the Collapse of the Spanish Empire, 1783–1829* (Chapel Hill: University of North Carolina Press, 1998).

43. TJ to Joseph Priestley, January 29, 1804.

44. For example, TJ to Jean Baptiste Say, February 1, 1804. See M. Andrew Holowchak, "Jefferson's Moral Agrarianism: Poetic Fiction or Moral Vision?" *Agriculture and Human Values* 28, no. 4 (2011): 497–506.

45. TJ to James Madison, January 30, 1787; and TJ to Edward Carrington, January 16, 1787.

46. He generally envisioned the "empire for liberty" to cover the North America, but in letters to Stuart and Monroe he saw two continents peopled by republican citizens, speaking the same language. See TJ to Archibald Stuart, January 25, 1786; and TJ to Gov. James Monroe, November 24, 1801.

47. Dumas Malone, *Jefferson and His Time*, vol. 6, *The Sage of Monticello* (Charlottesville: University of Virginia Press, 1981), 237.

48. TJ to Joseph C. Cabell, November 28, 1820.

49. See Holowchak, "Individual Liberty and Public Unity in an Expanding Nation."

50. TJ to Joseph C. Cabell, February 2, 1816.

51. For more on Jefferson's views on education, see M. Andrew Holowchak, *Thomas Jefferson's Philosophy of Education: A Utopian Dream* (London: Taylor & Francis, 2014).

52. Spelled out in his "Rockfish Gap Report."

53. "Jefferson's educational ideas," writes Charles Miller, "are those of the Scottish Enlightenment: calling for distinct levels of schools, the lowest level to include the

entire citizenry; advocating public rather than private education; transforming colleges that trained primarily for the ministry into full-fledged universities; and emphasizing science." Charles A. Miller, *Jefferson and Nature: An Interpretation* (Baltimore: Johns Hopkins University Press, 1988), 38.

54. Thomas Jefferson, "Bill for the More General Diffusion of Knowledge," in *Thomas Jefferson: Writings* ed. Peterson, 365–68.

55. Ibid., 367.

56. Thomas Jefferson, "Bill for Establishing a System of Public Education," in James B. Conant, *Thomas Jefferson and the Development of American Public Education* (Berkeley: University of California Press, 1962), 121–22.

57. Ibid., 122–23.

58. For a more detailed account of his varied views on geography in education, see William A. Koelsch, "Thomas Jefferson, American Geographers, and the Uses of Geography," *Geographical Review* 98, no. 2 (2008): 260–79.

59. Writes James Ronda: "Sweeping up to the Front Range of the Rockies and continuing again to the Pacific, the checkerboard look of the country repeats the Jeffersonian passion for straight lines, tidy corners, and the culture of agriculture. On in the mountain West is the pattern broken. And ever there, given half a chance, the lines and corners will reassert themselves on the land." James P. Ronda, *Jefferson's West: A Journey with Lewis and Clark* (Charlottesville, VA: Thomas Jefferson Foundation, 2000), 11.

60. "Who can assure me that your republican government will endure for long, if the education of its young people is not established on the set basis of republican principles, morality, and justice, and watched over by Congress, so that no professor may deviate from them? . . . Your true strength lies in the people living inland, where mores and social virtues capable of grandeur of soul and generosity, then you will reach you goal and see the emergence in your country of heroes as numerous as in Greece and wiser than in Rome." TJ to Thaddeus Kościuszko, February 1, 1812; Thomas Jefferson, *The Papers of Thomas Jefferson: Retirement Series*, vol. 4, June 18, 1811, to April 30, 1812, ed. J. Jefferson Looney (Princeton: Princeton University Press, 2007), 469–70.

61. TJ to Joseph C. Cabell, December 29, 1817.

62. Malone, *Sage of Monticello*, 245.

63. TJ to Joseph C. Cabell, January 14, 1818.

Chapter 10. "The Ablest . . . or None at All": Jefferson on Secondary Education for Sensitive Meritocracy

1. TJ to Peter Carr, September 7, 1814.

2. P. S. Dupont de Nemours to TJ, August 27, 1798.

3. P. S. Dupont de Nemours to TJ, April 21, 1800.

4. TJ to P. S. Dupont de Nemours, April 24, 1816.

5. Thomas Jefferson, "Bill for the More General Diffusion of Knowledge," in *Thomas Jefferson: Writings*, ed. Merrill D. Peterson (New York: Library of America, 1984), 365.

6. Thomas Jefferson, *Thomas Jefferson: Writings*, ed. Peterson, 459–60.

7. Thomas Jefferson, "The Report of the Commissioners Appointed to Fix the Site of the University of Virginia," in *Thomas Jefferson: Writings*, ed. Peterson, §3 and §4. In spite of the importance of university-level education, Jefferson was clear that primary-level education, through his system of wards, was more important for a thriving democracy than were universities. In a letter to Cabell (January 13, 1823), he states, "Were it necessary to give up either the Primaries or the University I would rather abandon the last, because it is safer to have a whole people respectably enlightened, than a few in a high state of science, and the many in ignorance. This last is the most dangerous in which a nation can be. The nations and governments of Europe are so many proofs of it."

8. Dumas Malone, *Jefferson the Virginian* (Boston: Little, Brown, 1948), 283.

9. Thomas Jefferson, "Rockfish Gap Report," in *Thomas Jefferson: Writings*, ed. Peterson, 461–62.

10. Joseph F. Kett, "Education," in *Thomas Jefferson: A Reference Biography*, ed. Merrill D. Peterson (New York: Charles Scribner's Sons, 1986), 241.

11. For example, TJ to George Washington, March 15, 1784; TJ to David Humphreys, June 23, 1791; TJ to Jean Baptiste Say, February 1, 1804; TJ to Thomas Leiper, January 21, 1809; TJ to Governor James Jay, April 7, 1809; and TJ to John Melish, January 13, 1813.

12. M. Andrew Holowchak, "Jefferson's Moral Agrarianism: Poetic Fiction or Moral Vision?" *Agriculture and Human Values* 28, no. 4 (2011): 477–97.

13. For more on the uniqueness of this letter, see M. Andrew Holowchak, *Jefferson's Philosophy of Education: A Utopian Dream* (London: Taylor & Francis, 2014), chap. 2.

14. Thomas Jefferson, *Jefferson's Literary Commonplace Book*, ed. Douglas L. Wilson (Princeton: Princeton University Press, 1898), §9.

15. He does list "Ideology," the science of thought, in his 1817 bill and "Rockfish Gap Report" one year later. Ideology had metaphysical content.

16. Thus, "[Jefferson] made selective use of the criterion of useful knowledge as a principle of exclusion," states Joseph Kett. Kett, "Education," 245.

17. Thomas Jefferson, "Query XIV," in *Notes on the State of Virginia*, in *Thomas Jefferson: Writings*, ed. Peterson, 274.

18. TJ to John Norvell, June 14, 1807.

19. TJ to Joseph Priestley, January 27, 1800.

20. Later called "colleges." The term *college* was no accident but was employed intentionally to show such secondary schools planted the seeds of a higher level of education. See Jennings L. Wagoner, *Jefferson and Education* (Chapel Hill: University of North Carolina Press, 2004), 84.

21. Jefferson, "Bill for the More General Diffusion of Knowledge," 368–71.

22. Ibid., 371.

23. Ibid., 371–72.

24. Ibid., 373.

25. Thomas Jefferson, "Bill for Establishing a System of Public Education," in James B. Conant, *Thomas Jefferson and the Development of American Public Education* (Berkeley: University of California Press, 1962), 124.

26. Ibid., 124.

27. The curriculum is extraordinarily broad and seems to fit better with university-level education or a trade school than with a grammar school. Here Jefferson is still involved with the proposed college at Albemarle—specifically the notion to turn Albemarle Academy into Central College—and the expansive curriculum seems for the sake of creating a topnotch, nonpareil grammar school, worthy of Jefferson's approbation, which leaves university-level schools for true specialization.

28. *Ideology*, coined by A. L. C. Destutt de Tracy, is an inquiry into the operations of the mind, knowledge, and types of proof—roughly, an admixture of psychology, epistemology, and logic. A. L. C. Destutt de Tracy, *Projet d'éléments d'idélogie* (Paris: Didot, 1801).

29. Lord Kames, *Elements of Criticism*, 5th ed. (Dublin: Charles Ingham, 1772), ii–v.

30. Meyer Reinhold, "The Classical World," in *Thomas Jefferson: A Reference Biography*, ed. Peterson, 135.

31. TJ to John Wayles Eppes, September 18, 1813. See also TJ to Joseph Priestley, January 27, 1800; and TJ to John Adams, December 10, 1819.

32. TJ to Monsieur A. Koraïs, October 31, 1823.

33. Thomas Jefferson, *Notes on the State of Virginia*, in *Thomas Jefferson: Writings*, ed. Peterson, 276.

34. Nonetheless, the college was unrivalled in its production of able statesmen. See Dumas Malone, *Jefferson and His Time*, vol. 1, *Jefferson the Virginian* (Boston: Little, Brown, 1948), 60.

35. Mark R. Wenger, "Thomas Jefferson, the College of William and Mary, and the University of Virginia," *Virginia Magazine of History and Biography* 103, no. 3 (1995): 347.

36. Ibid., 355–57.

37. TJ to Joseph C. Cabell, February 22, 1821.

38. Thomas Jefferson, "Query XV," in *Notes on the State of Virginia*, in *Thomas Jefferson: Writings*, ed. Peterson, 276–78.

39. Malone, *Jefferson the Virginian*, 284–85.

40. Thomas Jefferson, "Autobiography," in *Thomas Jefferson: Writings*, ed. Peterson, 43.

41. Merrill D. Peterson, *Thomas Jefferson & the New Nation: A Biography* (London: Oxford University Press, 1970), 149.

42. Charles Flynn Arrowood, *Thomas Jefferson and Education in a Republic* (New York: McGraw-Hill, 1970 [1930]), 30.

43. "Never was a commander-in-chief more fortunate in a field officer," writes Charles Arrowood. "Brave, patient, tactful, sagacious, resourceful, and of the highest integrity, Cabell was admired and trusted by everyone. His services to the University cannot be measured." Ibid., 31–32.

44. Wagoner, *Jefferson and Education*, 90–91.

45. Arrowood, *Thomas Jefferson and Education in a Republic*, 36.

46. Jefferson, "Rockfish Gap Report," 457.

47. TJ to Joseph C. Cabell, December 4, 1819.

48. Joseph C. Cabell to TJ, January 22, 1820.

49. It is clear also that he saw it as a bastion for Old Republicanism. See TJ to General James Breckinridge, February 15, 1821.

50. TJ to Joseph C. Cabell, February 15, 1820.

51. Wenger, "Thomas Jefferson, the College of William and Mary, and the University of Virginia," 367.

52. "By elaborating the colonnades where Greek philosophers used to teach into an 'academic village,'" writes Mayor, "he evolved for the University of Virginia a unity whose convenience, economy, and elegance are only just beginning to be appreciated by our college planners." A. Hyatt Mayor, "Jefferson's Enjoyment of the Arts," *Metropolitan Museum of Art Bulletin* 2, no. 4 (1943): 146.

53. Karl Lehmann, *Thomas Jefferson: American Humanist* (Charlottesville: University of Virginia Press, [1965] 1993), 185–86.

54. Jefferson, *Thomas Jefferson: Writings*, ed. Peterson, 457.

55. Frederick D. Nichols, "Architecture," in *Thomas Jefferson: A Reference Biography*, ed. Peterson, 226.

56. Joseph C. Cabell and Nathaniel Francis, eds., *Early History of the University of Virginia: As Contained in the Letters of Thomas Jefferson and Joseph C. Cabell, Hitherto Unpublished; With an Appendix Consisting of Mr. Jefferson's Bill for a Complete System of Education, and Other Illustrative Documents; And an Introduction Comprising a Brief Historical Sketch of the University, and a Biographical Notice of Joseph C. Cabell* (Richmond, VA: J. W. Randolph, 1856) , 174. See also George

Tucker, *Life of Thomas Jefferson*, vol. 2 (London: Charles Knight, 1837), 430–31; and Gilbert Chinard, *Thomas Jefferson: The Apostle of Americanism* (Ann Arbor: University of Michigan Press, [1929] 1962), 510.

57. Kett, "Education," 246.

58. Jefferson, "Rockfish Gap Report," 460–62.

59. TJ to Major John Cartwright, June 5, 1824; TJ to James Madison, January 8, 1825; and TJ to Joseph Cabell, February 3, 1825.

60. Wenger, "Thomas Jefferson, the College of William and Mary, and the University of Virginia," 368–69.

61. "Minutes of the Board of Visitors," October 4, 1824. Arrowood, *Thomas Jefferson and Education in a Republic*, 45–46.

62. For more on usefulness of education, see Holowchak, *Jefferson's Philosophy of Education*, chap. 4.

63. Joseph Kett writes: "Jefferson's conception was far more radical than that of the elective systems that gradually infiltrated American colleges during the nineteenth century. The latter allowed a growth of elective branches off a trunk of required courses. In contrast, Jefferson made no provision for required courses of any sort." Kett, "Education," 246.

64. Edwin Alderman became the first president of the university in 1904.

65. Arrowood, *Thomas Jefferson and Education in a Republic*, 19–20.

66. Nathaniel Cabell states: "In this feature is seen Mr. Jefferson's characteristic confidence in the capacity of individuals to determine for themselves what is best for them. He thought it safe to submit to the judgment of each student and his friends, the choice of the subject best adapted to the cast of his mind, and to his views in life. The results of the system are not wholly good, but the good preponderates." Nathaniel Cabell, *The Early History of the University of Virginia as Contained in the Letters of Thomas Jefferson and Joseph C. Cabell* (Richmond, VA: J. W. Randolph, 1856), 521–22.

67. "Minutes of the Board of Visitors," October 4, 1824. Writes historian Jennings L. Wagoner: "In an effort to encourage Virginia students to assume a sense of responsibility and maturity in matters of conduct, the Visitors had placed the reins of discipline in the students' own hands. Not the Board of Visitors or the faculty, but a student-run Board of Censors was to exist as the principal judicial body. Should sin or scandal dare emerge, this student court was to sit in judgment in all but extreme cases of misconduct." Jennings L. Wagoner, "Honor and Dishonor at Mr. Jefferson's University: The Antebellum Years," *History of Education Quarterly* 26, no. 2 (1986): 166.

68. Wenger, "Thomas Jefferson, the College of William and Mary, and the University of Virginia," 369. See also TJ to Ellen Randolph Coolidge, November 14, 1825.

69. Dumas Malone, *Jefferson and His Time*, vol. 6, *The Sage of Monticello* (Charlottesville: University of Virginia Press, 1981), 392–93.

70. Thomas C. Hunt and Jim Garrison, "Thomas Jefferson on Freedom of Religion and Inquiry: The Paradoxes of Liberal Modernity," *Freedom of Religion and Inquiry* 21, nos. 1–2 (1996): 35.

71. TJ to Francis Wayles Eppes, June 27, 1821.

72. Darren Staloff, "The Politics of Pedagogy," in *The Cambridge Companion to Thomas Jefferson*, ed. Frank Shuffleton (New York: Cambridge University Press, 2009), 138–39.

73. Conor Cruise O'Brien, *The Long Affair: Thomas Jefferson and the French Revolution, 1785–1800* (Lanham, MD: Rowman & Littlefield, 1996), 279.

74. TJ to Littleton Waller Tazewell, January 5, 1805; TJ to Joseph C. Cabell, February 2, 1816; and TJ to Joseph Cabell, January 13, 1823.

75. Jennings L. Wagoner states, "In creating his university, Jefferson had hoped to provide an intellectual and moral environment that would bring out the best, not the worst, habits and conduct on the part of the students." Wagoner, "Honor and Dishonor at Mr. Jefferson's University," 164–5.

76. That is why Jefferson embraced neology and so boldly opposed strict adherence to rules of grammar and preferred usage to give rules to grammar and not grammar to give rules to usage. What is grammatically expedient at one time might prove inexpedient at another time. TJ to John Waldo, August 16, 1813; and TJ to John Adams, August 15, 1820.

77. Kett, "Education," 247.

INDEX